D0800602

the Dehydrator bible

GLEN COVE PUBLIC LIBRARY
4 GLEN COVE AVENUE
GLEN COVE, NEW YORK 11542-2885

Jennifer MacKenzie, Jay Nutt & Don Mercer

Robert
ROSE

The Dehydrator Bible
Text copyright © 2009 Jennifer MacKenzie, Jay Nutt and Don Mercer
Photographs copyright © 2009 Robert Rose Inc.
Cover and text design copyright © 2009 Robert Rose Inc.

No part of this publication may be reproduced, stored in a retrieval system or transmitted, in any form or
by any means, without the prior written consent of the publisher or a licence from the Canadian Copyright
Licensing Agency (Access Copyright). For an Access Copyright licence, visit www.accesscopyright.ca
or call toll-free: 1-800-893-5777.

For complete cataloguing information, see page 361.

Disclaimer
The recipes in this book have been carefully tested by our kitchen and our tasters. To the best of our knowledge,
they are safe and nutritious for ordinary use and users. For those people with food or other allergies, or who have
special food requirements or health issues, please read the suggested contents of each recipe carefully and
determine whether or not they may create a problem for you. All recipes are used at the risk of the consumer.
Consumers should always consult their dehydrator manufacturer's manual for recommended procedures and
drying times.
    We cannot be responsible for any hazards, loss or damage that may occur as a result of any recipe use.
    For those with special needs, allergies, requirements or health problems, in the event of any doubt, please
contact your medical adviser prior to the use of any recipe.

Editor: Sue Sumeraj
Proofreader: Sheila Wawanash
Indexer: Gillian Watts
Design and Production: Joseph Gisini/PageWave Graphics Inc.
Photography: Colin Erricson
Food Styling: Kathryn Robertson
Prop Styling: Charlene Erricson

Cover image: Dried carrot slices (left), red bell pepper slices (right) and apple slices (rear)

We acknowledge the financial support of the Government of Canada through the Book Publishing Industry
Development Program (BPIDP) for our publishing activities.

Published by Robert Rose Inc.
120 Eglinton Avenue East, Suite 800, Toronto, Ontario, Canada M4P 1E2
Tel: (416) 322-6552 Fax: (416) 322-6936

Printed and bound in Canada

1 2 3 4 5 6 7 8 9 CP 17 16 15 14 13 12 11 10 09

Contents

3 1571 00277 5883

Introduction

Long before there was a refrigerator (or two) in every home, a deep-freezer in the basement and supermarkets full of pretty much anything in a box, package or jar, making food last between harvest seasons required a great deal of ingenuity. Early civilizations discovered that food left out in the sun was still edible after it was dry. With the advent of fire, drying and smoking became useful tools for food preservation between successful hunts and sustained ancient civilizations by providing a more consistent source of food. Today, we have the benefit of refrigeration, globalized food production, shipping and commercial processing, so we don't have to preserve our own food at all. But as the saying goes, everything old is new again.

Welcome to the new-old world of food dehydration. Whether you grow your own food, buy it locally from farmers' markets or farm stands, hunt for your own meat or even buy your food from a regular supermarket, seasonality still affects the price and abundance of food. It just makes sense to take advantage of food when it's abundant (and less expensive) and preserve it for times when it's not as plentiful, or not available at all. Drying food is a wonderful way to do this. Dried food storage is space-efficient, and individual dried ingredients can be used in a huge variety of ways, a bonus that other preservation techniques don't always offer. And when you're cooking with food you dried yourself, you know exactly where it came from and what's in it.

Modern appliances designed for food dehydration make this ancient preserving technique faster, more efficient, reliable and easy. We no longer have to worry about wild animals stealing food set out to dry or a sudden downpour ruining days of drying. A simple appliance with trays, a heat source and a fan takes away the elements of surprise and essentially allows you to put fresh food in and take dried food out. Of course, drying food does take some know-how and a little trial and error at times.

Cooking is a blend of science and art. Dehydrating food and turning it into delicious meals is an excellent example of that, and our team of authors has combined their expertise to maximize both aspects. Don Mercer is a professional engineer specializing in food science, with years of experience perfecting the technique of drying food in a lab and in practical settings (including his own backyard). Don teaches university food processing courses and has done work on food processing and drying around the world, helping developing communities implement the science of dehydration to sustain their food supply. Don has taken the guesswork out of drying foods so you can jump right in. Jennifer MacKenzie is a professional home economist with a bachelor of science in Foods and Nutrition. Through her expertise in recipe development, testing and writing, she knows both the science of how food works and the art of making it taste good — and how to write her techniques down so you can get the same results. Jay Nutt is a chef with years of experience cooking in restaurants and teaching cooking classes. He and Jennifer co-own their own restaurant and gourmet food store. Jay's flair for creating fabulous food that dazzles customers and keeps them coming back for more is incorporated into the recipes in this book, so you'll get the most out of your dried foods while making tasty dishes your family will love.

We've integrated the latest food safety information into our techniques (we've learned a few things since the earliest days of dehydrating), and have provided easy-to-follow drying instructions and time guidelines to give you the tools you need to preserve your own food safely at home. Once you've mastered the science of drying foods, you can explore the culinary art of cooking from your pantry full of preserved food. We've included recipes that use a mixture of dried and fresh ingredients, as well as recipes that primarily use dried ingredients; the latter are perfect for taking on the trail or road — or anywhere else without refrigeration.

When you've got your pantry stocked full of dried foods, and while the garden sleeps for the winter, you can take advantage of your dehydrator's versatility by using it to create homemade pet treats for your furry companions, to make gifts for family and friends, and even to dry special crafts and homemade decorations. We've created some recipes and instructions for you to try. Once you get going, you will likely think of even more uses for your dehydrator between gardening seasons.

We hope you'll enjoy incorporating the age-old practice of food dehydration into your modern life and taking advantage of what nature provides. So plant a few extra rows of tomatoes and beans, pick as many strawberries as possible when they're at their peak and buy that big basket of freshly harvested carrots. Then load up your dehydrator. You'll be thrilled to be cooking with your own dried foods the whole year through!

Acknowledgments

It takes quite a team to turn an idea into the book you're holding in your hands. From our team of authors, our thanks goes to the team at Robert Rose: our publisher, Bob Dees, for your vision and determination; Marian Jarkovich, for your marketing expertise; and Nina McCreath. To our editor, Sue Sumeraj, we could never have done this without your patience, attention to detail and wonderful way with words — and especially for deciphering what we were trying to say when we couldn't say it clearly ourselves.

The design and creative team took our recipes and instructions and created a lovely and useful book. Special thanks to Joseph Gisini and the PageWave Graphics team: Kevin Cockburn, Andrew Smith and Daniella Zanchetta. Thanks to photographer Colin Erricson, food stylist Kathryn Robertson and props stylist Charlene Erricson — making dried food look fantastic is no easy feat, but you did it. Thanks also to proofreader Sheila Wawanash and indexer Gillian Watts for adding that extra, important polish.

From Jennifer
To Mom and Dad, Brent, Alicia and John, I realize more and more each day just how lucky I am to have such a supportive, loving family. Thank you!

Jay, thank you for not running the other way when I suggested that you co-author a cookbook with me (in your other spare time) and for being there for me, always.

To Don, thank you for guiding us through the science of food drying. You helped us understand the "why" so we could better apply the "how."

Thank you to our family and friends who tasted our creations, offered ideas and suggestions and even picked up groceries for us (Ted, Shelly and Sami!).

From Jay
As with anyone who works with food, there are far more people who have influenced and shaped my career than can be mentioned here in these few words, so I extend my thanks to everyone I've worked with over the last twenty years in the restaurant and food service industry. They have collectively taught me more than I can possibly ever put to use.

Special thanks go to Stan Townsend, now the program head of the culinary program at Northern Alberta Institute of Technology, who provided a steadying hand at a time when I wasn't

sure I wanted to do this for a living, and to David MacGillivray for being a mentor not just as a chef, but as a Canadian chef.

Thanks to my dad, Joe, and my siblings, Dale, Rick and Melanie, who have not only encouraged my assorted successes, but also held me in check so I wouldn't believe my own press clippings. My appreciation to my late mother, Wendy, who taught me that any occasion involving food could be a special occasion.

Our staff and clientele at In A Nuttshell and Nuttshell Next Door Café deserve special thanks for humoring my whims, frustrations and idiosyncrasies during the formation of this book.

None of the above could have been accomplished without the support of my parents-in-law, Ken and Pat MacKenzie. I offer my love and gratitude for all you have done.

And finally, I must offer my love and thanks to my wife, Jennifer, whose passion for and knowledge of food and cooking help turn the gunpowder of my ideas from random explosions into orchestrated fireworks.

From Don
It has been a real joy for me to work with such creative individuals as Jennifer and Jay. As an associate professor in the Food Science Department at the University of Guelph, I tend to deal more with the scientific or mathematical aspects of drying and drying applications. Working on this book has been a refreshing and interesting experience.

I would like to thank my wife, Jane, for her abundant patience and understanding as I do solar drying experiments in the backyard, run various dehydrators in the garage, and sit down in the evening to enter data from laboratory experiments into spreadsheet programs on my laptop. It's also important to acknowledge the support of other family members: sincere thanks to our son Darren and his wife, Karren; to our son Geoffrey; and to our daughters, Andrea and Destiny. I would also like to welcome the newest addition to our family — our first grandchild, Ethan Douglas Mercer — who was born in April 2008. Of all the important things in this world, there is none as important as family.

To those of you reading this book, I hope you find pleasure and satisfaction as you dry your own products and enjoy using them to prepare the recipes. Happy drying!

PART 1

Dehydrating

Foods

Everything You Need to Know About Dehydrating Foods

What is Food Dehydration?

Basically, dehydration — or drying, as it is also called — is the process of removing water from a material. All food is composed of solids (starches, proteins, fiber, etc.) and a significant amount of water. In this book, we will look at the use of dried foods and explain how best to remove moisture from a wide variety of fruits, vegetables and herbs, as well as some prepared dishes, including meat.

The term "dehydration" is often used interchangeably with the term "drying." For our purposes, both words should be considered to mean the same thing.

The History of Drying Food

The origins of food drying predate recorded history. It is not hard to imagine primitive humans finding dried berries clinging to vines long after fresh berries had disappeared. These sweet, nutritious, sun-dried berries would have been a welcome food source during times of the year when other food was scarce. Natural drying processes were then duplicated by spreading fresh foods on the ground or on racks in the sun to dry. By preserving food in this way, early humans were not as vulnerable to food shortages as they had been. Almost every ancient culture developed some form of drying technology to preserve various foods, including fish and meat obtained from hunting. This is particularly true of those who lived in hot, dry regions of the world, where the abundant heat made drying relatively easy.

Not all drying relied on the sun's energy, however. Heat from fires was also an efficient and effective way to remove moisture — especially from meat, where smoke added to the preservation process.

Today, food dehydration is a science. We now understand the complexities of drying. Huge quantities of food can be dried in large commercial dryers, under highly controlled conditions, to produce shelf-stable products of uniformly high quality. One has only to walk through the supermarkets and look at the products on the shelves to see the impact of dried foods on our lives.

Advantages of Food Dehydration

By removing a major portion of the water from a food, we are able to reduce spoilage and increase the food's storage life. Without water, which is essential for their growth, many spoilage microorganisms cannot survive. Dried foods generally have little or no specialized storage requirements, but it is always best to keep them in a cool, dry location, out of direct sunlight, to maximize their shelf life.

Moisture removal also reduces weight and makes food easier to transport. This is of great importance to hikers and campers who have to carry their food supplies. Most of us are familiar with instant potatoes, which are simply potatoes with most of the water removed. Potatoes consist of about 80% water and 20% solids (mostly starches) when they are fresh. By removing most of the water, 5 pounds (2.5 kg) of fresh potatoes can be reduced to about 1 pound (0.5 kg) of dried potato flakes. Such a significant weight reduction is not only a boon to campers and hikers, but it also makes long-term storage more convenient, even in the comfort of home.

Some foods take on entirely different properties when dried. When dried under proper conditions, grapes become raisins, plums become prunes, fruit purées become fruit leathers and so on.

In addition, drying allows us to preserve

the food we grow in our gardens so that we can enjoy it throughout the year. There is something immensely satisfying about being able to cook with homegrown fruits and vegetables long after they have been harvested. We can also take advantage of the bounty of locally grown foods from farm stands and farmers' markets or a Community Supported Agriculture (CSA) program; by preserving these foods for when they are out of season, we can reduce our "food miles" while knowing exactly where our food came from.

Do-It-Yourself Food Dehydration

The do-it-yourself approach has become increasingly popular among homeowners and has worked its way into many aspects of our everyday lives. Food dehydration is no exception. With recent developments in equipment designed for home use, even the most inexperienced person can easily produce safe, high-quality dried foods. Easy-to-follow instructions are provided with most commercial home dehydrators to help you get started.

When you begin to dehydrate food, be prepared to make a few mistakes along the way. Remember, it is better to overdry a product than to underdry it. If you don't remove enough moisture, your product may spoil while in storage. An overly dried product, on the other hand, will not have enough moisture to support microbial growth, which means it will be "safer" than if too little moisture was removed. More liquid can always be added when you rehydrate the food, if necessary.

Always keep accurate records of what you have done. Important things to record are drying times, temperatures, details about the amount of product and how you prepared it, and the date on which the food was dried. It is a good idea to keep a

notebook listing this information for future reference, and for possible improvements in future drying applications. All dried products should be properly labeled and dated so that you can refer to your notes at a later time, if the need arises. If you are ever in doubt about the safety of a product, throw it out.

One mistake you may make early in your home food-drying work is comparing your results to those from large-scale commercial drying operations. Commercial products are prepared under conditions that meet exacting standards for which the dryer has been specifically designed. Home dehydrators cannot meet such rigorous standards. They are designed to provide flexibility and versatility for drying a wide range of products that would not normally be encountered in a commercial food processing facility. As well, many commercially dried foods have added sugar, sulphites and oil to further preserve the texture and color, making them softer and brighter-colored than home-dried foods. Home drying allows you to dry food without any additives, and you certainly know exactly what you're eating.

Equipment
Home Food Dehydrators

Drying can be accomplished in a variety of ways, using different forms of equipment. Some people might like to build their own food dryer, but the easiest and safest approach is to purchase one of the many models of home dehydrators that are now commercially available. An Internet search will turn up a wide variety of dehydrators, one of which may appeal to you.

When you're choosing a dehydrator, there are a few considerations that must be taken into account. First and foremost among these is whether the dehydrator has a fan to circulate heated air throughout the dryer and across all food surfaces. Units without a fan will take longer to dry the food to its final desired moisture content than a similarly sized unit equipped with a fan. There may also be an unevenness in the drying. In this book, times given for drying are based on tests conducted using food dehydrators with circulating fans. Some dehydrators have the fan mounted on the top of the machine, some at the back and some at the bottom. Each performs slightly differently, making the drying pattern different between the machines, but the final results are very similar.

Another factor in selecting a home food dehydrator is its heating capacity. A dehydrator with a 500-watt heater may be satisfactory for those who intend to dry only small amounts of product. Those who are drying larger volumes of product, or who might want to in the future, should consider a more powerful heater (e.g., 1 kilowatt).

Other considerations include the size of the machine (and how it will fit into the space you have available) and how easy it is to clean. Some people may want to look for features such as a digital temperature display and a timer that will automatically shut off the dryer after a desired time period.

Whatever your needs or desires, there is probably a dryer available to meet them. If you're new to drying, you may be tempted to buy a small machine, but once you embrace the idea of having your pantry stocked with home-dried foods, you'll likely want a dehydrator with a larger capacity. Many models come with the option to expand the capacity with additional trays; these are certainly something to consider when making your initial purchase.

After selecting a food dehydrator, you will have to experiment to identify the best conditions for the products you wish to dry. Do not be become discouraged by any failures or setbacks you may encounter; this is all part of the learning process. Once you get over your initial apprehension about doing your own food drying, you will begin to enjoy the opportunities it offers. We have made every effort to provide you with the information you need to successfully prepare each of the dried ingredients for the recipes presented here.

Other Essential Equipment

- **Airtight containers:** Glass jars or metal canisters with a tight-sealing lid or plastic containers designed for food storage provide the best protection to preserve dried foods.
- **Colander:** This should be sturdy and made of a heat-resistant material, such as stainless steel, enameled steel or silicone, for draining blanched or checked foods (the term "checking" is explained on page 19).
- **Fine-mesh tray liners (e.g., Clean-A-Screen):** Some dehydrators have trays with a fairly open mesh or rungs. For food that gets very small when dried, such as asparagus or grains, and for those that are higher in sugar and may stick, such as strawberries, the more flexible fine-mesh liners are essential for successful drying.
- **Heatproof metal strainer:** A long-handled mesh strainer made of stainless steel is useful when you're blanching and checking fruits and vegetables before drying. By using a strainer to lift the food out of the water, rather than dumping the pot of water and food into a colander, you can blanch multiple batches of produce in the same pot of water. After removing the food from the water, transfer it to a colander to continue draining.
- **Parchment paper:** Parchment paper has many uses in cooking and food preparation. It can be used in place of specialized leather sheets, to protect bakeware and to prevent foods from sticking to trays or pans when you're drying and cooking. It is available with other food wraps at most supermarkets.

- **Ruler:** A plastic or metal ruler that can be washed is best. Unless you're very experienced at gauging size by eye, use the ruler to make sure food slices and cubes are as close to exact as possible for even drying. We find it helpful to use a permanent marker to highlight the ¼-inch (0.5 cm) and ½-inch (1 cm) marks for easy viewing while chopping.
- **Sharp knives:** A good-quality chef's or French knife, paring knives and a serrated knife make preparation of foods much easier than poor-quality or dull knives.
- **Timer:** Look for electronic timers that can be set for up to 24 hours to remind you to check the foods in the dehydrator. It's easy to lose track of time, especially when you're adding items to the dryer at different times. We like to have a few timers on hand and stick a note on each timer that says what item it's for. Be sure to record what time you started drying as well, in case you need to add more time to the timer.
- **Vegetable peeler:** A sturdy, sharp vegetable peeler makes food preparation much easier. We prefer the Y-shaped peelers over the traditional straight style, because they tend to remove thinner peelings and are easier on the hands when you're peeling large amounts of produce. Peelers don't last forever; if you're not getting thin, cleanly cut pieces of peel, it's likely the blade is getting dull. It's worth investing in a new peeler.

Optional (But Helpful) Equipment

- **Immersion blender, mini chopper, food processor or blender:** An immersion blender (or hand blender) with a mini chopper attachment is the most versatile option. The wand attachment works well for puréeing foods for leathers and snacks, and the mini chopper attachment is the best tool for making powders from dried ingredients. A food processor or blender is useful for puréeing foods for leathers and snacks, but doesn't work as well for making powders.
- **Jerky gun:** This specially designed press for squeezing a ground meat mixture into thin strips is a terrific tool to have if you plan to make jerky with ground meats, as it makes shaping the strips fast and efficient.
- **Kitchen scissors:** Sharp scissors reserved for food are very handy for snipping dried foods into smaller pieces.
- **Leather, or "fruit roll," sheets:** These dehydrator accessories are handy when you're making fruit and vegetable leathers or snacks. They are available through dehydrator manufacturers or where dehydrators are sold. For most purposes, though, you can use parchment paper if you don't have leather sheets specifically designed for your machine.
- **Mandoline:** This manual slicing tool is ideal for cutting fruits and vegetables into thin, uniform slices. Mandolines range in price dramatically (from $20 to $200) and vary as much in quality. Seek out one that suits your needs and budget. If you frequently slice hard root vegetables, for example, a sturdy stainless steel model will be worth the investment. The Benriner mandoline, available at kitchenware stores and some Asian grocery stores, is our particular favorite for its economical price, effectiveness and compact size.
- **Salad spinner:** After you've washed herbs and other leafy greens, a salad spinner is an easy way to remove excess surface water without bruising the leaves.

Foods to Dehydrate

Most common foods are reasonably well suited to home dehydration. That being said, some are more easily dried than others, and there are some that you may wish to avoid altogether. Sliced apples are a wonderful starting point. Avocados and some meats and fish are not suited to home dehydration because they contain high levels of fat. High-fat products tend to spoil through a process known as oxidative rancidity: oxygen in the air reacts with the fats and oils to produce off-flavors and other undesirable traits. Because water is not a major factor in the spoilage of high-fat foods, removing it doesn't preserve the food.

Certain foods benefit from blanching, followed by quenching (see the definitions of these terms on pages 18 and 19), or from being fully cooked; these heat treatments improve the speed of drying and the final dried product. Foods that typically require heat treatment before drying include harder vegetables and those you don't generally eat raw; the blanching or cooking method is spelled out in the individual drying instructions when such treatment is needed.

Meat, poultry and fish must be fully cooked before they are dried. This was not considered necessary in the past, but we now have more knowledge about the risks of food-borne illnesses. Taking this extra precaution ensures that you'll have a good, safe dried product.

Some berries may be difficult to dry in your home dehydrator, but with a little perseverance and planning, most can be dried with a reasonable level of success. Fleshy berries, such as strawberries, are not generally a problem. They can be sliced and placed in the dryer. However, cranberries, blueberries and other fruits with a naturally occurring waxy coating and thick skin can take an extremely long time to dry unless certain pretreatment steps are followed. Drying rates can be greatly increased by disrupting the waxy surface coating, or by cutting the berries in half to expose a non-coated surface. Keep in mind that a waxy skin, and the peel on many fruits, is designed to prevent the loss of moisture so

that the seeds have nourishment to develop once the fruit is ripe. You are working against nature when you try to remove moisture from a berry or other thick-skinned fruit. Therefore, you must take special pretreatment measures, such as piercing the skin, cutting the berry or "checking" the berry's surface to create pathways for moisture removal (the term "checking" is explained on page 19).

Other berries, such as blackberries, are composed of many small segments or seed compartments. They do not dry well in their whole form and must be mashed to a purée to remove their moisture. (Although raspberries have the same composition, their surface is not as waxy as that of blackberries and they are easier to dry.)

Certain fruits and vegetables brown when exposed to air. Commercially dried fruits are often treated with sulfites to preserve the color; however, we prefer not to use this type of additive. To prevent browning, you can use a commercial ascorbic acid product (such as Fruit-Fresh), prepared according to package directions, or a mixture of $\frac{1}{4}$ cup (50 mL) lemon juice and 4 cups (1 L) water. As you slice the food, place it in the solution and leave it for about 10 minutes. Drain and shake off excess moisture, then place the sliced food on the drying trays. Whether you pretreat food this way is up to you: some pretreated foods stay much brighter in color; with others, pretreatment doesn't make much of a difference to the final product.

Drying Techniques

There are four key factors that will affect the success you have with food dehydration. These are:

1. Time
2. Temperature
3. Air speed or velocity
4. Raw material preparation

We have provided instructions on drying a wide variety of foods, explaining how best to prepare each food for dehydration and at what temperature to do the drying. We've included representative times, based on an average of tests conducted using several home dehydrators. Your drying times may vary, depending on the type of dryer you have and the properties of the food you are drying.

Even though it is the final item on our list, discussing raw material preparation first will allow us to examine the drying process in a more straightforward manner. The best way to begin is to visualize what water must do to escape from the food being dried. In most cases, moisture at the center of the food must travel to the surface by a process called diffusion. Once at the surface, this moisture is removed by the warm air in the dryer. Fruits such as apples can be cut into uniform slices of appropriate thickness to improve their drying. If the slices are too thick, they will take longer to dry. If they are too thin, the slices may not remain intact and will crumble or break easily. Based on our experience, we have found that $\frac{1}{4}$-inch (0.5 cm) thickness is suitable for most drying applications.

Generally, the more surface area exposed to the air in the dryer, the faster the drying will proceed. Just as cutting a turnip into small cubes speeds its cooking (compared to cooking a whole turnip), small cubes of turnip will dry far more quickly than thick slices.

In the home dehydrator, food to be dried is spread on trays or racks. These are then stacked on top of one another or inserted into a specially designed drying chamber. It is important to spread the food as evenly as possible to expose its entire surface to the heated air. In units equipped with a circulating fan, air is brought into the dryer by the fan and passed over a heating coil, where it is heated to the desired temperature (which you indicate by setting the thermostat on the dryer). The heated air then passes across the surface of the wet material, where it picks up moisture and exhausts it from the dryer. When you use open-mesh racks or trays, both the top and bottom surfaces of the food are exposed to the drying air. To ensure that all surfaces are exposed to the heated air and enhance the rate of drying, you may want to flip the food slices periodically during the drying process (or gently stir the bed of small food pieces if you are drying something like kernel corn or peas).

Some dryers may not have a completely uniform distribution of air throughout. There may be variations between the left and right sides of the trays, or between the front and back. This problem can be easily overcome by rotating the trays every few hours. Similarly, some dryers may have variable air circulation depending on whether the tray is located at the top, bottom or middle of the machine. By changing the order of the trays every few hours, this unevenness can be minimized. You may want to number the trays in your dryer so that you can keep track of the order in which they started and how you have rotated them.

Time is probably the most important factor in any drying process, but drying time is closely linked with temperature and air velocity, so we must consider some basic interactions of the three factors. The most common mistake in food drying is thinking you can rush the process by increasing the temperature, thereby reducing the time it takes to satisfactorily remove the desired amount of water. Don't give in to this temptation. The recommended temperature for drying most products is 130°F (55°C). For heat-sensitive products, such as herbs, 110°F (43°C) is appropriate. Meats are dried at a higher temperature, 155°F (68°C), to minimize bacterial growth.

Some instructions for dehydrating suggest using a slightly higher temperature during the first several hours of drying, when the moisture content of the food is at its highest, but for simplicity and uniformity, we recommend using the same temperature settings throughout the drying process. A higher initial temperature does not significantly reduce drying time, and if you forget to lower the temperature, you may reduce the quality of your finished product.

Excessively high temperatures may, in fact, actually slow the drying process. When exposed to very high heat, the surface of the food may dry to a leathery texture, creating a barrier to further water removal. This is known as case hardening. By maintaining lower drying temperatures, case hardening can be avoided and you'll get a better dried product in the end.

The speed at which heated air flows through the dryer is determined by the speed of the circulating fan on those units so equipped. On most dryers, the fan speed has been preset by the manufacturer and no adjustments are possible during use. It is important to have adequate movement of air across the surface of the food being dried. Where airflow is limited, moist air can stagnate at the surface of the food in the dryer and prevent the removal of additional moisture. With proper airflow, this stagnant layer of air is swept away and fresh heated air is brought in to replace it, thereby encouraging the removal of water from the food itself. In dehydrators not equipped with fans, drying times can be significantly increased due to air stagnation inside the drying chamber.

Laboratory tests have shown that air movement is a major factor in successful food drying. Combining adequate air movement with a suitable drying temperature is much better than trying to use high temperatures with poor air circulation.

Throughout the drying process, time is a critical factor. When fresh food is first placed in the dryer, there is often a great deal of moisture on its surface that is easily removed by the heated air moving through the dryer. This is where we see a rapid loss in moisture and a correspondingly rapid decrease in the weight of the material. Once the surface moisture is removed, moisture must then diffuse from the inner portions of the product to the surface. Moisture diffusion takes time and cannot be rushed. Even though the surface of the food may feel dry, there may still be moisture within the product that must be given time to reach the surface and be picked up by the heated air. Increasing the temperature of the air will not speed the process. Slicing your food to a suitable thickness (in general, ¼ inch/0.5 cm) is one of the few ways in which you can speed up moisture diffusion. Moisture has less distance to travel in thinner slices and can reach the surface more quickly.

You cannot simply touch the surface of the food to determine if it is completely dry, but you will learn to recognize the distinct signs that a product is dry enough to be removed from the dryer and packaged for storing. Some products, such as sliced apples, are firm and leathery when suitably dried. Other products, such as grated carrots, may be brittle. Some fruits that are high in sugar, such as grapes, will be soft and pliable even when completely dried; however, they won't feel juicy. This is something you'll get a feel for as you experiment with your dehydrator.

If you're not sure whether the food is dry inside, break or tear a piece open and squeeze the flesh. No liquid should come to the surface of the tear. If there is moisture inside, return the food to the dryer. Again, it is better to overdry than risk underdrying, which will lead to premature spoilage.

Storing Dehydrated Foods

Once you have dried your food, it is important to store it properly for future use. Take care to select appropriate storage containers that meet the needs of the product. In all cases, the containers should be completely clean and dry.

Factors that have a negative impact on the quality and storage life of dried foods include:

1. Exposure to moisture
2. Exposure to air
3. Exposure to heat
4. Exposure to sunlight
5. Time

During the drying process, every effort was made to remove moisture from the product. If the dried product is exposed to moisture during storage, it will pick up this moisture. If it picks up enough moisture, the food may begin to spoil or develop off-flavors and change in texture, in much the same way soda crackers diminish in quality during humid periods of the year. Therefore, we must protect dried foods from sources of moisture in the air. Although plastic bags with zip-lock or tie closures are convenient, they may allow air and moisture into the product over prolonged periods of time. For this reason, you may want to seal small quantities of dried foods in plastic bags and then place them in rigid airtight containers such as glass jars or metal canisters with tightly sealing lids. Larger quantities may simply be stored in these glass or metal containers.

If you are storing different dried foods in plastic bags and placing them in the same large container, be careful to include only foods that are compatible with each other. You do not want to risk a flavor or aroma transfer from strong spices or seasonings to more bland products (from onions to strawberries, for instance). You should also label each bag appropriately with a tag. Do not write on the plastic surface with a black ink marker, as this may affect the food inside the bag.

Air is another potential enemy of dried foods. Not only does air carry moisture, but about 20% of air is oxygen. Oxygen can react with various components in dried foods to produce off-flavors or promote other undesirable reactions, including color changes. To reduce the chance of air getting to your dried product, it is best to store it in tightly sealed glass or metal containers, just as you did to protect it from moisture. You can minimize the amount of air (and oxygen) in the headspace between the surface of the product and the lid of the container by completely filling your storage containers. If you use plastic bags, squeeze out as much air as possible before sealing the bag.

It is a good idea to let dried food cool before placing it in a sealed container for storage. Warm food products have a tendency to sweat, even though their moisture content is quite low. Any moisture that is given off can collect on the inside walls of the container and may lead to localized pockets of mold.

Once filled, storage containers should be placed in a cool, dry area. Most reactions within food products that ultimately lead to spoilage are sped up by heat. Keeping your dried product cool will help it retain its quality for a longer time. A cool pantry, lower cupboard or a storage bin placed well away from heat vents, water pipes, the stove or other sources of heat are good choices. Some people even place their dried product in the freezer to lengthen its storage life. Although freezing (or refrigeration) is not necessary, it does help preserve quality and is useful as extra insurance for meats, fish and dairy products.

Exposure to sunlight can have a negative effect on the flavor and color of dried foods. Even household lighting may reduce food quality over a prolonged time period. It is best to store your products in a dark area.

No matter how careful you are in storing your dried foods, there is always a limit to how long a food will retain its quality, though there are no definitive "best before" dates for each type of dried food. You can maximize storage life by properly drying the food and storing it under the best possible conditions. By comparing the quality of a dried food with the record you kept about its preparation and storage, you may be able to determine an appropriate expectation for its shelf life.

Rehydrating Dried Foods

Some dried foods are typically eaten in their dry form. Fruit purée made into leather is a perfect example of dried food meant to be eaten as is. Dried berries and pieces of fruit may be eaten as a snack or in a trail mix. Dried cucumber slices can be used with dips. However, many other foods must be rehydrated before they are consumed. Rehydration is the process of putting water back into a dried product and is really the reverse of the dehydration process.

Methods of food rehydration can be quite varied, but they are never very complicated. Some products can be rehydrated simply by soaking them in water at room temperature until they have absorbed as much water as possible. Others, such as dried tomatoes, rehydrate best when placed in heated liquid. This makes them ideal for stews: you can add dried tomatoes to the mixture and, as the mixture simmers, the tomatoes will absorb the necessary moisture. (Since the tomatoes are taking moisture from the stew, you must adjust your recipe to compensate for their water uptake). When rehydrating a dried product, you should not expect it to regain the moisture level and texture of the original fresh product — it will be slightly different but should be tender and palatable.

You may want to rehydrate certain dried foods with liquid other than water. For example, you can substitute fruit juices for water if you wish. By experimenting, you may be able to create some interesting and flavorful rehydrated products.

Many foods need to be rehydrated separately before they are added to recipes that call for fresh foods. It may take some trial and error before you get a feel for using home-dried foods in your favorite recipes. In Parts 2 and 3, we have included recipes developed specifically for home-dried foods, using the rehydration method that works best for those foods. These recipes will help you learn how to enjoy using your dried foods. From there, you can dry and cook away!

Troubleshooting

If the necessary precautions are taken during drying and storage, you should not have to worry about problems occurring later on. Most potential problems can be resolved before you finish drying the food — the key is to recognize the signs of these difficulties early enough to correct them.

Uneven drying is one of the most commonly observed problems. As mentioned above, food at one side of the dryer may dry more slowly than food on the other side of the same tray or rack. If you have a dehydrator with the fan mounted on the rear, you may notice that food near the back of the rack or tray dries faster than the food near the front. By rotating the trays every few hours, you can minimize uneven drying. In other cases, you may observe signs of uneven drying between trays or racks at the top and those in the middle or at the bottom of the dryer. By periodically moving the trays from one position to another, this unevenness can be successfully overcome.

There may be times when you notice that the outer surfaces of the food are dry and leathery but the inner portions are still soft and slightly moist. In all likelihood, the temperature of the air in the dryer was too high, causing case hardening. There is no easy fix for case hardening after the fact, but you may be able to continue drying the food at a lower temperature, recognizing that the drying process will be significantly slower than normal for this batch of product. If you suspect that the centers of your food pieces are still moist, do not package them for storage — they will probably spoil. You can either eat the food or use it in a recipe right away, or refrigerate it in an airtight container and use it within a few days.

If foods you have sliced and placed in the dryer are taking a long time to dry, check the temperature settings on the dryer and make sure that air is circulating inside. You'll know it is if you can feel air leaving the dryer through the vents. Consult the manufacturer's instructions if the air isn't flowing or the heat isn't working. If the dryer is functioning properly, the trouble may be caused by the food slices being too thick, or you may not have pretreated the food appropriately before putting it in the dryer.

Some products may change color during drying or storage when naturally occurring enzymes within them create undesirable pigments as the product ages. Uncooked dried cauliflower, for example, may turn a dark purple and then blacken. Proper blanching of the food before drying will destroy these enzymes.

If your storage containers are not airtight, off-flavors can develop as oxygen reacts with compounds in the food. You can reduce this problem by filling containers to the top and minimizing the amount of air trapped inside at the time of packaging.

It can be incredibly disheartening when your food visibly spoils after all your efforts to dry and store it. If the drying process has not removed enough moisture from the food, mold may grow, usually appearing as a fuzzy or furry gray patch on the surface of the food. You might also see molds of other colors. Regardless of the color, food showing signs of mold should be thrown away. You may be tempted to simply cut off the moldy portion of the food, but it is likely that there is more mold inside that you cannot see. Mold growth occurs where there is sufficient moisture to support it, so make every effort to minimize moisture by adequately drying the food, cooling it to prevent sweating and using thoroughly dried containers.

Some Definitions

Certain terms that you may not be familiar with will be used frequently throughout this book. Here's a brief explanation of what each term means:

Blanching: Blanching is a process that is carried out with many fresh vegetables to prepare them for drying or freezing. It is done by subjecting the vegetables to high temperatures for an appropriate length of time. The time depends on the vegetable itself and the size of the pieces that are being blanched. Blanching can be done by immersing the cut vegetables in boiling water or by exposing them to steam. The scalding action of the hot water destroys naturally occurring enzymes that contribute to flavor loss, texture changes and color changes during storage.

For water blanching, you can place the food directly into the boiling water and remove it with a strainer at the end of the blanching period. Alternatively, you can keep the food in the strainer during the blanching process as long as you keep the boiling water moving through the strainer and across the surface of the food pieces.

For steam blanching, you need to place the cut food in a basket, which is then set inside a pot containing a shallow layer of boiling water. Cover the pot with a tight-fitting lid to trap the steam.

Timing is important for blanching, as under-blanching will not destroy the enzymes and may even accelerate their activity. Over-blanching can begin to cook the fruits or vegetables and soften them excessively. You should only blanch small amounts of food at a time so that the temperature of the water does not fall too low below its boiling point. Start timing when the water comes back up to the boil. Steam blanching generally takes longer than water blanching and is not as easy to do as water blanching. For that reason, we recommend water blanching where applicable in our recipes.

Checking: Checking is a technique applied to berries with a waxy coating on their outer skin, such as grapes and blueberries. In the checking process, you are trying to create small disruptions in the waxy layer. These disruptions will appear as small cracks and may have a checkered appearance. Without these small breaks in their skin, many berries will not easily give up their moisture in the drying process.

To "check" berries, place a small batch in a heatproof strainer and dip them into a pot of boiling water for the recommended time. You must be careful not to heat them long enough to split the skins if you want the berries to maintain their shape and appearance. With a little trial and error, you will be able to determine the proper checking time for particular berries. The times given in this book are meant as guidelines only and are for representative berry samples. Your times may vary depending on the size and nature of the berries you are using.

If you find that checking does not work well for you, you may pierce the outer skin of each berry numerous times with a toothpick or the tines of a fork. This approach is particularly effective with grapes, which are large enough to easily pierce with a fork. We did notice some flavor loss in berries that were checked compared with those that were pierced with a toothpick. However, piercing individual berries is time-consuming, so you may decide that the slight flavor loss caused by checking is a minor sacrifice.

Quenching: After blanching or checking, it is necessary to stop the action of the heat on the food. Excessive exposure to heat can soften the outer portions of the food or cause the skin of berries to rupture. By plunging the hot food into a sink or basin of cold water, its temperature is lowered rapidly enough to stop the effects of heating in a very short time. Some sources refer to this process as "refreshing."

Cooking: Cooking also involves heating food and should not be confused with blanching or checking. Even though it is a word we routinely use in everyday conversation, defining the term "cooking" is not that easy to do, as it has different meanings to different people and can have different implications depending on the context in which it is used. Cooking is a very complex process that has various effects on food, ranging from altering its texture and appearance to rendering it safe from disease-causing microorganisms. While blanching and checking are generally short-term exposures to heat, cooking usually takes significantly longer and involves thoroughly heating the food until it reaches a relatively high temperature right through to its core.

Tips and Tricks

- As a general rule, when preparing vegetables for drying, if you wouldn't normally eat the vegetables raw (e.g., potatoes), you should blanch or precook them before drying. Blanching and cooking tenderize the cells and deactivate enzymes, which improves the quality of the dried product and makes vegetables more palatable once they're rehydrated.

- When drying foods that naturally vary in size, such as blueberries and asparagus, sort them into similar-sized pieces and place smaller or thinner ones on one drying tray, medium on another and larger or thicker ones on a third tray. This will make checking for doneness easier and more efficient.

- Strong foods such as garlic and onions can taint the plastic of the mesh trays or leather sheets, so you may prefer to use parchment paper or reserve some trays or sheets just for those foods by marking them with a heatproof permanent marker.

- When you're drying very small food items, such as rice, grains or peas, they may fall through the mesh — even fine mesh — to the bottom of the dryer. You have two options to help reduce this: line the tray with two mesh liners, slightly offset from each other to make the holes smaller; or line a drying tray with a leather sheet or parchment paper and place it below the mesh racks to catch any pieces that fall through. You can also dry small pieces directly on leather sheets, though this does slow the drying process considerably.

- If drying items that might drip, such as very juicy fruits or meats, place them on racks below other foods and place an empty tray lined with a leather sheet or parchment paper below the racks to keep the bottom of the dryer clean.

- When dehydrating pungent items, be sure there is good ventilation in the room or you'll be smelling the aroma for days. If the weather is moderate (60°F to 78°F/ 16°C to 26°C), you can use your dryer in the garage. Don't attempt this on particularly humid or wet days or days that are too hot or cold, as drying won't be very efficient. Never use an electric dehydrator outdoors.

- If using parchment paper to line trays for leathers or other puréed or small foods, secure the paper to the mesh tray with metal paper clips to prevent the paper from blowing and lifting in the dryer. Let paper clips cool before handling.

- Number your trays with a heatproof permanent marker on the outside edge so you can keep track of them easily when loading trays at different times or rearranging trays within the dryer.

- Think efficiency when you're using your dryer. Plan to fill the dryer with foods that require the same drying temperature. If drying different foods, start those that take the longest first, then add foods that require less time, timing it so everything is dry at approximately the same time.

- If you have a dryer with removable stacking trays, remove any trays that are not loaded with food. The air circulation and heat will be more concentrated, and drying will be faster.

- If using plastic storage bags to store dried foods, seal the bag almost completely, squeezing out air with your hands, then insert a straw in the small opening and suck out as much of the remaining air as possible. Quickly remove the straw and seal the opening. It's best to then place bags in an airtight container in case of small leaks.

- If you've packed your pantry full of dried foods, it's easy to forget what you've got on hand. Compile an inventory list of the items you have, as well as approximate amounts, and keep it somewhere handy, such as inside a kitchen cupboard, taped to the inside cover of this book or right in the pantry. When you're planning to cook, you can quickly glance at the list to see if you have the ingredients on hand. Don't forget to update the list each time you use some of your stores.

Dehydrating Fresh Produce

HERBS AND SEASONINGS

Basil

Preparation: Remove leaves from large stems. Small terminal leaf clusters can be left on thin stems.

Drying: Place on mesh drying trays. Dry at 110°F (43°C).

Time: 16 to 18 hours.

Doneness test: Leaves should be brittle and should crumble easily.

Tip

• Store dried basil leaves whole to preserve the most flavor. Crumble just before using.

Bay Leaves

Preparation: Cut leaves from branches, discarding branches.

Drying: Place on mesh drying trays. Dry at 110°F (43°C).

Time: 5 to 7 hours.

Doneness test: Leaves should be very crisp and should break easily when bent.

Tip

• Fresh bay leaves can be found with the other fresh herbs in some supermarkets, or you can grow your own bay laurel tree indoors.

Chives

Preparation: Trim off tough ends.

Drying: Place on mesh drying trays. Dry at 130°F (55°C).

Time: 5 to 6 hours.

Doneness test: Chives should be very crisp and should break easily when bent.

Tip

• It is easiest to dry chives whole and then snip them with scissors into small pieces to store and use.

Cilantro

Preparation: Remove leaves from large stems. Small terminal leaf clusters can be left on thin stems.

Drying: Place on mesh drying trays. Dry at 110°F (43°C).

Time: 8 to 10 hours.

Doneness test: Leaves should be brittle and should crumble easily.

Tip

• Store dried cilantro leaves whole to preserve the most flavor. Crumble just before using.

Curry Leaves

Preparation: Cut small sprigs of leaves from branches, discarding branches. Trim sprigs to lengths that fit easily on drying trays.

Drying: Place on mesh drying trays, overlapping as little as possible. Dry at 110°F (43°C).

Time: 5 to 7 hours.

Doneness test: Leaves should be very crisp and should break easily when bent.

Tip

• Strip dried leaves from stems before storing, discarding stems. The stems may hold some moisture that can lead to spoilage even though leaves are thoroughly dry.

Dill

Preparation: Cut long coarse stems off sprigs.

Drying: Place on mesh drying trays, overlapping as little as possible. Dry at 110°F (43°C).

Time: 7 to 8 hours.

Special instructions: Rearrange any overlapped sprigs as necessary to ensure even drying.

Doneness test: Sprigs should be dry and crisp, with no evidence of moisture inside.

Tip

• Store dried dill sprigs whole to preserve the most flavor. Crumble just before using.

Garlic

Slices

Preparation: Peel cloves and cut lengthwise into slices about $\frac{1}{8}$ inch (0.25 cm) thick.

Drying: Place on mesh drying trays. Dry at 130°F (55°C).

Time: 10 to 12 hours.

Doneness test: Slices should be dry, leathery and still pliable, with no evidence of moisture inside.

Tip

• You may want to dry garlic in the garage — or at least in a well-ventilated room — as the drying process is quite aromatic.

Roasted

Preparation: Wrap peeled garlic cloves in a large piece of foil. Roast in 350°F (180°C) oven for about 1 hour or until very soft. Let cool. Transfer to a food processor or use an immersion blender and purée until smooth.

Drying: Spread out to $\frac{1}{4}$-inch (0.5 cm) thickness, as evenly as possible, on leather sheets or on mesh drying trays lined with parchment paper, leaving it slightly thicker around the edges. Dry at 130°F (55°C).

Time: 14 to 18 hours.

Special instructions: Check after 10 hours. When top is very firm and edges start to lift, carefully peel leather from sheet, flip over and continue drying.

Doneness test: Garlic sheet should be dry, very firm and just slightly pliable.

Tip

• You can store roasted garlic as a sheet or, once cooled, transfer to a food processor or mini chopper and chop into small pieces.

Gingerroot

Slices

Preparation: Peel ginger and cut crosswise into slices about $\frac{1}{8}$ inch (0.25 cm) thick, cutting any slices that are larger than a quarter in half.

Drying: Place on mesh drying trays. Dry at 130°F (55°C).

Time: 3 to 4 hours.

Doneness test: Slices should be dry, leathery and still pliable, with no evidence of moisture inside.

Tips

• Use a sharp Y-shaped vegetable peeler to peel the gingerroot.
• Store dried ginger slices whole to preserve the most flavor. Chop or mince just before using.

Grated

Preparation: Peel gingerroot and grate the flesh on the coarse side of a box grater.

Drying: Spread on leather sheets or on mesh drying trays lined with parchment paper. Dry at 110°F (43°C).

Time: 6 to 8 hours.

Special instructions: Stir occasionally to break up any clumps and ensure even drying.

Doneness test: Pieces should be dry, leathery and still pliable, with no evidence of moisture inside.

Tip
- Fresh gingerroot has a taut, shiny skin and juicy flesh. Avoid wrinkled or moldy roots.

Lavender

Preparation: Cut any thick stems off sprigs so they fit easily on drying trays.

Drying: Place on mesh drying trays. Dry at 110°F (43°C).

Time: 8 to 10 hours.

Doneness test: Flowers and stems should be dry and crisp, and stems should break easily when bent.

Tips
- Cut fresh lavender just as the flowers are fully formed and colored but have not started to open.
- If you plan to use the flowers for cooking, strip them from the stems before storing, discarding stems or using for potpourri.

Mint

Preparation: Remove leaves from large stems. Small terminal leaf clusters can be left on thin stems.

Drying: Place on mesh drying trays. Dry at 110°F (43°C).

Time: 18 to 20 hours.

Special instructions: Be careful not to remove the mint leaves from the dryer too early. Even though they may feel dry to the touch after 10 hours or so, the leaves may not yet be adequately dried.

Doneness test: Leaves should be brittle and should crumble easily.

Tip
- Store dried mint leaves whole to preserve the most flavor. Crumble just before using.

Oregano and Marjoram

Preparation: Remove leaves from large stems. Small terminal leaf clusters can be left on thin stems.

Drying: Place on mesh drying trays. Dry at 110°F (43°C).

Time: 10 to 12 hours.

Doneness test: Leaves should be brittle and should crumble easily.

Tips
- For the best flavor, cut fresh oregano and marjoram when the leaves are fully formed but before flowers start to develop.
- Store dried oregano leaves whole to preserve the most flavor. Crumble just before using.

Parsley

Preparation: Cut long coarse stems off sprigs.

Drying: Place on mesh drying trays, overlapping as little as possible. Dry at 110°F (43°C).

Time: 6 to 8 hours.

Doneness test: Leaves should be brittle and should crumble easily, and stems should break when bent.

Tips
- Strip the dry leaf clusters from the stems for more space-efficient storage and just in case there is any moisture left in the stems that could spoil the leaves. Stems can be added to flavor stocks (freeze them for later use).
- Store dried parsley leaves whole to preserve the most flavor. Crumble just before using.

Rosemary

Preparation: Trim off any thick woody stems below the line of the leaves. Do not remove the leaves from the stems.

Drying: Place on mesh drying trays. Dry at 110°F (43°C).

Time: 10 to 12 hours.

Doneness test: The rosemary should be brittle, and the "leaves" should break away from the stem easily.

Tip
- Strip the dry leaves from the stems for more space-efficient storage and just in case there is any moisture left in the stems that could spoil the leaves. Stems can be added to flavor stocks (freeze them for later use).

Sage

Preparation: Remove leaves from large stems. Small terminal leaf clusters can be left on thin stems.

Drying: Place on mesh drying trays. Dry at 110°F (43°C).

Time: 12 to 14 hours.

Doneness test: Leaves should be brittle and should crumble easily.

Tip
- Store dried sage leaves whole to preserve the most flavor. Crumble just before using.

Savory

Preparation: Trim off thick ends of stems.

Drying: Place on fine-mesh drying trays (e.g., Clean-A-Screen). Dry at 110°F (43°C).

Time: 12 to 14 hours.

Doneness test: Leaves should be brittle and should crumble easily, and stems should break easily when bent.

Tip
- Strip the dry leaves from the stems for more space-efficient storage and just in case there is any moisture left in the stems that could spoil the leaves. Stems can be added to flavor stocks (freeze them for later use).

Tarragon

Preparation: Trim off thick ends of stems.

Drying: Place on mesh drying trays, overlapping as little as possible. Dry at 110°F (43°C).

Time: 10 to 12 hours.

Special instructions: Rearrange any overlapped sprigs as necessary to ensure even drying.

Doneness test: Leaves should be brittle and should crumble easily, and stems should break easily when bent.

Tips
- Strip the dry leaves from the stems for more space-efficient storage and just in case there is any moisture left in the stems that could spoil the leaves. Stems can be added to flavor stocks (freeze them for later use).
- Store dried tarragon leaves whole to preserve the most flavor. Crumble just before using.

Thyme

Preparation: Trim off thick woody stems below the leaves.

Drying: Place on mesh drying trays. Dry at 110°F (43°C).

Time: 12 to 14 hours.

Doneness test: Leaves should be brittle and should crumble easily, and stems should break easily when bent.

Tip
- Strip the dry leaves from the stems for more space-efficient storage and just in case there is any moisture left in the stems that could spoil the leaves. Stems can be added to flavor stocks (freeze them for later use).

FRUIT

Apples

Rings

Preparation: Peel apples, if desired, and remove core. Cut crosswise into rings about ¼ inch (0.5 cm) thick.

Pretreatment (optional): To prevent browning, dip apple rings in lemon juice or an ascorbic acid solution (see page 13) as you slice them. Drain well.

Drying: Place on mesh drying trays. Dry at 130°F (55°C).

Time: 5 to 6 hours.

Doneness test: Rings should feel dry and leathery and be spongy and still flexible.

Tips
- Choose apples that have a good flavor once heated, such as Granny Smith, McIntosh, Crispin, Cortland or Northern Spy. Apple varieties that are more suited to fresh eating, such as Royal Gala, don't have much flavor once dried.
- A mechanical apple peeler works well. It will peel, core and slice the apple all at once. They are available at hardware stores.

Slices

Preparation: Peel apples, if desired, and remove core. Cut lengthwise into slices about ¼ inch (0.5 cm) thick at the widest part.

Pretreatment (optional): To prevent browning, dip apple slices in lemon juice or an ascorbic acid solution (see page 13) as you slice them. Drain well.

Drying: Place on mesh drying trays. Dry at 130°F (55°C).

Time: 4 to 6 hours.

Doneness test: Slices should feel dry and leathery and be spongy and still flexible.

Tips
- Choose apples that have a good flavor once heated, such as Granny Smith, McIntosh, Crispin, Cortland or Northern Spy. Apple varieties that are more suited to fresh eating, such as Royal Gala, don't have much flavor once dried.
- Apple skin does toughen slightly when dried. If you're planning to rehydrate and cook the apples, you may wish to peel them before drying. If you're eating them as snacks, leave the skin on for extra fiber.

Apricots

Preparation: Cut lengthwise into quarters or wedges about ¼ inch (0.5 cm) thick at the widest part.

Pretreatment (optional): To prevent browning, dip apricots in lemon juice or an ascorbic acid solution (see page 13) as you slice them. Drain well.

Drying: Place on mesh drying trays. Dry at 130°F (55°C).

Time: 20 to 24 hours.

Doneness test: Slices should feel dry and leathery and still be flexible.

Tip
- Home-dried apricots will have a much dryer texture than those that are commercially dried.

Bananas

Preparation: Peel bananas and cut crosswise into slices about ¼ inch (0.5 cm) thick.

Pretreatment (optional): To prevent browning, dip banana slices in lemon juice or an ascorbic acid solution (see page 13) as you slice them. Drain well.

Drying: Place on mesh drying trays. Dry at 130°F (55°C).

Time: 8 to 10 hours.

Doneness test: Slices should feel dry and leathery and still be flexible.

Tip

- The bananas will be a bit sticky when fully dried. Peel them from the mesh drying trays as soon as you remove them from the dryer (while they're still warm) to prevent sticking.

Blueberries

Preparation: Check berries (see page 19) or, using a toothpick, pierce berries several times.

Drying: Spread on mesh drying trays. Dry at 130°F (55°C).

Time: 18 to 22 hours.

Doneness test: Berries should be slightly shriveled, firm and no longer juicy inside.

Tips

- Checking the berries is faster and easier than piercing, but there will be a slight loss in flavor.
- Sort the berries on the trays according to approximate size to make it easier to remove those that are done earlier.

Cantaloupe

Slices

Preparation: Using a serrated knife, cut skin and underlying green flesh from cantaloupe. Cut in half lengthwise and scoop out seeds and loose flesh. For larger melons, cut each half lengthwise into two or three wedges. Cut each wedge crosswise into slices about $\frac{1}{4}$ inch (0.5 cm) thick.

Drying: Place on mesh drying trays. Dry at 130°F (55°C).

Time: 12 to 14 hours.

Doneness test: Slices should feel dry and leathery and still be flexible.

Tips

- Use ripe, but not overripe cantaloupe. Ripe cantaloupe has a sweet aroma at the stem end, and the skin under the mesh will have turned from green to beige.
- Store slices whole to preserve the most flavor and best texture. Use scissors to snip into smaller pieces just before using.

Cubes

Preparation: Using a serrated knife, cut skin and underlying green flesh from cantaloupe. Cut in half lengthwise and scoop out seeds and loose flesh. For larger melons, cut each half lengthwise into two or three wedges. Cut each wedge crosswise into slices about $\frac{1}{4}$ inch (0.5 cm) thick. Cut slices into $\frac{1}{4}$-inch (0.5 cm) cubes.

Drying: Place on mesh drying trays. Dry at 130°F (55°C).

Time: 8 to 10 hours.

Doneness test: Cubes should feel dry and leathery, with no evidence of moisture inside.

Tip

- Use ripe, but not overripe cantaloupe. Ripe cantaloupe has a sweet aroma at the stem end, and the skin under the mesh will have turned from green to beige.

Cherries, Sweet or Sour (Tart)

Preparation: Cut cherries in half lengthwise around the pit and remove pit. Using a toothpick, pierce skin several times.

Drying: Place skin side down on mesh drying trays. Dry at 130°F (55°C).

Time: 14 to 24 hours.

Doneness test: Cherries should be leathery and pliable but no longer juicy inside.

Tips

- If cherries are very large, cut them into quarters to speed drying.
- Cherries can vary greatly in moisture level; therefore, the time range for drying is quite wide.

Citrus Fruits

Zest

Preparation: Using the coarse side of a box grater, scrape colored zest from the fruit. Alternatively, use a sharp Y-shaped vegetable peeler to remove thin strips of the colored zest. Be sure not to scrape through to the bitter white pith.

Drying: Spread on leather sheets. Dry at 130°F (55°C).

Time: 3 to 4 hours.

Special instructions: Stir occasionally to break up any clumps and ensure even drying.

Doneness test: Pieces should be firm, brittle and just slightly pliable.

Tip

- Store dried zest in larger pieces to preserve the most flavor. Using a sharp knife, chop finely just before using.

Slices

Preparation: Cut fruit crosswise into slices about $\frac{1}{4}$ inch (0.5 cm) thick.

Drying: Place on mesh drying trays. Dry at 130°F (55°C).

Time: Limes and oranges: 16 to 18 hours; lemons: 18 to 20 hours; grapefruit: 22 to 24 hours.

Special instructions: If possible, flip the slices several times so they dry evenly.

Doneness test: Slices should be firm, brittle and no longer pliable.

Tips

- The flesh may pull away from the center of the slices as they dry.
- Even though the fruit slices may feel dry, moisture from within the juice sacs can diffuse outwards upon cooling and make previously firm slices feel pliable. You may have to put slices back in the dryer after they have been stored overnight to finish the drying process.

Coconut

Preparation: Drill a hole in the end of the coconut shell and drain the liquid (or collect it for another use). Using a hammer, break the shell into pieces. Using the blunt point of a butter knife, pry the meat from the shell. Rinse coconut meat to remove shell debris and pat dry. Cut chunks into slices about $\frac{1}{4}$ inch (0.5 cm) thick.

Drying: Spread on mesh drying trays. Dry at 130°F (55°C).

Time: 6 to 8 hours.

Doneness test: Slices should be firm, brittle and just slightly pliable, with no evidence of moisture inside.

Tips

- If desired, use a vegetable peeler to peel off brown skin before cutting coconut meat into slices.
- Store dried coconut in larger pieces to preserve the most flavor. Using scissors or a sharp knife, snip or finely chop just before using.

Cranberries

Preparation: If using frozen berries, let thaw and drain off any excess liquid. Cut berries in half crosswise.

Drying: Place skin side down on mesh drying trays. Dry at 130°F (55°C).

Time: 10 to 14 hours.

Doneness test: Berries should be slightly shriveled, firm and no longer juicy inside.

Tips

- Berries that have been frozen and thawed will dry faster than fresh berries.
- Cutting berries crosswise, rather than lengthwise from the stem, exposes more surface area in the interior of the berry and speeds up the drying process.

Figs

Preparation: Cut figs lengthwise into wedges about $1/2$ inch (1 cm) thick at the widest part.

Drying: Place skin side down on mesh drying trays. Dry at 130°F (55°C).

Time: 16 to 20 hours.

Doneness test: Wedges should feel dry and leathery and still be flexible.

Tip

- Home-dried figs will have a much firmer, dryer texture than those that are commercially dried. Don't attempt to dry them whole — it will take an extremely long time.

Grapes

Whole

Preparation: Check grapes (see page 19) or, using a toothpick, pierce grapes all over.

Drying: Place on mesh drying trays. Dry at 130°F (55°C).

Time: 20 to 36 hours.

Doneness test: Grapes should be leathery and pliable but no longer juicy inside.

Tips

- The high sugar content and pulpy texture of grapes make them feel much softer when dried than other home-dried fruits; just make sure they're not juicy inside.

- Home-dried raisins may feel a little crispy on the outside when first dried but will become leathery upon cooling and storage.

Halves

Preparation: Cut grapes in half.

Drying: Place skin side down on mesh drying trays. Dry at 130°F (55°C).

Time: 18 to 20 hours.

Doneness test: Grapes should be leathery and pliable but no longer juicy inside.

Tip

- Halved grapes will produce unconventionally shaped raisins, but halving them does speed up drying.

Honeydew Melon

Preparation: Using a serrated knife, cut skin and underlying thick flesh from melon. Cut in half lengthwise and scoop out seeds and loose flesh. Cut each half lengthwise into three or four wedges. Cut each wedge crosswise into slices about $1/4$ inch (0.5 cm) thick.

Drying: Place on mesh drying trays. Dry at 130°F (55°C).

Time: 16 to 18 hours.

Doneness test: Slices should feel dry and leathery and still be flexible.

Tip

- Choose a melon that feels heavy for its size to avoid buying one that is dry and pulpy.

Kiwifruit

Preparation: Peel kiwis and cut crosswise into slices about $1/4$ inch (0.5 cm) thick.

Pretreatment (optional): To prevent browning, dip kiwi slices in lemon juice or an ascorbic acid solution (see page 13) as you slice them. Drain well.

Drying: Place on mesh drying trays. Dry at 130°F (55°C).

Time: 8 to 10 hours.

Doneness test: Slices should feel dry and leathery and still be flexible.

Tip

- Use a sharp Y-shaped vegetable peeler to peel the thin brown skin from kiwis.

Mangos

Preparation: Peel mangos. Holding the mango vertically, with the stem on the cutting board, cut lengthwise along both sides of the pit to make two "cheeks." Place cheeks cut side down and cut into slices about ¼ inch (0.5 cm) thick. Using a paring knife, cut remaining flesh from around the pit and cut into pieces about ¼ inch (0.5 cm) thick.

Drying: Place on mesh drying trays. Dry at 130°F (55°C).

Time: 10 to 12 hours.

Doneness test: Slices should feel dry and leathery and still be flexible.

Tips

- Choose firm, ripe mangos for drying. They should be fragrant, and the skin should yield lightly when pressed, but the flesh shouldn't be very soft or the slices will fall apart.
- Use a sharp Y-shaped vegetable peeler to peel the skin from mangos.

Papayas

Preparation: Using a serrated knife, cut skin and underlying green or yellow flesh from papayas. Cut in half lengthwise and scoop out seeds and loose flesh. Cut each half crosswise into slices about ¼ inch (0.5 cm) thick.

Drying: Place on mesh drying trays. Dry at 130°F (55°C).

Time: 12 to 14 hours.

Doneness test: Slices should feel dry and leathery and still be flexible.

Tip

- Use ripe, but not overripe papaya. The skin of ripe papaya yields slightly when pressed and there is a faint sweet aroma at the stem end. Signs of overripeness are dimpled or wrinkled skin or soft spots and a strong aroma.

Peaches and Nectarines

Preparation: If desired, peel peaches by blanching for 30 seconds. Using a slotted spoon, remove from boiling water and immediately plunge into cold water; let stand until cold. Drain well. Peel off skin. Cut lengthwise into wedges about ¼ inch (0.5 cm) thick at the widest part, or cut in half lengthwise around the pit, place cut side down on cutting board and cut into slices about ¼ inch (0.5 cm) thick.

Pretreatment (optional): To prevent browning, dip peach slices in lemon juice or an ascorbic acid solution (see page 13) as you slice them. Drain well.

Drying: Place on mesh drying trays. Dry at 130°F (55°C).

Time: 10 to 12 hours.

Doneness test: Wedges or slices should feel dry and leathery and still be flexible.

Tip

- The skin on peaches isn't too tough when dried and is perfectly fine for peaches that will be used dry. If you're planning to rehydrate and cook the peaches, you may wish to peel them before drying.

Pears

Preparation: Peel pears, if desired. Cut in half lengthwise, scoop out core and remove strings. Place cut side down on cutting board and cut into slices about ¼ inch (0.5 cm) thick at the widest part.

Pretreatment (optional): To prevent browning, dip pear slices in lemon juice or an ascorbic acid solution (see page 13) as you slice them. Drain well.

Drying: Place on mesh drying trays. Dry at 130°F (55°C).

Time: 12 to 14 hours.

Doneness test: Slices should feel dry and leathery and still be flexible.

Tip
• Pear skin is generally fairly tender but does toughen slightly when dried. If you're planning to rehydrate and cook the pears, you may wish to peel them before drying.

Pineapple

Rings

Preparation: Using a large serrated knife, cut skin from pineapple. Remove eyes with a paring knife. Cut pineapple crosswise into slices about $\frac{1}{4}$ inch (0.5 cm) thick. Cut out core.

Drying: Place on mesh drying trays. Dry at 130°F (55°C).

Time: 14 to 16 hours.

Doneness test: Rings should feel dry and leathery and still be flexible.

Tip
• If you plan to dry pineapple often, purchase a specially designed pineapple corer/peeler/slicer.

Quarter Rings

Preparation: Using a large serrated knife, cut skin from pineapple. Remove eyes with a paring knife. Cut pineapple lengthwise into quarters and cut off core. Cut quarters crosswise into slices about $\frac{1}{4}$ inch (0.5 cm) thick.

Drying: Place on mesh drying trays. Dry at 130°F (55°C).

Time: 14 to 16 hours.

Doneness test: Quarter rings should feel dry and leathery and still be flexible.

Tip
• To make cutting simple, purchase a peeled, cored pineapple, available at many supermarkets.

Pieces

Preparation: Using a large serrated knife, cut skin from pineapple. Remove eyes with a paring knife. Cut pineapple lengthwise into 8 wedges (if small) or 12 wedges (if large) and cut off core. Cut wedges crosswise into slices about $\frac{1}{4}$ inch (0.5 cm) thick.

Drying: Place on mesh drying trays. Dry at 130°F (55°C).

Time: 12 to 14 hours.

Doneness test: Pieces should feel dry and leathery and still be flexible.

Tip
• Peel pieces from the mesh drying trays as soon as you remove them from the dryer (while they're still warm) to prevent sticking.

Plums

Preparation: Cut plums lengthwise into quarters or wedges about $\frac{1}{2}$ inch (1 cm) thick at the widest part. Small plums can be cut in half; pierce the skin several times with a toothpick.

Drying: Place skin side down on mesh drying trays. Dry at 130°F (55°C).

Time: 18 to 20 hours.

Doneness test: Plums should feel dry and leathery and still be flexible.

Tip
• Firmer prune-style (blue, Italian) plums give the nicest texture when dried and have a flavor more like commercial prunes.

Raspberries

Preparation: None.

Drying: Place hollow side down on mesh drying trays. Dry at 130°F (55°C).

Time: 20 to 24 hours.

Doneness test: Berries should feel dry and crisp, with no evidence of moisture inside.

Tips

- Use fine-mesh tray liners (e.g., Clean-A-Screen) if necessary to prevent berries from sticking to tray. When removing dried berries, slide a dull metal spatula underneath to loosen and avoid crushing the berries.
- Locally grown, fresh-picked berries dry faster than varieties grown for shipping and a long shelf life.

Strawberries

Preparation: Hull strawberries and cut lengthwise into slices about $\frac{1}{4}$ inch (0.5 cm) thick.

Drying: Place cut side up on mesh drying trays. Dry at 130°F (55°C).

Time: 8 to 16 hours.

Doneness test: Slices should feel dry, leathery and no longer juicy but still slightly flexible.

Tips

- Use fine-mesh tray liners (e.g., Clean-A-Screen) if necessary to prevent berries from sticking to tray.
- Locally grown, fresh-picked berries dry faster than varieties grown for shipping and a long shelf life.

VEGETABLES

Asparagus

Preparation: Remove tough ends and any large scales. Cut spears into 1-inch (2.5 cm) sections.

Pretreatment: In a pot of boiling water, blanch asparagus for 3 minutes. Using a strainer, remove from boiling water and immediately plunge into cold water; let stand until cold. Drain well.

Drying: Place on mesh drying trays. Dry at 130°F (55°C).

Time: 12 to 14 hours.

Doneness test: Asparagus should feel dry and crisp and have no sign of moisture inside when broken open.

Tips

- Use fine-mesh tray liners (e.g., Clean-A-Screen) if necessary to prevent small pieces from falling through trays.

- Sort stalks on trays according to approximate thickness to make it easier to remove those that are done earlier.

Beans, Green and Yellow Wax

Preparation: Slice beans into 1-inch (2.5 cm) sections.

Pretreatment: In a pot of boiling water, blanch beans for 2 minutes. Using a strainer, remove from boiling water and immediately plunge into cold water; let stand until cold. Drain well.

Drying: Place on mesh drying trays. Dry at 130°F (55°C).

Time: 10 to 12 hours.

Doneness test: Beans should feel dry and crisp and have no sign of moisture inside when broken open.

Tip
* Use fine-mesh tray liners (e.g., Clean-A-Screen) if necessary to prevent small pieces from falling through trays.

Beans, Lima

Preparation: For fresh lima beans, remove beans from pods, discarding pods. For frozen lima beans, let thaw and drain off any excess liquid. For canned lima beans, drain and rinse beans.

Pretreatment: For fresh beans only, in a pot of boiling water, cook beans for 5 to 10 minutes (depending on size), or until tender. Using a strainer, remove from boiling water and immediately plunge into cold water; let stand until cold. Drain well.

Drying: Spread on mesh drying trays. Dry at 130°F (55°C).

Time: 5 to 12 hours.

Doneness test: Beans should feel dry and crisp and have no sign of moisture inside when broken open.

Tip
* The drying time will depend on what size beans you use; baby lima beans will dry in 5 to 6 hours; large lima beans will take 10 to 12 hours.

Beets

Preparation: Remove leaves, leaving 1 inch (2.5 cm) of stem on the beet. In a pot of boiling water, boil beets for 30 minutes, or until fork-tender. Using a strainer, remove from boiling water and immediately plunge into cold water; let stand until cold. Drain well. Cut off tops and remove skins. Cut into slices $\frac{1}{8}$ to $\frac{1}{4}$ inch (0.25 to 0.5 cm) thick.

Drying: Place on mesh drying trays. Dry at 130°F (55°C).

Time: 10 to 12 hours.

Doneness test: Slices should feel firm and leathery and still be flexible.

Tip
* Completely cooking the beets speeds up drying and provides a better texture once they're rehydrated.

Broccoli

Preparation: Break into 1-inch (2.5 cm) florets. Discard stems or reserve for another use.

Pretreatment: In a pot of boiling water, blanch broccoli for 2 minutes. Using a strainer, remove from boiling water and immediately plunge into cold water; let stand until cold. Drain well.

Drying: Place on mesh drying trays. Dry at 130°F (55°C).

Time: 6 to 8 hours.

Doneness test: Florets should feel dry and crisp and have no sign of moisture inside when broken open.

Tip
* Stems tend to remain tough after drying and rehydrating, so it's best to use just the florets. The stalks can be added to soups or peeled and cut up to serve with dip.

Carrots and Parsnips

Slices

Preparation: Peel carrots or parsnips and cut crosswise into slices about $\frac{1}{4}$ inch (0.5 cm) thick.

Pretreatment: In a pot of boiling water, blanch carrots for 3 minutes. Using a strainer, remove from boiling water and immediately plunge into cold water; let stand until cold. Drain well.

Drying: Place on mesh drying trays. Dry at 130°F (55°C).

Time: 6 to 8 hours.

Doneness test: Slices should feel dry and crisp but still be slightly flexible.

Tip

- The edges of sliced carrots will ripple when dried.

Thin Slices

Preparation: Peel carrots or parsnips and cut crosswise into slices about $1/8$ inch (0.25 cm) thick.

Pretreatment (optional): In a pot of boiling water, blanch carrots for 1 minute. Using a strainer, remove from boiling water and immediately plunge into cold water; let stand until cold. Drain well.

Drying: Place on mesh drying trays. Dry at 130°F (55°C).

Time: 4 to 6 hours.

Doneness test: Slices should feel dry and crisp but still be slightly flexible.

Tip

- Thin carrot slices will curl up when dried. Use fine-mesh tray liners (e.g., Clean-A-Screen) to prevent small pieces from falling through trays.

Pieces

Preparation: Peel carrots or parsnips and cut crosswise into large sections. Cut each section in half lengthwise. Cut thicker ends in half lengthwise again to make quarters. Cut crosswise into $1/4$-inch (0.5 cm) pieces.

Pretreatment (optional): In a pot of boiling water, blanch carrots for 3 minutes. Using a strainer, remove from boiling water and immediately plunge into cold water; let stand until cold. Drain well.

Drying: Place on mesh drying trays. Dry at 130°F (55°C).

Time: 4 to 5 hours.

Doneness test: Pieces should feel dry and crisp but still be slightly flexible.

Tips

- This is a more efficient way to cut carrots for drying than a conventional diced shape. True cubes will take considerably longer to dry.
- Use fine-mesh tray liners (e.g., Clean-A-Screen) to prevent small pieces from falling through trays.

Grated

Preparation: Grate carrots or parsnips on the coarse side of a box grater or using the shredding plate of a food processor.

Drying: Spread on fine-mesh drying trays (e.g., Clean-A-Screen). Dry at 130°F (55°C).

Time: 3 to 4 hours.

Special instructions: Stir occasionally to break up any clumps and ensure even drying.

Doneness test: Carrots should be shriveled, leathery and just slightly pliable.

Tip

- Remove carrots from the trays when warm and let cool in a shallow dish. If left to cool on the trays, they tend to stick.

Cauliflower

Preparation: Break cauliflower into 1-inch (2.5 cm) florets.

Pretreatment: In a pot of boiling water, blanch cauliflower for 4 minutes. Using a strainer, remove from boiling water and immediately plunge into cold water; let stand until cold. Drain well.

Drying: Place on mesh drying trays. Dry at 130°F (55°C).

Time: 8 to 10 hours.

Doneness test: Florets should feel dry and crisp and have no sign of moisture inside when broken open.

Tip

- Cauliflower florets will darken considerably as they dry, ending up an orangey-brown color, but will lighten up again when rehydrated.

Celery

Preparation: Trim ends and cut stalks crosswise into slices about $\frac{1}{4}$ inch (0.5 cm) thick.

Pretreatment (optional): In a pot of boiling water, blanch celery for 1 minute. Using a strainer, remove from boiling water and immediately plunge into cold water; let stand until cold. Drain well.

Drying: Place on mesh drying trays. Dry at 130°F (55°C).

Time: 6 to 8 hours.

Doneness test: Slices should feel dry and crisp and have no sign of moisture inside when broken open.

Tip

- Celery will shrink a lot as it dries. Use fine-mesh tray liners (e.g., Clean-A-Screen) to prevent small pieces from falling through trays.

Corn

Preparation: If using fresh corn, cook cobs in boiling water for 5 minutes. Let cool slightly and cut kernels from the cob. Let frozen corn thaw and drain off any excess liquid.

Drying: Spread on mesh drying trays. Dry at 130°F (55°C).

Time: 10 to 12 hours.

Doneness test: Corn should be shriveled, firm and brittle.

Tip

- To cut kernels from cobs, hold the wide end of the cob in your hand, placing the narrow end in a deep bowl, and use a small, flexible serrated knife to gently saw the kernels off the cob into the bowl.

Cucumbers, English and Field

Preparation: Trim ends and cut cucumbers crosswise into slices about $\frac{1}{4}$ inch (0.5 cm) thick. (Do not peel.)

Drying: Place on mesh drying trays. Dry at 130°F (55°C).

Time: 6 to 8 hours.

Doneness test: Slices should feel dry and crisp and have no sign of moisture inside when broken open.

Tip

- Some field cucumbers have very thick skins and tough seeds. Those with thinner skins and smaller seeds are better suited to drying.

Dandelion Greens

Preparation: Remove leaves from stalks.

Drying: Place on mesh drying trays. Dry at 110°F (43°C).

Time: 6 to 8 hours.

Special instructions: Rearrange leaves and flip over as necessary to ensure even drying.

Doneness test: Leaves should be crisp and brittle.

Tips

- If picking wild dandelion greens, be sure to use only those that haven't been sprayed with a pesticide.
- Dried greens add a boost of color and flavor to soups and stews.

Eggplant

Preparation: Peel eggplant and cut crosswise into slices about $\frac{1}{4}$ inch (0.5 cm) thick.

Pretreatment (optional): In a pot of boiling water, blanch eggplant for 1 minute. Using a strainer, remove from boiling water and immediately plunge into cold water; let stand until cold. Drain well.

Drying: Place on mesh drying trays. Dry at 130°F (55°C).

Time: 8 to 10 hours.

Doneness test: Slices should feel firm and leathery and still be flexible.

Tips

- Choose smaller eggplants, which tend to have fewer, smaller and less bitter seeds than larger eggplants.
- Use kitchen scissors to snip dried eggplant into smaller pieces before using.

Fennel

Preparation: Trim off root end and any tough outer layers. Cut crosswise into slices about $\frac{1}{4}$ inch (0.5 cm) thick. Cut slices into $\frac{1}{2}$-inch (1 cm) pieces.

Pretreatment: In a pot of boiling water, blanch fennel for 1 minute. Using a strainer, remove from boiling water and immediately plunge into cold water; let stand until cold. Drain well.

Drying: Place on mesh drying trays. Dry at 130°F (55°C).

Time: 6 to 8 hours.

Doneness test: Pieces should be dry, leathery and just slightly pliable, with no sign of moisture inside.

Tip

- The thick outer layers of fennel get quite stringy when dried. To avoid waste and use up the layers you've cut from the fresh fennel bulb, slice them very thinly and sauté or add to stock or soup.

Leeks

Slices

Preparation: Trim off roots and tough green tops of leeks. Cut in half lengthwise and rinse thoroughly between layers. Place cut side down and cut crosswise into $\frac{1}{4}$-inch (0.5 cm) slices.

Drying: Place on mesh drying trays. Dry at 130°F (55°C).

Time: 6 to 8 hours.

Doneness test: Slices should feel dry and crisp and have no sign of moisture inside when broken open.

Tip

- Be sure to rinse between the layers well, as there is often sand trapped deep inside.

Pieces

Preparation: Trim off roots and tough green tops of leeks. Cut in half lengthwise and rinse thoroughly between layers. Place cut side down and cut lengthwise, then crosswise into $\frac{1}{4}$- to $\frac{1}{2}$-inch (0.5 to 1 cm) pieces.

Drying: Place on mesh drying trays. Dry at 130°F (55°C).

Time: 6 to 8 hours.

Doneness test: Pieces should feel dry and crisp and have no sign of moisture inside when broken open.

Tip

- The green tops of leeks are very tough and stringy, so they are not suited to drying or regular cooking. You can wash them well and use them to flavor stocks.

Mushrooms

Preparation: Cut mushrooms lengthwise into slices about $\frac{1}{4}$ inch (0.5 cm) thick.

Drying: Place on mesh drying trays. Dry at 130°F (55°C).

Time: 8 to 14 hours.

Doneness test: Slices should feel dry and crisp and have no sign of moisture inside when broken open.

Tips

- These instructions will work for all types of mushrooms. If stems are thick and chewy, such as those on shiitake or portobello mushrooms, trim them off and dry only the caps. Stems can be used to flavor stocks.
- Mushrooms are easiest to dry in slices. For smaller mushroom pieces, crumble dried slices just before using.

Onions

Slices

Preparation: Remove the outer skin and first layer of the onion flesh. Cut into rings about $\frac{1}{4}$ inch (0.5 cm) thick, separating rings.

Drying: Place on mesh drying trays. Dry at 130°F (55°C).

Time: 6 to 8 hours.

Doneness test: Slices should feel dry and crisp and have no sign of moisture inside when broken open.

Tips

- Nest small rings inside larger rings to conserve space in the dryer.
- You may want to dry onions in the garage — or at least in a well-ventilated room — as the drying process is quite aromatic.

Pieces

Preparation: Remove the outer skin and first layer of the onion flesh. Cut into $\frac{1}{4}$- to $\frac{1}{2}$-inch (0.5 to 1 cm) pieces, separating layers.

Drying: Place on mesh drying trays. Dry at 130°F (55°C).

Time: 6 to 8 hours.

Doneness test: Pieces should feel dry and crisp and have no sign of moisture inside when broken open.

Tips

- To ensure even drying, stir periodically and separate any layers of onions that are stuck together.
- You may want to dry onions in the garage — or at least in a well-ventilated room — as the drying process is quite aromatic.

Roasted

Preparation: Remove the outer skin and first layer of the onion flesh. Cut into $\frac{1}{2}$-inch (1 cm) pieces, separating layers. For each $1\frac{1}{2}$ lbs (750 g) onions, add 2 tbsp (25 mL) balsamic, red wine, white wine or cider vinegar and salt and pepper to taste; toss to coat. Spread out on a baking sheet lined with parchment paper. Bake in a 350°F (180°C) oven for about 1 hour, stirring once, until browned and very tender.

Drying: Spread on fine-mesh drying trays (e.g., Clean-A-Screen). Dry at 130°F (55°C).

Time: 4 to 6 hours.

Doneness test: Onions should be shriveled, leathery and just slightly pliable.

Tip

- To ensure even drying, stir periodically and separate any layers of onions that are stuck together.

Peas, Green

Preparation: Remove fresh peas from pods, discarding pods. Let frozen peas thaw and drain off any excess liquid.

Pretreatment: If using fresh peas, blanch in a pot of boiling water for 3 minutes. Using a strainer, remove from boiling water and immediately plunge into cold water; let stand until cold. Drain well.

Drying: Spread on mesh drying trays. Dry at 130°F (55°C).

Time: 8 to 10 hours.

Doneness test: Peas should be shriveled, firm and brittle.

Peppers, Bell

Slices

Preparation: Cut peppers in half lengthwise. Cut out stem, core and seeds. Cut lengthwise or crosswise into $1/4$- to $1/2$-inch (0.5 to 1 cm) strips.

Drying: Place cut side down on mesh drying trays. Dry at 130°F (55°C).

Time: 14 to 18 hours.

Doneness test: Slices should feel dry and crisp and have no sign of moisture inside when broken open.

Tip

• Peppers vary quite a bit in the thickness of the flesh. Thicker, meatier peppers will take longer to dry. Thinner peppers may dry more quickly than the time specified.

Pieces

Preparation: Cut peppers in half lengthwise. Cut out stem, core and seeds. Cut lengthwise into $1/4$- to $1/2$-inch (0.5 to 1 cm) strips. Cut strips crosswise into $1/4$- to $1/2$-inch (0.5 to 1 cm) pieces.

Drying: Place skin side down on mesh drying trays. Dry at 130°F (55°C).

Time: 12 to 16 hours.

Doneness test: Pieces should feel dry and crisp and have no sign of moisture inside when broken open.

Peppers, Chile

Preparation: Cut peppers in half lengthwise. Cut out stem, core and seeds. Cut crosswise into slices about $1/4$ inch (0.5 cm) thick.

Drying: Place on mesh drying trays. Dry at 130°F (55°C).

Time: 12 to 18 hours.

Doneness test: Slices should feel dry and crisp and have no sign of moisture inside when broken open.

Tips

• When handling hot peppers, wear gloves to protect your hands from the peppers' oils and be careful not to touch your eyes.

• Use fine-mesh tray liners (e.g., Clean-A-Screen) if necessary to prevent peppers from falling through trays.

Potatoes

Slices

Preparation: Peel potatoes and cut crosswise into slices $1/8$ to $1/4$ inch (0.25 to 0.5 cm) thick.

Pretreatment: In a pot of boiling water, blanch potatoes for 5 minutes. Using a strainer, remove from boiling water and immediately plunge into cold water; let stand until cold. Drain well.

Drying: Place on mesh drying trays. Dry at 130°F (55°C).

Time: 8 to 10 hours.

Doneness test: Slices should feel dry and crisp and have no sign of moisture inside when broken open.

Tips

- Use a mandoline to make quick work of cutting thin, even slices of potato.
- Dried potato slices can be broken or cut into smaller pieces for rehydrating and cooking.

Cubes

Preparation: Peel potatoes and cut into $\frac{1}{2}$-inch (1 cm) cubes.

Pretreatment: In a pot of boiling water, boil potatoes for 10 minutes. Using a strainer, remove from boiling water and immediately plunge into cold water; let stand until cold. Drain well.

Drying: Place on mesh drying trays. Dry at 130°F (55°C).

Time: 12 to 16 hours.

Doneness test: Cubes should feel dry and crisp and have no sign of moisture inside when broken open.

Tip

- Be sure the potatoes are completely dry inside. They may feel firm on the outside when they still have moisture trapped within. It is better to leave them in the dryer longer to prevent premature spoilage.

Grated

Preparation: Peel potatoes, if desired, and shred on the coarse side of a box grater or using the shredding plate of a food processor.

Pretreatment: Place in a heatproof colander or strainer and check in boiling water (see page 19). Using a strainer, remove from boiling water and immediately plunge into cold water; let stand until cold. Gently press to squeeze out any excess liquid.

Drying: Spread on fine-mesh drying trays (e.g., Clean-A-Screen). Dry at 130°F (55°C).

Time: 2 to 3 hours.

Special instructions: Stir occasionally to break up any clumps and ensure even drying.

Doneness test: Potatoes should be dry, crisp and translucent.

Tip

- Remove potatoes from the trays when warm and let cool in a shallow dish. If left to cool on the screens, they tend to stick.

Pumpkin and Winter Squash

Slices

Preparation: Peel pumpkin or squash, cut in half lengthwise and scrape out seeds and loose flesh. Cut lengthwise into quarters or sixths, if desired. Cut crosswise into slices about $\frac{1}{4}$ inch (0.5 cm) thick.

Pretreatment: In a pot of boiling water, blanch pumpkin for 3 minutes. Using a strainer, remove from boiling water and immediately plunge into cold water; let stand until cold. Drain well.

Drying: Place on mesh drying trays. Dry at 130°F (55°C).

Time: 6 to 8 hours.

Doneness test: Slices should be dry, leathery and still pliable, with no evidence of moisture inside.

Tips

- Use only pie pumpkins or winter squash with firm, dense flesh. Pulpy jack-o'-lantern pumpkins and spaghetti squash, for example, don't dry well.
- Use a sharp Y-shaped vegetable peeler to peel hard pumpkins or squash. For the best texture, make sure to remove the thick layer just under the skin.

Cubes

Preparation: Peel pumpkin or squash and cut into $\frac{1}{4}$- to $\frac{1}{2}$-inch (0.5 to 1 cm) cubes.

Pretreatment: In a pot of boiling water, blanch pumpkin for 3 minutes. Using a strainer, remove from boiling water and immediately plunge into cold water; let stand until cold. Drain well.

Drying: Place on mesh drying trays. Dry at 130°F (55°C).

Time: 6 to 10 hours.

Doneness test: Cubes should feel dry and crisp and have no sign of moisture inside when broken open.

Grated

Preparation: Peel pumpkin or squash, cut in half lengthwise and scrape out seeds and loose flesh. Cut into chunks and shred on the coarse side of a box grater or using the shredding plate of a food processor.

Pretreatment: Place in a heatproof colander or strainer and check in boiling water (see page 19). Using a strainer, remove from boiling water and immediately plunge into cold water; let stand until cold. Gently press to squeeze out any excess liquid.

Drying: Spread on fine-mesh drying trays (e.g., Clean-A-Screen). Dry at 130°F (55°C).

Time: 2 to 3 hours.

Special instructions: Stir occasionally to break up any clumps and ensure even drying.

Doneness test: Pumpkin should be shriveled, leathery and just slightly pliable.

Tips
- Butternut squash is the easiest to use for grating because of its smooth shape and firm flesh.
- Remove pumpkin from the trays when warm and let cool in a shallow dish. If left to cool on the screens, it tends to stick.

Radishes

Preparation: Trim ends and cut radishes crosswise into slices about $\frac{1}{8}$ inch (0.25 cm) thick.

Drying: Place on mesh drying trays. Dry at 130°F (55°C).

Time: 5 to 6 hours.

Doneness test: Slices should feel dry and crisp and have no sign of moisture inside when broken open.

Tip
- Thin radish slices will curl up when dried. Use fine-mesh tray liners (e.g., Clean-A-Screen) to prevent small pieces from falling through trays.

Rhubarb

Thin slices

Preparation: Cut thin (less than $\frac{3}{4}$ inch/ 2 cm) stalks crosswise on a diagonal into $\frac{1}{2}$-inch (1 cm) slices.

Pretreatment: In a pot of boiling water, blanch rhubarb for 1 minute. Using a strainer, remove from boiling water and immediately plunge into cold water; let stand until cold. Drain well.

Drying: Place on mesh drying trays. Dry at 130°F (55°C).

Time: 8 to 10 hours.

Doneness test: Slices should feel dry and crisp and have no sign of moisture inside when broken open.

Tip
- Use fine-mesh tray liners (e.g., Clean-A-Screen) if necessary to prevent small pieces from falling through trays.

Thick slices

Preparation: Cut thick (larger than ¾ inch/2 cm) stalks crosswise on a diagonal into 1-inch (2.5 cm) slices.

Pretreatment: In a pot of boiling water, blanch rhubarb for 5 minutes. Using a strainer, remove from boiling water and immediately plunge into cold water; let stand until cold. Drain well.

Drying: Place on mesh drying trays. Dry at 130°F (55°C).

Time: 12 to 14 hours.

Doneness test: Slices should feel dry and crisp and have no sign of moisture inside when broken open.

Tip
* For best results, do not use rhubarb stalks that are very thick and woody.

Rutabaga and Turnips

Slices

Preparation: Peel rutabaga and cut in half lengthwise. Place cut side down and cut crosswise into slices about ¼ inch (0.5 cm) thick.

Pretreatment: In a pot of boiling water, blanch rutabaga for 3 minutes. Using a strainer, remove from boiling water and immediately plunge into cold water; let stand until cold. Drain well.

Drying: Place on mesh drying trays. Dry at 130°F (55°C).

Time: 6 to 8 hours.

Doneness test: Slices should be dry, leathery and still pliable, with no evidence of moisture inside.

Tip
* If rutabaga or turnips are large, you can cut them lengthwise into quarters to make smaller slices. The drying time will be about the same.

Cubes

Preparation: Peel rutabaga and cut into ¼- to ½-inch (0.5 to 1 cm) cubes.

Pretreatment: In a pot of boiling water, blanch rutabaga for 3 minutes. Using a strainer, remove from boiling water and immediately plunge into cold water; let stand until cold. Drain well.

Drying: Place on mesh drying trays. Dry at 130°F (55°C).

Time: 6 to 10 hours.

Doneness test: Cubes should feel dry and crisp and have no sign of moisture inside when broken open.

Tip
* Choose rutabaga and turnips that are heavy for their size and have no signs of shriveling, sprouting or mold.

Shallots

Slices

Preparation: Remove the outer skin of the shallots. Cut crosswise into slices about ¼ inch (0.5 cm) thick, separating rings.

Drying: Place on mesh drying trays. Dry at 130°F (55°C).

Time: 8 to 10 hours.

Doneness test: Shallots should be dry, leathery and just slightly pliable.

Tip
* Shallots are easiest to dry in rings. If you need chopped or finely chopped shallots, use scissors to cut dried rings into smaller pieces just before using.

Roasted

Preparation: Remove the outer skin of the shallots. Cut into ½-inch (1 cm) pieces, separating layers. For each 1 lb (500 g) shallots, add 2 tbsp (25 mL) red wine or white wine vinegar and salt and pepper to taste; toss to coat. Spread out on a baking sheet lined with parchment paper. Bake in a 350°F (180°C) oven for about 45 minutes, stirring once, until browned and very tender.

Drying: Spread on fine-mesh drying trays (e.g., Clean-A-Screen). Dry at 130°F (55°C).

Time: 4 to 6 hours.

Doneness test: Shallots should be shriveled, leathery and just slightly pliable.

Tip

- To ensure even drying, stir periodically and separate any layers of shallots that are stuck together.

Sweet Potatoes

Slices

Preparation: Bake sweet potatoes in a 350°F (180°C) oven for 45 minutes. Let rest until cool enough to touch, then remove the skins and cut flesh crosswise into slices about $\frac{1}{4}$ inch (0.5 cm) thick.

Drying: Place on mesh drying trays. Dry at 130°F (55°C).

Time: 10 to 12 hours.

Doneness test: Slices should feel firm and leathery and still be flexible.

Tip

- Roasting sweet potatoes before drying them helps maintain the shape much better than blanching and speeds up the drying process.

Cubes

Preparation: Bake sweet potatoes in a 350°F (180°C) oven for 45 minutes. Let rest until cool enough to touch, then remove the skins and cut flesh into $\frac{1}{2}$-inch (1 cm) cubes.

Drying: Place on mesh drying trays. Dry at 130°F (55°C).

Time: 12 to 14 hours.

Doneness test: Cubes should be shriveled and hard, with no sign of moisture inside.

Tip

- Roasting sweet potatoes before drying them helps maintain the shape much better than blanching and speeds up the drying process.

Tomatoes, Grape

Preparation: Cut tomatoes in half lengthwise.

Drying: Place on mesh drying trays. Dry at 130°F (55°C).

Time: 20 to 24 hours.

Doneness test: Tomatoes should feel dry, be just slightly pliable and have no sign of moisture inside when broken open.

Tip

- Home-dried tomatoes will be firmer than commercially dried tomatoes. If you don't dry them enough and leave them soft, they will spoil quickly.

Tomatoes, Plum (Roma)

Preparation: Cut smaller tomatoes lengthwise into 8 wedges; cut larger ones into 12 wedges.

Drying: Place skin side down on mesh drying trays. Dry at 130°F (55°C).

Time: 20 to 24 hours.

Doneness test: Wedges should feel dry, be just slightly pliable and have no sign of moisture inside when broken open.

Tips

- Point the thin part of the slices toward the center of the tray so that the air flow across the slices is not impeded by the thicker portion.
- Beefsteak-style tomatoes and juicy cherry tomatoes have a lot of moisture, so there's

very little tomato — and thus very little flavor — left after drying. Plum (Roma) or other paste-style tomatoes are better suited to drying.

- Home-dried tomatoes will be firmer than commercially dried tomatoes. If you don't dry them enough and leave them soft, they will spoil quickly.

Zucchini and Summer Squash

Slices

Preparation: Trim zucchini or squash and cut crosswise into slices about $\frac{1}{4}$ inch (0.5 cm) thick. (Do not peel.)

Drying: Place on mesh drying trays. Dry at 130°F (55°C).

Time: 6 to 10 hours.

Doneness test: Slices should feel dry and crisp and have no sign of moisture inside when broken open.

Tip
- Thinner zucchini are better for drying, as they tend to have firmer flesh and smaller seeds than large zucchini.

Grated

Preparation: Shred zucchini or squash on the coarse side of a box grater or using the shredding plate of a food processor. Place in a colander and gently press to squeeze out any excess liquid.

Drying: Spread on fine-mesh drying trays (e.g., Clean-A-Screen). Dry at 130°F (55°C).

Time: 2 to 3 hours.

Special instructions: Stir occasionally to break up any clumps and ensure even drying.

Doneness test: Zucchini should be shriveled, leathery and just slightly pliable.

Tip
- Remove zucchini from the trays when warm and let cool in a shallow dish. If left to cool on the screens, it tends to stick.

Making Fruit and Vegetable Leathers

Leather-Making Techniques and Tips

- A food processor is the best tool for puréeing thicker mixtures such as those used for leathers. If you don't have a food processor, an immersion blender in a tall cup works almost as well. If you only have a regular blender, you may need to add a bit of water to thin it out enough to blend; however, more water in the purée will increase the drying time.
- Use an offset spatula or a straight-edged dough scraper to spread the puréed mixture evenly on the sheet.
- It's best to press, rather than spread, thicker, dryer vegetable purées onto the sheet to help prevent fissures from forming as the purée dries. Some fissures will form in foods without pectin, creating cracked leather, and spreading tends to increase this chance.
- To determine whether the purée is spread to the right thickness, stick a toothpick straight down into the mixture and lift it out, then measure the moisture level on the toothpick.
- The thickness of the purée is more important than covering the entire leather sheet. Because sheets vary in size for different machines, you may need to use more than one, or cover only part of the sheet.
- Be sure to not to spread the purée too thin. Even though it will dry faster, it will be difficult to lift off the leather sheet and will likely tear into shreds.
- If you don't have leather sheets, you can use parchment paper. It does tend to wrinkle slightly with very moist purées, and the drying time may be quite a bit shorter, so start checking for dryness earlier. Tuck the edges of the parchment paper underneath the mesh on the drying tray, or use metal paper clips to secure the paper to the tray, to keep it from flying around in the circulating air.
- If you have hard plastic leather sheets or trays, drier mixtures such as vegetable leathers tend to stick. To prevent sticking, cut out a sheet of parchment paper the same size and shape as the sheet and line the sheet before spreading the purée.
- You don't have to flip the leather, but it does speed up drying.
- To make flipping the leather easier, invert the leather sheet onto another mesh drying tray, then carefully peel off the leather sheet. Alternatively, if the leather seems fragile, invert another mesh drying tray on top of the leather on sheet. Slide your hand under the leather sheet and flip both over so the leather is inverted on the mesh tray, then carefully peel off the leather sheet.
- Fruit leather can be sweetened to taste, but keep in mind that sugar will slow the drying process and that adding too much can make for a sticky product that may never get leathery.
- When testing for doneness, keep in mind that the leather will firm up more upon cooling. You want to make sure there are no moist patches, but overdried leather can become crispy.
- As soon as leather is dry, peel it off the sheet or tray while still warm and let cool. Place on a sheet of plastic wrap, parchment paper or waxed paper and roll up jellyroll-style, rolling wrap between layers of the leather to prevent it from sticking to itself. Place in an airtight container or sealable plastic bag and store at room temperature for up to 6 months.
- Vegetable leathers tend to get quite hard and dry, so they work best when turned into powder. Break cooled leather into pieces, chop in a mini chopper or spice grinder and process until finely chopped or to a powder. Add to soups, stews and rice.

FRUIT LEATHERS

Apple Cinnamon Leather

Preparation: In a bowl, combine 2 cups (500 mL) unsweetened applesauce and $\frac{1}{2}$ tsp (2 mL) ground cinnamon.

Drying: Spread out to $\frac{1}{4}$-inch (0.5 cm) thickness, as evenly as possible, on a leather sheet or a drying tray lined with parchment paper, leaving it slightly thicker around the edges. Dry at 130°F (55°C).

Time: 6 to 9 hours.

Special instructions: Start checking leather after 4 hours. When top is very firm and edges are easy to lift, carefully peel leather from sheet, flip over and continue drying.

Doneness test: Leather should be evenly translucent, with no visible moist spots, and should still be flexible.

Tip

- This works equally well with homemade or store-bought applesauce from a jar. Just be sure to read the label to make sure there's no added sugar. The amount of sugar added to commercial sauces interferes with proper drying.

Apricot Leather

Preparation: In a food processor, purée 2 cups (500 mL) halved apricots, 1 tbsp (15 mL) freshly squeezed lemon juice and 1 tbsp (15 mL) granulated sugar (if desired) until smooth.

Drying: Spread out to $\frac{1}{4}$-inch (0.5 cm) thickness, as evenly as possible, on a leather sheet or a drying tray lined with parchment paper, leaving it slightly thicker around the edges. Dry at 130°F (55°C).

Time: 5 to 7 hours.

Special instructions: Start checking leather after 3 hours. When top is very firm and edges are easy to lift, carefully peel leather from sheet, flip over and continue drying.

Doneness test: Leather should be evenly translucent, with no visible moist spots, and should still be flexible.

Tip

- Taste your apricots before puréeing them. Some are quite tart and will need some sugar; others are naturally quite sweet.

Strawberry Apple Leather

Preparation: In a food processor, purée 2 cups (500 mL) strawberries and 1 apple, peeled and chopped, until smooth.

Drying: Spread out to $\frac{1}{4}$-inch (0.5 cm) thickness, as evenly as possible, on a leather sheet or a drying tray lined with parchment paper, leaving it slightly thicker around the edges. Dry at 130°F (55°C).

Time: 6 to 8 hours.

Special instructions: Start checking leather after 5 hours. When top is very firm and edges are easy to lift, carefully peel leather from sheet, flip over and continue drying.

Doneness test: Leather should be evenly translucent, with no visible moist spots, and should still be flexible.

Tip

- Tart cooking apples that hold their flavor when heated, such as Granny Smith, Crispin and McIntosh, work best.

Banana Chocolate Leather

Preparation: In a food processor, purée 4 ripe bananas, broken into chunks, 2 tbsp (25 mL) unsweetened cocoa powder and 1 tbsp (15 mL) granulated sugar until smooth.

Drying: Spread out to ¼-inch (0.5 cm) thickness, as evenly as possible, on a leather sheet or a drying tray lined with parchment paper, leaving it slightly thicker around the edges. Dry at 130°F (55°C).

Time: 9 to 11 hours.

Special instructions: Start checking leather after 8 hours. When top is very firm and edges are easy to lift, carefully peel leather from sheet, flip over and continue drying.

Doneness test: Leather should be evenly firm, with no visible moist spots, and should still be flexible.

Tip
- Use very ripe bananas (with brown spots) for the best flavor. Underripe bananas aren't sweet or moist enough to make a nice leather.

Banana Nut Leather

Preparation: In a food processor, pulse ½ cup (125 mL) nuts (almonds, pecans, peanuts, hazelnuts) until finely chopped. Add 4 bananas, broken into chunks, and purée until fairly smooth.

Drying: Spread out to ¼-inch (0.5 cm) thickness, as evenly as possible, on a leather sheet or a drying tray lined with parchment paper, leaving it slightly thicker around the edges. Dry at 130°F (55°C).

Time: 9 to 11 hours.

Special instructions: Start checking leather after 7 hours. When top is very firm and edges are easy to lift, carefully peel leather from sheet, flip over and continue drying.

Doneness test: Leather should be evenly firm, with no visible moist spots, and should still be flexible.

Tips
- This leather tends to get crispy if overdried. If it does get crispy, break it into pieces and call it Banana Nut Crunch.
- The oil in the nuts reduces the shelf life of this leather. Store it at room temperature for up to 2 months or refrigerate for longer storage.

Cantaloupe Blueberry Leather

Preparation: In a food processor, purée 1½ cups (375 mL) chopped cantaloupe and 1 cup (250 mL) blueberries until smooth.

Drying: Spread out to ¼-inch (0.5 cm) thickness, as evenly as possible, on a leather sheet or a drying tray lined with parchment paper, leaving it slightly thicker around the edges. Dry at 130°F (55°C).

Time: 6 to 9 hours.

Special instructions: Start checking leather after 4 hours. When top is very firm and edges are easy to lift, carefully peel leather from sheet, flip over and continue drying.

Doneness test: Leather should be evenly firm, with no visible moist spots, and should still be flexible.

Tip
- Use a ripe and flavorful cantaloupe, but avoid an overripe melon, which can be pulpy or very juicy and give an unpleasant texture to the leather.

Mango Raspberry Leather

Preparation: In a food processor, purée 1$\frac{1}{2}$ cups (375 mL) chopped mango and 1 cup (250 mL) raspberries.

Drying: Spread out to $\frac{1}{4}$-inch (0.5 cm) thickness, as evenly as possible, on a leather sheet or a drying tray lined with parchment paper, leaving it slightly thicker around the edges. Dry at 130°F (55°C).

Time: 6 to 9 hours.

Special instructions: Start checking leather after 4 hours. When top is very firm and edges are easy to lift, carefully peel leather from sheet, flip over and continue drying.

Doneness test: Leather should be evenly translucent, with no visible moist spots, and should still be flexible.

Tip
- Use very ripe, soft mango for the best flavor and texture.

Peach Vanilla Leather

Preparation: In a food processor, purée 2$\frac{1}{2}$ cups (625 mL) chopped peaches, 1 tbsp (15 mL) granulated sugar or liquid honey, 1 tsp (5 mL) freshly squeezed lemon juice and $\frac{1}{4}$ tsp (1 mL) vanilla extract until smooth.

Drying: Spread out to $\frac{1}{4}$-inch (0.5 cm) thickness, as evenly as possible, on a leather sheet or a drying tray lined with parchment paper, leaving it slightly thicker around the edges. Dry at 130°F (55°C).

Time: 5 to 7 hours.

Special instructions: Start checking leather after 3$\frac{1}{2}$ hours. When top is very firm and edges are easy to lift, carefully peel leather from sheet, flip over and continue drying.

Doneness test: Leather should be evenly firm, with no visible moist spots, and should still be flexible.

Tip
- The peaches don't need to be peeled; just rub off any fuzz under running water before chopping.

Plum Cherry Leather

Preparation: In a food processor, purée 1$\frac{1}{2}$ cups (375 mL) chopped plums and 1 cup (250 mL) pitted sweet cherries until smooth.

Drying: Spread out to $\frac{1}{4}$-inch (0.5 cm) thickness, as evenly as possible, on a leather sheet or a drying tray lined with parchment paper, leaving it slightly thicker around the edges. Dry at 130°F (55°C).

Time: 7 to 9 hours.

Special instructions: Start checking leather after 5 hours. When top is very firm and edges are easy to lift, carefully peel leather from sheet, flip over and continue drying.

Doneness test: Leather should be evenly firm, with no visible moist spots, and should still be flexible.

Tip
- Purple or blue Italian-style plums have a deeper flavor than other plums; this flavor comes through nicely when the plums are dried.

Strawberry Banana Leather

Preparation: In a food processor, purée 2 cups (500 mL) strawberries and 1 ripe banana, broken into chunks, until smooth.

Drying: Spread out to ¼-inch (0.5 cm) thickness, as evenly as possible, on a leather sheet or a drying tray lined with parchment paper, leaving it slightly thicker around the edges. Dry at 130°F (55°C).

Time: 5 to 7 hours.

Special instructions: Start checking leather after 3 hours. When top is very firm and edges are easy to lift, carefully peel leather from sheet, flip over and continue drying.

Doneness test: Leather should be evenly firm, with no visible moist spots, and should still be flexible.

Tip

- Use very ripe bananas (with brown spots) for the best flavor. Underripe bananas aren't sweet or moist enough to make a nice leather.

Tropical Fruit Leather

Preparation: In a food processor, purée 1 cup (250 mL) chopped pineapple, 1 cup (250 mL) chopped mango and 1 ripe banana, broken into chunks, until smooth.

Drying: Spread out to ¼-inch (0.5 cm) thickness, as evenly as possible, on a leather sheet or a drying tray lined with parchment paper, leaving it slightly thicker around the edges. Dry at 130°F (55°C).

Time: 8 to 10 hours.

Special instructions: Start checking leather after 5 hours. When top is very firm and edges are easy to lift, carefully peel leather from sheet, flip over and continue drying.

Doneness test: Leather should be evenly firm, with no visible moist spots, and should still be flexible.

Tips

- Use ripe but not overripe fruit for the best flavor and texture.
- Sprinkle the purée with 2 tbsp (25 mL) sweetened shredded coconut, if desired.

VEGETABLE AND SAUCE LEATHERS

Tomato Pasta Sauce Leather

Preparation: Choose a homemade or prepared tomato pasta sauce with no meat, dairy or oil (or as little oil as possible). If sauce is chunky, purée in a food processor or blender until smooth.

Drying: Spread out to ¼-inch (0.5 cm) thickness, as evenly as possible, on a leather sheet or a drying tray lined with parchment paper, leaving it slightly thicker around the edges. Dry at 130°F (55°C).

Time: 12 to 16 hours.

Special instructions: Start checking leather after 10 hours. When top is very firm and edges are easy to lift, carefully peel leather from sheet, flip over and continue drying.

Doneness test: Leather should be evenly dry, with no visible moist spots, and should still be flexible.

Tip
- Starting with a thicker sauce will speed up the drying time. If you're making homemade sauce, simmer it a little longer to save time in the dryer.

Tomato Paste Leather

Preparation: None.

Drying: Press to $\frac{1}{4}$-inch (0.5 cm) thickness, as evenly as possible, on a leather sheet or a drying tray lined with parchment paper, leaving it slightly thicker around the edges. Dry at 130°F (55°C).

Time: 6 to 8 hours.

Special instructions: Start checking leather after 4 hours. When top is very firm and edges are easy to lift, carefully peel leather from sheet, flip over and continue drying.

Doneness test: Leather should be evenly dry, with no visible moist spots, and should still be flexible.

Salsa Leather

Preparation: Choose a homemade or prepared tomato salsa with no oil. If salsa is chunky, purée in a food processor or blender until smooth.

Drying: Spread out to $\frac{1}{4}$-inch (0.5 cm) thickness, as evenly as possible, on a leather sheet or a drying tray lined with parchment paper, leaving it slightly thicker around the edges. Dry at 130°F (55°C).

Time: 8 to 10 hours.

Special instructions: Start checking leather after 6 hours. When top is very firm and edges are easy to lift, carefully peel leather from sheet, flip over and continue drying.

Doneness test: Leather should be evenly dry, with no visible moist spots, and should still be flexible.

Tip
- Keep in mind that the flavor of the salsa will get very intense once dried. If you use a hot salsa, be prepared for the leather to be fiery.

Barbecue Sauce Leather

Preparation: In a saucepan, combine 1 clove garlic, minced, $\frac{1}{4}$ cup (50 mL) packed brown sugar, 1 tsp (5 mL) chili powder, $\frac{1}{2}$ tsp (2 mL) dry mustard, $\frac{1}{4}$ tsp (1 mL) each celery seed, salt and pepper, 1 cup (250 mL) tomato paste and $\frac{1}{4}$ cup (50 mL) each cider vinegar and water. Bring to a boil over medium heat, whisking constantly. Simmer, whisking, for 3 minutes to blend flavors.

Drying: Spread out to $\frac{1}{4}$-inch (0.5 cm) thickness, as evenly as possible, on a leather sheet or a drying tray lined with parchment paper, leaving it slightly thicker around the edges. Dry at 130°F (55°C).

Time: 16 to 20 hours.

Special instructions: Start checking leather after 12 hours. When top is very firm and edges are easy to lift, carefully peel leather from sheet, flip over and continue drying.

Doneness test: Leather should be evenly dry, with no visible moist spots, and should still be flexible.

Tip
- This barbecue sauce was specially created to make leather. Commercial sauces generally have too much sugar and thickeners to dry properly.

Carrot Leather

Preparation: In a saucepan, cover 4 cups (1 L) chopped carrots with water. Bring to a boil over high heat. Reduce heat and boil gently for about 7 minutes or until carrots are very soft. Drain, reserving cooking liquid. In a food processor, purée carrots, adding as much of the reserved cooking liquid as necessary to make a smooth, thick paste. Season to taste with salt and pepper, if desired.

Drying: Press to $\frac{1}{4}$-inch (0.5 cm) thickness, as evenly as possible, on a leather sheet or a drying tray lined with parchment paper, leaving it slightly thicker around the edges. Dry at 130°F (55°C).

Time: 6 to 9 hours.

Special instructions: Start checking leather after 4 hours. When top is very firm and edges are easy to lift, carefully peel leather from sheet, flip over and continue drying.

Doneness test: Leather should be evenly dry, with no visible moist spots, and should still be flexible.

Tip
- This leather tastes terrific on its own or can be broken into pieces or finely chopped and added to soups or stews.

Sweet Potato and Red Pepper Leather

Preparation: Pierce 1 large sweet potato (about 1 lb/500 g) all over with a fork. Place on a baking sheet and bake in a 350°F (180°C) oven for about 1 hour or until fork-tender. Let cool. Peel and cut into chunks. In a food processor, purée sweet potato and 1 cup (250 mL) chopped red bell pepper until smooth. Season to taste with salt and pepper, if desired.

Drying: Press to $\frac{1}{4}$-inch (0.5 cm) thickness, as evenly as possible, on a leather sheet or a drying tray lined with parchment paper, leaving it slightly thicker around the edges. Dry at 130°F (55°C).

Time: 6 to 9 hours.

Special instructions: Start checking leather after 4 hours. When top is very firm and edges are easy to lift, carefully peel leather from sheet, flip over and continue drying.

Doneness test: Leather should be evenly dry, with no visible moist spots, and should still be flexible.

Tip
- This leather tastes terrific on its own or can be broken into pieces or finely chopped and added to soups or stews.

Green Pea Leather

Preparation: In a food processor, purée 2 cups (500 mL) cooked or thawed frozen green peas until smooth, adding a little water if necessary. Season to taste with salt and pepper, if desired.

Drying: Press to $\frac{1}{4}$-inch (0.5 cm) thickness, as evenly as possible, on a leather sheet or a drying tray lined with parchment paper, leaving it slightly thicker around the edges. Dry at 130°F (55°C).

Time: 8 to 10 hours.

Special instructions: Start checking leather after 5 hours. When top is very firm and edges are easy to lift, carefully peel leather from sheet, flip over and continue drying.

Doneness test: Leather should be evenly dry and crisp.

Tip
- Green pea leather is quite hard, so it is best used as a powder or broken into small pieces. Add to soups and stews.

Roasted Winter Squash or Pumpkin Leather

Preparation: On a baking sheet lined with parchment paper, toss 4 cups (1 L) cubed winter squash ($\frac{1}{2}$-inch/1 cm cubes) with 2 tbsp (25 mL) cider vinegar. Roast in a 350°F (180°C) oven for about 30 minutes or until browned and tender. Let cool. In a food processor, purée roasted squash until smooth. Season to taste with salt and pepper, if desired.

Drying: Press to $\frac{1}{4}$-inch (0.5 cm) thickness, as evenly as possible, on a leather sheet or a drying tray lined with parchment paper, leaving it slightly thicker around the edges. Dry at 130°F (55°C).

Time: 8 to 10 hours.

Special instructions: Start checking leather after 6 hours. When top is very firm and edges are easy to lift, carefully peel leather from sheet, flip over and continue drying.

Doneness test: Leather should be evenly dry, with no visible moist spots, and should still be flexible.

Tip
- Butternut squash is the easiest to peel and chop and has a drier texture than some other squash. Avoid soft, pulpy squash, as they can make a crumbly leather.

Mushroom Leather

Preparation: In a skillet, over medium-high heat, sauté 1 lb (500 g) mushrooms, chopped, $\frac{1}{2}$ cup (125 mL) chopped onion, 3 cloves garlic, minced, and $\frac{1}{2}$ tsp (2 mL) crumbled dried rosemary for about 10 minutes or until liquid is evaporated and mushrooms start to brown. Let cool. In a food processor, purée until fairly smooth. Season to taste with salt and pepper, if desired.

Drying: Press to $\frac{1}{4}$-inch (0.5 cm) thickness, as evenly as possible, on a leather sheet or a drying tray lined with parchment paper, leaving it slightly thicker around the edges. Dry at 130°F (55°C).

Time: 8 to 10 hours.

Special instructions: Start checking leather after 5 hours. When top is very firm and edges are easy to lift, carefully peel leather from sheet, flip over and continue drying.

Doneness test: Leather should be evenly dry and slightly flexible.

Tip
- Use pieces of this leather in soups and stews — or add some when making vegetable stock to boost the flavor.

Spinach Leather

Preparation: In a food processor, purée 2 cups (500 mL) drained cooked or thawed frozen spinach (about 12 oz/ 375 g) until fairly smooth. Season to taste with salt and pepper, if desired.

Drying: Press to $\frac{1}{4}$-inch (0.5 cm) thickness, as evenly as possible, on a leather sheet or a drying tray lined with parchment paper, leaving it slightly thicker around the edges. Dry at 130°F (55°C).

Time: 8 to 10 hours.

Special instructions: Start checking leather after 5 hours. When top is very firm and edges are easy to lift, carefully peel leather from sheet, flip over and continue drying.

Doneness test: Leather should be evenly dry and crisp.

Tip
- Dried spinach is best used as a powder. Break cooled leather into chunks and chop in a food processor to a fine powder. Add to soups, rice, stews or eggs.

Dehydrating Beans, Tofu, Grains and Dairy

Beans and Tofu

Cooked Grains and Pasta

Dairy

BEANS AND TOFU

Canned or Cooked Beans

Preparation: Drain and rinse canned or cooked black beans, kidney beans, white pea (navy) beans, Romano beans or chickpeas. Drain well.

Drying: Place on mesh drying trays. Dry at 130°F (55°C).

Time: 5 to 6 hours.

Doneness test: Beans should be light, crisp and dry throughout.

Tip
- Some beans burst open and crumble slightly while drying. Just scoop up all of the small bits and add to the beans when packaging. The small bits help thicken recipes that use dried cooked beans.

Basic Veggie Burger Blend

Preparation: In a food processor, combine 1 cup (250 mL) cooked long-grain brown rice, 1 cup (250 mL) drained, rinsed canned or cooked chickpeas and 1 cup (250 mL) drained, rinsed canned or cooked brown lentils. Pulse until finely chopped but not puréed.

Drying: Spread out to ¼-inch (0.5 cm) thickness, as evenly as possible, on a fine-mesh drying tray, a leather sheet or a drying tray lined with parchment paper. Dry at 130°F (55°C).

Time: 4 to 6 hours.

Doneness test: Pieces should be very crisp and dry throughout.

Tip
- The small pieces may fall through even a fine-mesh drying tray, so the leather sheet or parchment may work better for you, though they do slow drying time. If using the fine-mesh tray, place a leather sheet on an empty rack below to catch any pieces that fall through.

Tofu

Slices

Preparation: Use extra-firm or firm tofu. Remove from package and rinse well. Cut into slices about ¼ inch (0.5 cm) thick.

Drying: Place on mesh drying trays. Dry at 130°F (55°C).

Time: 12 to 14 hours.

Special instructions: After about 8 hours, flip the tofu pieces to speed up drying, if desired.

Doneness test: Slices should feel very dry and firm and should break easily when bent.

Tips
- For extra flavor, marinate tofu in any of the jerky marinades or rubs (pages 64 to 68) for 30 minutes; drain off excess, if necessary, before drying.
- Because tofu contains fat, it is best stored in the refrigerator, where it will keep for up to 6 months; it can be stored at room temperature for up to 2 weeks.

Crumbled

Preparation: Use extra-firm or firm tofu. Remove from package and rinse well. Break into ¼- to ½-inch (0.5 to 1 cm) pieces.

Drying: Spread out as thinly and evenly as possible on fine-mesh drying trays. Dry at 130°F (55°C).

Time: 12 to 14 hours.

Special instructions: During drying, rearrange tofu on the tray to separate any clumps.

Doneness test: Pieces should feel very dry and firm.

Tips

- For even drying, make sure the tofu pieces are uniform in size.
- For extra flavor, marinate tofu in any of the jerky marinades or rubs (pages 64 to 68) for 30 minutes; drain off excess, if necessary, before drying.
- Because tofu contains fat, it is best stored in the refrigerator, where it will keep for up to 6 months; it can be stored at room temperature for up to 2 weeks.

Shredded

Preparation: Use extra-firm or firm tofu. Remove from package and rinse well. Using the coarse side of a box cheese grater, grate into shreds.

Drying: Spread out as thinly and evenly as possible on fine-mesh drying trays. Dry at 130°F (55°C).

Time: 10 to 12 hours.

Special instructions: During drying, rearrange tofu on the tray to separate any clumps.

Doneness test: Shredded tofu should feel very dry and firm.

Tips

- The color of tofu will darken considerably as it dries.

- Use fine-mesh tray liners (e.g., Clean-A-Screen) if necessary to prevent pieces from falling through trays.
- Because tofu contains fat, it is best stored in the refrigerator, where it will keep for up to 6 months; it can be stored at room temperature for up to 2 weeks.

Puréed

Preparation: Use firm tofu. Remove from package and rinse well. In a food processor, purée until smooth.

Drying: Spread out to ¼-inch (0.5 cm) thickness, as evenly as possible, on leather sheets or on drying trays lined with parchment paper, leaving it slightly thicker around the edges. Dry at 130°F (55°C).

Time: 12 to 14 hours.

Special instructions: Start checking tofu after 8 hours. When top is firm and edges are easy to lift, carefully peel from trays, flip over and continue drying.

Doneness test: Sheets should be evenly dry and crisp.

To use: Sheets can be crumbled into pieces or ground in a food processor or mini chopper, then added to recipes.

Tips

- Be sure there are no lumps in the purée, as they will not dry properly.
- Because tofu contains fat, it is best stored in the refrigerator, where it will keep for up to 6 months; it can be stored at room temperature for up to 2 weeks.

COOKED GRAINS AND PASTA

White Rice

Preparation: Cook long-grain white rice according to package directions until tender. Rinse under cold running water to cool and rinse off excess starch. Drain well.

Drying: Spread out as evenly as possible on fine-mesh drying trays. Dry at 130°F (55°C).

Time: 5 to 6 hours.

Special instructions: Stir occasionally to break up any clumps and ensure even drying.

Doneness test: Rice should be translucent, very firm and dry throughout.

Tip
• Use fine-mesh tray liners (e.g., Clean-A-Screen) if necessary to prevent rice from falling through trays.

Brown Rice

Preparation: Cook long-grain brown rice according to package directions until tender. Rinse under cold running water to cool and rinse off excess starch. Drain well.

Drying: Spread out as evenly as possible on fine-mesh drying trays. Dry at 130°F (55°C).

Time: 6 to 8 hours.

Special instructions: Stir occasionally to break up any clumps and ensure even drying.

Doneness test: Rice should be translucent, very firm and dry throughout.

Tip
• Use fine-mesh tray liners (e.g., Clean-A-Screen) if necessary to prevent rice from falling through trays.

Wild Rice

Preparation: Cook wild rice according to package directions until tender. Rinse under cold running water to cool and rinse off excess starch. Drain well.

Drying: Spread out as evenly as possible on fine-mesh drying trays. Dry at 130°F (55°C).

Time: 6 to 8 hours.

Special instructions: Stir occasionally to break up any clumps and ensure even drying.

Doneness test: Rice grains should be firm, should snap easily when bent and should be dry throughout.

Tips
• Wild rice is rather expensive. You may want to experiment with small amounts to perfect your drying technique before drying larger quantities.
• Some wild rice grains are much larger than others. Large grains will take longer to cook and to dry.

Wheat Berries

Preparation: Cook wheat berries until tender. Rinse under cold running water to cool and rinse off excess starch. Drain well.

Drying: Spread out as evenly as possible on fine-mesh drying trays. Dry at 130°F (55°C).

Time: 3 to 4 hours.

Special instructions: Stir occasionally to break up any clumps and ensure even drying.

Doneness test: Wheat berries should be very firm and dry throughout.

Tips

- Wheat berries are whole kernels of wheat. They can be found at natural food stores and bulk stores, or where other whole grains are sold.
- Use fine-mesh tray liners (e.g., Clean-A-Screen) if necessary to prevent grains from falling through trays.

Barley

Preparation: Cook whole (hulled) barley, pot barley or pearl barley until tender. Drain and rinse under cold running water. Drain well.

Drying: Spread out as evenly as possible on fine-mesh drying trays. Dry at 130°F (55°C).

Time: 3 to 4 hours.

Special instructions: Stir occasionally to break up any clumps and ensure even drying.

Doneness test: Barley should be very firm and dry throughout.

Tips

- Use fine-mesh tray liners (e.g., Clean-A-Screen) if necessary to prevent grains from falling through trays.
- Whole barley is less refined than pot or pearl barley, so it takes longer to cook, but the extra nutrition is worth it.

Whole Oats

Preparation: Cook whole (hulled) oats until tender. Drain and rinse under cold running water. Drain well.

Drying: Spread out as evenly as possible on fine-mesh drying trays. Dry at 130°F (55°C).

Time: 3 to 4 hours.

Special instructions: Stir occasionally to break up any clumps and ensure even drying.

Doneness test: Oats should be very firm and dry throughout.

Tip

- Use fine-mesh tray liners (e.g., Clean-A-Screen) if necessary to prevent oats from falling through trays.

Steel-Cut Oats

Preparation: Cook steel-cut oats according to package directions until thickened and tender.

Drying: Spread out to 1/4-inch (0.5 cm) thickness, as evenly as possible, on leather sheets or on drying trays lined with parchment paper, leaving it slightly thicker around the edges. Dry at 130°F (55°C).

Time: 7 to 10 hours.

Special instructions: Start checking oats after 5 hours. When top is very firm and edges are easy to lift, carefully peel from leather sheets, flip over and continue drying.

Doneness test: Sheets should be evenly dry and crisp and should break easily when bent.

To use: Break sheets into small pieces and process in a mini chopper, food processor or blender until fairly finely chopped and about one-quarter is powdery. Rehydrate by soaking 1 part ground oats in 3 parts water for 20 minutes, then bring to a boil.

Tip

- Cooked large-flake rolled oats can also be dried in this way.

Elbow Macaroni

Preparation: Cook pasta according to package directions until tender but firm (al dente). Rinse well under cold running water to remove excess starch. Drain well.

Drying: Place on fine-mesh drying trays. Dry at 130°F (55°C).

Time: 2 to 4 hours.

Special instructions: Rearrange pasta on the tray as necessary to separate pieces.

Doneness test: Pasta should be very light, evenly firm and dry throughout.

To use: Soak dried cooked pasta in room-temperature water for about 30 minutes. Or add to boiling water and boil for 3 to 5 minutes.

Tips
- Use fine-mesh tray liners (e.g., Clean-A-Screen) if necessary to prevent pasta from falling through trays.
- Dried cooked pasta doesn't shrink much in size but does rehydrate easily with room-temperature water, making it perfect for eating away from home.

Fusilli or Rotini Pasta

Preparation: Cook pasta according to package directions until tender but firm (al dente). Rinse well under cold running water to remove excess starch. Drain well.

Drying: Place on mesh drying trays. Dry at 130°F (55°C).

Time: 2 to 4 hours.

Special instructions: Rearrange pasta on the tray as necessary to separate pieces.

Doneness test: Pasta should be very light, evenly firm and dry throughout.

To use: Soak dried cooked pasta in room-temperature water for about 30 minutes. Or add to boiling water and boil for 3 to 5 minutes.

Tip
- Open pasta shapes with a lot of surface area work best for drying and rehydrating.

Bread Crumbs

Preparation: Cut fresh bread, buns or rolls into slices about $1/2$ inch (1 cm) thick.

Drying: Place on mesh drying trays. Dry at 155°F (68°C).

Time: 1 to 3 hours.

Doneness test: Slices should be very firm and crisp throughout.

To store: Let dried bread cool completely. Transfer to a bowl and crumble to coarse crumbs, or in a food processor, process to fine crumbs. Store in an airtight container at room temperature for up to 6 months.

Tip
- Crumbs made from breads with nuts or seeds will not keep as long because of the oils. Store crumbs made from these breads in the freezer.

DAIRY

Cottage Cheese

Preparation: Use 1% (low-fat) cottage cheese. Stir to blend evenly.

Drying: Spread out to $\frac{1}{4}$-inch (0.5 cm) thickness, as evenly as possible, on leather sheets or on drying trays lined with parchment paper, leaving it slightly thicker around the edges. Dry at 130°F (55°C).

Time: 10 to 14 hours.

Special instructions: If possible, flip over after 5 to 6 hours or once the cheese is easy to lift from the leather sheets; this will speed up drying.

Doneness test: Sheets should be thoroughly dry and very hard.

To use: Break dried cottage cheese into small pieces to simmer in sauces. Use a mini chopper to grind dried cottage cheese to a powder for use in other recipes.

Tips
- For maximum shelf life, dried cottage cheese is best stored in the refrigerator, where it will keep for up to 6 months; it can be stored at room temperature for up to 1 week.
- Do not attempt to use higher-fat cottage cheese, as it may go rancid quickly when heated and stored at room temperature.

Puréed

Preparation: Use 1% (low-fat) cottage cheese. Using an immersion blender in a tall cup, or in a food processor or blender, purée cottage cheese until smooth.

Drying: Spread out to $\frac{1}{4}$-inch (0.5 cm) thickness, as evenly as possible, on leather sheets or on drying trays lined with parchment paper, leaving it slightly thicker around the edges. Dry at 130°F (55°C).

Time: 10 to 14 hours.

Special instructions: If possible, flip over after 5 to 6 hours or once the cheese is easy to lift from the leather sheets; this will speed up drying.

Doneness test: Sheets should be thoroughly dry and very hard.

To use: Break dried cottage cheese into small pieces to simmer in sauces. Use a mini chopper to grind dried cottage cheese to a powder for use in other recipes.

Tips
- For maximum shelf life, dried cottage cheese is best stored in the refrigerator, where it will keep for up to 6 months; it can be stored at room temperature for up to 1 week.
- Do not attempt to use higher-fat cottage cheese, as it may go rancid quickly when heated and stored at room temperature.

Yogurt

Plain

Preparation: Use 1% (low-fat) yogurt. Stir until smooth and blended.

Drying: Spread out to $\frac{1}{4}$-inch (0.5 cm) thickness, as evenly as possible, on leather sheets or on drying trays lined with parchment paper, leaving it slightly thicker around the edges. Dry at 130°F (55°C).

Time: 12 to 14 hours.

Special instructions: If possible, flip over after about 8 hours or once the yogurt is easy to lift from the leather sheets; this will speed up drying.

Doneness test: Sheets should be firm and should break easily.

Tips

- Avoid any yogurts with gelatin or other thickeners, as they won't dry thoroughly.
- Do not attempt to use higher-fat yogurt, as it may go rancid quickly when heated and stored at room temperature.
- For maximum shelf life, dried yogurt is best stored in the refrigerator, where it will keep for up to 6 months; it can be stored at room temperature for up to 1 week.

Fruit-Flavored

Preparation: Use 1% (low-fat) fruit-flavored yogurt. Stir until smooth and blended.

Drying: Spread out to ¼-inch (0.5 cm) thickness, as evenly as possible, on leather sheets or on drying trays lined with parchment paper, leaving it slightly thicker around the edges. Dry at 130°F (55°C).

Time: 14 to 20 hours.

Special instructions: Start checking yogurt after 10 hours. When top is very firm and edges start to lift, carefully peel from leather sheets, flip over and continue drying. Or, if desired, you can cut sheet into small pieces and transfer pieces to a mesh drying tray for a chewy snack.

Doneness test: Dried yogurt should be evenly dry and firm but still flexible.

Tips

- Avoid any yogurts with gelatin or other thickeners, as they won't dry thoroughly.
- Flavored yogurts contain varying amounts of added sugars. Those higher in sugar will take longer to dry. Avoid yogurts with artificial sweeteners.
- For maximum shelf life, dried yogurt is best stored in the refrigerator, where it will keep for up to 6 months; it can be stored at room temperature for up to 1 week.

Dehydrating Meat, Poultry and Fish

Making Jerky

Dried meat, fish and poultry have sustained people around the world for centuries. Leftover meat that wasn't eaten right away was cut into strips and left to dry, sometimes over a fire, for later use. Removing the moisture made it last longer and made it lighter to pack and carry for nomadic populations. We have learned from those historical populations to preserve meat, fish and poultry and have expanded the practice by making it taste even more delicious by adding flavorful marinades and rubs.

In this chapter, we have provided some recipes for jerky strips and ground meat jerky. You can certainly experiment with the flavors, but the method should be followed carefully to make sure the jerky you make at home gets preserved properly and is safe to eat. Use only fresh meat, poultry or fish that you are confident is of the highest quality.

Lean cuts are necessary to make jerky that lasts. Higher-fat cuts do not dry properly, and the residual fats in the meat will go rancid and spoil the jerky. Cuts with marbling of fat through the meat also tend to break apart as the meat is cooked and dried, and the fat leaches out, so you don't end up with nice strips.

All meat, poultry and fish (even the lean cuts) will have a small amount of fat that cooks out when the strips are first baked, and some may continue to rise to the surface during drying. These small amounts of fat are easy to blot off with paper towels after cooking and during drying to ensure a high-quality jerky.

Jerky recipes made with ground meats also benefit from the use of lean meat. Ground meat jerky is easiest if you have a specially designed jerky gun, but with some patience you can hand-shape strips with a piping bag or simple spoons. The advantage of making jerky with ground meats is that you can incorporate seasoning elements right into the meat for extra flavor. Jerky made with ground meat is also much more tender, which is particularly good for kids and those who don't like the toothsome texture of traditional jerky made from meat strips.

For the utmost food safety, we recommend that only fully cooked meats, poultry and fish be used to make jerky at home. Historically, raw meats have been used, but new research suggests that, to protect against food-borne illnesses, the only safe way to make jerky is to cook the meat to well done before drying it.

Storing Jerky

To store jerky, once it has cooled, place it in an airtight container lined with a paper towel. Check it periodically to see if any more fat has come out of the jerky; if so, replace the paper towel with a fresh one. When storing jerky, keep different flavors separate to be sure the flavors stay true.

Commercial jerky generally contains nitrites as a preservative, which creates a softer texture, brighter color and longer shelf life. We prefer not to use any preservatives, other than common salt; therefore, the recipes have been tested without added nitrites. For that reason, we recommend storing at room temperature for a maximum of 1 month. However, jerky can be safely refrigerated for up to 6 months or frozen for up to 1 year.

Dried products take up much less space in the fridge or freezer than fresh and are stable for packing without refrigeration for a short time, making them perfect for camping and hiking.

Suitable Cuts for Jerky Strips

Any of these cuts can be used to make jerky strips (pages 64 to 68).

Beef, Venison, Elk, Moose, Bison

- flank steak
- eye of round
- outside round
- sirloin tip

Chicken, Turkey, Farmed Duck, Wild Goose

- boneless skinless breast

Ostrich, Emu

- fan (thigh)
- inside strip
- outside strip
- top strip
- back tender

Fish

- low-fat fish fillets, such as catfish, cod, ocean perch, pickerel (northern pike), pollock, rainbow trout, striped bass, rock bass or tilapia
- salmon fillets are traditional for jerky, but their fat content makes them unsuitable for room-temperature storage; store salmon jerky in the refrigerator for up to 1 month or in the freezer for up to 6 months

Before purchasing fish, always learn what you can about sustainability and fishing practices. Good North American resources are
- www.montereybayaquarium.org/cr/ SeafoodWatch/wcb/sfw_regional.aspx
- www.seachoice.org

Using Bottled Marinades to Prepare Jerky

Look for bottled marinades or sauces that don't contain a high amount of sugar, as sugar tends to lengthen the drying time significantly. Many bottled products also contain some amount of oil, which will decrease the shelf life of the jerky, as oils tend to go rancid over time. Choose oil-free marinades or those with as little oil as possible. Be judicious in your use of bottled marinade: excess marinade tends to congeal and clump, forming overly intense flavor in those spots.

Sea Salt and Peppercorn Jerky

A light seasoning makes this jerky versatile: you can use it in a wide array of recipes or simply enjoy it as is.

Makes about 24 strips

• *Large rimmed baking sheets, lined with parchment paper*

1 lb	meat, poultry or fish, trimmed	500 g
1 tsp	sea salt	5 mL
1/2 tsp	freshly ground black pepper	2 mL

1. For easier slicing, put the meat in the freezer for about 25 minutes or until firm but not solid. Meanwhile, preheat oven to 350°F (180°C).

2. Using a sharp knife, cut meat into strips about 1/4 inch (0.5 cm) thick, cutting with the grain for chewy strips or across the grain for more brittle strips (which will be easier to chew).

3. In a bowl, toss meat strips with salt and pepper, coating evenly. Arrange on prepared baking sheets, leaving space between each strip.

4. Bake in preheated oven for 10 minutes or until meat is no longer pink inside (or fish is firm and opaque). Transfer to a baking sheet lined with paper towels, turning to blot both sides.

5. Place cooked meat strips on mesh drying trays. Dry at 155°F (68°C) for 6 to 8 hours, occasionally blotting any fat that rises to the surface with paper towels, until jerky is firm and flexes and cracks, but doesn't break, when gently bent. Transfer to a clean baking sheet lined with paper towels and let cool completely, turning once to blot thoroughly.

Cajun Jerky

Sweetness, spice and heat combine to make a zesty jerky.

Makes about 24 strips

Tips

Experiment with your favorite prepared dry rubs and spice blends. On average, use about 1/3 cup (75 mL) per pound (500 g) meat, poultry or fish.

Fish, chicken breasts and tender ostrich and emu cuts only need to stand in the rub for 15 minutes to 1 hour. For other meats, refrigerate for 30 minutes or longer.

• *Large rimmed baking sheets, lined with parchment paper*

1 lb	meat, poultry or fish, trimmed	500 g
2 tbsp	sweet paprika	25 mL
4 tsp	packed brown sugar	20 mL
2 tsp	salt	10 mL
2 tsp	dry mustard	10 mL
1/2 tsp	ground ginger	2 mL
1/2 tsp	cayenne pepper	2 mL
1/4 tsp	ground allspice	1 mL

1. For easier slicing, put the meat in the freezer for about 25 minutes or until firm but not solid.

2. Using a sharp knife, cut meat into strips about 1/4 inch (0.5 cm) thick, cutting with the grain for chewy strips or across the grain for more brittle strips (which will be easier to chew).

3. In a bowl, combine paprika, brown sugar, salt, mustard, ginger, cayenne and allspice. Add meat strips and toss to coat. Let stand at room temperature for 15 minutes, or cover and refrigerate for up to 8 hours (see tip, at left). Meanwhile, preheat oven to 350°F (180°C).

4. Arrange meat strips on prepared baking sheets, leaving space between each strip. Bake in preheated oven for 10 minutes or until meat is no longer pink inside (or fish is firm and opaque). Transfer to a baking sheet lined with paper towels, turning to blot both sides.

5. Place cooked meat strips on mesh drying trays. Dry at 155°F (68°C) for 6 to 8 hours, occasionally blotting any fat that rises to the surface with paper towels, until jerky is firm and flexes and cracks, but doesn't break, when gently bent. Transfer to a clean baking sheet lined with paper towels and let cool completely, turning once to blot thoroughly.

Maple and Grainy Dijon Jerky

This jerky marinade gives the classic honey-mustard idea a gourmet twist by combining sweet maple syrup with tangy mustard.

Makes about 24 strips

Tip

Fish, chicken breast and tender ostrich and emu cuts only need to marinate for 15 minutes to 1 hour. For other meats, marinate for 30 minutes or longer.

• *Large rimmed baking sheets, lined with parchment paper*

1 lb	meat, poultry or fish, trimmed	500 g
$\frac{1}{4}$ tsp	salt	1 mL
2 tbsp	grainy Dijon mustard	25 mL
2 tbsp	pure maple syrup	25 mL

1. For easier slicing, put the meat in the freezer for about 25 minutes or until firm but not solid.

2. Using a sharp knife, cut meat into strips about $\frac{1}{4}$ inch (0.5 cm) thick, cutting with the grain for chewy strips or across the grain for more brittle strips (which will be easier to chew).

3. In a bowl, combine salt, mustard and maple syrup. Add meat strips and toss to coat. Let stand at room temperature for 15 minutes, or cover and refrigerate for up to 8 hours (see tip, at left). Meanwhile, preheat oven to 350°F (180°C).

4. Remove meat from marinade, discarding excess marinade and accumulated juices. Arrange meat strips on prepared baking sheets, leaving space between each strip. Bake in preheated oven for 10 minutes or until meat is no longer pink inside (or fish is firm and opaque). Transfer to a baking sheet lined with paper towels, turning to blot both sides.

5. Place cooked meat strips on mesh drying trays. Dry at 155°F (68°C) for 6 to 8 hours, occasionally blotting any fat that rises to the surface with paper towels, until jerky is firm and flexes and cracks, but doesn't break, when gently bent. Transfer to a clean baking sheet lined with paper towels and let cool completely, turning once to blot thoroughly.

Teriyaki Jerky

Teriyaki is one of the most popular seasonings for jerky, and once you taste this version you'll know why. This marinade gives a depth of flavor you just don't get from bottled sauces.

Makes about 24 strips

Tip

Fish, chicken breast and tender ostrich and emu cuts only need to marinate for 15 minutes to 1 hour. For other meats, marinate for 30 minutes or longer.

• *Large rimmed baking sheets, lined with parchment paper*

1 lb	meat, poultry or fish, trimmed	500 g
2 tbsp	packed brown sugar	25 mL
1/2 tsp	ground ginger	2 mL
1/2 tsp	freshly ground black pepper	2 mL
2 tbsp	soy sauce	25 mL
1 tsp	Asian chili sauce	5 mL
1 tsp	rice vinegar	5 mL

1. For easier slicing, put the meat in the freezer for about 25 minutes or until firm but not solid.

2. Using a sharp knife, cut meat into strips about 1/4 inch (0.5 cm) thick, cutting with the grain for chewy strips or across the grain for more brittle strips (which will be easier to chew).

3. In a bowl, combine brown sugar, ginger, pepper, soy sauce, chili sauce and vinegar. Add meat strips and toss to coat. Let stand at room temperature for 15 minutes, or cover and refrigerate for up to 8 hours (see tip, at left). Meanwhile, preheat oven to 350°F (180°C).

4. Remove meat from marinade, discarding excess marinade and accumulated juices. Arrange meat strips on prepared baking sheets, leaving space between each strip. Bake in preheated oven for 10 minutes or until meat is no longer pink inside (or fish is firm and opaque). Transfer to a baking sheet lined with paper towels, turning to blot both sides.

5. Place cooked meat strips on mesh drying trays. Dry at 155°F (68°C) for 6 to 8 hours, occasionally blotting any fat that rises to the surface with paper towels, until jerky is firm and flexes and cracks, but doesn't break, when gently bent. Transfer to a clean baking sheet lined with paper towels and let cool completely, turning once to blot thoroughly.

Jerk Jerky

A little taste of Jamaica spices up jerky nicely. If you like it hot, hot, hot, use the Scotch bonnet pepper.

Makes about 24 strips

Tip

Fish, chicken breast and tender ostrich and emu cuts only need to marinate for 15 minutes to 1 hour. For other meats, marinate for 30 minutes or longer.

• *Large rimmed baking sheets, lined with parchment paper*

1 lb	meat, poultry or fish, trimmed	500 g
1 tbsp	minced garlic	15 mL
1 tsp	ground allspice	5 mL
1 tsp	ground coriander	5 mL
$\frac{1}{2}$ tsp	cayenne pepper (or $\frac{1}{2}$ Scotch bonnet pepper, minced)	2 mL
$\frac{1}{2}$ tsp	freshly ground black pepper	2 mL
$\frac{1}{4}$ tsp	ground nutmeg	1 mL
$\frac{1}{4}$ cup	freshly squeezed lime juice	50 mL

1. For easier slicing, put the meat in the freezer for about 25 minutes or until firm but not solid.

2. Using a sharp knife, cut meat into strips about $\frac{1}{4}$ inch (0.5 cm) thick, cutting with the grain for chewy strips or across the grain for more brittle strips (which will be easier to chew).

3. In a bowl, combine garlic, allspice, coriander, cayenne, black pepper, nutmeg and lime juice. Add meat strips and toss to coat. Let stand at room temperature for 15 minutes, or cover and refrigerate for up to 8 hours (see tip, at left). Meanwhile, preheat oven to 350°F (180°C).

4. Remove meat from marinade, discarding excess marinade and accumulated juices. Arrange meat strips on prepared baking sheets, leaving space between each strip. Bake in preheated oven for 10 minutes or until meat is no longer pink inside (or fish is firm and opaque). Transfer to a baking sheet lined with paper towels, turning to blot both sides.

5. Place cooked meat strips on mesh drying trays. Dry at 155°F (68°C) for 6 to 8 hours, occasionally blotting any fat that rises to the surface with paper towels, until jerky is firm and flexes and cracks, but doesn't break, when gently bent. Transfer to a clean baking sheet lined with paper towels and let cool completely, turning once to blot thoroughly.

Herb and Garlic Ground Meat Jerky

Garden-fresh herbs season the ground meat just enough to add interest, but not so much that they overwhelm the meat. You can substitute other herbs for the oregano and sage to vary the flavor.

Makes about 6 oz (175 g)

Tips

If you don't have a jerky gun or piping bag, use a rubber spatula and a small spoon to spoon meat mixture into strips on prepared baking sheets.

To flatten strips that are piped or spooned onto baking sheets, place another sheet of parchment paper on top and press as evenly as possible. Ensure that the strips don't touch each other.

It is best to err on the side of caution and cook the beef a little longer, if necessary, to make sure it is well done.

- *Preheat oven to 400°F (200°C)*
- *Jerky gun or piping bag fitted with a large round tip*
- *Large rimmed baking sheets, lined with parchment paper*

1 lb	lean ground beef, venison, lamb or pork	500 g
$\frac{1}{2}$ cup	chopped onion	125 mL
6	cloves garlic	6
1 cup	chopped fresh parsley	250 mL
1 tbsp	chopped fresh oregano	15 mL
1 tbsp	chopped fresh sage	15 mL
$1\frac{1}{2}$ tsp	salt	7 mL
$\frac{1}{2}$ tsp	freshly ground black pepper	2 mL

1. In a food processor, combine beef, onion, garlic, parsley, oregano, sage, salt and pepper. Process until onion, garlic and herbs are finely chopped and mixture has a paste-like consistency.

2. Fill jerky gun according to manufacturer's directions, or using a piping bag, pipe strips of beef mixture onto prepared baking sheets, leaving at least $\frac{1}{2}$ inch (1 cm) between strips. Flatten, if necessary, to $\frac{1}{4}$-inch (0.5 cm) thickness (see tip, at left).

3. Bake in preheated oven for about 20 minutes or until beef is well done. Transfer strips to a plate lined with paper towels and blot dry.

4. Place cooked strips on mesh drying trays. Dry at 155°F (68°C) for 5 to 6 hours, occasionally blotting any fat that rises to the surface with paper towels, until jerky is firm and flexes and cracks, but doesn't break, when gently bent. Transfer to a clean baking sheet lined with paper towels and let cool completely, turning once to blot thoroughly.

Peppercorn Ground Meat Jerky

This jerky is definitely for fans of the bold peppercorn! Use high-quality peppercorns and coarsely grind it just before using for the best flavor.

Makes about 6 oz (175 g)

Tips

If you don't have a jerky gun or piping bag, use a rubber spatula and a small spoon to spoon meat mixture into strips on prepared baking sheets.

To flatten strips that are piped or spooned onto baking sheets, place another sheet of parchment paper on top and press as evenly as possible. Ensure that the strips don't touch each other.

It is best to err on the side of caution and cook the beef a little longer, if necessary, to make sure it is well done.

- Preheat oven to 400°F (200°C)
- Jerky gun or piping bag fitted with a large round tip
- Large rimmed baking sheets, lined with parchment paper

1 lb	lean ground beef, venison, lamb or pork	500 g
$\frac{1}{2}$ cup	chopped onion	125 mL
6	cloves garlic	6
$1\frac{1}{2}$ tsp	salt	7 mL
2 tsp	coarsely ground black pepper (approx.), divided	10 mL

1. In a food processor, combine beef, onion, garlic, salt and 1 tsp (5 mL) of the pepper. Process until onion and garlic are finely chopped and mixture has a paste-like consistency.

2. Fill jerky gun according to manufacturer's directions, or using a piping bag, pipe strips of beef mixture onto prepared baking sheets, leaving at least $\frac{1}{2}$ inch (1 cm) between strips. Flatten, if necessary, to $\frac{1}{4}$-inch (0.5 cm) thickness (see tip, at left). Sprinkle remaining pepper liberally over meat strips.

3. Bake in preheated oven for about 20 minutes or until beef is well done. Transfer strips to a plate lined with paper towels and blot dry.

4. Place cooked strips on mesh drying trays. Dry at 155°F (68°C) for 5 to 6 hours, occasionally blotting any fat that rises to the surface with paper towels, until jerky is firm and flexes and cracks, but doesn't break, when gently bent. Transfer to a clean baking sheet lined with paper towels and let cool completely, turning once to blot thoroughly.

Maple and Whisky Ground Meat Jerky

Maple and whisky add a rustic Canadian touch to jerky. You might just be able to imagine yourself trekking through the back woods when you taste this one. And if you eat it while actually trekking in the woods, it'll be all the more terrific.

Makes about 6 oz (175 g)

Tips

If you don't have a jerky gun or piping bag, use a rubber spatula and a small spoon to spoon meat mixture into strips on prepared baking sheets.

To flatten strips that are piped or spooned onto baking sheets, place another sheet of parchment paper on top and press as evenly as possible. Ensure that the strips don't touch each other.

It is best to err on the side of caution and cook the beef a little longer, if necessary, to make sure it is well done.

- *Preheat oven to 400°F (200°C)*
- *Jerky gun or piping bag fitted with a large round tip*
- *Large rimmed baking sheets, lined with parchment paper*

1 lb	lean ground beef, venison, lamb or pork	500 g
1/2 cup	chopped onion	125 mL
1 1/2 tsp	salt	7 mL
1 tsp	coarsely ground black pepper	5 mL
2 tbsp	pure maple syrup	25 mL
2 tbsp	Canadian whisky (rye) or bourbon	25 mL

1. In a food processor, combine beef, onion, salt, pepper, maple syrup and whisky. Process until onion is finely chopped and mixture has a paste-like consistency.

2. Fill jerky gun according to manufacturer's directions, or using a piping bag, pipe strips of beef mixture onto prepared baking sheets, leaving at least 1/2 inch (1 cm) between strips. Flatten, if necessary, to 1/4-inch (0.5 cm) thickness (see tip, at left).

3. Bake in preheated oven for about 20 minutes or until beef is well done. Transfer strips to a plate lined with paper towels and blot dry.

4. Place cooked strips on mesh drying trays. Dry at 155°F (68°C) for 5 to 6 hours, occasionally blotting any fat that rises to the surface with paper towels, until jerky is firm and flexes and cracks, but doesn't break, when gently bent. Transfer to a clean baking sheet lined with paper towels and let cool completely, turning once to blot thoroughly.

Asian Ground Meat Jerky

Sweet, sour, salty and a touch of heat — your taste buds are sure to be satisfied when you're snacking on this jerky. It also provides a great boost of flavor when used in recipes.

Makes about 6 oz (175 g)

Tips

If you don't have a jerky gun or piping bag, use a rubber spatula and a small spoon to spoon meat mixture into strips on prepared baking sheets.

To flatten strips that are piped or spooned onto baking sheets, place another sheet of parchment paper on top and press as evenly as possible. Ensure that the strips don't touch each other.

It is best to err on the side of caution and cook the beef a little longer, if necessary, to make sure it is well done.

- Preheat oven to 400°F (200°C)
- Jerky gun or piping bag fitted with a large round tip
- Large rimmed baking sheets, lined with parchment paper

1 lb	lean ground beef, venison, lamb or pork	500 g
1/2 cup	chopped onion	125 mL
6	cloves garlic	6
1 tbsp	packed brown sugar	15 mL
1 tsp	ground ginger	5 mL
1 tsp	coarsely ground black pepper	5 mL
1/2 tsp	salt	2 mL
2 tbsp	soy sauce	25 mL
1 tbsp	rice vinegar or freshly squeezed lime juice	15 mL

1. In a food processor, combine beef, onion, garlic, brown sugar, ginger, pepper, salt, soy sauce and vinegar. Process until onion and garlic are finely chopped and mixture has a paste-like consistency.

2. Fill jerky gun according to manufacturer's directions, or using a piping bag, pipe strips of beef mixture onto prepared baking sheets, leaving at least 1/2 inch (1 cm) between strips. Flatten, if necessary, to 1/4-inch (0.5 cm) thickness (see tip, at left).

3. Bake in preheated oven for about 20 minutes or until beef is well done. Transfer strips to a plate lined with paper towels and blot dry.

4. Place cooked strips on mesh drying trays. Dry at 155°F (68°C) for 5 to 6 hours, occasionally blotting any fat that rises to the surface with paper towels, until jerky is firm and flexes and cracks, but doesn't break, when gently bent. Transfer to a clean baking sheet lined with paper towels and let cool completely, turning once to blot thoroughly.

Southwestern Ground Meat Jerky

With a touch of chili, cumin and lime, this jerky is a flavorful snack and a super starter for chili, soups and other Southwestern favorites.

Makes about 6 oz (175 g)

Tips

If you don't have a jerky gun or piping bag, use a rubber spatula and a small spoon to spoon meat mixture into strips on prepared baking sheets.

To flatten strips that are piped or spooned onto baking sheets, place another sheet of parchment paper on top and press as evenly as possible. Ensure that the strips don't touch each other.

It is best to err on the side of caution and cook the beef a little longer, if necessary, to make sure it is well done.

- *Preheat oven to 400°F (200°C)*
- *Jerky gun or piping bag fitted with a large round tip*
- *Large rimmed baking sheets, lined with parchment paper*

1 lb	lean ground beef, venison, lamb or pork	500 g
1/2 cup	chopped onion	125 mL
6	cloves garlic	6
2 tsp	chili powder	10 mL
1 1/2 tsp	salt	7 mL
1 tsp	coarsely ground black pepper	5 mL
1 tsp	ground cumin	5 mL
1 tbsp	freshly squeezed lime juice	15 mL

1. In a food processor, combine beef, onion, garlic, chili powder, salt, pepper, cumin and lime juice. Process until onion and garlic are finely chopped and mixture has a paste-like consistency.

2. Fill jerky gun according to manufacturer's directions, or using a piping bag, pipe strips of beef mixture onto prepared baking sheets, leaving at least 1/2 inch (1 cm) between strips. Flatten, if necessary, to 1/4-inch (0.5 cm) thickness (see tip, at left).

3. Bake in preheated oven for about 20 minutes or until beef is well done. Transfer strips to a plate lined with paper towels and blot dry.

4. Place cooked strips on mesh drying trays. Dry at 155°F (68°C) for 4 to 6 hours, occasionally blotting any fat that rises to the surface with paper towels, until jerky is firm and flexes and cracks, but doesn't break, when gently bent. Transfer to a clean baking sheet lined with paper towels and let cool completely, turning once to blot thoroughly.

Ground Beef

Makes about 4 oz (125 g)

	extra-lean ground beef	500 g
1 lb		

Salt and freshly ground black pepper

Tips

Small pieces may fall through even a fine-mesh drying tray, so place a leather sheet on an empty rack below to catch any pieces that fall through.

1. In a large skillet, over medium heat, cook beef, breaking up with a spoon, for about 8 minutes or until no longer pink and liquid has evaporated. Transfer to a baking sheet lined with paper towels and top with more paper towels to blot any excess moisture. Season to taste with salt and pepper.

2. Place cooked meat on fine-mesh drying trays (e.g., Clean-A-Screen). Dry at 155°F (68°C) for 6 to 8 hours, rearranging occasionally as necessary to break up any clumps, until meat is very firm and dry throughout. Let cool completely.

Dried Shrimp

Makes about 3 oz (90 g)

1 lb	medium or large shrimp	500 g

Tips

Jumbo or extra-large shrimp tend to get tough when cooked and dried; medium or large shrimp are better suited to drying.

A non-acidic marinade can be used before drying. Avoid any marinades with citrus juice or vinegar, as these will toughen shrimp. Coat cooked shrimp with marinade, cover and refrigerate for 30 to 60 minutes. Drain well.

1. Peel and devein shrimp. Cut in half lengthwise.

2. In a large pot of boiling salted water, cook shrimp for 2 to 3 minutes or just until firm and opaque. Using a strainer, remove from boiling water and immediately plunge into ice water; let stand until cold. Drain well and pat dry with paper towels.

3. Place on mesh drying trays. Dry at 155°F (68°C) for 4 to 5 hours or until very firm and just slightly pliable. Let cool completely.

PART 2

Cooking at Home with Dehydrated Foods

Using Dehydrated Foods in Everyday Cooking

About the Recipes

You've been peeling, slicing, blanching and drying, and now you've got a stockpile of dried foods ready to be enjoyed. It's time to put those wonderful ingredients to use in your everyday cooking. This part of the book features recipes that have been adapted from classics traditionally made with fresh ingredients, as well as some that are specially designed to highlight the flavors and characteristics of home-dried foods.

In these recipes, we've used a combination of fresh and dried ingredients. One of the benefits of cooking with a mixture of fresh and dried foods is that you don't have to rely as much on seasonality — you can mix foods that are in season in June with foods harvested in the fall without breaking the bank. In addition, these recipes allow you to plan your meals around the dried ingredients you have in your pantry, supplementing them with a few fresh ingredients. You don't need to have dried a huge variety of foods, or to dry more just to use the ones you have. As with all styles of cooking, there are techniques that work better for some ingredients than others; these recipes focus on making the most of the texture and flavor of dried ingredients, with a little help from ingredients that are better used fresh.

We've included tips and variations to make the recipes easy to follow and versatile, and we hope that once you've gotten a feel for the way dried foods rehydrate and work in recipes, you'll get creative, adding your own touches to expand your repertoire.

Ingredient Pointers

When it comes to how we call for ingredients in our recipes, we've made a few assumptions you'll need to know when preparing them:

- **Produce:** All fresh produce is washed first and any inedible parts, such as stems, seeds, skin, pits and cores, are removed unless otherwise specified. We assume that you will peel vegetables that are commonly peeled (such as carrots), and instruct you to peel those that can be eaten either way (such as potatoes and apples) when peeling is necessary.
- **Tomatoes:** When we call for dried tomatoes, we are referring to plum (Roma) tomatoes. These are the easiest and most economical to dry, but if you have a surplus of dried grape tomatoes, they will work interchangeably.
- **Beans and other legumes:** When we call for "dry beans," we mean beans that are purchased dry and aren't yet cooked. If we intend for you to use beans that you have cooked and dehydrated, we specify "dried cooked beans."
- **Chicken, beef and vegetable stock:** The recipes were tested with commercially prepared, high-quality stock in the form of ready-to-use broth and/or condensed broth diluted according to label directions. Sodium-reduced stock is preferred for many recipes and is noted accordingly. If you use homemade unsalted stock, you will need to add more salt than we've specified to enhance the other flavors.
- **Meat and poultry:** The recipes were tested with fresh unseasoned meat and poultry (except where dried meats are used). If you use seasoned meat that is infused with sodium phosphate, the cooking time, salt level and moisture level of recipes will be affected. Be sure to read fresh meat labels carefully before purchasing.
- **Chicken:** We prefer to use air-chilled chicken for the best flavor and texture. Conventional water-chilled chicken will work but can make sauces a little more watery, and the chicken may be chewy when simmered.
- **Eggs:** The recipes were tested using large fresh eggs unless otherwise specified.

- **Milk:** The recipes were tested with 2% milk. Other types of milk will work, although fat-free (skim) milk may cause sauces to be thin and look less appetizing, and can cause a slightly tougher texture in baked goods.
- **Butter:** We use real butter, and the recipes were tested with salted butter. If using unsalted butter, you may need to slightly increase the amount of salt (add about ¼ tsp/1 mL salt per 1 cup/250 mL butter).
- **Vegetable oil:** Use whichever type of vegetable oil you prefer. A plain-flavored oil, such as canola, works well as an everyday, all-purpose oil.
- **Olive oil:** Regular, virgin or "pure" olive oil is fine for most regular cooking and can be substituted where vegetable oil is called for. If you prefer to use olive oil, use a very light-tasting oil to avoid overpowering the flavor of the other ingredients. Extra-virgin olive oil adds a wonderful flavor to certain recipes, and we've called for it where we feel the flavor of the dish benefits.
- **Salt:** There are numerous types of salt available these days. Use whatever type you prefer, whether it is table salt, sea salt or kosher salt. In a few recipes that benefit from the fresher taste and crispy texture of sea salt or kosher salt, we've specified these.

  Many of the recipes add a measured amount of salt in the cooking process and then suggest adding more to taste at the end. This allows for variability in the salt level of added ingredients (stock, tomatoes, etc.). Adding salt at the end of cooking also heightens the flavors of the dish. If you leave salt out, the spices and other flavorings will be very dull.

  To add salt to taste, first sample the cooked dish. If you are not sure whether it needs more salt, spoon a small amount into a bowl and add a pinch of salt. Stir it in and taste again. If the salt has brightened the flavors, add more salt to the pot — ¼ tsp

(1 mL) at a time is a good start. Stir and taste after each addition until you're happy with the flavor. Adding small amounts at a time and tasting each time is much better than adding a lot at once. If you over-salt, there is no remedy!

- **Pepper:** We prefer black pepper that we keep in a grinder and grind just before using. The flavor is far superior to that of preground pepper. Bottled or packaged ground pepper can taste harsh, strong and sometimes dusty.
- **Pasta:** Unless otherwise specified, the recipes were tested with traditional dried pasta available at regular supermarkets.

Measuring Primer

We've also made some assumptions when it comes to measuring ingredients:

- Produce is medium-sized unless otherwise specified.
- Where the exact quantity of vegetables or fruits is important, a volume is given (e.g., ½ cup/125 mL chopped onions). When it isn't imperative, a number is given.
- Dry ingredients are measured in nesting-style dry measuring cups. This includes chopped vegetables and fruit, both dry and fresh. Ingredients such as flour are spooned in and leveled off, not tapped or packed. Brown sugar is packed into the cup just enough that it holds its shape when dumped out, but not so tightly that it is difficult to remove from the cup.
- Liquid ingredients are measured in a liquid measuring cup with graduated volume markings, generally with a handle and a spout. The volume is read at eye level.
- Measuring spoons are used for quantities less than ¼ cup (50 mL).
- Both imperial and metric quantities are provided in the recipes. They are not, however, interchangeable. If using imperial measures, measure all ingredients in imperial. If using metric, measure all ingredients in metric.

Breakfast

Tomato and Basil Quiche

The intense flavor of dried tomatoes bursts through in this simple quiche.

Serves 4 to 6

Tip

If the dried tomatoes are leathery, use kitchen scissors to cut them into small pieces, wiping the blades with a hot cloth as necessary to remove stickiness.

Variation

Add 2 slices of crumbled cooked bacon or pancetta with the vegetables in step 2.

• *Preheat oven to 375°F (190°C)*

¼ cup	chopped dried tomatoes	50 mL
1 tsp	crumbled dried basil	5 mL
½ tsp	finely chopped dried garlic	2 mL
½ cup	boiling water	125 mL
¼ cup	shredded Asiago, provolone or mozzarella cheese	50 mL
1	9-inch (23 cm) pie crust, unbaked	1
4	eggs	4
½ tsp	salt	2 mL
¼ tsp	freshly ground black pepper	1 mL
1¼ cups	milk	300 mL

1. In a heatproof bowl, combine tomatoes, basil, garlic and boiling water. Let stand for 15 minutes or until vegetables are softened. Strain through a fine-mesh sieve to drain off any excess liquid (do not squeeze vegetables).

2. Sprinkle cheese over bottom of pie crust; sprinkle vegetables over cheese.

3. In a bowl, whisk together eggs, salt, pepper and milk until blended and slightly foamy. Pour over vegetables in crust.

4. Bake in lower third of preheated oven for about 40 minutes or until crust is golden and a knife inserted in the center comes out clean. Let cool on a rack for 10 minutes. Serve hot or warm.

Ratatouille Vegetable Quiche

A French-influenced vegetable medley shines in this quiche. For a satisfying lunch or light dinner, add a leafy green salad with balsamic vinaigrette on the side.

Serves 4 to 6

Variation

For a richer quiche, use half-and-half (10%) or table (18%) cream in place of the milk.

● Preheat oven to 375°F (190°C)

2 tbsp	chopped dried eggplant	25 mL
2 tbsp	chopped dried tomatoes	25 mL
1 tbsp	chopped dried zucchini	15 mL
1 tbsp	dried onion pieces	15 mL
1/2 tsp	finely chopped dried garlic	2 mL
1/2 tsp	crumbled dried thyme or oregano	2 mL
3/4 cup	boiling water	175 mL
2 tbsp	freshly grated Parmesan cheese or crumbled goat cheese	25 mL
1	9-inch (23 cm) pie crust, unbaked	1
4	eggs	4
1/2 tsp	salt	2 mL
1/4 tsp	freshly ground black pepper	1 mL
1 cup	milk	250 mL

1. In a heatproof bowl, combine eggplant, tomatoes, zucchini, onion, garlic, thyme and boiling water. Let stand for 15 minutes or until vegetables are softened. Strain through a fine-mesh sieve to drain off any excess liquid (do not squeeze vegetables).

2. Sprinkle cheese over bottom of pie crust; sprinkle vegetables over cheese.

3. In a bowl, whisk together eggs, salt, pepper and milk until blended and slightly foamy. Pour over vegetables in crust.

4. Bake in lower third of preheated oven for about 40 minutes or until crust is golden and a knife inserted in the center comes out clean. Let cool on a rack for 10 minutes. Serve hot or warm.

Mushroom and Thyme Omelet

An omelet is just the thing to make when there doesn't seem to be anything good to eat in the house. This one takes advantage of the full flavor of dried mushrooms and herbs.

Serves 2

Variations

You can add up to 2 tbsp (25 mL) other chopped dried vegetables you have on hand. Try bell peppers, zucchini or crumbled dried potatoes. Increase the boiling water to ¹⁄₂ cup (50 mL) if adding extra vegetables.

Sprinkle ¹⁄₄ cup (50 mL) shredded sharp cheese or crumbled feta cheese over eggs when you finish stirring in step 4.

2 tbsp	crumbled dried mushrooms	25 mL
¹⁄₄ tsp	crumbled dried thyme	1 mL
¹⁄₄ cup	boiling water	50 mL
4	eggs	4
¹⁄₄ tsp	salt	1 mL
	Freshly ground black pepper	
2 tsp	butter or vegetable oil	10 mL

1. In a heatproof bowl, combine mushrooms, thyme and boiling water. Let stand for 20 minutes or until mushrooms are plump and soft. Strain through a fine-mesh sieve to drain off any excess liquid (do not squeeze mushrooms).

2. In a bowl, whisk together eggs, salt and pepper to taste until blended but not foamy.

3. In a small nonstick skillet, melt butter over medium heat. Add mushroom mixture and sauté for about 2 minutes or until hot.

4. Reduce heat to low. Add egg mixture and cook, stirring gently with a rubber spatula, for about 2 minutes or until eggs are about half set. Cook, without stirring, for about 3 minutes or just until eggs are set. Flip omelet into a roll or divide in half and slide flat onto a plate.

Baked Sweet and Chile Pepper Omelet

Baking this omelet means you can pop it in the oven and get a salad ready while it cooks to perfection. Leftovers are terrific served cold for lunch, too.

Serves 4

Tip

Leftover omelet can be cooled, wrapped and refrigerated for up to 2 days.

Variation

Add ¼ cup (50 mL) chopped dried shrimp with the peppers in step 1 and increase the boiling water to 1 cup (250 mL). Alternatively, add 1 cup (250 mL) chopped cooked fresh shrimp with the vegetables in step 2.

- *Preheat oven to 350°F (180°C)*
- *9-inch (23 cm) glass pie plate, greased*

½ cup	dried red or green bell pepper pieces	125 mL
2 tbsp	dried onion pieces	25 mL
1 to 2 tbsp	dried hot chile peppers, chopped	15 to 25 mL
¾ cup	boiling water	175 mL
6	eggs	6
½ tsp	salt	2 mL
¼ tsp	freshly ground black pepper	1 mL
¼ cup	milk	50 mL
1 cup	shredded Swiss or Cheddar cheese	250 mL

1. In a heatproof bowl, combine bell peppers, onion, chile peppers to taste and boiling water. Let stand for 15 minutes or until vegetables are softened. Strain through a fine-mesh sieve to drain off any excess liquid (do not squeeze vegetables).

2. In a bowl, whisk together eggs, salt, pepper and milk until blended but not foamy. Pour into prepared pie plate and sprinkle with vegetables and cheese.

3. Bake in preheated oven for about 30 minutes or until puffed and golden and a knife inserted in the center comes out clean. Let cool on a rack for 5 minutes before cutting into wedges.

Breakfast Fajitas with Black Beans, Corn and Salsa

Perk up your breakfast with these colorful, flavorful fajitas. They'll be a welcome change from the same old scrambled eggs.

Serves 4

Tip

To save time in the morning, soak and drain the dried vegetables the night before. Cover and refrigerate overnight or for up to 2 days. Add to the skillet and sauté to heat up before adding the eggs in step 4.

Variations

Substitute $1/3$ cup (75 mL) dry Anytime Salsa (page 161), rehydrated according to recipe directions, for the prepared salsa in this recipe.

In place of dried cooked black beans, use $1/2$ cup (125 mL) drained and rinsed canned or cooked black beans and add with the vegetables in step 4. Reduce the boiling water to 1 cup (250 mL).

- *Preheat oven or toaster oven to 350°F (180°C)*

$1/4$ cup	chopped dried tomatoes	50 mL
$1/4$ cup	dried cooked black beans	50 mL
$1/4$ cup	dried corn kernels	50 mL
2 tsp	finely chopped dried hot chile peppers (optional)	10 mL
$1\frac{1}{2}$ cups	boiling water	375 mL
4	large whole wheat flour tortillas (or 8 small)	4
6	eggs	6
$1/2$ tsp	salt	2 mL
$1/4$ tsp	freshly ground black pepper	1 mL
1 tbsp	chopped fresh cilantro (optional)	15 mL
1 tbsp	butter or vegetable oil	15 mL
$3/4$ cup	prepared salsa	175 mL
$1/2$ cup	shredded Monterey Jack or sharp (old) Cheddar cheese	125 mL

1. In a heatproof bowl, combine tomatoes, beans, corn, chile peppers (if using) and boiling water. Let stand for 30 minutes or until vegetables are softened. Strain through a fine-mesh sieve to drain off any excess liquid (do not squeeze vegetables).

2. Meanwhile, stack tortillas on a large piece of foil, moistening each lightly with wet fingers to prevent sticking. Wrap tightly and warm in preheated oven for 10 minutes.

3. In a bowl, whisk together eggs, salt, pepper and cilantro (if using) until blended but not foamy.

4. In a large nonstick skillet, melt butter over medium-high heat. Reduce heat to medium-low and add eggs. Cook, stirring gently, for about 1 minute or until starting to set. Stir in vegetables and cook, stirring, for about 1 minute or until eggs are set.

5. Spoon egg mixture in a strip along the center of each tortilla and top with salsa and cheese. Fold up one end and fold in both sides to enclose filling.

Asparagus and Tomato Strata with Herbs

This is the perfect dish to make for breakfast entertaining — it's really savory French toast with a fancy name. Assemble it the night before, pop it in the oven in the morning, and your guests will awake to a sumptuous meal. They'll think you're hiding a five-star chef in your pantry!

Serves 6 to 8

Tip
Use a dense, crusty bread for the best texture. Egg bread, sourdough or multigrain bread all work well.

- 13- by 9-inch (3 L) glass baking dish, greased

1 cup	chopped dried tomatoes	250 mL
½ cup	dried asparagus pieces	125 mL
1½ cups	boiling water	375 mL
12	slices bakery-style sandwich bread	12
6	eggs	6
1 tbsp	crumbled dried parsley	15 mL
1 tsp	salt	5 mL
1 tsp	crumbled dried basil or oregano	5 mL
½ tsp	crumbled dried rosemary or thyme	2 mL
½ tsp	freshly ground black pepper	2 mL
2 cups	milk	500 mL
1 cup	shredded provolone, fontina or Oka cheese	250 mL

1. In a heatproof bowl, combine tomatoes, asparagus and boiling water. Let stand for 20 minutes or until vegetables are softened. Strain through a sieve to drain off any excess liquid (do not squeeze vegetables).

2. In prepared baking dish, arrange slices of bread attractively, overlapping as necessary. Sprinkle with vegetables.

3. In a bowl, whisk together eggs, parsley, salt, basil, rosemary, pepper and milk until blended and slightly foamy. Pour evenly over bread, pressing down with a rubber spatula to help liquid soak into bread. Cover and refrigerate for at least 2 hours or for up to 12 hours.

4. Preheat oven to 350°F (180°C).

5. Uncover baking dish and press again with spatula to moisten top layer of bread. Sprinkle with cheese. Bake for about 50 minutes or until top is golden and puffed and a knife inserted in the center comes out clean. Let cool on a rack for 10 minutes.

Banana Almond Pancakes

Bananas and almonds give new life to this breakfast staple. Serve with classic maple syrup or drizzle with honey.

Serves 4

Tip

To toast almonds, spread whole raw almonds on a baking sheet and bake in a 375°F (190°C) oven, stirring once or twice, for about 8 minutes or until nuts are toasted and fragrant. Watch carefully, as they burn easily. Transfer to a bowl and let cool.

● *Preheat oven to 300°F (150°C)*

¹⁄₂ cup	dried banana slices	125 mL
2 cups	milk	500 mL
1¾ cups	all-purpose flour	425 mL
2 tsp	baking powder	10 mL
¹⁄₄ tsp	salt	1 mL
¹⁄₂ cup	toasted almonds (see tip, at left)	125 mL
2	eggs	2
1 tbsp	packed brown sugar	15 mL
¹⁄₄ cup	butter, melted, or vegetable oil	50 mL
	Butter or vegetable oil	

1. In a glass measuring cup or a saucepan, combine bananas and milk. Heat in microwave on Medium (50%) power or over medium heat for about 3 minutes or just until steaming. Remove from heat and let cool almost to room temperature.

2. In a large bowl, whisk together flour, baking powder and salt.

3. Add almonds to banana mixture and, using an immersion blender, purée until fairly smooth (or transfer to a blender). Pulse in eggs, sugar and butter until blended. Pour over dry ingredients and stir just until moistened.

4. Heat a large nonstick skillet over medium heat until small drops of water splashed on the surface evaporate almost immediately. Brush lightly with butter. Add about ¹⁄₄ cup (50 mL) of batter per pancake and cook for 2 to 3 minutes or until bubbles just start to break in batter and bottom is golden brown. Flip and cook the other side for about 1 minute or until golden brown. Keep warm on rack in oven. Repeat with remaining batter, buttering pan and adjusting heat as necessary between batches.

Blueberry Ricotta Pancakes

These rich pancakes have the flavor of cheese blintzes, but are easier to make. You can use other dried berries in addition to, or instead of, the blueberries.

Serves 4

Variation

Substitute ¼ cup (50 mL) powdered dried puréed cottage cheese and ¾ cup (175 mL) water for the ricotta cheese.

- Preheat oven to 300°F (150°C)
- Steamer basket or heatproof sieve

⅓ cup	dried blueberries	75 mL
2 cups	all-purpose flour	500 mL
2 tsp	baking powder	10 mL
¼ tsp	salt	1 mL
2	eggs	2
¼ cup	granulated sugar	50 mL
1 cup	milk	250 mL
1 cup	ricotta cheese (preferably extra-smooth)	250 mL
2 tbsp	butter, melted, or vegetable oil	25 mL
	Butter or vegetable oil	

1. In steamer basket or heatproof sieve set over a saucepan of simmering water, steam blueberries, covered, for about 5 minutes or until soft and plump. Transfer to a plate lined with paper towels and let cool.

2. In a large bowl, whisk together flour, baking powder and salt.

3. In another bowl, whisk together eggs, sugar, milk, ricotta and butter until blended. Pour over dry ingredients and sprinkle with blueberries. Stir just until moistened.

4. Heat a large nonstick skillet over medium heat until small drops of water splashed on the surface evaporate almost immediately. Brush lightly with butter. Add about ¼ cup (50 mL) of batter per pancake and cook for 2 to 3 minutes or until bubbles just start to break in batter and bottom is golden brown. Flip and cook the other side for about 1 minute or until golden brown. Keep warm on rack in oven. Repeat with remaining batter, buttering pan and adjusting heat as necessary between batches.

Oatmeal with Fruit and Maple

This warm, hearty breakfast is made special by the addition of dried fruit and maple sugar. Use your favorite dried fruit, or a mixture.

Serves 4 to 6

Tip

Any type of dried fruit works well in this recipe. Just chop different fruits into pieces of the same size so they all get plump and tender at the same time.

1 cup	steel-cut oats	250 mL
¹⁄₂ tsp	salt	2 mL
¹⁄₄ tsp	ground cinnamon	1 mL
3¹⁄₄ cups	cold water	800 mL
¹⁄₂ cup	chopped dried fruit	125 mL
¹⁄₂ cup	boiling water	125 mL
	Maple sugar granules or brown sugar	
	Milk (optional)	

1. In a large saucepan, combine oats, salt, cinnamon and cold water. Bring to a boil over high heat. Reduce heat to low and cook, stirring often, for 20 minutes.

2. Meanwhile, in a heatproof bowl, combine dried fruit and boiling water. Let stand for 15 minutes.

3. Stir dried fruit and soaking water into oats and cook, stirring often, for about 10 minutes or until oats are tender and thick and fruit is plump.

4. Spoon into bowls and sprinkle with maple sugar. Serve with milk, if desired.

Citrus Ginger Creamy Wheat

Creamy wheat porridge has always been one of Jennifer's favorites on cold winter mornings. This version has an updated twist with the infusion of citrus and ginger.

Serves 4

Tip

Make sure you don't use instant or 1-minute cereal. It doesn't cook the same way, and you'll end up with something closer to wallpaper paste than to cereal.

2	slices dried gingerroot	2
2	strips dried orange zest	2
1	strip dried lemon zest	1
1¹⁄₂ cups	water	375 mL
1 cup	milk	250 mL
Pinch	salt	Pinch
¹⁄₂ cup	Cream of Wheat cereal (farina)	125 mL
	Honey or brown sugar (optional)	

1. In a saucepan, combine ginger, orange zest, lemon zest and water. Bring to a boil over medium heat. Reduce heat to low, cover and simmer for 5 minutes or until fragrant.

2. Increase heat to medium and stir in milk and salt. Return just to a simmer, stirring often. Gradually pour in cereal in a thin, steady stream, stirring constantly. Reduce heat and simmer, stirring often, for about 5 minutes or until cereal is soft and thickened. Discard ginger, orange zest and lemon zest. Sweeten each serving to taste with honey (if using).

Apple, Cranberry and Oat Breakfast Crumble

Leftover apple crumble for breakfast is one of Jennifer's guilty pleasures. This version is a little less sweet than a dessert crumble and incorporates dried fruit and grains into a healthy breakfast dish.

Serves 4

Tip

This crumble can be baked, cooled, covered and refrigerated for up to 2 days. Reheat, covered in foil, in a 350°F (180°C) oven for about 30 minutes, or reheat individual portions in the microwave on Medium (50%) power for 2 to 3 minutes.

Variations

Substitute barley, triticale or other rolled grains for all or some of the rolled oats.

Replace half or all of the dried apples with dried sliced pears and use ground ginger instead of cinnamon.

- 8-inch (2 L) glass baking dish, greased

1 1/2 cups	dried apple slices	375 mL
1/3 cup	dried cranberries	75 mL
1/4 tsp	ground cinnamon	1 mL
1 3/4 cups	unsweetened apple juice, divided	425 mL
1 cup	quick-cooking or large-flake rolled oats	250 mL
2 tbsp	whole wheat flour	25 mL
2 tbsp	liquid honey or maple syrup	25 mL
	Flavored yogurt	

1. In prepared baking dish, combine apples, cranberries and cinnamon. Pour in 1 1/2 cups (375 mL) of the apple juice. Cover and refrigerate for at least 8 hours or for up to 12 hours.

2. Preheat oven to 375°F (190°C).

3. In a bowl, combine oats, flour, honey and the remaining apple juice, stirring until crumbly. Sprinkle over apple mixture.

4. Bake for about 20 minutes or until fruit is hot and bubbling and topping is crispy. Serve hot or warm, with a dollop of yogurt.

"Bird Seed" Squares

The funny name for these squares comes from Jay's friend Kirby, who claims they look like bird seed. He sure doesn't complain when he eats them every chance he gets, though! They're full of protein, energy and vitamins and make a great start to the day or a snack any time.

Makes 16 squares

Tips

Use your favorite flake cereal for these squares, or use a mixture, such as corn, wheat and bran flakes. Keep in mind, bran flakes alone would be quite dense. We like a multigrain cereal called Weetabix High Fiber Crisp (GrainShop) or Ultima Organic High Fiber.

Use any mixture of dried fruits you like. For the best texture, choose those that are soft and pliable. If using dry, crisp fruit, steam it lightly over simmering water and pat dry before adding in step 2.

- 8-inch (2 L) square baking pan or dish, lined with greased foil with a 2-inch (5 cm) overhang

3 cups	ready-to-eat flake cereal (see tip, at left)	750 mL
1/4 cup	roasted sunflower seeds or pumpkin seeds	50 mL
1/4 cup	chopped toasted pecans or almonds (see tip, page 86)	50 mL
2 tbsp	flax seeds	25 mL
1 tbsp	sesame seeds	15 mL
1/2 cup	corn syrup	125 mL
1/2 cup	smooth peanut butter	125 mL
3/4 cup	chopped dried fruit (see tip, at left)	175 mL
1 tbsp	butter	15 mL

1. In a large bowl, combine cereal, sunflower seeds, pecans, flax seeds and sesame seeds.

2. In a saucepan, over medium heat, combine corn syrup and peanut butter. Heat, stirring often, until peanut butter is melted. Remove from heat and add fruit and butter. Stir until butter is melted. Pour over cereal mixture and stir until evenly coated.

3. Press into prepared pan. Refrigerate for about 1 hour or until firm and set. Using foil overhang as handles, remove from pan and transfer to a cutting board. Cut into squares. Squares can be refrigerated in an airtight container or individually wrapped for up to 2 weeks.

Soups

Apple, Fennel and Celery Soup

This soup offers a unique blend of flavors with a Mediterranean feel. The fennel adds a subtle licorice taste. Serve with toasted baguette and Brie or goat cheese for a lovely summer lunch.

Serves 4

1 cup	dried potato slices	250 mL
1/2 cup	dried apple slices, chopped	125 mL
1/2 cup	dried celery slices	125 mL
1/2 cup	dried onion pieces	125 mL
1/2 cup	dried fennel cubes	125 mL
1 tsp	minced dried garlic	5 mL
7 cups	water, vegetable stock or chicken stock	1.75 L
1 cup	dry white wine	250 mL
1 tsp	salt (or to taste)	5 mL
1/4 tsp	freshly ground black pepper	1 mL

1. In a large pot, combine potatoes, apples, celery, onions, fennel, garlic, water and wine; bring to a boil over high heat. Reduce heat and simmer, stirring occasionally, for about 40 minutes or until vegetables are soft and flavor is well blended.

2. Using an immersion blender in the pot, or transferring in batches to a blender or food processor, purée soup until silky smooth. Return to pot, if necessary.

3. Return to a simmer, stirring often, for 10 minutes or until you're pleased with the consistency. Stir in salt and pepper.

Asparagus, Morel and Herb Soup

Asparagus and morels lend a subtle but rich flavor to this soup, which is just begging to be served on a special occasion. You don't have to wait until spring for these delicacies if you have them dried.

Serves 4

Variation

When they're in season, add blanched fresh asparagus tips or sliced fresh morels sautéed in butter to each serving.

½ cup	dried asparagus pieces	125 mL
½ cup	dried morel mushroom slices (or other exotic mushrooms)	125 mL
½ cup	dried leek pieces	125 mL
¼ cup	dried celery slices	50 mL
½ tsp	chopped dried garlic	2 mL
1 tbsp	crumbled dried parsley	15 mL
1 tsp	crumbled dried basil	5 mL
1 tsp	crumbled dried tarragon	5 mL
8 cups	water or vegetable stock	2 L
1 tsp	salt (or to taste)	5 mL
¼ tsp	freshly ground black pepper	1 mL
2 tbsp	half-and-half (10%), table (18%) or whipping (35%) cream	25 mL

1. In a large pot, combine asparagus, morels, leeks, celery, garlic, parsley, basil, tarragon and water; bring to a boil over high heat. Reduce heat and simmer, stirring occasionally, for 30 to 35 minutes or until vegetables are soft and flavor is well blended.

2. Using an immersion blender in the pot, or transferring in batches to a blender or food processor, purée soup until silky smooth. Return to pot, if necessary.

3. Return to a simmer, stirring often, for 10 to 15 minutes or until you're pleased with the consistency. Stir in salt and pepper.

4. Ladle into bowls and drizzle each serving with cream.

Carrot and Ginger Soup

This soup always gives Jay a warm, happy feeling, not just because it tastes great, but also because it reminds him of a favorite children's book: The Tawny Scrawny Lion.

Serves 4

Variation
After puréeing the soup, add about ½ cup (125 mL) cooked rice, wild rice or barley.

2 cups	dried carrot pieces or slices	500 mL
½ cup	dried onion pieces	125 mL
½ cup	each dried celery and leek slices	125 mL
1 tsp	minced fresh gingerroot	5 mL
Pinch	cayenne pepper	Pinch
8 cups	water or vegetable stock	2 L
1 tbsp	freshly squeezed lemon juice	15 mL
1 tsp	salt (or to taste)	5 mL
¼ tsp	freshly ground black pepper	1 mL

1. In a large pot, combine carrots, onions, celery, leeks, ginger, cayenne and water; bring to a boil over high heat. Reduce heat and simmer, stirring occasionally, for about 40 minutes or until vegetables are soft and flavor is well blended.

2. Using an immersion blender in the pot, or transferring in batches to a blender or food processor, purée soup until silky smooth. Return to pot, if necessary.

3. Return to a simmer, stirring often, for 15 minutes or until you're pleased with the consistency. Stir in lemon juice, salt and black pepper.

Summer Green Pea and Mint Soup

As John Lennon may or may not have suggested, "Give peas a chance." This is a light, refreshing soup that requires very little work. The bright green color and fresh pea flavor are accented by a touch of mint. A little bit of cream drizzled over each serving lifts the soup into the ethereal.

Serves 4

2 cups	dried green peas	500 mL
½ cup	dried celery slices	125 mL
½ cup	dried onion pieces	125 mL
7 cups	chicken or vegetable stock	1.75 L
1 tsp	crumbled dried mint	5 mL
	Salt and freshly ground black pepper	

1. In a large pot, combine peas, celery, onions and chicken stock; bring to a boil over high heat. Reduce heat and simmer, stirring occasionally, for 20 to 25 minutes or until vegetables are soft and flavor is well blended. Stir in mint.

2. Using an immersion blender in the pot, or transferring in batches to a blender or food processor, purée soup until silky smooth. Return to pot, if necessary.

3. Reheat over medium heat until steaming, stirring often. Season to taste with salt and pepper.

Curried Cauliflower Soup

This soup is a variation on a classic curry pairing. It's a good one to make a day or two in advance, to let the flavors blend together.

Serves 4

Tip

If making ahead, let soup cool, transfer to an airtight container and refrigerate for up to 2 days. Return to pot and reheat over medium heat until steaming. Adjust seasoning, if necessary, with salt and pepper.

1 tbsp	Indian yellow curry paste	15 mL
2 cups	dried cauliflower florets	500 mL
1/2 cup	dried celery slices	125 mL
1/2 cup	dried onion pieces	125 mL
1/2 cup	dried cooked chickpeas	125 mL
2 tbsp	crumbled dried parsley	25 mL
8 cups	water or vegetable stock	2 L
1 cup	unsweetened apple juice	250 mL
1 tsp	salt (or to taste)	5 mL
1/4 tsp	freshly ground black pepper	1 mL

1. In a large pot, over low heat, sauté curry paste for about 30 seconds or until fragrant. Stir in cauliflower, celery, onions, chickpeas, parsley, water and apple juice; bring to a boil over high heat. Reduce heat and simmer, stirring occasionally, for 25 to 30 minutes or until vegetables are tender and flavor is well blended. Stir in salt and pepper.

Three Sisters Soup

Many ancient cultures refer to three sisters; in Native North American history, the three sisters are represented by corn, beans and squash, which rely on each other to survive and to enrich the earth even as they draw nutrients from it.

Serves 4

Tip

For the squash, you can use butternut or acorn squash, or even pumpkin, depending on what's in your pantry.

1/2 cup	dried corn kernels	125 mL
1/2 cup	dried green bean pieces	125 mL
1/3 cup	dried winter squash cubes	75 mL
1/3 cup	dried potato cubes	75 mL
1 tbsp	dried celery slices	15 mL
1 tbsp	dried onion pieces	15 mL
1/2 tsp	minced dried garlic	2 mL
1 tbsp	crumbled dried parsley	15 mL
1/2 tsp	crumbled dried thyme	2 mL
9 cups	water or vegetable stock	2.25 L
1 tsp	salt (or to taste)	5 mL
1/2 tsp	freshly ground black pepper	2 mL

1. In a large pot, combine corn, beans, squash, potatoes, celery, onions, garlic, parsley, thyme and water; bring to a boil over high heat. Reduce heat and simmer, stirring occasionally, for about 45 minutes or until potatoes are tender and flavor is well blended. Stir in salt and pepper.

Mushroom, Garlic and Rosemary Soup

This easy yet elegant soup makes a prefect starter for a sit-down dinner.

Serves 4

Tips

Regular white button mushrooms add plenty of flavor, but feel free to use exotic mushrooms as well for an even richer, woodsy taste.

Always purée soup longer than you think is necessary; the silky smooth result will raise your soup to five-star level.

Variation

For a richer, more luxurious soup, drizzle each serving with half-and-half (10%), table (18%) or whipping (35%) cream.

1 tbsp	olive oil	15 mL
1/2 cup	diced onions	125 mL
1/4 cup	diced celery	50 mL
2	cloves garlic, chopped	2
1/2 cup	dry white wine	125 mL
2 cups	dried mushroom slices	500 mL
1 tsp	fresh rosemary leaves (or 1/2 tsp/2 mL crumbled dried rosemary)	5 mL
8 cups	water or vegetable stock	2 L
1 tsp	salt (or to taste)	5 mL
1/4 tsp	freshly ground black pepper	1 mL

1. In a large pot, heat oil over medium heat. Add onions, celery and garlic; sauté for 5 to 7 minutes or until translucent. Add wine and simmer, stirring often, until the liquid has almost evaporated. Add mushrooms, rosemary and water; bring to a boil over high heat. Reduce heat and simmer, stirring occasionally, for about 20 minutes or until mushrooms are soft and flavor is well blended.

2. Using an immersion blender in the pot, or transferring in batches to a blender or food processor, purée soup until silky smooth. Return to pot, if necessary.

3. Return to a simmer, stirring often, for 15 minutes or until you're pleased with the consistency. Stir in salt and pepper.

Red Pepper Bisque

Although bisque is traditionally made with seafood, this gorgeous vegetarian version relies on the rich flavor of the roasted vegetables to help it rise to the occasion.

Serves 4

Variations

Replace fresh tomatoes, red bell peppers and garlic with 1 cup (250 mL) chopped dried tomatoes, $\frac{1}{2}$ cup (125 mL) dried red bell pepper pieces and 1 tsp (5 mL) minced dried garlic. Omit the oil and skip step 1. Increase the water to 10 cups (2.5 L). The flavor won't be quite as rich as with the roasted vegetables.

For real decadence, garnish each serving with cooked shrimp or lobster chopped small enough to fit on a spoon.

- Preheat oven to 400°F (200°C)
- Rimmed baking sheet

6	plum (Roma) tomatoes, chopped	6
4	cloves garlic	4
2	red bell peppers, chopped	2
1 tbsp	olive oil	15 mL
$\frac{1}{2}$ cup	dried onion pieces	125 mL
$\frac{1}{4}$ cup	dried celery slices	50 mL
$\frac{1}{4}$ cup	dried carrot pieces	50 mL
$\frac{1}{2}$ tsp	crumbled dried rosemary	2 mL
$\frac{1}{2}$ tsp	crumbled dried thyme	2 mL
8 cups	water or vegetable stock	2 L
	Salt and freshly ground black pepper	
4	slices baguette	4
2 tbsp	crumbled feta or goat cheese or freshly grated Parmesan cheese	25 mL

1. In a bowl, combine tomatoes, garlic, red peppers and olive oil, tossing to coat thoroughly. Spread in a single layer on baking sheet and roast in preheated oven for 15 to 20 minutes or until vegetables are lightly caramelized.

2. In a large pot, combine roasted vegetables, onions, celery, carrots, rosemary, thyme and water; bring to a boil over high heat. Reduce heat and simmer, stirring occasionally, for 20 to 25 minutes or until vegetables are soft and flavor is well blended.

3. Using an immersion blender in the pot, or transferring in batches to a blender or food processor, purée soup until silky smooth. Return to pot, if necessary.

4. Return to a simmer, stirring often, for 10 to 15 minutes or until you're pleased with the consistency. Stir in salt and pepper.

5. Just before serving, preheat broiler. On a clean baking sheet, toast baguette slices on both sides. Sprinkle with cheese and broil just until melted.

6. Ladle soup into bowls and float a crouton on top of each serving.

Tomato Soup with Basil and Garlic

Sometimes simple is best. This soup captures the memory of childhood, with the sophistication of adulthood.

Serves 4

Tip

To bring those memories rushing back, serve with your favorite grilled cheese sandwich, such as sharp Cheddar on multigrain bread.

2 cups	dried plum (Roma) tomatoes	500 mL
1 cup	dried onion pieces	250 mL
1/2 cup	dried celery slices	125 mL
1 tsp	chopped dried garlic	5 mL
7 cups	water or vegetable stock	1.75 L
2 tbsp	finely chopped fresh basil	25 mL
1 tsp	salt (or to taste)	5 mL
1/4 tsp	freshly ground black pepper	1 mL

1. In a large pot, combine tomatoes, onions, celery, garlic and water; bring to a boil over high heat. Reduce heat and simmer, stirring occasionally, for about 25 minutes or until vegetables are soft and flavor is well blended.

2. Using an immersion blender in the pot, or transferring in batches to a blender or food processor, purée soup until silky smooth. Return to pot, if necessary.

3. Reheat over medium heat until steaming, stirring often. Stir in basil, salt and pepper.

Chicken, Lemon and Rice Soup

This recipe is based on a terrific soup Jay learned to make when he worked in a Greek restaurant in Edmonton, Alberta. This soup really is good for all that ails you.

Serves 4

Variations

After Thanksgiving or Christmas, substitute cooked turkey for the chicken.

Replace the white rice with brown or wild rice.

1 cup	dried cooked long-grain white rice	250 mL
1/2 cup	dried onion pieces	125 mL
1/2 cup	dried celery slices	125 mL
6 cups	chicken stock	1.5 L
	Grated zest and juice of 1 lemon	
2 cups	diced cooked chicken	500 mL
2 tbsp	chopped fresh parsley	25 mL
2	eggs, whisked	2
	Salt and freshly ground black pepper	

1. In a pot, combine rice, onions, celery, chicken stock and lemon juice; bring to a boil over high heat. Reduce heat and simmer for 20 to 25 minutes or until rice is tender.

2. Stir in lemon zest, chicken and parsley; simmer for 5 to 10 minutes or until chicken is heated through.

3. Gradually drizzle eggs into the hot broth, stirring constantly to create threads of cooked egg. Season to taste with salt and pepper. Serve immediately.

Squash and Apple Soup

This hearty soup with a hint of fruit can be either left chunky or puréed until smooth. It goes well with a meal where you are serving wine.

Serves 4

Tip

If you find the apples are sour, try adding 1 tsp (5 mL) pure maple syrup or honey to smooth out the flavor.

1/4 tsp	ground cumin	1 mL
1/4 tsp	ground coriander	1 mL
1 cup	dried winter squash cubes	250 mL
1 cup	chopped dried apples	250 mL
1/4 cup	dried carrot pieces	50 mL
1/4 cup	dried celery slices	50 mL
1/4 cup	dried onion pieces	50 mL
1/2 tsp	minced dried garlic	2 mL
1/2 tsp	mustard seeds	2 mL
1/4 tsp	crumbled dried sage	1 mL
6 cups	water or vegetable stock	1.5 L
1 cup	unsweetened apple juice or cider	250 mL
1 tsp	salt (or to taste)	5 mL
1/2 tsp	freshly ground black pepper	2 mL

1. In a large pot, over low heat, toast cumin and coriander, stirring constantly, for about 1 minute or until fragrant. Remove from heat.

2. Add squash, apples, carrots, celery, onions, garlic, mustard seeds, sage and water; bring to a boil over high heat. Reduce heat and simmer, stirring occasionally, for 40 minutes. Add apple juice, salt and pepper; simmer for 10 minutes or until vegetables are soft and flavor is well blended.

3. For a smooth soup, using an immersion blender in the pot, or transferring in batches to a blender or food processor, purée soup until silky smooth. Return to pot, if necessary, and reheat over medium heat until steaming, stirring often.

Pumpkin Soup

Pumpkin makes a great autumn or winter soup with a lovely color, velvety texture and enticing aroma.

Serves 4

Variations

For a richer, more luxurious soup, drizzle each serving with half-and-half (10%), table (18%) or whipping (35%) cream and sprinkle with toasted green pumpkin seeds (pepitas).

Pumpkin also works well when matched with curry; substitute 1 tsp (5 mL) of curry paste for the cinnamon, paprika and cumin. Skip step 1 and add the curry paste with pumpkin.

½ tsp	ground cumin	2 mL
¼ tsp	ground cinnamon	1 mL
¼ tsp	paprika	1 mL
2 cups	dried pumpkin cubes	500 mL
¼ cup	dried carrot pieces	50 mL
¼ cup	dried celery slices	50 mL
¼ cup	dried onion pieces	50 mL
½ tsp	minced dried garlic	2 mL
6 cups	water or vegetable stock	1.5 L
1 cup	unsweetened apple juice	250 mL
1 tsp	salt (or to taste)	5 mL
¼ tsp	freshly ground black pepper	1 mL

1. In a large pot, over low heat, toast cumin, cinnamon and paprika, stirring constantly, for about 1 minute or until fragrant. Remove from heat.

2. Add pumpkin, carrots, celery, onion, garlic, water and apple juice; bring to a boil over high heat. Reduce heat and simmer, stirring occasionally, for about 35 minutes or until vegetables are soft and flavor is well blended.

3. Using an immersion blender in the pot, or transferring in batches to a blender or food processor, purée soup until silky smooth. Return to pot, if necessary.

4. Return to a simmer, stirring often, for 10 to 15 minutes or until you're pleased with the consistency. Stir in salt and pepper.

Sweet Potato and Chile Pepper Soup

Loosely based on Central and South American flavors, this soup provides not just warmth, but also a little heat to help keep the cold out.

Serves 4

Tips

The sautéed fresh vegetables add depth of flavor to the soup, but if you want to substitute dried vegetables, use about one-quarter the amount and rehydrate in warm water for about 15 minutes. Drain, then sauté as directed.

Use peppers within your own tolerance range; however, if you use habaneros or Scotch bonnets and your family or guests aren't used to them, you're likely to leave them in tears.

1 tbsp	vegetable oil	15 mL
1/2 cup	diced onion	125 mL
1/4 cup	sliced leek (white and light green part only)	50 mL
1/4 cup	diced celery	50 mL
1/4 cup	diced carrot	50 mL
2	cloves garlic, minced	2
1/4 tsp	ground cumin	1 mL
1/4 tsp	ground coriander	1 mL
2 cups	dried sweet potato cubes or slices	500 mL
1 tbsp	chopped dried hot chile peppers (see tip, at left)	15 mL
8 cups	water or vegetable stock	2 L
1/4 cup	finely chopped fresh parsley	50 mL
2 tbsp	freshly squeezed lime juice	25 mL
1 tsp	salt (or to taste)	5 mL
1/2 tsp	freshly ground black pepper	2 mL

1. In a large pot, heat oil over medium heat. Add onion, leek, celery, carrot and garlic; sauté for 5 to 7 minutes or until translucent. Reduce heat to low. Add cumin and coriander; sauté for 2 minutes.

2. Add sweet potatoes, chile peppers and water; bring to a boil over high heat. Reduce heat and simmer for about 20 minutes or until sweet potatoes are soft and flavor is well blended.

3. Using an immersion blender in the pot, or transferring in batches to a blender or food processor, purée soup until silky smooth. Return to pot, if necessary.

4. Return to a simmer, stirring often, for 15 to 20 minutes or until you're pleased with the consistency. Stir in parsley, lime juice, salt and pepper.

Summer Vichyssoise

Enjoy this soup on those sultry hot summer days when a chilled bowl of vichyssoise is exactly what you need to re-energize your appetite.

Serves 4

Variation

For a sophisticated approach, add 1 ripe pear, peeled and chopped, or 1/4 cup (50 mL) chopped dried pears with the vegetables, and crumble some blue cheese and toasted pecans over the top before serving.

2 cups	dried potato cubes	500 mL
1/2 cup	dried leek slices	125 mL
1/2 cup	dried onion pieces	125 mL
1/4 cup	dried celery slices	50 mL
1 tsp	crumbled dried dill	5 mL
8 cups	water or vegetable stock	2 L
1 cup	whipping (35%) cream	250 mL
1 tbsp	freshly squeezed lemon juice	15 mL
1 tsp	salt (or to taste)	5 mL
1/4 tsp	freshly ground black pepper	1 mL
1 tbsp	finely chopped fresh chives	15 mL

1. In a large pot, combine potatoes, leeks, onions, celery, dill and water; bring to a boil over high heat. Reduce heat and simmer, stirring occasionally, for about 45 minutes or until vegetables are soft and flavor is well blended.

2. Using an immersion blender in the pot, or transferring in batches to a blender or food processor, purée soup until silky smooth. Return to pot, if necessary.

3. Return to a simmer, stirring often, for 10 to 15 minutes or you're pleased with the consistency. Remove from heat and let cool.

4. Transfer to a bowl or airtight container, cover and refrigerate for about 4 hours, until chilled, or overnight.

5. Just before serving, stir in cream, lemon juice, salt and pepper. Ladle into bowls and garnish with chives.

Roasted Onion and Potato Soup

In this variation on classic leek and potato soup, the roasting brings out a rich caramel flavor that is complemented by the tang of the vinegar. The combination of fresh and dried vegetables adds to the depth of flavor.

Serves 4

Tip

Use this as a base soup to create other soups. Add spinach and pears, or corn and bacon, or blue cheese . . . the options are endless.

- Preheat oven to 400°F (200°C)
- Rimmed baking sheet

2 cups	diced peeled potatoes	500 mL
1 cup	diced onions	250 mL
2 tbsp	olive oil	25 mL
1 tbsp	balsamic vinegar	15 mL
1/4 cup	dried leek slices	50 mL
1/4 cup	dried celery slices	50 mL
1/2 tsp	crumbled dried thyme	2 mL
1/2 tsp	minced dried garlic	2 mL
8 cups	water or vegetable stock	2 L
1 tsp	salt (or to taste)	5 mL
1/2 tsp	freshly ground black pepper	2 mL

1. In a large bowl, combine potatoes, onions, oil and vinegar, tossing to coat thoroughly. Spread evenly on baking sheet in a single layer and roast in preheated oven for 15 to 20 minutes or until golden brown and tender.

2. In a large pot, combine roasted vegetables, leeks, celery, thyme, garlic and water; bring to a boil over high heat. Reduce heat and simmer, stirring occasionally, for about 30 minutes or until vegetables are soft and flavor is well blended.

3. Using an immersion blender in the pot, or transferring in batches to a blender or food processor, purée soup until silky smooth. Return to pot, if necessary.

4. Reheat over medium heat until steaming, stirring often. Stir in salt and pepper.

French-Style Three-Onion Soup

No soup chapter would be complete without a French onion soup recipe. Our version incorporates red and yellow onions, as well as shallots, for a deep onion broth that pairs well with the cheese croutons.

Serves 4

Tips

To maximize the flavor of this soup, use the best-quality stock you can find. Some supermarkets and specialty shops carry homemade stocks that have less additives and sodium.

Dark vegetable stock is made by roasting the vegetables before simmering them with water to make the stock. It adds a depth of flavor that can't be beat!

Variation

Use $1/2$ cup (125 mL) freshly grated Parmesan cheese or crumbled blue cheese for the topping.

- Four 2-cup (500 mL) ovenproof soup bowls
- Baking sheet

1 cup	dried red onion slices	250 mL
1 cup	dried onion slices	250 mL
2 tbsp	finely chopped dried shallots	25 mL
1 tsp	dried garlic slices	5 mL
$1/2$ tsp	crumbled dried thyme	2 mL
$1/2$ cup	dry sherry or brandy	125 mL
8 cups	beef stock or dark vegetable stock (preferably sodium-reduced)	2 L
	Salt and freshly ground pepper	
4	slices dry sourdough bread, cut to the size of your soup bowls	4
1 cup	finely shredded Swiss, Gruyère or Emmental cheese	250 mL

1. In a large pot, combine red onions, onions, shallots, garlic, thyme and sherry; bring to a boil over medium heat, stirring often. Sauté for about 5 minutes or until the liquid is absorbed and onions have started to turn golden brown.

2. Stir in beef stock and bring to a boil over high heat. Reduce heat and simmer for 30 to 40 minutes or until onions are very soft and soup is slightly thickened. Season to taste with salt and pepper.

3. Just before serving, preheat broiler.

4. Ladle soup into bowls. Place bread on soup and sprinkle cheese over top to cover the surface. Broil for 2 to 3 minutes or until cheese is bubbling and golden brown.

Leek and Wild Rice Soup with Herbs

The sherry adds a touch of class to this soup, perfect for serving to company.

Serves 4

Tip

Using dried cooked wild rice decreases the cooking time for this soup considerably. If you don't have it, boil 2 tbsp (25 mL) wild rice in a saucepan of water for 15 minutes, drain and then add with the vegetables in step 1 and simmer for a total of 40 minutes.

Variation

When in season, add 1 cup (250 mL) blanched chopped asparagus or fiddleheads with the cream.

¼ cup	dried leek slices	50 mL
¼ cup	dried onion pieces	50 mL
¼ cup	dried celery slices	50 mL
1 tsp	minced dried garlic	5 mL
1 tsp	crumbled dried parsley	5 mL
½ tsp	crumbled dried thyme	2 mL
½ tsp	crumbled dried basil	2 mL
6 cups	water or vegetable stock	1.5 L
¼ cup	dry sherry or white wine	50 mL
¼ cup	dried cooked wild rice	50 mL
1 cup	whipping (35%) cream	250 mL
1 tsp	salt (or to taste)	5 mL
¼ tsp	freshly ground black pepper	1 mL

1. In a large pot, combine leeks, onions, celery, garlic, parsley, thyme, basil, water and sherry; bring to a boil over high heat. Reduce heat and simmer, stirring occasionally, for 20 minutes.

2. Stir in rice and simmer for about 20 minutes or until vegetables and rice are tender and flavor is well blended. Stir in cream, salt and pepper. Reheat until steaming, stirring often.

Black Bean Soup with Chipotle and Lime

This soup features a classic pairing of chiles and lime. Serve it in the summer with corn tortilla chips and either margaritas or very cold beer.

Serves 4

Tip

Chipotle peppers are smoked jalapeños and are available dried at specialty food stores, some well-stocked supermarkets and spice emporiums. If dried aren't available, they are often available in cans, packed in adobo sauce. You can use one canned chipotle, drained and minced, and add it with the lime zest.

½ tsp	ground coriander	2 mL
½ tsp	ground cumin	2 mL
2 cups	dried cooked black beans	500 mL
½ cup	dried celery slices	125 mL
½ cup	dried onion pieces	125 mL
1	dried chipotle pepper (see tip, at left)	1
9 cups	water or vegetable stock	2.25 L
	Grated zest and juice of 1 lime	
1 tsp	salt (or to taste)	5 mL
½ tsp	freshly ground black pepper	2 mL

Garnish (optional)

2 tbsp	shredded Cheddar cheese	25 mL
2 tbsp	sour cream	25 mL
2 tbsp	guacamole	25 mL

1. In a large pot, over low heat, toast cumin and coriander, stirring constantly, for about 1 minute or until fragrant. Remove from heat.

2. Add black beans, celery, onions, chipotle and water; bring to a boil over high heat. Reduce heat and simmer, stirring occasionally, for about 40 minutes or until vegetables are soft and flavor is well blended. Discard chipotle. Stir in lime zest, lime juice, salt and pepper.

3. Ladle into bowls and, if desired, garnish with cheese, sour cream and guacamole.

Three-Bean Minestrone

This classic peasant-style tomato vegetable soup is quick and easy, and will satisfy your craving for comfort food.

Serves 4

Tip

Nearly any of the beans or vegetables can be exchanged for similar items that you have available; the exception is the tomatoes, as they're the base flavor.

1 cup	dried plum (Roma) tomatoes, chopped	250 mL
¼ cup	dried celery slices	50 mL
¼ cup	dried onion pieces	50 mL
¼ cup	dried green bean pieces	50 mL
¼ cup	dried cooked kidney beans	50 mL
¼ cup	dried cooked navy beans	50 mL
1 tsp	minced dried garlic	5 mL
1 tbsp	crumbled dried parsley	15 mL
8 cups	water or vegetable stock	2 L
¼ cup	small pasta (shells, ziti or macaroni)	50 mL
1 tsp	salt (or to taste)	5 mL
½ tsp	freshly ground black pepper	2 mL
	Freshly grated Parmesan cheese	

1. In a large pot, combine tomatoes, celery, onions, green beans, kidney beans, navy beans, garlic, parsley and water; bring to a boil over high heat. Reduce heat and simmer for 20 minutes.

2. Stir in pasta and simmer for about 20 minutes or until vegetables and pasta are tender and flavor is well blended. Stir in salt and pepper. Serve sprinkled with cheese.

Hot-and-Sour Tofu and Mushroom Soup

This Asian-influenced soup, featuring sweet, sour, salty, bitter and umami, is good in both cold and hot weather.

Serves 4

Tips

We like to use the small dried red chile peppers that are common in Asian cooking. They're available at Asian grocery stores and in well-stocked supermarkets. If you prefer to use your own dried hot chile peppers, use 1 tsp (5 mL) minced.

If you love the salty flavor of fish sauce, you can increase the amount to taste.

To prepare lemongrass, trim off tough outer layers. Cut remaining stalk into 2-inch (5 cm) sections. Smash each piece with the broad side of a knife to bruise; this will help release the flavor when the lemongrass is cooked.

Variation

For a more substantial soup, add 1 cup (250 mL) cooked noodles or cubed cooked chicken or shrimp.

1 cup	dried tofu cubes	250 mL
½ cup	dried carrot pieces	125 mL
½ cup	dried celery slices	125 mL
½ cup	dried mushroom slices	125 mL
3	wild lime leaves	3
2	small dried chile peppers, stem and seeds removed, crumbled	2
1	stalk lemongrass, chopped into 2-inch (5 cm) pieces	1
8 cups	vegetable stock, chicken stock or water	2 L
3 tbsp	chopped fresh Thai basil	45 mL
2 tbsp	chopped fresh cilantro	25 mL
1 tsp	Thai fish sauce (nam pla)	5 mL

1. In a large pot, combine tofu, carrots, celery, mushrooms, lime leaves, chile peppers, lemongrass and vegetable stock; bring to a boil over high heat. Reduce heat and simmer, stirring occasionally, for 25 to 30 minutes or until vegetables are tender and flavor is well blended. Discard lemongrass and lime leaves. Stir in basil, cilantro and fish sauce.

Sweet Corn and Bell Pepper Chowder

Jay and Jennifer adore fresh corn from the Jacksons' farm near their home and enjoy it frequently through the summer and then dry some to use after the fresh corn season has passed. This soup will both warm you up and bring back memories of warmer days.

Serves 4

Tip

While chowders are usually cream- or tomato-based, and this is neither, they almost always contain potatoes, as this one does.

Variation

A great addition to this soup would be ¹⁄₂ cup (125 mL) diced ham or ¹⁄₄ cup (50 mL) crumbled crisp bacon.

¹⁄₄ tsp	ground coriander	1 mL
¹⁄₄ tsp	ground cumin	1 mL
¹⁄₂ cup	dried corn kernels	125 mL
¹⁄₂ cup	dried sweet potato cubes	125 mL
¹⁄₄ cup	dried red bell pepper pieces	50 mL
1 tbsp	dried celery slices	15 mL
1 tbsp	dried onion pieces	15 mL
1 tsp	crumbled dried parsley	5 mL
¹⁄₂ tsp	minced dried garlic	2 mL
8 cups	water or vegetable stock	2 L
2 tbsp	freshly squeezed lime juice	25 mL
³⁄₄ tsp	salt (or to taste)	3 mL
¹⁄₄ tsp	freshly ground black pepper	1 mL
	Hot pepper sauce (optional)	

1. In a large pot, over low heat, toast cumin and coriander, stirring constantly, for about 1 minute or until fragrant. Remove from heat.

2. Add corn, sweet potatoes, red peppers, celery, onion, parsley, garlic and water; bring to a boil over high heat. Reduce heat and simmer, stirring occasionally, for about 20 minutes or until vegetables are tender and flavor is well blended. Stir in lime juice, salt and pepper. Add hot pepper sauce to taste (if using), or pass it at the table.

Shrimp Chowder

This recipe is based on a seafood chowder Jay tried in San Francisco. There, the flavor of the chowder is highlighted by the addition of warm sourdough bread to soak up the juice in the bottom of the bowl. You can do the same at home.

Serves 4

Variation

Substitute 4 oz (125 g) fresh shrimp, mussels, scallops or cubed white fish for the dried shrimp, or add fresh fish in addition to the dried shrimp.

½ cup	dried cooked shrimp, chopped	125 mL
¼ cup	dried tomatoes, chopped	50 mL
¼ cup	dried celery slices	50 mL
¼ cup	dried leek slices	50 mL
¼ cup	dried onion pieces	50 mL
¼ cup	dried potato cubes	50 mL
½ tsp	minced dried garlic	2 mL
1 tsp	crumbled dried basil	5 mL
1 tsp	crumbled dried parsley	5 mL
¼ tsp	paprika	1 mL
⅛ tsp	cayenne pepper	0.5 mL
8 cups	water or vegetable stock	2 L
2 tbsp	freshly squeezed lemon juice	25 mL
¾ tsp	salt (or to taste)	3 mL
¼ tsp	freshly ground black pepper	1 mL

1. In a large pot, combine shrimp, tomatoes, celery, leeks, onions, potatoes, garlic, basil, parsley, paprika, cayenne and water; bring to a boil over high heat. Reduce heat and simmer, stirring occasionally, for about 35 minutes or until potatoes are soft and flavor is well blended. Stir in lemon juice, salt and black pepper.

One-Dish Meals

Corn and Three-Bean Chili

A medley of beans and the sweetness of corn work well in this hearty vegetarian chili.

Serves 4

Tip

For a flavorful garnish, make *Chili-Lime Sour Cream*: Combine 1 cup (250 mL) sour cream, grated zest and juice of 1 lime and ¼ tsp (1 mL) hot pepper sauce. Spoon a dollop on top of each bowl of chili.

Variation

In place of dry beans, use 1 cup (250 mL) each canned beans or peas, drained and rinsed (or a total of 3 cups/ 750 mL any mixture), and skip steps 1 and 2.

¼ cup	dry black-eyed peas	50 mL
¼ cup	dry chickpeas	50 mL
¼ cup	dry navy (white pea) beans	50 mL
	Cold water	
6 cups	water, divided	1.5 L
2 tbsp	olive oil	25 mL
2	cloves garlic, chopped	2
1	onion, chopped	1
1 tbsp	chili powder	15 mL
1 tbsp	crumbled dried oregano	15 mL
½ cup	dried corn kernels	125 mL
¼ cup	dried carrot slices	50 mL
¼ cup	dried celery slices	50 mL
2 cups	chopped seeded tomatoes (about 3)	500 mL
¼ cup	chopped fresh parsley (or 2 tbsp/ 25 mL crumbled dried)	50 mL
1½ tsp	salt (or to taste)	7 mL
1 tsp	freshly ground black pepper (or to taste)	5 mL

1. In a bowl, combine black-eyed peas, chickpeas, navy beans and enough cold water to cover by at least 2 inches (5 cm). Cover and let soak at room temperature for at least 8 hours or overnight. Drain and rinse well; drain again.

2. In a saucepan, bring 3 cups (750 mL) of the water to a boil. Add bean mixture and boil gently for about 1 hour or until beans are tender. Drain well.

3. Meanwhile, in a large pot, heat oil over medium heat. Add garlic, onion, chili powder and oregano; sauté for about 5 minutes or until onion is softened. Add corn, carrots, celery, tomatoes and the remaining water; bring to a boil. Reduce heat and simmer, stirring occasionally, for about 30 minutes or until vegetables are tender.

4. Add beans and simmer, stirring occasionally, for about 30 minutes or until vegetables and beans are soft and flavor is blended. Stir in parsley, salt and pepper.

Spicy Tofu Chili

This is a great one-step vegetarian dish that provides plenty of protein — and lots of flavor, too.

Serves 4

Variation

You could also do this in a slow cooker on Low for 6 to 8 hours, letting it simmer nice and slow all day so it's ready when you come in from the cold.

12 oz	soy ground beef replacement, crumbled	375 g
½ cup	dried onion pieces	125 mL
½ cup	dried celery slices	125 mL
½ cup	dried mushroom slices	125 mL
1	jalapeño pepper, finely chopped	1
1	can (28 oz/796 mL) diced tomatoes, with juice	1
1	can (14 to 19 oz/398 to 540 mL) white beans, drained and rinsed	1
1	can (14 to 19 oz/398 to 540 mL) chickpeas, drained and rinsed	1
1 tbsp	chili powder	15 mL
1½ tsp	salt (or to taste), divided	7 mL
1 tsp	freshly ground black pepper	5 mL
2 cups	water	500 mL

Toppings (optional)

Sour cream
Shredded Cheddar cheese
Chopped green onions

1. In a large pot, combine ground beef replacement, onions, celery, mushrooms, jalapeño, tomatoes with juice, beans, chickpeas, chili powder, 1 tsp (5 mL) of the salt, pepper and water; bring to a simmer over medium-high heat, stirring often. Reduce heat and simmer, stirring occasionally, for about 40 minutes or until vegetables are tender and chili is thickened. Season with the remaining salt.

2. Ladle into bowls and, if desired, top with sour cream, cheese and green onions.

Aloo Tari

The unusual name of this recipe loosely translates to "curried vegetable stew," but it is certainly much more enticing. Serve this fragrantly spiced, hearty vegetarian dish over steamed basmati rice and with a dollop of yogurt for a satisfying meal.

Serves 4

Tips

To substitute dried garlic and onion for the fresh, pour 1 cup (250 mL) boiling water over 12 slices dried garlic and ¼ cup (50 mL) dried onion pieces and let stand for 30 minutes or until softened. Drain well and pat dry before using together in step 2.

If you prefer to use dried cooked chickpeas, pour 1 cup (250 mL) boiling water over ½ cup (125 mL) and let stand for 1 hour or until tender. Drain well and add in step 3.

1 cup	dried sweet potato slices	250 mL
½ cup	dried carrot slices	125 mL
2½ cups	boiling water, divided	625 mL
½ cup	dried cauliflower florets	125 mL
1 tbsp	vegetable oil	15 mL
1	onion, chopped (see tip, at left)	1
3	cloves garlic, minced (see tip, at left)	3
1 tbsp	Indian yellow curry paste or powder	15 mL
½ tsp	cumin seeds	2 mL
Pinch	cayenne pepper (optional)	Pinch
1	can (28 oz/796 mL) diced tomatoes, with juice	1
1½ cups	rinsed drained cooked or canned chickpeas (see tip, at left)	375 mL
	Salt and freshly ground black pepper	
¼ cup	chopped fresh cilantro	50 mL

1. Using kitchen scissors, cut any large sweet potato slices into quarters or halves. In a heatproof bowl, combine sweet potatoes, carrots and 2 cups (500 mL) of the boiling water. In a separate heatproof bowl, combine cauliflower and the remaining ½ cup (125 mL) boiling water. Let both stand for 30 minutes.

2. In a large saucepan, heat oil over medium heat. Add onion and sauté for about 3 minutes or until starting to soften. Add garlic, curry paste, cumin seeds and cayenne (if using); sauté for 2 minutes or until softened and fragrant. Add tomatoes with juice and bring to a boil, scraping up any brown bits stuck to pot. Reduce heat and boil gently for 5 minutes or until slightly reduced.

3. Add sweet potatoes and carrots with soaking water and chickpeas. Boil gently, stirring occasionally, for about 15 minutes or until vegetables are almost tender. Gently stir in cauliflower with soaking liquid; boil gently, stirring occasionally, for about 5 minutes or until vegetables are tender. Season to taste with salt and black pepper. Serve sprinkled with cilantro.

Mexican Squash Stew with Chiles and Quinoa

A robust and satisfying stew with the taste of Mexico makes for a healthy vegetarian main course. It's got so much flavor, meat eaters won't miss the meat.

Serves 4

Tips

The heat of jalapeños can vary, with some being fairly mild and some fiery hot. Taste your jalapeños before using (if you dare) and adjust the amount to your taste. Alternatively, add only 1 jalapeño pepper and season to taste with hot pepper sauce at the end.

Use leftover stew as a filling for a vegetable burrito. Fill a flour tortilla with stew and wrap to enclose filling. Place in a greased baking dish and spread with salsa. Sprinkle with shredded cheese and heat in the microwave or in a 350°F (180°C) oven. Serve with guacamole.

1 cup	quinoa, rinsed and drained	250 mL
2 tsp	ground coriander	10 mL
1 tsp	ground cumin	5 mL
1 cup	dried butternut squash or pumpkin cubes	250 mL
1/2 cup	dried potato cubes	125 mL
1/4 cup	dried onion pieces	50 mL
1/4 cup	chopped dried tomatoes	50 mL
1/4 cup	dried green bean pieces	50 mL
1 to 2	jalapeño peppers, seeded and finely chopped	1 to 2
4 cups	water or vegetable stock	1 L
1/2 tsp	salt	2 mL
1/4 tsp	freshly ground black pepper	1 mL
	Grated zest and juice of 1 lime	

1. In a large saucepan, over medium heat, toast quinoa, coriander and cumin, stirring constantly, for about 2 minutes or until fragrant. Transfer to a bowl and set aside.

2. Add squash, potatoes, onions, tomatoes, green beans, jalapeños to taste and water to the pot and bring to a boil over medium-high heat, stirring often. Reduce heat and boil gently for 15 minutes or until vegetables are slightly softened.

3. Add quinoa mixture, salt and pepper; return to a boil. Cover, reduce heat to low and simmer for 20 minutes or until quinoa and vegetables are tender and stew is thickened. Stir in lime zest and juice. Season to taste with salt and pepper.

Chicken Stew with Dumplings

For Jay, this old-fashioned recipe brings back memories of Sunday dinners after spending a chilly day on the backyard skating rink.

Serves 4

Tips

For an easy take-to-work lunch, make a double recipe of the stew and, before adding dumplings, remove half from the pot and let cool. Portion into small microwave-safe containers and freeze for up to 3 months. Reheat in the microwave or a saucepan.

To use dried leek slices, add $\frac{1}{2}$ cup (125 mL) in step 2 and increase the stock by $\frac{1}{4}$ cup (50 mL).

2 tbsp	vegetable oil	25 mL
1 lb	boneless skinless chicken thighs, cut into chunks	500 g
2	leeks, light and white green parts only, thinly sliced	2
$\frac{1}{2}$ cup	dried mushroom slices	125 mL
$\frac{1}{2}$ cup	dried green peas	125 mL
$\frac{1}{2}$ cup	dried carrot pieces	125 mL
1 tbsp	crumbled dried parsley	15 mL
1 tsp	crumbled dried tarragon or oregano	5 mL
1 tsp	crumbled dried thyme	5 mL
2 cups	chicken stock (preferably sodium-reduced)	500 mL
$\frac{1}{2}$ cup	dry white wine	125 mL
	Salt and freshly ground black pepper	

Dumplings

$1\frac{1}{2}$ cups	all-purpose flour	375 mL
1 tbsp	crumbled dried parsley	15 mL
2 tsp	baking powder	10 mL
$\frac{1}{2}$ tsp	salt	2 mL
$\frac{1}{8}$ tsp	freshly ground black pepper	0.5 mL
$1\frac{1}{4}$ cups	milk or beer	300 mL
2 tbsp	butter, melted	25 mL

1. In a large pot, heat oil over medium-high heat until very hot but not smoking. Add chicken and cook, turning often, until browned on all sides. Add leeks and sauté for about 2 minutes or until softened.

2. Add mushrooms, peas, carrots, parsley, tarragon, thyme, chicken stock and wine; bring to a simmer, scraping up any brown bits stuck to pot. Reduce heat and simmer, stirring often, for 25 to 30 minutes or until vegetables are tender and chicken is no longer pink inside. Season with salt and pepper.

3. *Meanwhile, prepare the dumplings:* In a bowl, combine flour, parsley, baking powder, salt and pepper. Pour in milk and butter. Using a fork, stir just until evenly moistened but some lumps remain.

4. Drop dumpling batter by large spoonfuls onto surface of simmering stew. Cover, reduce heat to low and simmer for about 15 minutes or until a toothpick inserted in the center of a dumpling comes out clean.

Chicken Pot Pie

Jay and Jennifer's store, In a Nuttshell, has served a variation of this chicken pot pie in the fall and winter since its very first year, and it remains a staple for many of their customers.

Serves 8

Tips

Use the best-quality chicken stock possible. If you don't have reduced-sodium stock, use 3 cups (750 mL) regular stock and 1 cup (250 mL) water.

The chicken filling can be made ahead through step 2. Let cool and store in an airtight container in the refrigerator for up to 2 days or in the freezer for up to 3 months. If frozen, thaw overnight in the refrigerator. Proceed with step 3 and increase the baking time to about 45 minutes if necessary to heat the filling.

● *13- by 9-inch (3 L) glass baking dish, greased*

8	baby red potatoes, quartered	8
1 cup	dried carrot pieces	250 mL
1 cup	dried mushroom slices	250 mL
1/2 cup	dried onion pieces	125 mL
1/2 cup	dried celery slices	125 mL
1 tsp	crumbled dried sage	5 mL
1 tsp	crumbled dried tarragon or basil	5 mL
4 cups	chicken stock (preferably sodium-reduced)	1 L
1/4 cup	all-purpose flour	50 mL
1/4 cup	vegetable oil	50 mL
4 cups	chopped cooked chicken breasts or thighs (about 1 1/2 lbs/750 g)	1 L
1/2 tsp	salt (or to taste)	2 mL
1/2 tsp	freshly ground black pepper (or to taste)	2 mL
1	package (14 to 16 oz/400 to 500 g) frozen puff pastry, thawed	1
2 tbsp	milk	25 mL

1. In a large pot, combine potatoes, carrots, mushrooms, onions, celery, sage, tarragon and chicken stock; bring to a boil over medium-high heat. Reduce heat and boil gently for about 20 minutes or until potatoes are tender.

2. In a small bowl, whisk together flour and oil to make a smooth paste. Gradually whisk into the simmering vegetable mixture and simmer, stirring, until stock is thickened. Remove from heat and stir in chicken, salt and pepper.

3. Spread chicken filling in prepared baking dish and let cool slightly. Meanwhile, preheat oven to 350°F (180°C).

4. On a floured surface, roll puff pastry into a rectangle about 1 inch (2.5 cm) larger than the top of the dish. Place pastry over the filling in the dish and crimp the edges, tucking to fit just inside the dish. Brush pastry with milk.

5. Bake for 35 minutes or until filling is bubbling and pastry is golden brown. Let cool on a rack for 10 minutes before serving.

Hamburger Stew

This is a good standby for those nights when you need something fast and easy that everyone in the family will enjoy.

Serves 4

Variations

Add ¼ cup (50 mL) brewed coffee with the beef stock to give an interesting depth of flavor to this stew.

Southwestern Hamburger Stew: Replace the carrots with dried corn kernels and add 1 tbsp (15 mL) chopped dried chile peppers. Garnish each serving with fresh lime juice and cilantro.

1 lb	lean ground beef	500 g
½ cup	dried potato cubes	125 mL
¼ cup	dried onion slices	50 mL
¼ cup	dried celery slices	50 mL
¼ cup	dried carrot pieces	50 mL
1 tsp	minced dried garlic	5 mL
2 cups	beef stock (preferably sodium-reduced)	500 mL
1 cup	water	250 mL
1	can (28 oz/796 mL) diced tomatoes, drained (or 2 cups/500 mL chopped fresh)	1
2 tbsp	crumbled dried parsley (or ¼ cup/50 mL chopped fresh)	25 mL
½ tsp	salt (or to taste)	2 mL
½ tsp	freshly ground black pepper	2 mL

1. In a large pot, over medium-high heat, brown ground beef, breaking up with a spoon, for about 7 minutes or until no longer pink.

2. Add potatoes, onions, celery, carrots and garlic, stirring until fully combined. Add beef stock and water; bring to a boil, scraping up any brown bits stuck to pot. Reduce heat and simmer for 25 to 30 minutes or until potatoes are tender and stew is thickened.

3. Stir in tomatoes and parsley and simmer for about 5 minutes or until heated through. Season with salt and pepper.

Beef and Potato Stew

This simple but filling dish will satisfy your hunger on a cold day.

Serves 4 to 6

Tips

For a richer flavor, use a dark beer, such as Guinness.

Fresh herbs add a nice touch at the end of cooking, but you can use ¼ tsp (1 mL) dried instead and add with the potatoes.

2 lbs	stewing beef, cut into 1-inch (2.5 cm) pieces	1 kg
¼ cup	all-purpose flour	50 mL
2 tbsp	vegetable oil (approx.), divided	25 mL
½ cup	dried potato cubes	125 mL
¼ cup	dried onion pieces	50 mL
¼ cup	dried carrot pieces	50 mL
¼ cup	dried celery slices	50 mL
½ tsp	minced dried garlic	2 mL
1	can (14 to 19 oz/398 to 540 mL) stewed tomatoes	1
2 cups	beer or beef stock (preferably sodium-reduced)	500 mL
2 cups	water	500 mL
1 tsp	salt (or to taste)	5 mL
½ tsp	freshly ground black pepper (or to taste)	2 mL
½ tsp	finely chopped fresh rosemary or thyme	2 mL

1. In a bowl, toss beef with flour. In a large pot, heat half the oil over medium-high heat. Add beef, in small batches, and brown on all sides, adding more oil to the pot as necessary between batches. Transfer browned meat to a bowl.

2. Reduce heat to medium-low and add potatoes, onions, carrots, celery and garlic to the pot. Add tomatoes, beer and water; bring to a boil, scraping up any brown bits stuck to pot. Return the beef and any accumulated juices to the pot. Reduce heat and simmer, stirring often, for about 1½ hours or until vegetables and beef are tender. Season with salt and pepper and stir in rosemary.

Beef and Beer Stew with Turnips, Squash and Onions

Although turnips are less appreciated in North America, they have been popular in central and northern Europe for thousands of years. This recipe combines turnips with the tartness of hops and the sweetness of malt found in most lager beers to make a rich winter stew.

Serves 4 to 6

Tip

Make sure you have a good crusty bread for mopping up the juices at the bottom of the bowl.

2 lbs	stewing beef, cut into 1-inch (2.5 cm) pieces	1 kg
1/4 cup	all-purpose flour	50 mL
2 tbsp	vegetable oil (approx.), divided	25 mL
1/2 cup	dried butternut squash cubes	125 mL
1/2 cup	dried onion pieces	125 mL
1/2 cup	dried turnip or rutabaga cubes	125 mL
1/2 cup	chopped dried apples (optional)	125 mL
1/4 cup	dried celery slices	50 mL
1 tsp	crumbled dried thyme	5 mL
1	clove garlic, minced	1
1	bottle (12 oz/341 mL) lager beer	1
3 cups	beef stock (preferably sodium-reduced)	750 mL
2	potatoes, diced	2
1 tsp	salt (or to taste)	5 mL
1/2 tsp	freshly ground black pepper	2 mL

1. In a bowl, toss beef with flour. In a large pot, heat half the oil over medium-high heat. Add beef, in small batches, and brown on all sides, adding more oil to the pot as necessary between batches. Transfer browned meat to a bowl.

2. Add squash, onions, turnip, apples (if using), celery, thyme, garlic, beer and beef stock to the pot and bring to a boil, scraping up any brown bits stuck to pot. Return the beef and any accumulated juices to the pot. Reduce heat and simmer, stirring often, for about 1 hour or until the beef is slightly tender.

3. Stir in potatoes, salt and pepper; simmer, stirring occasionally, for about 30 minutes or until beef and potatoes are fork-tender and liquid has thickened to a rich stew consistency. Season with salt and pepper.

Beef Tenderloin and Mushroom Ragoût

Ragoût is an elegant way to elevate a humble stew into something worthy of a special event. At a hotel Jay worked at, they served it in a little puff pastry shell and garnished it with fresh herbs.

Serves 4

Tips

Serve with boiled new potatoes, rice, egg noodles or little dumplings, such as spaetzle.

Leftovers are super served on toasted bread for a hot beef sandwich.

Variation

For a deeper mushroom flavor, use half shiitake or cremini mushrooms and half regular mushrooms.

1 cup	dried mushroom slices	250 mL
1/2 cup	dried onion pieces	125 mL
1/2 cup	dried celery slices	125 mL
1 cup	water	250 mL
1 lb	beef tenderloin, cubed	500 g
1/4 cup	all-purpose flour	50 mL
2 tbsp	vegetable oil (approx.), divided	25 mL
1 tsp	minced dried garlic	5 mL
1/4 tsp	crumbled dried thyme (or 1/2 tsp/2 mL chopped fresh)	1 mL
Pinch	crumbled dried rosemary (or 1/4 tsp/1 mL chopped fresh)	Pinch
2 cups	dark beer	500 mL
1/2 tsp	salt (or to taste)	2 mL
1/4 tsp	freshly ground black pepper	1 mL

1. In a bowl, combine mushrooms, onions, celery and water. Let stand for 20 minutes or until vegetables start to soften. Drain, reserving soaking liquid.

2. In a bowl, toss beef with flour. In a large pot, heat half the oil over medium-high heat. Add beef, in small batches, and brown on all sides, adding more oil to the pot as necessary between batches. Transfer browned meat to a bowl.

3. Reduce heat to medium-low, add mushroom mixture, garlic, thyme and rosemary to the pot and cook, stirring, for 2 minutes. Add reserved soaking liquid and beer; bring to a boil, scraping up any brown bits stuck to pot. Return the beef and any accumulated juices to the pot. Reduce heat and simmer, stirring often, for about 30 minutes or until vegetables and beef are tender. Season with salt and pepper.

Teriyaki Orange Simmered Beef

This Japanese-inspired dish is quick, easy and out of the ordinary. Serve over fluffy steamed rice or cooked noodles.

Serves 4

Tips

Look for a thick teriyaki sauce (sometimes called a stir-fry sauce) for the best texture. If you only have thin sauce, whisk in 1 tsp (5 mL) cornstarch before stirring the sauce into the pan and cook for about 1 minute.

Substitute ⅓ cup (175 mL) dried broccoli for the fresh. Soak it in water for 15 minutes; drain and add in step 2.

1 cup	Teriyaki Beef Jerky, broken into pieces	250 mL
½ cup	dried onion slices	125 mL
¼ cup	dried celery slices	50 mL
1 tsp	minced gingerroot	5 mL
	Grated zest and juice of 1 orange	
2 cups	water	500 mL
1 cup	small broccoli florets	250 mL
½ cup	snow peas, trimmed	125 mL
½ cup	thick teriyaki sauce	125 mL

1. In a skillet, combine beef jerky, onions, celery, ginger, orange juice and water; bring to a simmer over medium heat. Simmer, stirring occasionally, for about 15 minutes or until vegetables are tender.

2. Add broccoli and snow peas; simmer, stirring often, for 5 to 7 minutes or until broccoli is tender-crisp. Stir in teriyaki sauce and orange zest.

Peppercorn Ground Beef Jerky Shepherd's Pie

Cooking the beef jerky with the dried vegetables creates the gravy in this simple version of shepherd's pie. The cheese in the potatoes gives it a rich finish.

Serves 8

Tip

The beef mixture can be made ahead. Let cool and store in an airtight container in the refrigerator for up to 2 days. Reheat until steaming in a pot over medium heat before assembling in step 4.

Variation

For more adventurous palates, use crumbled blue cheese or shredded Gruyère in the mashed potatoes.

- 13- by 9-inch (3 L) glass baking dish, greased

2 cups	chopped Peppercorn Ground Beef Jerky	500 mL
¾ cup	dried corn kernels	175 mL
¾ cup	dried onion pieces	175 mL
½ cup	dried celery slices	125 mL
1 tsp	chopped dried garlic	5 mL
1 tsp	crumbled dried thyme	5 mL
8 cups	water	2 L
6	oblong or Yukon gold potatoes, peeled and cut into chunks	6
1 cup	milk or half-and-half (10%) cream	250 mL
½ cup	freshly grated Parmesan cheese	125 mL
½ tsp	salt	2 mL
½ tsp	freshly ground black pepper	2 mL

1. In a large pot, combine beef jerky, corn, onions, celery, garlic, thyme and water. Let stand for 15 minutes or until vegetables start to soften. Bring to a boil over medium-high heat, stirring often. Reduce heat and boil gently, stirring occasionally, for 15 to 20 minutes or until corn is tender and sauce is slightly thickened. Remove from heat.

2. Meanwhile, in a pot, cover potatoes with cold water and bring to a boil over high heat. Reduce heat and boil gently for about 20 minutes or until potatoes are fork-tender. Drain, return to pot and let air-dry for 10 minutes. Using a potato masher, mash potatoes until lumps are gone; gradually mash in milk, cheese, salt and pepper.

3. Preheat oven to 375°F (190°C).

4. Spread beef mixture in prepared baking dish. Spread mashed potatoes over beef. Bake for 25 to 30 minutes or until potatoes are golden brown and crispy on top.

Cassoulet with Beans, Sausage and Bread Crumbs

Traditional French cassoulet includes duck and pork and takes all day to make. This version is a little lower in fat and is streamlined while keeping the spirit of the dish intact.

Serves 8

Tips

For the sausage, use Merguez sausage (made from lamb) or your favorite cooked or smoked sausage. Make sure to drain the fat from cooked sausage.

If not using smoked sausage, add ¼ cup (50 mL) diced smoked bacon or ham with the sausage for extra flavor.

Variation

In place of dry beans, use 6 cups (1.5 L) drained and rinsed canned white beans (about four 14-oz/398 mL cans or three 19-oz/540 mL cans) and skip steps 1 and 2.

• *13- by 9-inch (3 L) glass baking dish, greased*

2 cups	dry navy (pea) or white kidney beans	500 mL
	Cold water	
1 cup	dried onion pieces	250 mL
½ cup	each dried celery and carrot slices	125 mL
1	can (14 to 19 oz/398 to 540 mL) stewed tomatoes	1
1 lb	cooked or smoked spicy sausage, sliced	500 g
1 tbsp	crumbled dried parsley	15 mL
1 tsp	crumbled dried thyme	5 mL
½ tsp	crumbled dried rosemary	2 mL
1 cup	dry white wine	250 mL
2 cups	coarse dried bread crumbs	500 mL
¼ cup	butter, melted	50 mL
2	cloves garlic, minced	2
	Salt and freshly ground black pepper	

1. In a large pot, combine beans and enough cold water to cover; bring to a boil over high heat. Boil for 3 minutes. Remove from heat and let stand for 1 hour. (Alternatively, cover beans with cold water by at least 2 inches/5 cm and let soak for at least 8 hours or overnight.) Drain and rinse well; drain again.

2. In a clean pot, combine beans and 12 cups (3 L) water; bring to a boil over high heat. Reduce heat, cover, leaving lid slightly ajar, and boil gently for about 45 minutes or until beans are almost tender. Drain well.

3. Preheat oven to 350°F (180°C).

4. In prepared baking dish, combine beans, onions, celery, carrots, tomatoes, sausage, parsley, thyme, rosemary, wine and 2 cups (500 mL) water. Cover with foil and bake for 1 hour or until vegetables are tender and mixture has thickened.

5. Meanwhile, in a bowl, combine bread crumbs, butter, garlic and salt and pepper to taste.

6. Remove foil and season cassoulet with salt and pepper to taste. Sprinkle with bread crumbs. Bake, uncovered, for 15 minutes or until bread crumbs are golden brown.

Pepperette Sausage, Pepper and Onion Jambalaya

Based on the New Orleans classic, this variation relies on flavorful pepperette sausages instead of the traditional ham. The brown rice makes for a more substantial serving, sure to leave you satisfied.

Serves 4

Tip

Like many dishes, jambalaya was originally designed to use up leftover bits and pieces around the kitchen. To jazz it up, add some cooked shrimp, mussels or crayfish with the tomatoes and cook just long enough to heat through.

1 cup	chopped pepperette sausages or ground meat jerky	250 mL
$\frac{1}{2}$ cup	dried green bell pepper pieces	125 mL
$\frac{1}{2}$ cup	dried red bell pepper pieces	125 mL
$\frac{1}{4}$ cup	dried celery slices	50 mL
$\frac{1}{4}$ cup	dried onion pieces	50 mL
2 tsp	minced dried garlic	10 mL
$\frac{1}{4}$ tsp	cayenne pepper	1 mL
2 cups	tomato juice	500 mL
1 cup	water	250 mL
2	tomatoes, seeded and chopped	2
$\frac{1}{4}$ cup	chopped fresh parsley (or 1 tbsp/ 15 mL crumbled dried)	50 mL
	Salt and freshly ground black pepper	
	Hot pepper sauce	
3 cups	hot cooked brown rice (about 1 cup/ 250 mL raw)	750 mL

1. In a large pot, over medium heat, combine sausages, red and green peppers, celery, onions, garlic, cayenne, tomato juice and water. Let stand for 15 minutes or until vegetables start to soften.

2. Bring to a boil over medium-high heat, stirring often. Reduce heat and simmer, stirring occasionally, for about 15 minutes or until vegetables are tender and sauce is slightly thickened.

3. Stir in tomatoes and parsley. Season to taste with salt, black pepper and hot pepper sauce. Serve over rice and pass more hot pepper sauce at the table.

Shrimp and Sausage Saffron Paella

Traditionally, this Spanish dish is made in a single pan designed especially for paella, but it will work in a regular skillet, too. With dried ingredients, you can make this almost entirely with items from your pantry.

Serves 4

Tip

The saffron is a signature of the dish and gives it the distinct yellow color. Saffron can be found in the spice section of large supermarkets, at specialty stores and at some well-stocked bulk stores. It is expensive, but a little goes a long way and the flavor is worth it.

Variations

Paella can also include cooked chicken, ham and/or shellfish for a more sumptuous version. Feel free to add what you have on hand with or in place of the sausage.

Replace the dried shrimp with 8 oz (250 g) fresh medium or large shrimp, peeled and deveined. Add with the sausage in step 3 and cook just until shrimp are pink and opaque.

½ cup	dried cooked shrimp, finely chopped	125 mL
½ cup	dried tomatoes, slivered	125 mL
½ cup	dried green bell pepper pieces	125 mL
½ cup	dried onion pieces	125 mL
2 tbsp	crumbled dried parsley	25 mL
1 tsp	minced dried garlic	5 mL
Pinch	saffron threads	Pinch
4 cups	water	1 L
1 cup	dry white wine	250 mL
1 cup	parboiled long-grain white rice	250 mL
½ tsp	salt	2 mL
½ tsp	freshly ground black pepper	2 mL
1 cup	chopped cooked or smoked spicy sausage	250 mL

1. In a large skillet, combine shrimp, tomatoes, green peppers, onions, parsley, garlic, saffron and water; bring to a boil over medium-high heat. Reduce heat and boil gently for 5 minutes or until vegetables start to soften.

2. Stir in rice, salt and pepper; return to a boil. Reduce heat to low, cover and simmer for 20 minutes or until rice is tender and most of the liquid is absorbed.

3. Stir in sausage and simmer, uncovered, stirring gently occasionally, for about 5 minutes or until sausage is heated through. Season to taste with salt and pepper.

Angel Hair Pasta with Tomatoes, Asparagus and Peas

This pasta dish makes a nice light lunch or dinner and is perfect for enjoying al fresco on a sunny day.

Serves 4

Tip

Remember, don't cook with a wine that you wouldn't enjoy drinking from a glass. Cooking enhances bad flavors as much as it does good ones.

Variation

For a richer sauce, replace $\frac{1}{2}$ cup (125 mL) of the wine with whipping (35%) cream.

$\frac{1}{2}$ cup	chopped dried tomatoes	125 mL
$\frac{1}{2}$ cup	dried asparagus pieces	125 mL
$\frac{1}{4}$ cup	dried green peas	50 mL
1 tsp	minced dried garlic	5 mL
$\frac{1}{4}$ tsp	crumbled dried tarragon	1 mL
$1\frac{1}{2}$ cups	water	375 mL
1 cup	dry white wine	250 mL
12 oz	angel hair pasta	375 g
	Salt and freshly ground black pepper	
$\frac{1}{4}$ cup	freshly grated Parmesan cheese	50 mL

1. In a saucepan, combine tomatoes, asparagus, peas, garlic, tarragon, and water. Let stand for 30 minutes or until vegetables start to soften.

2. Add wine and bring to a boil over high heat. Reduce heat and boil gently, stirring occasionally, for 7 to 10 minutes or until vegetables are tender and liquid is reduced by about half.

3. Meanwhile, in a large pot of boiling salted water, cook pasta for about 6 minutes, or according to package directions, until al dente (tender to the bite). Drain well, reserving 1 cup (250 mL) of the pasta water, and return pasta to the pot.

4. Add vegetable mixture to the pasta and toss gently to coat, adding enough of the reserved pasta water to moisten. Season to taste with salt and pepper. Divide among heated serving bowls and serve sprinkled with cheese.

Spaghetti with Mushrooms, Thyme and Garlic

A must for the mushroom lovers in your life, this recipe brings the earthiness of mushrooms together with the richness of goat cheese.

Serves 4

Variation

If you're not a fan of goat cheese, replace it with 1/2 cup (125 mL) soft cheese, such as ricotta or mascarpone.

1/4 cup	dried shiitake mushroom slices	50 mL
1/4 cup	dried cremini mushroom slices	50 mL
1/4 cup	dried oyster mushroom slices	50 mL
1 cup	boiling water	250 mL
1 tsp	minced dried garlic	5 mL
1/2 tsp	crumbled dried thyme	2 mL
1 cup	dry white wine	250 mL
12 oz	spaghetti	375 g
1 cup	whipping (35%) cream	250 mL
1/4 cup	crumbled soft goat cheese	50 mL
	Salt and freshly ground black pepper	

1. In a saucepan, combine shiitake, cremini and oyster mushrooms and boiling water. Let stand for 20 minutes or until mushrooms start to soften.

2. Add garlic, thyme and wine; bring to a boil over medium-high heat, stirring often. Reduce heat and simmer, stirring occasionally, for about 10 minutes or until mushrooms are tender and liquid is reduced by about half.

3. Meanwhile, in a large pot of boiling salted water, cook spaghetti for about 8 minutes, or according to package directions, until al dente (tender to the bite). Drain well and return to the pot.

4. Stir cream and goat cheese into the mushroom mixture and bring back to a simmer, stirring until cheese is melted. Season to taste with salt and pepper. Add to the spaghetti and toss gently to coat.

Apple, Cranberry and Oat
Breakfast Crumble (page 89)

Dried Carrot Slices (page 33)

Three Sisters Soup (page 95)

Dried Mushrooms (page 37) and Sweet Potato Cubes (page 42)

Aloo Tari (page 114)

Dried Apple Slices (page 26), Leek Pieces
(page 36), Plum (Roma) Tomatoes (page 42)
and Red Bell Pepper Slices (page 38)

Angel Hair Pasta with Tomatoes, Asparagus and Peas (page 127)

Dried Zucchini Slices
(page 43), Broccoli (page 33),
Green Peas (page 38) and
Celery (page 35)

Penne with Tomatoes, Artichokes and Basil

Here's a great pasta for a grown-up palate. The dried tomatoes create a deep-flavored sauce, and artichoke hearts are always a favorite in pastas for Jay's customers at Nuttshell Next Door Café.

Serves 4

Variations

For a more substantial meal, add 1½ cups (375 mL) diced cooked chicken breast or cooked shrimp with the artichokes.

For a roasted flavor accent, replace the onions with dried roasted onions and the garlic with 1 tbsp (15 mL) crumbled dried roasted garlic.

1 cup	dried tomatoes, slivered	250 mL
¼ cup	dried onion pieces	50 mL
1 tsp	chopped dried garlic	5 mL
Pinch	hot pepper flakes	Pinch
2 cups	water	500 mL
12 oz	penne or other short pasta	375 g
1	can (14 oz/398 mL) artichoke hearts, drained and quartered	1
2 tbsp	extra-virgin olive oil	25 mL
¼ cup	chopped fresh basil	50 mL
	Salt and freshly ground black pepper	
¼ cup	freshly grated Parmesan cheese	50 mL

1. In a saucepan, combine tomatoes, onions, garlic, hot pepper flakes and water. Let stand for 15 minutes or until tomatoes are starting to soften.

2. Bring to a boil over medium-high heat. Reduce heat and simmer, stirring occasionally, for about 15 minutes or until onions are soft and sauce is thickened.

3. Meanwhile, in a large pot of boiling salted water, cook penne for 10 minutes, or according to package directions, until al dente (tender to the bite). Drain well, reserving 1 cup (250 mL) of the pasta water, and return pasta to the pot.

4. Add artichokes and olive oil to the tomato mixture and simmer for 5 minutes or until heated through. Pour over pasta and add basil; toss gently to coat, adding enough of the reserved pasta water to moisten. Season to taste with salt and pepper. Serve sprinkled with Parmesan cheese.

Vegetable Lasagna

You can never go wrong with a classic lasagna. It'll be a hit for a weeknight meal or for entertaining.

Serves 8

Tip

Let leftover lasagna cool completely, then cut it into individual portions. Wrap in plastic wrap, place in airtight containers or freezer bags and freeze for up to 6 months. Thaw overnight in the refrigerator or in the microwave before reheating.

• *13- by 9-inch (3 L) glass baking dish, greased*

1 cup	dried tomatoes	250 mL
1 cup	chopped dried eggplant	250 mL
$1/2$ cup	dried red bell pepper slices	125 mL
3 cups	boiling water, divided	750 mL
1 cup	dried mushroom slices	250 mL
$1/2$ cup	dried onion slices	125 mL
2	eggs	2
1 cup	ricotta cheese	250 mL
2 cups	chopped fresh spinach	500 mL
12	oven-ready lasagna noodles	12
5 cups	tomato pasta sauce (approx.)	1.25 L
1 cup	shredded Cheddar cheese	250 mL
1 cup	shredded mozzarella cheese	250 mL

1. In a heatproof bowl, combine tomatoes, eggplant, red peppers and 2 cups (500 mL) of the boiling water. In another heatproof bowl, combine mushrooms, onions and the remaining boiling water. Let both stand for about 30 minutes or until vegetables are softened and water has cooled to room temperature. Keeping bowls of vegetables separate, drain vegetables through a sieve, reserving excess soaking water. Set vegetables and water aside.

2. Preheat oven to 350°F (180°C).

3. In a small bowl, using a fork, combine eggs and ricotta until blended. Stir in the spinach and set aside.

4. In a large measuring cup, stir reserved soaking water into tomato sauce, adding more sauce as necessary to make 6 cups (1.5 L) total.

5. Spread $1^1/2$ cups (375 mL) of the tomato sauce in the bottom of prepared baking dish. Place 3 lasagna noodles on top of the sauce, breaking to fit as necessary. Spread $1^1/2$ cups (375 mL) tomato sauce over the noodles and arrange tomatoes, eggplant and red peppers over the sauce. Place a layer of noodles over the vegetables. Spread $1^1/2$ cups (375 mL) tomato sauce over the noodles and arrange mushrooms and onions over the sauce. Place another layer of noodles over the vegetables. Spread with

the ricotta mixture and arrange another layer of noodles over top. Spread the remaining tomato sauce over the noodles and sprinkle with Cheddar and mozzarella cheese.

6. Cover with foil and bake for 35 to 40 minutes or until sauce is bubbling. Uncover and bake for about 15 minutes or until cheese is golden brown and vegetables and noodles are tender. Let cool on a rack for 10 minutes before serving.

Curried Tofu with Mushrooms and Lentils

This lightly curried dish is an excellent way to introduce tofu to your family. Make sure to use firm tofu, so that the texture holds through the cooking process.

Serves 4

Tip
Add your favorite seasonal fresh vegetables, such as snow peas, baby corn or chopped red bell peppers, during the last 5 minutes of cooking.

1 tbsp	vegetable oil	15 mL
$\frac{1}{2}$ cup	red lentils, rinsed and drained	125 mL
1 tsp	Indian yellow curry paste	5 mL
$\frac{1}{2}$ cup	dried mushroom slices	125 mL
$\frac{1}{2}$ cup	dried onion slices	125 mL
$\frac{1}{4}$ cup	dried carrot slices	50 mL
$\frac{1}{4}$ cup	dried celery slices	50 mL
4 cups	water or vegetable stock	1 L
8 oz	firm tofu, drained and cubed	250 g
2	green onions, thinly sliced	2
	Plain yogurt (optional)	
1	lime, quartered	1

1. In a saucepan, heat oil over medium heat. Add lentils and curry paste; sauté for 30 seconds or until fragrant. Add mushrooms, onions, carrots, celery and water; bring to a boil, stirring often. Stir in tofu. Reduce heat to low, cover, leaving lid slightly ajar, and simmer, stirring occasionally, for about 25 minutes or until lentils and vegetables are tender.

2. Sprinkle each serving with green onions and top with a dollop of yogurt, if desired. Serve with a wedge of lime to squeeze over top.

Baked Macaroni Tuna Casserole

Classic comfort food can't be beat — especially when made nutritiously from scratch with your own home-dried vegetables.

Serves 4

Tip

The casserole can be made ahead through step 5. Let cool, cover and refrigerate for up to 1 day. Cover with foil and bake in a 350°F (180°C) for about 30 minutes or until hot in the center. Uncover and proceed with step 6.

• 8-inch (2 L) square glass baking dish, greased

1/2 cup	dried mushroom slices	125 mL
1/4 cup	dried celery slices	50 mL
1/4 cup	dried onion pieces	50 mL
1/4 cup	dried green peas	50 mL
1 1/2 cups	water	375 mL
8 oz	macaroni or small pasta shells	250 g
1/4 cup	all-purpose flour	50 mL
2 1/2 cups	milk	625 mL
2	cans (each 6 oz/175 g) tuna, drained	2
1 tsp	grated lemon zest	5 mL
2 tbsp	freshly squeezed lemon juice	25 mL
1 cup	shredded Cheddar or mozzarella cheese, divided	250 mL
	Salt and freshly ground black pepper	
1 cup	coarse dried bread crumbs	250 mL

1. In a saucepan, combine mushrooms, celery, onions, peas and water. Let stand for about 30 minutes or until vegetables start to soften.

2. Meanwhile, in a large pot of boiling salted water, cook macaroni for about 6 minutes, or according to package directions, until almost tender (do not overcook). Drain and rinse well and return to the pot. Set aside.

3. Preheat oven to 350°F (180°C).

4. Bring vegetable mixture to a boil over medium heat. Whisk flour into milk and gradually whisk into saucepan. Reduce heat and simmer, whisking constantly, for about 10 minutes or until vegetables are tender and sauce is thickened. Remove from heat. Stir in tuna, lemon zest, lemon juice and 3/4 cup (175 mL) of the cheese.

5. Add tuna mixture to the macaroni and toss gently to coat. Season to taste with salt and pepper. Spread in prepared baking dish.

6. Sprinkle casserole with bread crumbs and the remaining cheese. Bake for 10 to 15 minutes or until bread crumbs are crispy and cheese is melted.

Side Dishes

Ratatouille

A medley of vegetables with a Mediterranean touch becomes an easy side with plenty of flavor.

Serves 4

Tips

Cook the mixture until thick enough to mound on a spoon and serve as a side for grilled meats or poultry, or leave it saucy to use as a topping for cooked pasta.

Chop the vegetables very small and simmer the ratatouille until very thick, and you can use it as a bruschetta topping, sprinkled with mozzarella or Parmesan cheese.

½ cup	dried eggplant slices	125 mL
¼ cup	chopped dried tomatoes	50 mL
¼ cup	dried zucchini slices	50 mL
2 tbsp	dried red and/or green bell pepper pieces	25 mL
2 tbsp	dried onion pieces	25 mL
1 tsp	minced dried garlic	5 mL
1 tsp	crumbled dried basil	5 mL
¼ tsp	crumbled dried thyme	1 mL
¼ tsp	salt	1 mL
Pinch	cayenne pepper (optional)	Pinch
	Freshly ground black pepper	
2 cups	reduced-sodium vegetable stock or water	500 mL

1. In a saucepan, combine eggplant, tomatoes, zucchini, bell peppers, onions, garlic, basil, thyme, salt, cayenne, black pepper to taste and vegetable stock; bring to a boil over medium heat, stirring often. Reduce heat to low, cover and simmer, stirring occasionally, for about 10 minutes or until vegetables are plump and tender.

2. Uncover, increase heat to medium and simmer, stirring often, for 5 to 10 minutes or until thickened to desired consistency. Season to taste with salt and black pepper.

Cauliflower and Broccoli Gratin

Classic vegetables in a classic Cheddar gratin make for a tasty side dish that will be welcome at any meal.

Serves 4

Tip

To prevent the sauce from being lumpy and to keep the milk from splitting, it is essential that you add the milk to the pan gradually while whisking constantly.

Variation

Omit the bread crumb topping for simple vegetables with cheese sauce. Add the full 1 cup (250 mL) cheese in step 3 and skip steps 4 and 5, heating the vegetables slightly in the saucepan if necessary.

- 4-cup (1 L) shallow baking dish

½ cup	dried cauliflower florets	125 mL
½ cup	dried broccoli florets	125 mL
1 tbsp	dried onion pieces	15 mL
1 cup	boiling water	250 mL
1 tbsp	butter	15 mL
2 tbsp	all-purpose flour	25 mL
1½ cups	milk	375 mL
1 cup	shredded sharp (old) Cheddar cheese, divided	250 mL
1 tsp	Dijon mustard	5 mL
	Salt and freshly ground black pepper	
1 cup	coarse dried bread crumbs	250 mL
2 tbsp	chopped fresh parsley (optional)	25 mL

1. In baking dish, combine cauliflower, broccoli, onions and boiling water. Cover and let stand for 30 minutes or until vegetables are plump. Drain off liquid.

2. Meanwhile, preheat oven to 375°F (190°C).

3. In a saucepan, melt butter over medium heat. Add flour and cook, stirring, for 1 minute. Gradually whisk in milk. Cook, whisking constantly, for about 5 minutes or until bubbling and thickened. Remove from heat and whisk in ¾ cup (175 mL) of the cheese and the mustard. Season to taste with salt and pepper. Pour over vegetables in baking dish and toss gently to coat.

4. In a bowl, combine the remaining cheese, bread crumbs and parsley (if using). Sprinkle over vegetables.

5. Bake for about 20 minutes or until sauce is hot and bubbling, topping is golden brown and cheese is melted.

Curry-Roasted Squash and Chickpeas

Serve this flavorful dish along with other curries or as an accompaniment to grilled or roast chicken or pork.

Serves 4

Variation

For added flavor and crunch, sprinkle vegetables with 2 tbsp (25 mL) chopped almonds or peanuts for the last 5 minutes of roasting.

- 6-cup (1.5 L) shallow baking dish

1/2 cup	dried butternut squash cubes	125 mL
1/4 cup	dried onion slices	50 mL
2 tbsp	dried red bell pepper slices	25 mL
2 cups	boiling water, divided	500 mL
1 cup	rinsed drained canned or cooked chickpeas	250 mL
1 tbsp	vegetable oil	15 mL
2 tsp	Indian yellow curry paste or powder	10 mL
1/2 tsp	crumbled dried mint	2 mL
1/4 tsp	salt	1 mL
2 tbsp	chopped dried apricots	25 mL

1. In a heatproof bowl, combine squash, onions, red peppers and 1¾ cups (425 mL) of the boiling water; cover and let stand for 30 minutes or until vegetables are soft. Drain, reserving ¼ cup (50 mL) of the soaking liquid.

2. Meanwhile, preheat oven to 400°F (200°C).

3. In baking dish, combine soaked vegetables, reserved liquid, chickpeas, oil, curry paste, mint and salt. Roast, stirring twice, for about 30 minutes or until starting to brown.

4. Meanwhile, in a heatproof bowl, combine apricots and the remaining boiling water; let stand for 15 to 30 minutes or until softened.

5. Stir apricot mixture into vegetables and season to taste with salt.

Corn and Black Bean Succotash

This colorful mixture of vegetables and beans adds good nutrition and flavor to a simple roast chicken breast, pork chop or fish fillet.

Serves 4

Tip

Soaking the vegetables at room temperature does take a little longer, but it gives a nicer texture to the squash. If you're in a hurry, you can boil the stock before adding it to the vegetables and reduce the soaking time to 10 minutes.

Variation

Add a hint of smoky flavor by using ¼ tsp (1 mL) smoked paprika instead of the cayenne pepper.

½ cup	dried corn kernels	125 mL
½ cup	dried butternut squash cubes	125 mL
¼ cup	dried onion pieces	50 mL
2 tbsp	dried red bell pepper pieces	25 mL
2 tbsp	dried green bell pepper pieces	25 mL
1 tbsp	crumbled dried parsley	15 mL
½ tsp	salt (or to taste)	2 mL
¼ tsp	crumbled dried thyme	1 mL
¼ tsp	cayenne pepper	1 mL
2 cups	reduced-sodium vegetable or chicken stock	500 mL
1 cup	rinsed drained canned or cooked black beans	250 mL
1 tbsp	butter	15 mL

1. In a saucepan, combine corn, squash, onions, red peppers, green peppers, parsley, salt, thyme, cayenne and vegetable stock. Cover and let stand for 30 minutes or until corn starts to soften.

2. Uncover and bring to a boil over medium heat, stirring often. Stir in beans. Reduce heat and boil gently, stirring occasionally, for about 15 minutes or until vegetables are soft and liquid is almost absorbed. Remove from heat and stir in butter until melted. Season to taste with salt.

Zucchini and Red Pepper Fritters

These are a cross between a vegetable and a bread and make for a nice change from the usual rice or potatoes.

Serves 4

Tip

Serve fritters as an appetizer with hot tomato pasta sauce for dipping.

¼ cup	dried grated zucchini	50 mL
2 tbsp	dried red bell pepper pieces	25 mL
½ tsp	crumbled dried oregano or basil	2 mL
1 cup	boiling water	250 mL
¾ cup	all-purpose flour	175 mL
¼ cup	freshly grated Parmesan cheese	50 mL
1 tsp	granulated sugar	5 mL
1 tsp	baking powder	5 mL
½ tsp	salt	2 mL
¼ tsp	freshly ground black pepper	1 mL
1	egg	1
	Vegetable oil	

1. In a heatproof bowl, combine zucchini, red peppers, oregano and boiling water. Cover and let stand for about 30 minutes or until vegetables are very soft and cooled to room temperature.

2. Meanwhile, in a bowl, combine flour, Parmesan cheese, sugar, baking powder, salt and pepper.

3. Using a fork, stir egg into vegetable mixture until blended. Pour over dry ingredients and stir with a fork just until moistened and some lumps remain, adding a little more water if necessary to make a thick, spoonable batter, similar to dumplings.

4. In a large skillet, heat about ½ inch (1 cm) of oil over medium heat until a small amount of batter turns golden in a few seconds. Using two spoons, one to hold batter and one to slide it into the oil, carefully drop heaping tablespoonfuls (15 mL) of batter into the oil for each fritter (without crowding the pan). Fry for about 2 minutes per side, turning once, or until deep golden brown. Using a slotted spoon, transfer to a plate lined with paper towels. Repeat with the remaining batter, adding more oil and adjusting the heat as necessary between batches.

Vegetable and Ricotta Strudel

This recipes is so versatile for entertaining menus, you'll make it over and over again. Jennifer and Jay serve it alongside grilled meats, as a vegetarian main course with tomato sauce, or on top of greens for a hearty salad.

Serves 4

Tips

Strudels can be assembled, covered and refrigerated for up to 8 hours.

When working with phyllo, keep it covered with a slightly damp tea towel to prevent it from drying out.

• *Baking sheet, lined with parchment paper*

½ cup	chopped dried tomatoes	125 mL
¼ cup	dried zucchini slices, chopped	50 mL
2 tbsp	dried red bell pepper pieces	25 mL
1 tbsp	dried onion pieces	15 mL
2 tsp	crumbled dried basil	10 mL
1 tsp	crumbled dried oregano	5 mL
¾ cup	reduced-sodium vegetable stock	175 mL
1 tbsp	balsamic vinegar	15 mL
	Salt and freshly ground black pepper	
1 cup	ricotta cheese	250 mL
1	egg	1
8	sheets phyllo pastry	8
3 tbsp	melted butter or olive oil	45 mL
⅓ cup	cornmeal or fine dried bread crumbs	75 mL

1. In a saucepan, combine tomatoes, zucchini, red peppers, onions, basil, oregano and vegetable stock; bring to a boil over medium heat. Reduce heat and boil gently, stirring often, for about 10 minutes or until vegetables are soft and most of the liquid is absorbed. Remove from heat and stir in vinegar. Let cool to room temperature. Season to taste with salt and pepper.

2. In a bowl, using a fork, combine ricotta and egg until blended. Season to taste with pepper.

3. Preheat oven to 425°F (220°C).

4. Lay one sheet of phyllo on a large work surface and brush lightly with butter. Place a second sheet on top and brush with butter. Starting about 1 inch (2.5 cm) from one long side of sheet, in the center, sprinkle one-quarter of the cornmeal in a 6-inch (15 cm) square. Spoon one-quarter of the vegetable mixture over the closest half of the cornmeal. Top with one-quarter of the ricotta mixture. Starting at the edge closest to you, fold pastry and filling over so filling is surrounded by cornmeal. Fold both short ends toward the center. Roll up and place seam side down on prepared baking sheet. Brush outside of strudel with butter. Repeat to make 3 more strudels.

5. Bake strudels for about 15 minutes or until golden brown. Using a serrated knife, cut strudels in half on a diagonal.

Barley and Beet Risotto

This isn't really risotto, since there is no rice, but the cooking method creates a creamy grain dish that is just like risotto but with the added toothsome texture and deep flavor of barley. The beets and a touch of orange are lovely accents.

Serves 4 to 6

Tip

Heating the stock and keeping it hot is important for risotto. If you add unheated stock, it cools down the rice — or in this case, barley — with each addition, and you don't get the signature creamy texture of a good risotto.

½ cup	dried beet slices, cut into cubes	125 mL
½ tsp	minced dried garlic	2 mL
2 cups	boiling water	500 mL
3 cups	reduced-sodium vegetable or chicken stock	750 mL
1 tbsp	butter or olive oil	15 mL
1	onion, chopped	1
¼ tsp	salt	1 mL
¼ tsp	freshly ground black pepper	1 mL
1 cup	pot barley, rinsed and drained	250 mL
2 tbsp	freshly squeezed orange or lemon juice	25 mL
	Freshly grated Parmesan cheese	

1. In a heatproof bowl or measuring cup, combine beets, garlic and boiling water. Cover and let stand for 30 minutes or until beets are softened.

2. Meanwhile, in a saucepan, bring vegetable stock to a boil over high heat. Reduce heat to low and keep hot.

3. In a deep saucepan, melt butter over medium heat. Add onion, salt and pepper; sauté for 5 minutes or until onion is softened. Add barley and stir until well coated. Add beet mixture, with soaking liquid, and 1 cup (250 mL) of the hot stock; bring to a boil, stirring often. Cover, reduce heat to medium-low and cook, stirring occasionally, for 25 minutes.

4. Uncover and simmer, stirring often and adding the remaining stock about ½ cup (125 mL) at a time as the previous addition is absorbed, for about 20 minutes or until barley is just tender with a slight bite and beets are tender. Adjust the heat as necessary to keep the pot at a steady simmer. Stir in orange juice and season to taste with salt and pepper. Serve sprinkled with cheese.

Asparagus Risotto

This risotto recipe takes a few shortcuts to make it easier and quicker than the traditional method. Best of all, the creaminess and terrific flavor remain intact.

Serves 4 to 6

Tips

For superior flavor, use the best-quality stock available. It really makes a difference when you're making risotto.

If you don't have dried lemon zest, add ¹⁄₂ tsp (2 mL) fresh grated lemon zest with the Parmesan.

1 tbsp	butter or olive oil	15 mL
1 cup	short-grain white rice (such as Arborio)	250 mL
¹⁄₄ cup	dried onion pieces	50 mL
1 tsp	minced dried garlic	5 mL
¹⁄₄ tsp	salt (or to taste)	1 mL
4 cups	reduced-sodium vegetable or chicken stock	1 L
¹⁄₄ cup	dry white wine	50 mL
¹⁄₃ cup	dried asparagus pieces	75 mL
1 tsp	crumbled dried lemon zest	5 mL
¹⁄₂ cup	boiling water (approx.)	125 mL
¹⁄₄ cup	freshly grated Parmesan cheese	50 mL
	Freshly ground black pepper	

1. In a deep saucepan, melt butter over medium heat. Add rice and sauté for 2 minutes or until rice is coated and looks glassy. Add onions, garlic, salt, vegetable stock and wine; bring to a boil, stirring often. Stir in asparagus and lemon zest. Cover, reduce heat to low and cook, stirring twice, for about 20 minutes or until rice and asparagus are almost tender.

2. Uncover and stir in boiling water. Cook, stirring, for about 5 minutes or until rice is just tender to the bite and is a creamy consistency, adding a little more boiling water as necessary. Stir in Parmesan and season to taste with salt and pepper.

Mushroom and Herb Risotto

Dried mushrooms have such a rich flavor you need only a few simple herbs and a splash of sherry to make a hearty-tasting risotto.

Serves 4 to 6

Tips

Use a blend of dried mushrooms, such as button, cremini and shiitake, for the most robust, woodsy flavor.

Heating the stock and keeping it hot is important for risotto. If you add unheated stock, it cools the rice down with each addition, and you don't get the signature creamy texture of a good risotto.

1/3 cup	dried mushroom slices (see tip, at left)	75 mL
1 cup	boiling water	250 mL
4 cups	reduced-sodium vegetable or chicken stock, divided	1 L
1 tbsp	butter or olive oil	15 mL
1 cup	short-grain white rice (such as Arborio)	250 mL
1/4 cup	dried onion pieces	50 mL
2 tsp	minced dried garlic	10 mL
1 tsp	crumbled dried tarragon or thyme	5 mL
1/2 tsp	crumbled dried rosemary	2 mL
1/4 tsp	salt (or to taste)	1 mL
1/4 cup	dry sherry or white wine	50 mL
1/4 cup	freshly grated Asiago or Parmesan cheese	50 mL
	Freshly ground black pepper	

1. In a heatproof bowl or measuring cup, combine mushrooms and boiling water; let stand for 15 minutes or until mushrooms start to soften.

2. Meanwhile, in a saucepan, bring stock to a boil over high heat. Reduce heat to low and keep hot.

3. In a deep saucepan, melt butter over medium heat. Add rice and sauté for 2 minutes or until rice is coated and looks glassy. Add half of the hot stock, onions, garlic, tarragon, rosemary, salt and sherry; bring to a boil, stirring often.

4. Stir in mushrooms, with soaking liquid. Reduce heat and simmer, stirring often and adding more stock about 1/2 cup (125 mL) at a time as the previous addition is absorbed, for about 30 minutes or until rice is just tender to the bite and is a creamy consistency. Stir in cheese and season to taste with salt and pepper.

Sweet Pepper Rice Pilaf

The confetti of peppers in this simple rice dish will make it a highlight on the plate. It's a fabulous accompaniment for grilled or pan-seared fish or poultry.

Serves 4

Tip

The color and flavor of this rice match particularly well with fish that is blackened or heavily spiced. Soothe the heat by garnishing the fish with your favorite fruit chutney.

Variation

Substitute long-grain brown rice for the white, increase the stock to 4 cups (1 L) and increase the cooking time to about 40 minutes.

1 tbsp	olive oil	15 mL
1 cup	long-grain white rice, rinsed and drained	250 mL
$\frac{1}{4}$ cup	dried yellow bell pepper pieces	50 mL
$\frac{1}{4}$ cup	dried red bell pepper pieces	50 mL
$\frac{1}{4}$ cup	dried onion pieces	50 mL
1 tsp	minced dried garlic	5 mL
$\frac{1}{4}$ tsp	salt (or to taste)	1 mL
$\frac{1}{4}$ tsp	paprika	1 mL
$\frac{1}{4}$ tsp	freshly ground black pepper	1 mL
$2\frac{3}{4}$ cups	reduced-sodium chicken stock	675 mL

1. In a saucepan, heat oil over medium heat. Add rice and sauté for about 2 minutes or until rice is coated and looks glassy. Add yellow and red peppers, onions, garlic, salt, paprika, pepper and chicken stock; increase heat to high and bring to a boil. Reduce heat to low, cover with a tight-fitting lid and cook for about 20 minutes or until rice and vegetables are tender and liquid is absorbed.

2. Remove from heat and let stand, covered, for 5 minutes. Fluff with a fork and season to taste with salt.

Mushroom Herb Rice Pilaf

Add savory herbs and mushrooms to nutritious brown rice, and you have a wonderful side dish for chicken or pork.

Serves 4 to 6

Tip

Use a brown and wild rice blend or your favorite mixed rice blend for this recipe.

1 tbsp	olive oil	15 mL
1 cup	long-grain brown rice, rinsed and drained	250 mL
1/4 cup	dried onion pieces	50 mL
1/4 cup	dried red bell pepper pieces	50 mL
1/4 cup	dried shiitake mushroom slices	50 mL
1/4 cup	dried button mushroom slices	50 mL
1 tbsp	crumbled dried parsley	15 mL
1 tsp	crumbled dried oregano	5 mL
1/2 tsp	crumbled dried thyme	2 mL
1/4 tsp	salt (or to taste)	1 mL
3 1/4 cups	reduced-sodium chicken stock	800 mL
1/4 tsp	freshly ground black pepper	1 mL

1. In a saucepan, heat oil over medium heat. Add rice and sauté for about 2 minutes or until rice is coated and looks glassy. Add onions, red peppers, shiitake and button mushrooms, parsley, oregano, thyme, salt, pepper and chicken stock; increase heat to high and bring to a boil. Reduce heat to low, cover with a tight-fitting lid and cook for about 40 minutes or until rice and vegetables are tender and liquid is absorbed.

2. Remove from heat and let stand, covered, for 5 minutes. Fluff with a fork and season to taste with salt.

Wild Rice and Cranberry Pilaf

This colorful side dish is perfect for festive occasions like Thanksgiving or Christmas. Wild rice is a traditional Native American harvest, gathered from the canoe.

Serves 6

Tip

Wild rice will generally quadruple in volume, and may take longer to cook depending upon its source. Depending on the size and density of the grain, some of the liquid may not be absorbed during cooking. Just drain off any excess liquid, reserving it to add to a soup or stew, if desired.

1 cup	wild rice	250 mL
1/4 cup	dried leek slices	50 mL
1/4 cup	dried onion pieces	50 mL
1/4 cup	dried carrot pieces	50 mL
1/4 tsp	freshly ground black pepper	1 mL
2 cups	sodium-reduced vegetable or chicken stock	500 mL
2 cups	water	500 mL
1/4 cup	dried cranberries	50 mL
1 tbsp	crumbled dried parsley	15 mL
	Salt	

1. In a saucepan, combine wild rice, leeks, onions, carrots, pepper, vegetable stock and water; bring to a boil over high heat. Reduce heat to medium-low, cover, leaving lid slightly ajar, and boil gently for 30 minutes. Stir in cranberries and parsley; cover, leaving lid slightly ajar and boil gently for about 30 minutes or until rice is tender.

2. Remove from heat and let stand, covered, for 5 minutes. Season to taste with salt.

Wild Rice Cakes

If you have dried cooked wild rice in your pantry, these interesting pancakes can be whipped up in no time. They make a fantastic side dish for baked salmon, pan-seared chicken or pork chops.

Serves 4

Variations

Substitute dried cooked long-grain brown rice or barley for the wild rice.

Add 1 tsp (5 mL) Indian yellow curry paste with the rice and omit the thyme.

$\frac{1}{2}$ cup	dried cooked wild rice	125 mL
2 tbsp	dried grated zucchini	25 mL
1 tbsp	dried grated carrots	15 mL
1 tbsp	dried red bell pepper pieces, minced	15 mL
$\frac{1}{2}$ tsp	crumbled dried thyme or basil	2 mL
1 cup	boiling water	250 mL
$1\frac{1}{4}$ cups	all-purpose flour	300 mL
$\frac{1}{2}$ tsp	salt	2 mL
$\frac{1}{2}$ tsp	baking soda	2 mL
$\frac{1}{3}$ cup	plain yogurt (approx.)	75 mL
	Vegetable oil	

1. In a heatproof 2-cup (500 mL) liquid measuring cup, combine rice, zucchini, carrots, red peppers, thyme and boiling water. Let stand for about 30 minutes or until rice and vegetables are very soft and cooled to room temperature.

2. Meanwhile, in a bowl, combine flour, salt and baking soda.

3. Add enough yogurt to the rice mixture to make 2 cups (500 mL) total and stir until well blended. Pour over dry ingredients and stir just until moistened.

4. Preheat oven to 300°F (150°C).

5. Heat a large nonstick skillet over medium heat until small drops of water splashed on the surface evaporate almost immediately. Brush lightly with oil. Add about $\frac{1}{4}$ cup (50 mL) of batter per pancake and, using the bottom of a metal ladle or measuring cup, gently spread to about $3\frac{1}{2}$ inches (8.5 cm) in diameter. Cook for 2 to 3 minutes or until bubbles just start to break in batter and bottom is golden brown. Flip and cook the other side for about 1 minute or until golden brown. Keep warm on rack in preheated oven. Repeat with remaining batter, oiling pan and adjusting heat as necessary between batches.

Rösti Potato Cakes

Golden, crispy potato cakes are a nice side dish for breaded veal or pork cutlets or grilled fish. A little dollop of sour cream or applesauce is always a welcome addition.

Serves 4

Variation

Make 8 to 12 small cakes and use for appetizers, topped with cream cheese and smoked salmon.

1/2 cup	dried grated potatoes	125 mL
1 cup	boiling water	250 mL
1	egg	1
2 tbsp	all-purpose flour	25 mL
2 tsp	snipped dried chives	10 mL
1/2 tsp	salt	2 mL
1/4 tsp	freshly ground black pepper	1 mL
	Vegetable oil	

1. In a heatproof bowl, combine potatoes and boiling water. Cover and let stand for about 30 minutes or until potatoes are very soft and cooled to room temperature. Drain well, squeezing out excess liquid.

2. Meanwhile, preheat oven to 350°F (180°C).

3. In another bowl, whisk together egg, flour, chives, salt and pepper. Add potatoes and toss with a fork until evenly coated.

4. In a large skillet, heat a thin layer of oil over medium heat until hot but not smoking. Spoon one-quarter of the potato mixture into pan and spread to about 1/2-inch (1 cm) thickness. Cook for 3 to 4 minutes per side, turning once, or until golden brown. Using a spatula, transfer to a plate lined with paper towels, turning once to blot. Keep warm on another plate in preheated oven. Repeat with remaining potato mixture, adding and reheating oil as necessary between batches.

Classic Scalloped Potatoes

You can never go wrong with scalloped potatoes to accompany ham, roast chicken, pork chops, roast beef . . . pretty much anything! With dried potatoes and onions on hand, they're a cinch to make.

Serves 4

Variation
Replace ½ cup (125 mL) of the potatoes with dried sweet potato slices.

- Preheat oven to 400°F (200°C)
- 8-cup (2 L) shallow glass baking dish, greased

2 cups	dried potato slices	500 mL
¼ cup	dried onion slices	50 mL
1 cup	water	250 mL
1 cup	table (18%) or whipping (35%) cream	250 mL
½ tsp	Dijon or dry mustard	2 mL
2 tbsp	all-purpose flour	25 mL
½ tsp	salt	2 mL
¼ tsp	freshly ground black pepper	1 mL
2 tbsp	butter, cut into small pieces	25 mL
¼ cup	freshly grated Parmesan cheese (optional)	50 mL

1. In prepared baking dish, combine potatoes and onions.

2. In a measuring cup or bowl, combine water, cream and mustard. Whisk in flour, salt and pepper. Pour over potato mixture. Cover and bake in preheated oven for 30 minutes or until sauce is bubbling and starting to thicken.

3. Uncover, sprinkle butter over potatoes and bake for about 20 minutes or until potatoes are fork-tender, sauce is thickened and top is golden brown. Sprinkle with Parmesan (if using) and broil for 1 to 2 minutes, if desired. Let stand for 5 minutes before serving.

Potato and Herb Gratin

With dried potato slices, this dish is ready to pop into the oven in minutes, but the fragrant aroma of herbs wafting through the kitchen will make everyone think you toiled for hours.

Serves 4

Variation
Use ¼ cup (50 mL) crumbled blue cheese instead of the Swiss for a bolder flavor.

- Preheat oven to 400°F (200°C)
- 4-cup (1 L) shallow glass baking dish

2 cups	dried potato slices	500 mL
¼ tsp	crumbled dried rosemary	1 mL
¼ tsp	crumbled dried thyme	1 mL
Pinch	freshly ground black pepper	Pinch
2 cups	reduced-sodium vegetable or chicken stock	500 mL
½ cup	coarse dried bread crumbs	125 mL
½ cup	shredded Swiss cheese	125 mL

1. In baking dish, combine potatoes, rosemary, thyme, pepper and vegetable stock. Cover and bake in preheated oven for about 25 minutes or until potatoes are fork-tender. Uncover and bake for 30 minutes or until potatoes are soft and most of the liquid is absorbed.

2. In a bowl, combine bread crumbs and cheese; sprinkle over potatoes. Bake for 15 minutes or until topping is golden and cheese is bubbly. Let stand for 5 minutes before serving.

Cheddar Herb Mashed Potatoes

When you have dried potato cubes in your pantry, mashed potatoes are easy to whip up any time. The cheese and herbs give them a special flavor.

Serves 4

Variation
For a smoky kick, add 1 tbsp (15 mL) chipotle barbecue sauce with the cheese.

1 cup	dried potato cubes	250 mL
½ tsp	crumbled dried basil	2 mL
¼ tsp	crumbled dried rosemary	1 mL
1 cup	water	250 mL
¼ cup	milk (approx.)	50 mL
½ cup	shredded sharp (old) Cheddar cheese	125 mL
	Salt and freshly ground black pepper	

1. In a saucepan, combine potatoes, basil, rosemary and water; bring to a boil over medium heat. Reduce heat, cover, leaving lid slightly ajar, and boil gently for about 10 minutes or until potatoes are soft. Remove from heat.

2. Using a potato masher, mash potatoes until smooth, gradually adding enough milk to make a soft consistency. Mash in cheese until blended. Season to taste with salt and pepper.

Sweet Potatoes with Browned Butter and Sage

The nutty flavor of browned butter enhances sweet potatoes beautifully, especially when it's accented by sage. These are a nice change from traditional mashed sweet potatoes.

Serves 4

Tips

Soaking the sweet potatoes at room temperature helps to rehydrate them without letting them get mushy. It does take a little longer, but the superior texture is worth it.

Warm a serving dish with hot water, drain well and dry before adding the finished sweet potatoes to keep them nice and hot at the table.

2 cups	dried sweet potato slices	500 mL
2 cups	water	500 mL
¼ cup	butter	50 mL
1	clove garlic, minced	1
1 tsp	crumbled dried sage	5 mL
2 tbsp	chopped almonds or pecans	25 mL
2 tbsp	freshly squeezed lemon juice	25 mL
	Salt and freshly ground black pepper	

1. In a shallow dish, combine sweet potatoes and water. Let stand for 30 minutes or until potatoes are plump and soft. Drain well.

2. In a large skillet, melt butter over medium-low heat. Add garlic and sage; sauté for about 2 minutes or until garlic is fragrant and just starts to turn golden brown. Stir in almonds and lemon juice; sauté for about 2 minutes or until butter is browned.

3. Gently stir in sweet potatoes and cook, shaking pan occasionally, for 5 to 10 minutes or until potatoes are hot and starting to brown. Season to taste with salt and pepper.

Dried Tomato and Basil Polenta

Polenta is Italian comfort food, and with the addition of flavorful dried tomatoes and seasonings, it becomes a side dish fit for any dinner party.

Serves 4 to 6

Tip

The key to smooth, creamy polenta without lumps is to have the liquid at a full boil and pour in the cornmeal in a thin, steady stream, stirring all the while. Keep stirring while it cooks to prevent sticking.

Variation

To make grilled polenta squares, pour very thick hot polenta into a buttered 8-cup (2 L) shallow baking dish, smoothing top. Let cool, cover and refrigerate until firm. Cut into squares, brush both sides with vegetable oil and grill over medium-high heat or broil until hot and browned.

1/3 cup	chopped dried tomatoes	75 mL
2 tbsp	dried onion pieces	25 mL
1 tsp	crumbled dried basil	5 mL
1/2 tsp	minced dried garlic	2 mL
2 1/2 cups	water	625 mL
2 cups	vegetable or chicken stock	500 mL
1 cup	cornmeal	250 mL
1/2 cup	whipping (35%) cream (optional)	125 mL
	Salt and freshly ground black pepper	
	Freshly grated Parmesan cheese	

1. In a saucepan, combine tomatoes, onions, basil, garlic, water and vegetable stock; bring to a full rolling boil over medium heat. Gradually pour in cornmeal, stirring constantly.

2. Reduce heat and simmer, stirring almost constantly, for about 20 minutes or until thickened and cornmeal and vegetables are soft. Stir in cream (if using) and season to taste with salt and pepper. Serve sprinkled with cheese.

Egg Noodles with Peas and Carrots

Buttery noodles and tender vegetables prove that even the simplest of side dishes can perk up an everyday meal. This one is perfect with roast or grilled beef, pork or sausages.

Serves 4

Variation

Add 1 tbsp (15 mL) dried red bell pepper pieces with the vegetables, replace the dill with basil or oregano and sprinkle each serving with freshly grated Parmesan cheese.

¼ cup	dried green peas	50 mL
¼ cup	dried carrot pieces	50 mL
1 cup	water	250 mL
6 oz	broad egg noodles (about 3 cups/ 750 mL)	175 g
2 tbsp	butter	25 mL
1 tbsp	crumbled dried parsley	15 mL
½ tsp	crumbled dried dill	2 mL
	Salt and freshly ground black pepper	

1. In a measuring cup or bowl, combine peas, carrots and water; let stand for 20 minutes or until vegetables start to soften. Drain, reserving soaking water.

2. In a large pot of boiling salted water, cook vegetables and noodles, stirring occasionally, for about 5 minutes or until noodles are just tender. Drain well.

3. In the same pot, melt butter over medium heat. Add noodle mixture, parsley and dill, tossing gently just until noodles are well coated in butter, adding enough of the soaking water to moisten as desired. Season to taste with salt and pepper.

Linguini with Red Peppers, Garlic and Rosemary

Pasta as a side dish adds visual interest and flavor to the plate, and this one is just as easy to prepare as a rice or potato dish. It pairs nicely with fish, poultry or veal.

Serves 4 to 6

Tip

Turn this into a main course by adding sliced grilled chicken or shrimp on top of each serving.

8 oz	linguini	250 g
1/2 cup	dried red bell pepper slices	125 mL
1 tsp	minced dried garlic	5 mL
1/4 tsp	crumbled dried rosemary	1 mL
1/2 cup	water	125 mL
1/2 cup	whipping (35%) cream	125 mL
1/4 cup	crumbled soft goat cheese or mascarpone cheese	50 mL
1 tbsp	red wine vinegar	15 mL
	Salt and freshly ground black pepper	

1. In a large pot of boiling salted water, cook linguine for about 10 minutes, or according to package directions, until al dente (tender to the bite).

2. Meanwhile, in a saucepan, combine red peppers, garlic, rosemary and water; bring to a boil over high heat. Reduce heat and simmer, stirring occasionally, for about 5 minutes or until peppers are softened and liquid is slightly reduced

3. Drain pasta and return to the pot over low heat. Add red pepper mixture, cream and cheese; toss gently to coat. Stir in vinegar and season to taste with salt and pepper.

Orzo Pasta with Basil, Pine Nuts and Raisins

Orzo may look like rice, but it has quite a different texture. Seasoned with these classic Mediterranean flavors, it's sure to become a regular feature at your dinner table.

Serves 4

Tips

Pine nuts are best stored in the freezer or refrigerator, as they can go rancid quickly. Buy small amounts from a store with high turnover. Chopped or slivered almonds are a good substitute.

To toast pine nuts: In a small dry skillet, over medium heat, toast pine nuts, stirring constantly, for about 3 minutes or until golden and fragrant.

¼ cup	dried carrot pieces	50 mL
¼ cup	dried leek slices	50 mL
1 tsp	crumbled dried basil	5 mL
½ tsp	minced dried garlic	2 mL
1 cup	reduced-sodium vegetable or chicken stock	250 mL
6 oz	orzo	175 g
1 tbsp	extra-virgin olive oil	15 mL
¼ cup	raisins	50 mL
	Salt and freshly ground black pepper	
2 tbsp	toasted pine nuts (see tips, at left)	25 mL

1. In a small saucepan, combine carrots, leeks, basil, garlic and vegetable stock. Let stand for 15 minutes or until vegetables start to soften.

2. Bring vegetable mixture to a boil over medium heat. Reduce heat to low, cover and simmer for about 10 minutes or until vegetables are tender and liquid is slightly reduced.

3. Meanwhile, in a pot of boiling salted water, cook orzo, stirring often, for about 8 minutes, or according to package directions, until al dente (tender to the bite).

4. Drain orzo and return to the pot. Add vegetable mixture, oil and raisins; toss gently to coat. Season to taste with salt and pepper. Serve sprinkled with pine nuts.

Salad Dressings, Sauces and Fillings

Sweet Red Pepper and Basil Vinaigrette

The vibrant flavor and color of this vinaigrette is delicious on any type of salad: simple greens, pasta salad or marinated vegetables.

**Makes about
¾ cup (175 mL)**

2 tbsp	dried red bell pepper pieces	25 mL
½ tsp	crumbled dried basil	2 mL
¼ tsp	salt	1 mL
Pinch	freshly ground black pepper	Pinch
¼ cup	white wine vinegar, red wine vinegar or balsamic vinegar	50 mL
½ cup	olive oil	125 mL
1 tsp	liquid honey or pure maple syrup (approx.)	5 mL

1. In a tall cup (to use an immersion blender) or in a blender, combine red peppers, basil, salt, pepper and vinegar. Let stand for about 1 hour or until peppers are soft.

2. Add oil and honey and purée until smooth. Season to taste with more honey and pepper. Use immediately or store in an airtight container in the refrigerator for up to 2 weeks.

Roasted Onion Vinaigrette

The rich flavor of dried roasted onion adds a flavor dimension to this dressing that you just can't get with fresh onions.

**Makes about
¾ cup (175 mL)**

1 tbsp	dried roasted onion pieces	15 mL
½ tsp	granulated sugar (approx.)	2 mL
¼ tsp	salt	1 mL
Pinch	freshly ground black pepper	Pinch
¼ cup	balsamic vinegar, white wine vinegar or red wine vinegar	50 mL
½ cup	olive oil	125 mL
½ tsp	Dijon or dry mustard	2 mL

1. In a tall cup (to use an immersion blender) or in a blender, combine onions, sugar, salt, pepper and vinegar. Let stand for about 1 hour or until onions are soft.

2. Add oil and mustard and purée until smooth. Season to taste with more sugar and pepper. Use immediately or store in an airtight container in the refrigerator for up to 2 weeks.

Sweet and Tangy Ginger Vinaigrette

A pleasant ginger flavor in a sweet and tangy vinaigrette makes a refreshing salad dressing. Use it on thinly sliced carrots and cucumbers, mixed greens or an Asian noodle salad.

Makes about 1 cup (250 mL)

Variation

Ginger Wasabi Vinaigrette: Add ¹/₂ tsp (2 mL) wasabi powder or paste with the ginger.

3	slices dried gingerroot	3
2 tbsp	granulated sugar (approx.)	25 mL
¹/₄ tsp	salt	1 mL
¹/₃ cup	rice vinegar	75 mL
¹/₂ cup	vegetable oil	125 mL

1. In a tall cup (to use an immersion blender) or in a blender, combine ginger, sugar, salt and vinegar. Let stand for about 1 hour or until ginger is soft.

2. Add oil and purée until smooth. Season to taste with more sugar. Use immediately or store in an airtight container in the refrigerator for up to 2 weeks.

Curry Mango Vinaigrette

Use this subtly spiced, fruity dressing on greens, as a dip for satays or as an interesting twist to shrimp cocktail.

Makes about ³⁄₄ cup (175 mL)

Variation

Use ¹⁄₂ tsp (2 mL) crumbled dried mint or 1 tsp (5 mL) chopped fresh mint in place of the cilantro.

¼ cup	chopped dried mangos	50 mL
½ tsp	Indian yellow curry paste or powder	2 mL
¼ tsp	salt	1 mL
⅓ cup	rice, white wine or cider vinegar	75 mL
¼ cup	water (approx.)	50 mL
1 tsp	crumbled dried cilantro (or 1 tbsp/ 15 mL fresh)	5 mL
⅓ cup	vegetable oil	75 mL

1. In a saucepan, combine mangos, curry paste, salt, vinegar and water. Let stand for 15 minutes or until mangos start to soften.

2. Bring to a simmer over medium heat. Reduce heat and simmer for about 5 minutes or until mangos are very soft. Let cool completely.

3. In a tall cup (to use an immersion blender) or in a blender, combine mango mixture, cilantro and oil. Purée until smooth, adding more water to thin, if desired. Use immediately or store in an airtight container in the refrigerator for up to 1 week.

Roasted Garlic Dressing

Add a new dimension to your Caesar salad, potato salad or pasta salad with this robust dressing.

Makes about ²⁄₃ cup (150 mL)

Tip

Break dried roasted garlic into chunks and finely chop in a spice grinder or using a mortar and pestle before measuring.

1 tbsp	finely chopped dried roasted garlic	15 mL
½ tsp	granulated sugar (approx.)	2 mL
¼ tsp	salt	1 mL
Pinch	freshly ground black pepper	Pinch
3 tbsp	cider vinegar or white wine vinegar	45 mL
¼ cup	olive oil	50 mL
½ tsp	Dijon or dry mustard	2 mL
¼ cup	mayonnaise	50 mL

1. In a tall cup (to use an immersion blender) or in a blender, combine garlic, sugar, salt, pepper and vinegar. Let stand for about 1 hour or until garlic is soft.

2. Add oil and mustard and purée until smooth. Add mayonnaise and pulse just until blended. Season to taste with more sugar and pepper. Use immediately or store in an airtight container in the refrigerator for up to 2 weeks.

Apple, Cranberry and Sage Relish

Not just cranberry sauce, not just applesauce — this tangy relish will be a hit at your next holiday meal, or even spread on a sandwich.

Makes about ¾ cup (175 mL)

Tip

Soaking the fruit mixture in room-temperature water or in the fridge gives this relish a fresher flavor than if the mixture were soaked in boiling water. But if you're in a hurry, you can use boiling water and let stand for 20 to 30 minutes.

½ cup	dried apple slices	125 mL
¼ cup	dried cranberries	50 mL
1 tbsp	dried onion pieces	15 mL
½ tsp	crumbled dried sage	2 mL
1 cup	water	250 mL
2 tsp	granulated sugar	10 mL
¼ tsp	salt	1 mL
Pinch	freshly ground black pepper	Pinch
¼ cup	unsweetened apple cider or juice	50 mL

1. In a tall cup (to use an immersion blender) or in a blender, combine apples, cranberries, onions, sage and water. Let stand for about 1 hour, until fruit is very soft, or cover and refrigerate overnight.

2. Pulse fruit mixture until finely chopped but not puréed. Transfer to a small saucepan and add sugar, salt, pepper and cider; bring to a boil over medium heat. Reduce heat and simmer, stirring often, for about 5 minutes or until slightly thickened. Serve warm or let cool, transfer to an airtight container and refrigerate for up to 3 days.

Pear, Raisin and Walnut Chutney

This chutney is quick to prepare when you use dried fruits and is full of flavor and texture. It is just the thing to perk up chicken, pork or fish and is wonderful on top of cheese and crackers for a simple appetizer.

Makes about 1 cup (250 mL)

Tip

The flavor of chutney does improve on standing, so if you have time, make this 1 to 2 days before serving.

½ cup	chopped dried pear slices	125 mL
¼ cup	raisins	50 mL
2 tbsp	granulated sugar	25 mL
¼ tsp	salt	1 mL
Pinch	ground cinnamon	Pinch
Pinch	cayenne pepper	Pinch
1 cup	water	250 mL
¼ cup	cider vinegar	50 mL
¼ cup	chopped toasted walnuts	50 mL

1. In a saucepan, combine pears, raisins, sugar, salt, cinnamon, cayenne and water; bring to a boil over medium heat. Reduce heat to low, cover, leaving lid slightly ajar, and simmer, stirring occasionally, for about 15 minutes or until fruit is soft and liquid is slightly reduced.

2. Add vinegar and increase heat to medium-low. Simmer, stirring often, for 5 to 10 minutes or until liquid is almost all absorbed. Remove from heat and stir in walnuts. Use immediately or let cool, transfer to an airtight container and refrigerate for up to 5 days.

Onion Marmalade

Onion marmalade is one of Jay's trademark recipes and is a perennial favorite in the gourmet takeout meals he makes. Serve it on grilled salmon, poultry or pork or with warmed Brie cheese for an appetizer.

**Makes about
²/₃ cup (150 mL)**

Tip

Use dried red onions for a lovely color, if you have them.

1 cup	dried onion slices	250 mL
1 cup	water	250 mL
¼ tsp	salt	1 mL
	Freshly ground black pepper	
¼ cup	liquid honey or packed brown sugar	50 mL
¼ cup	cider vinegar or red wine vinegar	50 mL

1. In a saucepan, combine onions and water; bring to a boil over medium heat. Reduce heat to low, cover, leaving lid slightly ajar, and simmer, stirring occasionally, for about 10 minutes or until onions are soft.

2. Stir in salt, pepper to taste, honey and vinegar; increase heat just enough to bring to a gentle boil. Boil gently, stirring often, for about 10 minutes or until marmalade is slightly jammy (it will thicken more upon cooling). Use immediately or let cool, transfer to an airtight container and refrigerate for up to 5 days.

Anytime Salsa

With dried vegetables on hand, you can make this salsa any time. It's super with chips for dipping or to add a zesty flavor to recipes.

Makes about 1 cup (250 mL)

Tip

If you like a fiery salsa, increase the chile pepper slices to 1 to 1½ tsp (5 to 7 mL) in step 1 or season with hot pepper sauce to taste in step 2.

¼ cup	dried tomatoes	50 mL
2 tbsp	dried red bell pepper pieces	25 mL
2 tbsp	dried green bell pepper pieces	25 mL
1 tbsp	dried onion pieces	15 mL
½ tsp	dried hot chile pepper slices (or to taste)	2 mL
½ tsp	crumbled dried oregano	2 mL
1 cup	boiling water	250 mL
½ tsp	salt (or to taste)	2 mL
1 tbsp	freshly squeezed lime juice or red wine vinegar	15 mL

1. In a food processor or mini chopper, combine tomatoes, red and green bell peppers, onions, hot peppers and oregano. Pulse until finely chopped.

2. Transfer to a heatproof bowl and pour in boiling water. Cover and let stand for 30 minutes or until vegetables are soft and liquid is absorbed. Season with salt and stir in lime juice. Use immediately or transfer to an airtight container and refrigerate for up to 5 days.

Dried Herb Pesto

Use this pesto spread on fish before roasting or grilling, add to chopped fresh tomatoes for a quick bruschetta topping, or toss with hot cooked pasta.

**Makes about
¹⁄₂ cup (125 mL)**

Variation

For a bit of a kick, add ¹⁄₂ tsp (2 mL) minced dried hot chile peppers or ¹⁄₄ tsp (1 mL) hot pepper flakes with the herbs.

¹⁄₄ cup	crumbled dried parsley	50 mL
2 tbsp	crumbled dried basil	25 mL
2 tbsp	crumbled dried oregano	25 mL
2 tsp	crumbled dried rosemary	10 mL
1 tsp	crumbled dried thyme or savory	5 mL
¹⁄₄ cup	olive oil	50 mL
¹⁄₄ cup	freshly grated Parmesan cheese	50 mL
2 tbsp	toasted pine nuts or chopped walnuts	25 mL

1. In a small saucepan, combine parsley, basil, oregano, rosemary, thyme and oil; heat over low heat just until bubbles start to form around the edge of the pan. Remove from heat, cover and let stand for at least 2 hours, until herbs are very soft and fragrant, or for up to 1 day.

2. In a blender, mini chopper or small food processor, purée herb mixture and cheese until smooth. Add pine nuts and purée until nuts are very finely chopped and pesto is thickened. Use immediately or transfer to an airtight container and refrigerate for up to 2 weeks. Let warm to room temperature before using.

Dried Tomato Pesto

There's no need to spend a lot of money on commercially prepared tomato pesto when you've got your own dried tomatoes and this easy recipe.

Makes about ½ cup (125 mL)

Variation

Add 2 tbsp (25 mL) freshly grated Parmesan cheese in step 2.

2	slices dried garlic	2
½ cup	chopped dried tomatoes	125 mL
1 tbsp	crumbled dried basil	15 mL
¼ tsp	salt	1 mL
Pinch	freshly ground black pepper	Pinch
¼ cup	olive oil	50 mL
1 tbsp	red wine vinegar	15 mL

1. In a small saucepan, combine garlic, tomatoes, basil, salt, pepper and oil; heat over low heat just until bubbles start to form around the edge of the pan. Remove from heat, cover and let stand for at least 4 hours, until tomatoes are very soft and oil is well flavored, or for up to 1 day.

2. In a blender, mini chopper or small food processor, purée tomato mixture and vinegar until fairly smooth. Use immediately or transfer to an airtight container and refrigerate for up to 2 weeks. Let warm to room temperature before using.

Apple, Onion and Leek Sauce

A cream sauce splashed with apple and two types of onions is simple to put together but adds "wow" to the plate. Serve it with pork roast or chops, poultry or a smoked ham.

Makes about 1½ cups (375 mL)

Tips

Use scissors to easily cut dried apples into small pieces.

Cut the onions into smaller pieces if you have large rings.

½ cup	dried apple slices, chopped	125 mL
¼ cup	dried leek slices	50 mL
¼ cup	dried onion slices	50 mL
1 cup	vegetable or chicken stock	250 mL
1 cup	whipping (35%) cream	250 mL
1 tsp	Dijon mustard	5 mL
	Salt and freshly ground black pepper	

1. In a saucepan, combine apples, leeks, onions and vegetable stock; bring to a boil over medium heat. Reduce heat and boil gently, stirring occasionally, for about 15 minutes or until onions are softened.

2. Stir in cream and mustard and return to a boil. Boil gently, stirring often, for 5 to 10 minutes or until slightly thickened. Season to taste with salt and pepper.

Mushroom and White Wine Sauce

This sauce is so versatile you'll find yourself making it over and over again. It's a dazzling addition to simple roast chicken, pork or veal, and you can even use it as a pasta sauce.

Makes about 2 cups (500 mL)

Tip
Mashing the flour with softened butter is an easy way to thicken a hot sauce without getting lumps. The butter also adds a nice flavor.

1/2 cup	dried mushroom slices	125 mL
2 tbsp	dried onion pieces	25 mL
1 tbsp	crumbled dried parsley	15 mL
1 tsp	minced dried garlic	5 mL
1 tsp	crumbled dried tarragon, basil or thyme	5 mL
1 1/2 cups	vegetable or chicken stock	375 mL
1/3 cup	dry white wine	75 mL
1 tbsp	all-purpose flour	15 mL
1 tbsp	butter, softened	15 mL
	Salt and freshly ground black pepper	

1. In a saucepan, combine mushrooms, onions, parsley, garlic, tarragon, vegetable stock and wine; bring to a boil over medium heat. Reduce heat and boil gently, stirring often, for about 20 minutes or until mushrooms are soft.

2. In a small bowl, mash flour with butter until blended. Whisk into saucepan until blended. Boil gently, stirring constantly, for about 5 minutes or until sauce is thickened. Season to taste with salt and pepper.

Mushroom, Beer and Onion Sauce

This sauce is just asking for a juicy grilled steak or roast beef. It's also nice on sausages and pork chops.

Makes about 2 cups (500 mL)

Variation
Omit the flour and stir 2 tbsp (25 mL) crumbled blue cheese into the sauce after you remove it from the heat, stirring until melted.

1/2 cup	dried mushroom slices	125 mL
1/2 cup	dried onion pieces	125 mL
1 tsp	minced dried garlic	5 mL
	Salt and freshly ground black pepper	
1	bottle (12 oz/341 mL) dark or red beer	1
2 tbsp	all-purpose flour	25 mL
2 tbsp	water	25 mL
1 tbsp	grainy Dijon mustard	15 mL
1/4 tsp	hot pepper sauce (or to taste)	1 mL

1. In a saucepan, combine mushrooms, onions, garlic, salt, pepper and beer; bring to a boil over medium heat. Reduce heat and boil gently, stirring often, for about 20 minutes or until mushrooms are soft.

2. In a small bowl, whisk flour with water and mustard until blended. Whisk into saucepan until blended. Boil gently, stirring constantly, for about 5 minutes or until sauce is thickened. Season with hot pepper sauce.

Dried Tomato and Herb Sauce

Whip up a thick, rich sauce for pasta or pizza any time with dried tomatoes and herbs. You can simmer it to the consistency you like best.

Makes about 3 cups (750 mL) (or about 2 cups/500 mL thick sauce)

Tips

If you prefer a chunky sauce, mince the garlic and finely chop the dried tomatoes before adding them to the saucepan, and omit the puréeing.

The sugar helps to smooth out the flavor and enhances the tomatoes and herbs. Just a little really makes a big difference.

Variation

For an even richer flavor, use dried roasted onion pieces and 2 tsp (10 mL) crumbled dried roasted garlic.

3	slices dried garlic	3
1 cup	dried tomatoes	250 mL
2 tbsp	dried onion pieces	25 mL
1 tbsp	crumbled dried parsley	15 mL
1 tsp	crumbled dried basil	5 mL
1 tsp	crumbled dried oregano	5 mL
½ tsp	salt	2 mL
¼ tsp	freshly ground black pepper	1 mL
4 cups	water	1 L
	Granulated sugar (optional)	

1. In a saucepan, combine garlic, tomatoes, onions, parsley, basil, oregano, salt, pepper and water; bring to a boil over medium heat. Reduce heat to low, cover, leaving lid slightly ajar, and simmer, stirring occasionally, for about 20 minutes or until tomatoes are very soft and starting to break down.

2. Using an immersion blender in the pan, or transferring to a blender, purée sauce until fairly smooth. Return to pan, if necessary.

3. For a thicker sauce, return to a simmer over medium heat. Reduce heat and simmer, uncovered, stirring often, for about 15 minutes or until desired consistency. Season to taste with salt, pepper and sugar (if using).

Tomato, Cottage Cheese and Herb Stuffing

Use this light, creamy stuffing to stuff chicken breasts, pork chops, roasted zucchini, cannelloni or giant pasta shells.

Makes about 1 cup (250 mL)

Tips

Draining the cottage cheese prevents the stuffing from oozing all over the place when it's stuffed into meats.

This amount of stuffing can be used to stuff 6 chicken breasts, pork chops or zucchini halves. For cannelloni or giant pasta shells, you may want to double the recipe.

¾ cup	cottage cheese	175 mL
2 tbsp	finely chopped dried tomatoes	25 mL
1 tbsp	crumbled dried parsley	15 mL
2 tsp	crumbled dried oregano	10 mL
¼ tsp	crumbled dried rosemary	1 mL
2 tbsp	boiling water	25 mL
1	egg	1
Pinch	freshly ground black pepper	Pinch

1. In a fine-mesh sieve set over a bowl, drain cottage cheese for at least 30 minutes or until excess liquid drains off (or cover and refrigerate overnight). If desired, for a smoother texture, purée in a mini chopper or with an immersion blender.

2. Meanwhile, in a small heatproof bowl, combine tomatoes, parsley, oregano, rosemary and boiling water. Cover and let stand for about 30 minutes or until tomatoes are soft and water is absorbed.

3. Whisk in cottage cheese, egg and pepper until blended. Use immediately or cover and refrigerate for up to 1 day. For best results, let stand at room temperature for about 15 minutes to take off the chill before stuffing meats.

Dried Tomato, Basil and Garlic Goat Cheese Stuffing

The tang of goat cheese marries beautifully with the Mediterranean flavors in this stuffing. Use it for veal or chicken roulades, eggplant pinwheels or cannelloni.

Makes about 1 cup (250 mL)

Variation
Replace the goat cheese with softened cream cheese or mashed softened feta cheese.

¼ cup	finely chopped dried tomatoes	50 mL
1 tsp	crumbled dried basil	5 mL
¼ cup	boiling water	50 mL
½ cup	crumbled soft goat cheese	125 mL
¼ cup	fine dried bread crumbs or cracker crumbs	50 mL
⅛ tsp	freshly ground black pepper or cayenne pepper	0.5 mL

1. In a small heatproof bowl, combine tomatoes, basil and boiling water. Cover and let stand for about 30 minutes or until tomatoes are soft and water is absorbed. (If all of the water isn't absorbed in this time, carefully drain it off, trying not to lose the herbs.)

2. Mash in goat cheese, bread crumbs and pepper until blended. Use immediately or cover and refrigerate for up to 1 day. For best results, let stand at room temperature for about 15 minutes to take off the chill before stuffing meats.

Mushroom, Cream Cheese and Herb Stuffing

Spread this stuffing on butterflied pork tenderloin, in a pocket of thick chicken breasts or between stacked roasted eggplant or zucchini slices and warm gently.

Makes about 1 cup (250 mL)

Tips

This is the perfect time to use exotic dried mushrooms, such as cremini, shiitake or morels, for a deep, woodsy flavor.

Be sure not to use light or non-fat cream cheese. The thickeners can react differently when cheese is heated, causing the cheese to break down.

2	slices dried garlic	2
1/4 cup	dried mushroom slices	50 mL
1/2 cup	boiling water	125 mL
3/4 cup	cream cheese, softened	175 mL
1 tsp	crumbled dried oregano, tarragon or basil	5 mL
1/4 tsp	crumbled dried rosemary	1 mL
1/4 tsp	salt	1 mL
1/4 tsp	freshly ground black pepper	1 mL

1. In a small heatproof bowl, combine garlic, mushrooms and boiling water. Cover and let stand for about 30 minutes or until mushrooms are very soft. Drain, squeezing out excess moisture. Finely chop garlic and mushrooms. Return to bowl.

2. Mash in cream cheese, oregano, rosemary, salt and pepper until blended. Use immediately or cover and refrigerate for up to 1 day. For best results, let stand at room temperature for about 15 minutes to take off the chill before stuffing meats.

Spinach, Leek and Wild Rice Stuffing

The combination of brown and wild rice, leeks and fresh spinach makes an elegant stuffing for pork, turkey or chicken, or shines as a simple side dish.

Makes about 2 cups (500 mL)

Tip

This is enough stuffing for one spiral-stuffed butterflied pork loin roast or boneless turkey breast or 2 to 3 pork tenderloins. You can also use it to stuff a 2- to 3-lb (1 to 1.5 kg) roasting chicken.

Variation

Add 4 slices prosciutto or smoked bacon, chopped and sautéed until crisp, with the wine.

• *Large shallow baking dish*

¼ cup	wild rice	50 mL
½ cup	long-grain brown rice	125 mL
2 cups	reduced-sodium vegetable or chicken stock	500 mL
½ cup	dried leek slices	125 mL
¼ cup	dried celery slices	50 mL
1 tsp	crumbled dried rosemary	5 mL
4 cups	fresh spinach, trimmed (about 4 oz/125 g)	1 L
2 tbsp	dry white wine (or 1 tbsp/15 mL white wine vinegar)	25 mL
	Salt and freshly ground black pepper	

1. In a sieve, rinse wild rice under running water. Drain and set aside. Rinse brown rice until water runs clear; drain and set aside separately.

2. In a saucepan with a tight-fitting lid, bring vegetable stock to a boil over high heat. Stir in wild rice, reduce heat and boil gently for 15 minutes. Stir in brown rice, leeks, celery and rosemary; reduce heat to low, cover and simmer for about 45 minutes or until rice is tender and most of the liquid is absorbed. Remove from heat. Add spinach, cover and let stand for about 5 minutes or until spinach is wilted.

3. Using a fork, fluff rice mixture, stirring in wine, and season to taste with salt and pepper. Spread out in baking dish and let cool.

Cranberry, Wild Rice and Herb Stuffing

Combining wild rice and bread makes for a less dense stuffing than using all rice. The cranberries and herbs add a lovely flavor and color.

Makes about 4 cups (1 L)

Tip

This is enough to stuff 1 large roasting chicken. Double or triple it if you want to stuff a turkey. Alternatively, bake it in a buttered casserole dish, covered, in a 325°F to 375°F (160°C to 190°C) oven for 20 to 30 minutes or until hot.

½ cup	wild rice	125 mL
½ cup	dried onion pieces	125 mL
½ cup	dried celery slices	125 mL
¼ tsp	freshly ground black pepper	1 mL
2½ cups	reduced-sodium vegetable or chicken stock (approx.), divided	625 mL
½ cup	dried cranberries	125 mL
2 tbsp	crumbled dried parsley	25 mL
1 tbsp	crumbled dried oregano or marjoram	15 mL
1 tsp	crumbled dried sage or rosemary	5 mL
3 cups	cubed day-old crusty bread	750 mL
	Salt	

1. In a saucepan, combine wild rice, onions, celery, pepper and 2 cups (500 mL) of the stock; bring to a boil over high heat. Reduce heat to medium-low, cover, leaving lid slightly ajar, and boil gently for 30 minutes.

2. Stir in cranberries and boil gently for about 30 minutes or until rice is tender. Stir in parsley, oregano and sage. Remove from heat and let stand, covered, for 5 minutes.

3. Transfer to a bowl and let cool completely. Add bread and toss gently to combine, adding enough of the remaining stock to moisten. Season to taste with salt.

Cornbread, Apple and Sausage Stuffing

This classic stuffing is made even better with homemade cornbread spiked with sage and garlic. Use it to stuff chicken, turkey or a crown roast of pork, or bake it as a side dish.

Makes about 12 cups (3 L)

Tip

This stuffing can be used for a 10- to 15-lb (5 to 7.5 kg) turkey or for two 4- to 5-lb (2 to 2.5 kg) chickens, with extra to bake on the side. Alternatively, the stuffing can be baked separately. Lightly pack into a buttered 12-cup (3 L) casserole dish, drizzle with an extra $\frac{1}{2}$ cup (125 mL) stock and bake in a 325°F to 375°F (160°C to 190°C) oven for 20 to 30 minutes or until hot and crispy.

$\frac{1}{2}$ cup	chopped dried apples	125 mL
1 cup	chicken or vegetable stock (approx.)	250 mL
8 oz	sausage (any flavor), removed from casings	250 g
2	stalks celery, chopped	2
1	onion, chopped	1
	Salt and freshly ground black pepper	
1	loaf Crisp Savory Cornbread (see recipe, page 200), cut into 1-inch (2.5 cm) cubes	1

1. In a measuring cup or bowl, combine apples and stock; set aside.

2. In a large skillet, over medium-high heat, cook sausage, breaking up with a spoon, for about 5 minutes or until no longer pink inside and starting to brown. Reduce heat to medium-low and add celery and onion; sauté for about 7 minutes or until softened. Add apple mixture and bring to a simmer, scraping up any bits stuck to pan.

3. Transfer to a large bowl, add cornbread and toss gently to coat. The cornbread should be moistened but not soggy. Add a little more stock to moisten, if necessary. Let cool completely before stuffing poultry.

Lemon, Leek and Thyme Bread Crumb Crust

A plain chicken breast, pork chop or roast gets a gourmet twist when you add a crumb crust. Press the crust on before roasting to add color, texture and fabulous flavor.

Makes about 1 cup (250 mL)

Tip

This recipe makes enough for 4 chicken breasts or pork chops. If you want to coat a larger roast, double the recipe.

3	strips (about 1 1/2 by 1/2 inch/3.5 by 1 cm) dried lemon zest	3
2 tbsp	dried leek slices	25 mL
1/2 tsp	crumbled dried thyme	2 mL
1/4 cup	boiling water	50 mL
1 cup	coarse dried bread crumbs	250 mL
1/8 tsp	salt	0.5 mL
Pinch	freshly ground black pepper	Pinch
1 tbsp	butter, melted	15 mL

1. In a tall cup (to use an immersion blender) or in a mini chopper or blender, combine lemon zest, leeks, thyme and boiling water. Let stand for about 30 minutes or until leeks are soft.

2. Pulse leek mixture until finely chopped but not puréed. Transfer to a bowl and add bread crumbs, salt, pepper and butter, tossing to evenly combine. Use immediately or cover and refrigerate for up to 1 day.

Snacks

Dried Tomato, Basil and Peppercorn Rollups

The intense flavor of dried tomatoes with a few simple ingredients added will make these little nibbles one of your must-have snacks.

Makes about 24 pieces

Tip

The tortillas can be filled, rolled, wrapped and refrigerated for up to 4 hours before serving. Cut just before serving.

1/4 cup	finely chopped dried tomatoes	50 mL
1 tsp	crumbled dried basil	5 mL
1/2 tsp	cracked black peppercorns	2 mL
1/4 cup	boiling water	50 mL
4 oz	cream cheese, softened	125 g
2 tbsp	freshly grated Parmesan or Asiago cheese	25 mL
4	6-inch (15 cm) flour tortillas	4

1. In a heatproof bowl, combine tomatoes, basil, peppercorns and boiling water. Let stand for about 30 minutes or until tomatoes are very soft. Mash in cream cheese and Parmesan until blended.

2. Place tortillas on a cutting board. Spread with cheese mixture, leaving a 1/2-inch (1 cm) border. Roll up jellyroll-style and cut into 1-inch (2.5 cm) pieces. Place cut side up on a platter to serve.

Savory Apple Rings

These make for a nice change to garnish a soup, as an addition to a cheese or pâté tray or simply as a snack, with a cold beer.

Makes about 36 rings

Tip

Use Granny Smith, Northern Spy, Cortland, Empire or other tart apples that hold their shape and flavor when cooked.

4	large tart cooking apples	4
2 tsp	crumbled dried thyme or sage	10 mL
1/2 tsp	salt	2 mL
1/2 tsp	freshly ground black pepper	2 mL
1/2 cup	cider vinegar or white wine vinegar	125 mL

1. Peel apples and remove cores. Cut crosswise into rings about 1/8 inch (2.5 cm) thick.

2. In a shallow dish, combine thyme, salt, pepper and vinegar. Dip apple rings in this mixture, one at a time, shaking off excess.

3. Place apple rings on mesh drying trays. Dry at 155°F (68°C) for about 4 hours or until firm and crisp. Remove from trays, transfer to a wire rack and let cool completely. Serve immediately or store in an airtight container at room temperature for up to 3 months.

Apple Rollups with Mustard, Thyme and Maple

You can create dazzling appetizers in minutes when you have this savory leather on hand.

Makes about 16 pieces

Tips

Depending on the size and shape of your dehydrator and leather sheets, you may get slightly larger or smaller squares, which will work just fine. If your sheets make a rounded ring of leather, cut the ring into quarters and start rolling from the wider side. There's no need to square the pieces off.

The savory leather can be cooled, wrapped and stored in an airtight container at room temperature for up to 3 months.

Rolls can be filled, wrapped and refrigerated for up to 8 hours. Cut into pieces just before serving.

Variation

Replace the ham with thin slices of Swiss or Havarti cheese.

- Leather sheets or parchment paper

2 cups	unsweetened applesauce	500 mL
2 tbsp	Dijon or grainy mustard	25 mL
1/2 tsp	crumbled dried thyme (or 1 1/2 tsp/ 7 mL finely chopped fresh)	2 mL
1/4 tsp	salt	1 mL
1/4 tsp	freshly ground black pepper	1 mL
1 tbsp	pure maple syrup	15 mL
4	thin slices smoked ham	4

1. In a bowl, combine applesauce mustard, thyme, salt and pepper. Spread out to 1/4-inch (0.5 cm) thickness, as evenly as possible, on leather sheets, leaving it slightly thicker around the edges. Dry at 130°F (55°C) for 4 to 5 hours or until top is very firm and edges are easy to lift. Carefully peel leather from sheet, flip over and continue drying for about 2 hours or until evenly translucent and still flexible, with no visible moist spots. Peel off sheets and let cool on a cutting board.

2. Cut leather into 4-inch (10 cm) squares. Brush smooth side with maple syrup. Top each square with a piece of ham, trimming edges to fit. Roll up jellyroll-style and cut crosswise into 1-inch (2.5 cm) pieces. Secure each roll with a toothpick, if necessary.

Cajun-Spiced Dried Onion Rings

These peppy snacks call for some sour cream dip and a frosty beer.

Makes about 3 cups (750 mL)

Variation

For a smoky touch, replace ¹⁄₂ tsp (2 mL) of the sweet paprika with smoked paprika.

6	small onions	6
2 tbsp	sweet paprika	25 mL
1 tsp	salt	5 mL
1 tsp	finely crumbled dried thyme	5 mL
¹⁄₂ tsp	cayenne pepper	2 mL
¹⁄₄ cup	red wine vinegar or white vinegar	50 mL

1. Cut onions crosswise into rings about ¹⁄₈ inch (0.25 cm) thick. Carefully separate layers into individual rings.

2. In a shallow dish, combine onions, paprika, salt, thyme, cayenne and vinegar. Cover and let stand for at least 1 hour or for up to 4 hours.

3. Drain onions, discarding marinade. Place onions on mesh drying trays, setting smaller rings inside larger rings to save space. Dry at 130°F (55°C) for 8 to 10 hours or until rings are dry and crisp, with no sign of moisture inside. Let cool completely on trays or transfer to a cool container. Serve immediately or store in an airtight container at room temperature for up to 6 months.

Balsamic-Marinated Onion Rings

Use these as garnish for soup, on a cheese platter or even just for munching.

Makes about 3 cups (750 mL)

Tip

These onion rings can also be rehydrated for use in recipes.

4	small red onions	4
¹⁄₄ tsp	salt	1 mL
¹⁄₄ tsp	freshly ground black pepper	1 mL
¹⁄₄ cup	balsamic vinegar	50 mL

1. Cut onions crosswise into rings about ¹⁄₈ inch (0.25 cm) thick. Carefully separate layers into individual rings.

2. In a shallow dish, combine onions, salt, pepper and vinegar. Cover and let stand for at least 1 hour or for up to 4 hours.

3. Drain onions, discarding marinade. Place onions on mesh drying trays, setting smaller rings inside larger rings to save space. Dry at 130°F (55°C) for 8 to 10 hours or until rings are dry and crisp, with no sign of moisture inside. Let cool completely on trays or transfer to a cool container. Serve immediately or store in an airtight container at room temperature for up to 6 months.

Parmesan Cheese and Herb Breadstick Bites

Crunchy breadsticks flavored with olive oil, herbs and Parmesan are divine with a glass of wine for hors d'oeuvres, on top of a salad or to accompany a bowl of soup.

Makes about 48 pieces

Tips

A day-old (or even 2-day-old) baguette is much easier to cut into sticks. If it's too fresh, the sticks won't be as nicely shaped and will take longer to dry.

This is the time to use good-quality extra-virgin oil for terrific flavor. Because the oil reduces the storage time, however, they're best enjoyed within a week.

Variation

To use dried herbs, combine oil and black pepper with 1 tsp (5 mL) crumbled dried parsley, ½ tsp (2 mL) crumbled dried basil and ¼ tsp (1 mL) crumbled dried rosemary or thyme. Let stand for at least 30 minutes or for up to 4 hours to infuse the oil with flavor before brushing it onto bread.

1	day-old baguette (about 12 oz/375 g)	1
1 tbsp	finely chopped fresh parsley	15 mL
1 tbsp	finely chopped fresh basil	15 mL
1 tsp	finely chopped fresh rosemary or thyme	5 mL
¼ tsp	freshly ground black pepper	1 mL
⅓ cup	olive oil	75 mL
1 cup	freshly grated Parmesan cheese	250 mL

1. Cut baguette in half lengthwise. Cut each half crosswise into 3-inch (7.5 cm) sections. Cut sections lengthwise into ½-inch (1 cm) sticks.

2. In a bowl, combine parsley, basil, rosemary, pepper and oil. Brush over cut sides of baguette sticks. Dip oiled sides in Parmesan cheese, pressing slightly to help it stick and shaking off excess.

3. Place breadsticks crust side down on mesh drying trays. Dry at 155°F (68°C) for about 3 hours or until firm and crisp. Let cool completely on trays or on wire racks. Serve immediately or store in a cookie tin at room temperature for up to 1 week.

Seasoned Bagel Bites

Don't let day-old bagels go to waste. Season them up and dry them to make these addictive little bites. You'll find yourself buying extra bagels just to make another batch.

Makes about 12 dozen pieces

4	day-old bagels	4
1 tsp	sea salt	5 mL
1/2 tsp	freshly ground black pepper	2 mL
1/2 cup	malt vinegar, cider vinegar or white vinegar	125 mL

1. Cut bagels crosswise into slices about 1/4 inch (0.5 cm) thick and spread out on a cutting board.

2. In a bowl, combine salt, pepper and vinegar, stirring to dissolve salt. Brush over both sides of bagel slices. Cut each slice into 6 wedges.

3. Place bagel wedges on mesh drying trays. Dry at 155°F (68°C) for about 2 hours or until firm and crisp. Let cool completely on trays or on wire racks. Serve immediately or store in an airtight container at room temperature for up to 2 months.

Mexican Tortilla Triangles

Zesty, crispy tortilla triangles make a super dipper for guacamole, your favorite sour cream dip or salsa. You can also use them as garnish for taco salad or on top of soup.

Makes 48 pieces

1 tbsp	chili powder	15 mL
1/2 tsp	ground cumin	2 mL
1/2 tsp	salt	2 mL
1/4 tsp	chipotle pepper powder (optional)	1 mL
2 tbsp	freshly squeezed lime juice	25 mL
4	small flour tortillas	4

1. In a small bowl, combine chili powder, cumin, salt, chipotle powder (if using) and lime juice, stirring to dissolve salt. Brush over both sides of tortillas. Stack tortillas and cut into 12 triangles.

2. Place tortilla triangles on mesh drying trays. Dry at 155°F (68°C) for about 2 hours or until firm and crisp. Let cool completely on trays or on wire racks. Serve immediately or store in an airtight container at room temperature for up to 2 months.

Greek Pita Chips

With just a few ingredients, you can easily create your own savory chips with the classic Greek flavors of oregano and lemon. Use them as dippers for tzatziki or hummus, or as croutons on a salad or soup.

Makes 64 pieces

Tip

Drying these chips without added oil gives them a longer shelf life. For extra flavor, brush lightly with extra-virgin olive oil just before serving.

4	8-inch (20 cm) pitas (with pocket)	4
2 tsp	finely crumbled dried oregano	10 mL
$\frac{1}{2}$ tsp	sea salt	2 mL
$\frac{1}{2}$ tsp	freshly ground black pepper	2 mL
$\frac{1}{2}$ cup	freshly squeezed lemon juice	125 mL

1. Using a small serrated knife, cut pitas around the edge into two circles. Place interior side up on a cutting board.

2. In a bowl, combine oregano, salt, pepper and lemon juice, stirring to dissolve salt. Brush over tops of pitas. Cut each circle into 8 wedges.

3. Place pita wedges seasoned side up on mesh drying trays. Dry at 155°F (68°C) for about 1 hour or until firm and crisp. Let cool completely on trays or on wire racks. Serve immediately or store in an airtight container at room temperature for up to 2 months.

Apple Cinnamon Oat Crisps

These crispy snacks, made with the fantastic flavor of apple and cinnamon and a touch of brown sugar, can be enjoyed at home or on the go.

Makes about 50 crisps

Tip

Use a clean plastic ruler, the straight edge of a dough scraper or an offset spatula to spread the mixture evenly on the sheets.

• *Leather sheets or parchment paper*

1 cup	steel-cut oats	250 mL
½ tsp	salt	2 mL
3 cups	water	750 mL
2	apples, chopped	2
¼ cup	packed brown sugar or liquid honey	50 mL
¾ tsp	ground cinnamon	3 mL

1. In a saucepan, combine oats, salt and water. Bring to a boil over high heat. Reduce heat to low and cook, stirring often, for about 30 minutes or until oats are tender and thick. Measure out 3 cups (750 mL) and transfer to a shallow dish; let cool. Reserve any extra for another use.

2. In a food processor, combine apples, sugar and cinnamon; pulse until very finely chopped. Add oats and pulse until mixture is fairly smooth and a paste consistency.

3. Spread out to ¼-inch (0.5 cm) thickness, as evenly as possible, on leather sheets, leaving it slightly thicker around the edges. Dry at 130°F (55°C) for 5 to 8 hours or until top is very firm and it is easy to lift from the sheet. Flip onto a cutting board and cut into 1½-inch (4 cm) square pieces.

4. Transfer pieces to mesh drying trays, moist side down, and dry for about 2 hours or until firm and crisp. Let cool completely on trays or on wire racks. Serve immediately or store in a cookie tin at room temperature for up to 2 months.

Brown Rice, Cinnamon and Raisin Crisps

These are a not-too-sweet, biscotti-like snack. Doing the second "baking" in the dehydrator rather than the oven prevents the crisps from getting over-baked, while drying them to a perfect crispiness. They're terrific topped with soft cheese or pâté, spread with nut butter or on their own.

Makes about 120 small crisps

Variations

For savory crisps, replace the cinnamon with ½ tsp (2 mL) crumbled dried rosemary and add ½ tsp (2 mL) freshly ground black pepper.

Add ½ cup (125 mL) roasted salted sunflower seeds with the raisins in either the sweet or the savory version.

- *Preheat oven to 350°F (180°C)*
- *Baking sheet, lined with parchment paper*

1	egg	1
1 cup	cooked brown rice, cooled	250 mL
¼ cup	packed brown sugar or liquid honey	50 mL
1¾ cups	whole wheat flour	425 mL
1 tsp	ground cinnamon	5 mL
½ tsp	baking powder	2 mL
½ tsp	salt	2 mL
1 cup	raisins	250 mL

1. In a food processor, purée egg, rice and sugar until fairly smooth. Add flour, cinnamon, baking powder and salt; pulse until combined and a crumbly dough forms. Add raisins and pulse just until evenly distributed and slightly chopped.

2. Divide dough in half and squeeze each half into a log about 10 inches (25 cm) long. Place on prepared baking sheet, leaving at least 3 inches (7.5 m) between logs. Press down until logs are about ¾ inch (2 cm) thick. Bake in preheated oven for about 30 minutes or until firm and a tester inserted in the center comes out clean. Let cool on pan on a rack for 10 minutes.

3. Transfer logs to a cutting board. Using a serrated knife and a gentle sawing motion, cut crosswise into slices about ⅛ inch (0.25 cm) thick.

4. Place slices on mesh drying trays. Dry at 155°F (68°C) for 2 to 4 hours or until firm and very crisp. Let cool completely on trays or on wire racks. Serve immediately or store in a cookie tin at room temperature for up to 2 months.

Wild Rice, Cranberry and Cashew Chews

The nuttiness of wild rice and cashews and the tang of cranberries and apples complement each other well in these decidedly different, toothsome snacks.

Makes about 48 small pieces

Tip
You'll need about $\frac{1}{2}$ cup (125 mL) raw wild rice to get 2 cups (500 mL) cooked.

Variation
Use almonds, brazil nuts, walnuts or pecans in place of the cashews. To enhance the flavor, toast nuts in a dry skillet over medium heat, stirring constantly, for about 3 minutes or until fragrant.

• Leather sheets or parchment paper

2 cups	cooked wild rice, cooled	500 mL
1 cup	cranberries (fresh or frozen and thawed)	250 mL
1 cup	chopped apple	250 mL
$\frac{1}{4}$ cup	roasted salted cashews	50 mL
2 tbsp	liquid honey	25 mL
1 tbsp	unsweetened apple juice or cranberry juice (approx.)	15 mL

1. In a food processor or in a tall cup (to use an immersion blender), pulse rice, cranberries, apple, cashews and honey until finely chopped. Add just enough apple juice to make a thick, fairly smooth paste.

2. Drop by heaping teaspoonfuls (5 mL), at least 1 inch (2.5 cm) apart, onto leather sheets. Using a moistened spatula, press to $\frac{1}{4}$-inch (0.5 cm) thickness. Dry at 130°F (55°C) for 3 to 4 hours or until tops are firm and edges are easy to lift.

3. Lift carefully and transfer to mesh drying trays, moist side down. Dry for 2 to 3 hours or until firm inside and out but still slightly flexible. Lift from mesh trays to loosen and let cool completely on trays or on wire racks. Serve immediately or store in an airtight container at room temperature for up to 1 month.

Peanut Banana Chews

A portable snack with the classic flavors of peanut and banana is sure to satisfy you, whether you're on the trail or on the road.

Makes about 70 pieces

Tips

Use ripe bananas (with brown spots) for the best flavor and texture.

For an extra treat, spread melted chocolate on the bottom side of one chew and sandwich with another.

- *Leather sheets or parchment paper*

1½ cups	roasted salted peanuts	375 mL
3	bananas	3
1 tbsp	packed brown sugar	15 mL

1. In a food processor, pulse peanuts until finely chopped. Add bananas and brown sugar; purée until fairly smooth.

2. Drop by heaping teaspoonfuls (5 mL) onto leather sheets, at least 2 inches (5 cm) apart. Using a spatula, spread to ⅛-inch (0.25 cm) thickness. Dry at 130°F (55°C) for 4 to 5 hours or until tops are firm and edges are easy to lift.

3. Lift carefully and transfer to mesh drying trays, moist side down. Dry for 3 to 4 hours or until firm but still slightly flexible, with no sign of moisture inside. Lift from mesh trays to loosen and let cool completely on trays or on wire racks. Serve immediately or store in an airtight container at room temperature for up to 1 month.

Angel Food Cake Dipping Bites

Fat-free angel food cake makes crisp, sweet little bites that are perfect for dipping into fruit yogurt, chocolate fondue or a cream cheese dip. They make a fun snack or dessert.

Makes about 72 pieces

Tip

This is a perfect way to use up leftover angel food cake. Just don't use it if there is icing on or filling in the cake.

1	7-inch (18 cm) angel food cake	1

1. Freeze cake for about 30 minutes or until slightly firm. Using a serrated knife, cut cake in half crosswise. Place each half cut side down and cut crosswise into slices about ½ inch (1 cm) thick. Cut each slice into ¾-inch (2 cm) wedges or fingers.

2. Place cake pieces on mesh drying trays. Dry at 155°F (68°C) for about 2 hours or until firm and crisp. Let cool completely on trays or on wire racks. Serve immediately or store in an airtight container at room temperature for up to 1 month.

Sweet and Salty Snack Mix

A different taste in every bite will make for happy snacking with this easy blend of sweet and salty ingredients.

Makes about 3 cups (750 mL)

Tip

Substitute your favorite ready-to-eat cereals and dried fruits. Keep in mind that hard, crunchy cereals work best.

• *Leather sheet or parchment paper*

2 tbsp	packed brown sugar	25 mL
¼ tsp	cayenne pepper	1 mL
¼ cup	soy sauce	50 mL
1 tsp	Worcestershire sauce (optional)	5 mL
1 cup	O-shaped oat cereal	250 mL
½ cup	shredded wheat squares cereal (Shreddies or Chex)	125 mL
½ cup	pretzel sticks	125 mL
½ cup	raisins	125 mL
½ cup	chopped dried pineapple	125 mL

1. In a bowl, combine brown sugar, cayenne, soy sauce and Worcestershire sauce (if using), stirring until sugar is dissolved. Add oat cereal, wheat cereal, pretzels, raisins and pineapple; toss to coat evenly.

2. Spread mixture onto leather sheets. Dry at 135°F (58°C), stirring and spreading out pieces once or twice, for 2 to 3 hours or until no longer sticky. Let cool completely on trays. Serve immediately or store in an airtight container at room temperature for up to 1 month.

Baked Goods

Peach Vanilla Muffins

The floral flavor of peaches is enhanced by the vanilla in these muffins. They are nice for breakfast or as an afternoon snack.

Makes 12 muffins

Tip

Muffins are best within a day of baking. Wrap extra cooled muffins individually in plastic wrap, then place in an airtight container or freezer bag and freeze for up to 2 months.

Variations

For extra vanilla punch, use vanilla-flavored yogurt and reduce the sugar to $2/3$ cup (150 mL).

Add $1/4$ cup (50 mL) dried blueberries with the chopped peaches.

- *Preheat oven to 375°F (190°C)*
- *12-cup muffin pan, greased or lined with silicone or paper liners*

$3/4$ cup	dried peach slices, divided	175 mL
$3/4$ cup	boiling water	175 mL
$2^1/2$ cups	all-purpose flour	625 mL
$1^1/2$ tsp	baking powder	7 mL
$1/2$ tsp	salt	2 mL
$1/4$ tsp	baking soda	1 mL
Pinch	ground nutmeg	Pinch
$3/4$ cup	packed brown sugar	175 mL
1	egg	1
$3/4$ cup	plain yogurt (not fat-free)	175 mL
$1/4$ cup	butter, melted, or vegetable oil	50 mL
1 tbsp	vanilla extract	15 mL

1. In a large heatproof measuring cup or bowl, combine $1/2$ cup (125 mL) of the peaches and the boiling water; let stand for 30 minutes or until peaches are soft and water has cooled to room temperature.

2. Meanwhile, preheat oven to 375°F (190°C).

3. Using an immersion blender, or transferring to a blender, purée peach mixture until fairly smooth. Return to the cup or bowl, if necessary. Using scissors, cut the remaining peaches into small pieces and stir into purée. Set aside.

4. In a large bowl, whisk together flour, baking powder, salt, baking soda and nutmeg. Set aside.

5. Whisk brown sugar, egg, yogurt, butter and vanilla into peach mixture. Pour over dry ingredients and stir just until moistened.

6. Spoon batter evenly into prepared muffin pan. Bake in preheated oven for 20 to 25 minutes or until tops are firm to the touch. Let cool in pan on a wire rack for 10 minutes. Transfer muffins to rack to cool completely.

Apricot Almond Muffins

Apricots and almonds add flavor, crunch and color to these satisfying muffins. They improve after sitting, so make them a day ahead to maximize the flavor.

Makes 12 muffins

Tips

To toast almonds, spread whole raw almonds on a baking sheet and bake in a 375°F (190°C) oven, stirring once or twice, for about 8 minutes or until nuts are toasted and fragrant. Watch carefully, as they burn easily. Transfer to a bowl and let cool, then chop.

Muffins are best within a day of baking. Wrap extra cooled muffins individually in plastic wrap, then place in an airtight container or freezer bag and freeze for up to 2 months.

- *Preheat oven to 375°F (190°C)*
- *12-cup muffin pan, greased or lined with silicone or paper liners*

1/2 cup	dried apricot slices, chopped	125 mL
1 cup	unsweetened applesauce	250 mL
3/4 cup	milk	175 mL
1 1/2 cups	all-purpose flour	375 mL
1 cup	whole wheat flour	250 mL
2 tsp	baking powder	10 mL
1/2 tsp	baking soda	2 mL
1/2 tsp	salt	2 mL
1/2 tsp	ground nutmeg	2 mL
2/3 cup	chopped toasted almonds, divided	150 mL
2/3 cup	granulated sugar	150 mL
1	egg	1
1/4 cup	butter, melted, or vegetable oil	50 mL

1. In a measuring cup or bowl, combine apricots, applesauce and milk; let stand for 15 minutes.

2. In a large bowl, whisk together all-purpose and whole wheat flours, baking powder, baking soda, salt and nutmeg. Stir in 1/2 cup (125 mL) of the almonds. Set aside.

3. Whisk sugar, egg and butter into apricot mixture. Pour over dry ingredients and stir just until moistened.

4. Spoon batter evenly into prepared muffin pan. Sprinkle remaining almonds on top. Bake in preheated oven for 20 to 25 minutes or until tops are firm to the touch. Let cool in pan on a wire rack for 10 minutes. Transfer muffins to rack to cool completely.

Strawberry Yogurt Muffins

Fresh strawberries don't hold up well in quick breads, but once dried, they add a burst of color and flavor that can't be beat.

Makes 12 muffins

Tips

When baking, avoid fat-free yogurt and any yogurt that contains gelatin, as it doesn't react well to heat and can cause rubbery baked goods.

Muffins are best within a day of baking. Wrap extra cooled muffins individually in plastic wrap, then place in an airtight container or freezer bag and freeze for up to 2 months.

- *Preheat oven to 375°F (190°C)*
- *12-cup muffin pan, greased or lined with silicone or paper liners*

½ cup	dried strawberry slices, chopped	125 mL
1 cup	plain yogurt (not fat-free)	250 mL
¾ cup	milk	175 mL
1½ cups	all-purpose flour	375 mL
1¼ cups	whole wheat flour	300 mL
2 tsp	baking powder	10 mL
½ tsp	baking soda	2 mL
½ tsp	salt	2 mL
½ tsp	ground cinnamon	2 mL
⅔ cup	granulated sugar	150 mL
1	egg	1
¼ cup	butter, melted, or vegetable oil	50 mL

1. In a measuring cup or bowl, combine strawberries, yogurt and milk; let stand for 10 minutes.

2. In a large bowl, whisk together all-purpose and whole wheat flours, baking powder, baking soda, salt and cinnamon. Set aside.

3. Whisk sugar, egg and butter into strawberry mixture. Pour over dry ingredients and stir just until moistened.

4. Spoon batter evenly into prepared muffin pan. Bake in preheated oven for 20 to 25 minutes or until tops are firm to the touch. Let cool in pan on a wire rack for 10 minutes. Transfer muffins to rack to cool completely.

Cranberry Pecan Muffins

Cranberries and pecans are a classic combination and work brilliantly together in these nutritious muffins.

Makes 12 muffins

Tips

To toast pecans, spread pecan halves on a baking sheet and bake in a 375°F (190°C) oven, stirring once or twice, for 5 to 7 minutes or until nuts are toasted and fragrant. Watch carefully, as they burn easily. Transfer to a bowl and let cool, then chop.

Muffins are best within a day of baking. Wrap extra cooled muffins individually in plastic wrap, then place in an airtight container or freezer bag and freeze for up to 2 months.

- 12-cup muffin pan, greased or lined with silicone or paper liners

½ cup	dried cranberry halves	125 mL
¾ cup	boiling water	175 mL
1½ cups	all-purpose flour	375 mL
1 cup	whole wheat flour	250 mL
2 tsp	baking powder	10 mL
½ tsp	baking soda	2 mL
½ tsp	salt	2 mL
½ tsp	ground ginger	2 mL
¾ cup	packed brown sugar	175 mL
1	egg	1
1 cup	unsweetened applesauce	250 mL
¼ cup	butter, melted, or vegetable oil	50 mL
½ cup	chopped toasted pecans	125 mL
12	pecan halves (optional)	12

1. In a large heatproof measuring cup or bowl, combine cranberries and boiling water; let stand for 30 minutes or until cranberries are soft and water has cooled to room temperature.

2. Meanwhile, preheat oven to 375°F (190°C).

3. In a large bowl, whisk together all-purpose and whole wheat flours, baking powder, baking soda, salt and ginger. Set aside.

4. Whisk brown sugar, egg, applesauce and butter into cranberry mixture. Pour over dry ingredients, sprinkle with chopped pecans and stir just until moistened.

5. Spoon batter evenly into prepared muffin pan. If desired, press a pecan half lightly on top of each muffin. Bake for 20 to 25 minutes or until tops are firm to the touch. Let cool in pan on a wire rack for 10 minutes. Transfer muffins to rack to cool completely.

Pumpkin Cranberry Muffins

Pumpkin adds moisture and a rich flavor to these muffins, and the combination of pumpkin and cranberries is not only colorful but delicious too!

Makes 12 muffins

Tip

Muffins are best within a day of baking. Wrap extra cooled muffins individually in plastic wrap, then place in an airtight container or freezer bag and freeze for up to 2 months.

Variations

Replace the pumpkin with dried butternut squash slices or cubes.

Replace the cranberries with chopped dried apples or pears.

- 12-cup muffin pan, greased or lined with silicone or paper liners

¾ cup	dried pumpkin slices or cubes	175 mL
1½ cups	boiling unsweetened apple juice or water, divided	375 mL
½ cup	dried cranberry halves	125 mL
1½ cups	all-purpose flour	375 mL
1 cup	whole wheat flour	250 mL
2 tsp	baking powder	10 mL
½ tsp	salt	2 mL
½ tsp	ground cinnamon	2 mL
½ tsp	ground ginger	2 mL
¾ cup	packed brown sugar	175 mL
1	egg	1
¼ cup	butter, melted, or vegetable oil	50 mL

1. In a large heatproof measuring cup or bowl, combine pumpkin and 1¼ cups (300 mL) of the boiling apple juice. In a separate heatproof measuring cup or bowl, combine cranberries and the remaining boiling apple juice. Let both stand for 30 minutes or until pumpkin and cranberries are soft and water has cooled to room temperature.

2. Meanwhile, preheat oven to 375°F (190°C).

3. Using an immersion blender, or transferring to a blender, purée pumpkin mixture until fairly smooth. Return to the cup or bowl, if necessary, and stir in cranberry mixture. Set aside.

4. In a large bowl, whisk together all-purpose and whole wheat flours, baking powder, salt, cinnamon and ginger. Set aside.

5. Whisk brown sugar, egg and butter into pumpkin mixture. Pour over dry ingredients and stir just until moistened.

6. Spoon batter evenly into prepared muffin pan. Bake for about 25 minutes or until tops are firm to the touch. Let cool in pan on a wire rack for 10 minutes. Transfer muffins to rack to cool completely.

Carrot Pineapple Muffins

It sounds strange, but the dried carrot and pineapple make these muffins really moist once they're soaked and puréed. The muffins benefit from standing, so make them the day before you plan to serve them for the best texture.

Makes 12 muffins

Tip
Wrap extra cooled muffins individually in plastic wrap, then place in an airtight container or freezer bag and freeze for up to 2 months.

Variations
Substitute dried mango or papaya slices for all or some of the pineapple.

Add ¼ cup (50 mL) sweetened flaked coconut with the flour and sprinkle a little more on top of each muffin before baking.

- *12-cup muffin pan, greased or lined with silicone or paper liners*

½ cup	dried pineapple rings	125 mL
¼ cup	dried carrot slices	50 mL
1¼ cups	boiling water	300 mL
2½ cups	all-purpose flour	625 mL
½ cup	natural bran	125 mL
2 tsp	baking powder	10 mL
½ tsp	baking soda	2 mL
½ tsp	salt	2 mL
½ tsp	ground ginger or nutmeg	2 mL
¾ cup	packed brown sugar	175 mL
1	egg	1
¾ cup	plain yogurt (not fat-free)	175 mL
¼ cup	butter, melted, or vegetable oil	50 mL

1. In a large heatproof measuring cup or bowl, combine pineapple, carrots and boiling water; let stand for 30 minutes or until carrots are soft and water has cooled to room temperature.

2. Meanwhile, preheat oven to 375°F (190°C).

3. Using an immersion blender, or transferring to a blender, purée pineapple mixture until pineapple and carrots are finely chopped. Return to the cup or bowl, if necessary. Set aside.

4. In a large bowl, whisk together flour, bran, baking powder, baking soda, salt and ginger. Set aside.

5. Whisk brown sugar, egg, yogurt and butter into pineapple mixture. Pour over dry ingredients and stir just until moistened.

6. Spoon batter evenly into prepared muffin pan. Bake for 20 to 25 minutes or until tops are firm to the touch. Let cool in pan on a wire rack for 10 minutes. Transfer muffins to rack to cool completely.

Banana-Banana Muffins

A double hit of banana makes these moist muffins even more satisfying. Serve them with a cold glass of milk or a bowl of yogurt for breakfast.

Makes 12 muffins

Tips

For an added touch, place a dried banana slice on top of each muffin before baking.

Muffins are best within a day of baking. Wrap extra cooled muffins individually in plastic wrap, then place in an airtight container or freezer bag and freeze for up to 2 months.

Variation

Banana Nut Muffins: Add ½ cup (125 mL) chopped toasted walnuts or pecans, stirring them in as you combine the wet and dry ingredients.

- *12-cup muffin pan, greased or lined with silicone or paper liners*

¾ cup	dried banana slices, divided	175 mL
1 cup	boiling water	250 mL
1½ cups	all-purpose flour	375 mL
1 cup	whole wheat flour	250 mL
2 tsp	baking powder	10 mL
½ tsp	salt	2 mL
¼ tsp	baking soda	1 mL
¼ tsp	ground cinnamon or nutmeg	1 mL
⅔ cup	packed brown sugar	150 mL
1	egg	1
½ cup	milk	125 mL
¼ cup	butter, melted, or vegetable oil	50 mL

1. In a large heatproof measuring cup or bowl, combine ½ cup (125 mL) of the bananas and the boiling water; let stand for 30 minutes or until bananas are soft and water has cooled to room temperature.

2. Meanwhile, preheat oven to 375°F (190°C).

3. Using an immersion blender, or transferring to a blender, purée banana mixture until smooth. Return to the cup or bowl, if necessary. Finely chop the remaining banana slices and stir into purée. Set aside.

4. In a large bowl, whisk together all-purpose and whole wheat flours, baking powder, salt, baking soda and cinnamon. Set aside.

5. Whisk brown sugar, egg, milk and butter into banana mixture. Pour over dry ingredients and stir just until moistened.

6. Spoon batter evenly into prepared muffin pan. Bake for 20 to 25 minutes or until tops are firm to the touch. Let cool in pan on a wire rack for 10 minutes. Transfer muffins to rack to cool completely.

Muesli Muffins

Turn the flavors of muesli cereal into a hearty, energy-packed muffin. Use your favorite dried fruits, such as peaches, pears, apricots, cherries and berries, alone or in combination.

Makes 12 muffins

Tips

Toasting the oats and almonds adds depth of flavor, but you can skip that step if you're in a hurry.

If your dried fruit is very firm and crispy, you may want to steam it over simmering water for a few minutes to plump it before adding it in step 2.

Muffins are best within a day of baking. Wrap extra cooled muffins individually in plastic wrap, then place in an airtight container or freezer bag and freeze for up to 2 months.

Variation

Use fruit-flavored yogurt in place of the plain and reduce the sugar to 3 tbsp (45 mL).

- *Preheat oven to 375°F (190°C)*
- *Rimmed baking sheet*
- *12-cup muffin pan, greased or lined with silicone or paper liners*

1 cup	quick-cooking rolled oats	250 mL
1/2 cup	chopped almonds or pecans	125 mL
3/4 cup	mixed dried fruit, chopped	175 mL
1 cup	plain yogurt (not fat-free)	250 mL
3/4 cup	milk	175 mL
1 1/2 cups	all-purpose flour	375 mL
1/2 cup	whole wheat flour	125 mL
2 tsp	baking powder	10 mL
1 tsp	ground cinnamon	5 mL
1/4 tsp	baking soda	1 mL
1/4 tsp	salt	1 mL
1/3 cup	granulated sugar	75 mL
1	egg	1
1/3 cup	liquid honey	75 mL
1/4 cup	butter, melted, or vegetable oil	50 mL

1. Spread oats and almonds in a single layer on baking sheet. Bake in preheated oven, stirring twice, for about 7 minutes or until toasted and fragrant. Transfer to a large bowl and let cool. (Leave the oven on.)

2. Meanwhile, in a measuring cup or bowl, combine dried fruit, yogurt and milk; let stand for 10 minutes.

3. Set 1/4 cup (50 mL) of the oat mixture aside. Add all-purpose and whole wheat flours, baking powder, cinnamon, baking soda and salt to the remaining oat mixture. Set aside.

4. Whisk sugar, egg, honey and butter into fruit mixture. Pour over dry ingredients and stir just until moistened.

5. Spoon batter evenly into prepared muffin pan. Sprinkle reserved oat mixture on top, pressing lightly so it sticks. Bake for 20 to 25 minutes or until tops are firm to the touch. Let cool in pan on a wire rack for 10 minutes. Transfer muffins to rack to cool completely.

Blueberry Scones

A light steaming brings out the intense flavor of dried blueberries, and when they're added to these buttery scones, it's pure delight.

Makes 8 large scones

Tips

You can use a food processor to combine the dry ingredients and cut in the butter. Use the pulse function to incorporate the butter just until the mixture starts to clump together, then transfer to a bowl and stir in the milk.

Extra scones can be cooled completely, individually wrapped in plastic and then placed in a freezer bag or an airtight container and frozen for up to 2 months. Reheat wrapped in foil in a 350°F (180°C) oven or let thaw at room temperature.

Variation

Replace the milk and lemon juice with 1 cup + 2 tbsp (275 mL) buttermilk.

- Preheat oven to 400°F (200°C)
- Steamer basket or heatproof sieve
- Baking sheet, lined with parchment paper

$^1/_3$ cup	dried blueberries	75 mL
1 cup	milk	250 mL
2 tbsp	freshly squeezed lemon juice	25 mL
3 cups	all-purpose flour	750 mL
$^1/_3$ cup	granulated sugar	75 mL
$2^1/_2$ tsp	baking powder	12 mL
$^1/_2$ tsp	baking soda	2 mL
$^1/_2$ tsp	salt	2 mL
$^3/_4$ cup	cold butter, cut into cubes	175 mL
	Milk or any type of cream (optional)	
	Granulated sugar (optional)	

1. In steamer basket set over a saucepan of simmering water, steam blueberries, covered, for about 5 minutes or until soft and plump. Transfer to a plate lined with paper towels and let cool.

2. In a measuring cup or bowl, combine milk and lemon juice; let stand for 5 minutes.

3. In a large bowl, combine flour, sugar, baking powder, baking soda and salt. Using a pastry blender or two knives, cut in butter until crumbly and dough starts to clump together. Using a fork, stir in milk mixture just until moistened.

4. Turn out onto a lightly floured surface and gently knead in blueberries just until evenly distributed and dough holds together. Pat into a circle about 1 inch (2.5 cm) thick. Using a sharp knife, cut circle into 8 wedges.

5. Place wedges at least 1 inch (2.5 cm) apart on prepared baking sheet. If desired, brush tops with milk and sprinkle lightly with sugar. Bake in preheated oven for about 20 minutes or until puffed and golden brown. Let cool on pan on a wire rack for 10 minutes. Serve warm or transfer scones to rack to cool completely.

Ginger Lemon Scones

The zingy flavors of ginger and lemon make these scones a teatime treat. Try them spread with herbed cream cheese for an interesting sandwich.

Makes 8 large scones

Tip

Extra scones can be cooled completely, individually wrapped in plastic and then placed in a freezer bag or an airtight container and frozen for up to 2 months. Reheat wrapped in foil in a 350°F (180°C) oven or let thaw at room temperature.

Variation

Lemon-Glazed Ginger Lemon Scones: Mix 2 tbsp (25 mL) icing (confectioner's) sugar with 1 to 2 tsp (5 to 10 mL) freshly squeezed lemon juice, or just enough to make a drizzling consistency. Drizzle over cooled scones and let stand for 15 minutes before serving.

- *Preheat oven to 400°F (200°C)*
- *Baking sheet, lined with parchment paper*

1 tbsp	dried gingerroot slices	15 mL
1 tbsp	chopped dried lemon zest	15 mL
¼ cup	boiling water	50 mL
¾ cup	milk	175 mL
3 cups	all-purpose flour	750 mL
⅓ cup	packed brown sugar	75 mL
1 tbsp	baking powder	15 mL
½ tsp	salt	2 mL
¾ cup	cold butter, cut into cubes	175 mL
	Milk or any type of cream (optional)	
	Granulated sugar (optional)	

1. In a large heatproof measuring cup or bowl, combine ginger, lemon zest and boiling water; let stand for 15 minutes or until ginger and lemon are soft and water has cooled to room temperature.

2. Add milk and, using an immersion blender or transferring to a blender, purée until fairly smooth. Return to the cup or bowl, if necessary. Set aside.

3. In a large bowl, combine flour, brown sugar, baking powder and salt. Using a pastry blender or two knives, cut in butter until crumbly and dough starts to clump together. Using a fork, stir in milk mixture just until moistened.

4. Turn out onto a lightly floured surface and gently knead just until dough holds together. Pat into a circle about 1 inch (2.5 cm) thick. Using a sharp knife, cut circle into 8 wedges.

5. Place wedges at least 1 inch (2.5 cm) apart on prepared baking sheet. If desired, brush tops with milk and sprinkle lightly with granulated sugar. Bake in preheated oven for about 20 minutes or until puffed and golden brown. Let cool on pan on a wire rack for 10 minutes. Serve warm or transfer scones to rack to cool completely.

Savory Tomato Herb Scones

Fresh-baked scones add a nice touch to a bowl of homemade soup. They are also lovely with a slice of cheese and a salad for lunch.

Makes 8 large scones

Tip

Extra scones can be cooled completely, individually wrapped in plastic and then placed in a freezer bag or an airtight container and frozen for up to 2 months. Reheat wrapped in foil in a 350°F (180°C) oven or let thaw at room temperature.

Variations

Bacon and Tomato Herb Scones: Add ¼ cup (50 mL) crumbled cooked bacon with the tomatoes in step 5.

Ham and Tomato Herb Scones: Add ½ cup (125 mL) diced cooked ham with the tomatoes in step 5.

• *Baking sheet, lined with parchment paper*

¼ cup	dried tomatoes, chopped	50 mL
2 tsp	crumbled dried basil	10 mL
¼ tsp	crumbled dried rosemary or thyme	1 mL
¼ cup	boiling water	50 mL
¾ cup	milk	175 mL
2 tbsp	white wine vinegar	25 mL
3 cups	all-purpose flour	750 mL
2½ tsp	baking powder	12 mL
1 tsp	granulated sugar	5 mL
½ tsp	baking soda	2 mL
½ tsp	salt	2 mL
¼ tsp	freshly ground black pepper	1 mL
¾ cup	cold butter, cut into cubes	175 mL
¼ cup	freshly grated Parmesan cheese (optional)	50 mL

1. In a large heatproof measuring cup or bowl, combine tomatoes, basil, rosemary and boiling water; let stand for 30 minutes or until tomatoes are soft and water has cooled to room temperature.

2. In a measuring cup or bowl, combine milk and vinegar; let stand for 5 minutes. Pour any excess liquid from tomatoes into milk mixture.

3. Meanwhile, preheat oven to 400°F (200°C).

4. In a large bowl, combine flour, baking powder, sugar, baking soda, salt and pepper. Using a pastry blender or two knives, cut in butter until crumbly and dough starts to clump together. Using a fork, stir in milk mixture just until moistened.

5. Turn out onto a lightly floured surface and gently knead in tomatoes just until evenly distributed and dough holds together. Pat into a circle about 1 inch (2.5 cm) thick. Using a sharp knife, cut circle into 8 wedges.

6. Place wedges at least 1 inch (2.5 cm) apart on prepared baking sheet. If desired, sprinkle tops with Parmesan cheese. Bake for about 20 minutes or until puffed and golden brown. Let cool on pan on a wire rack for 10 minutes. Serve warm or transfer scones to rack to cool completely.

Apricot Tea Cake

This slightly sweet soda bread–style cake is quick to make and gets dressed up with the addition of sweet and tangy apricots.

Makes 1 loaf, 8 to 10 slices

Tips

Use scissors to cut the apricots into small pieces, wiping the blades with a hot cloth periodically if they get sticky.

If you don't have buttermilk, place 2 tbsp (25 mL) freshly squeezed lemon juice in a measuring cup and add enough milk to make $1\frac{1}{2}$ cups (375 mL). Alternatively, use $1\frac{1}{4}$ cups (300 mL) milk and $\frac{1}{4}$ cup (50 mL) plain yogurt or sour cream (not fat-free).

- *Preheat oven to 375°F (190°C).*
- *Baking sheet, lined with parchment paper*

$\frac{1}{2}$ cup	dried apricot slices, chopped	125 mL
$1\frac{1}{2}$ cups	buttermilk (see tip, at left)	375 mL
3 cups	all-purpose flour	750 mL
$\frac{1}{2}$ cup	granulated sugar	125 mL
1 tsp	baking powder	5 mL
1 tsp	baking soda	5 mL
$\frac{1}{2}$ tsp	salt	2 mL
$\frac{1}{4}$ cup	cold butter, cut into cubes	50 mL
	Buttermilk or milk	
	Granulated or coarse sugar	

1. In a large measuring cup or bowl, combine apricots and buttermilk; let stand for 15 minutes or until apricots are softened.

2. In a large bowl, combine flour, sugar, baking powder, baking soda and salt. Using a pastry blender or two knives, cut in butter until crumbly and dough starts to clump together. Using a fork, stir in buttermilk mixture just until moistened.

3. Turn out onto a lightly floured surface and gently knead just until dough holds together. Place in the center of prepared baking sheet and gently pat into a circle about $1\frac{1}{2}$ inches (4 cm) thick. Brush top with buttermilk and sprinkle with sugar. Using a serrated knife, score top of loaf with a large X.

4. Bake in preheated oven for about 45 minutes or until golden brown and a tester inserted in the center comes out clean. Let cool on pan on a wire rack for 10 minutes. Serve warm or transfer cake to a rack to cool completely.

Lemon Zucchini Loaf

The bounty of zucchini from a summer garden can be enjoyed all year in this moist, easy-to-make loaf. It's as good for breakfast as it is spread with cream cheese for lunch.

Makes 1 loaf, about 12 slices

Variations

Replace the fresh lemon zest and juice with 1 tbsp (15 mL) crumbled dried lemon zest, adding it with the zucchini, and replace the milk with 1 cup + 2 tbsp (275 mL) buttermilk.

Add 1 tsp (5 mL) chopped fresh thyme or lemon thyme with the lemon zest.

- 9- by 5-inch (2 L) metal loaf pan, greased or lined with parchment paper

¾ cup	dried zucchini slices	175 mL
1 cup	milk	250 mL
1 tsp	grated lemon zest	5 mL
2 tbsp	freshly squeezed lemon juice	25 mL
2 cups	all-purpose flour	500 mL
¾ cup	whole wheat flour	175 mL
1 tsp	baking powder	5 mL
1 tsp	baking soda	5 mL
½ tsp	salt	2 mL
1 cup	packed brown sugar	250 mL
½ cup	cold butter, cut into pieces	125 mL
1	egg	1
2 tsp	vanilla extract	10 mL

1. In a saucepan, combine zucchini and milk; heat over medium heat just until bubbles form around the edge of the pan. Remove from heat and stir in lemon juice. Let stand for about 30 minutes or until zucchini is soft and mixture is cooled to room temperature.

2. Meanwhile, preheat oven to 350°F (180°C).

3. In a large bowl, combine all-purpose and whole wheat flours, baking powder, baking soda and salt. Set aside.

4. In tall measuring cup (to use an immersion blender) or in a blender or food processor, combine zucchini mixture, lemon zest, brown sugar and butter. Pulse until zucchini and butter are finely chopped. Add egg and vanilla; process until blended. Pour over dry ingredients and stir just until moistened.

5. Spread batter in prepared pan, smoothing top. Bake for about 1 hour or until a tester inserted in the center comes out clean. Let cool in pan on a wire rack for 10 minutes. Transfer loaf to rack to cool completely.

Apple and Dried Plum Loaf

The apples and plums not only give a lovely flavor to this loaf, but also add moisture that replaces some of the fat used in traditional loafs.

Makes 1 loaf, about 12 slices

Tip

If your loaf pan is black or dark gray, the outside of the loaf may get too dark and crispy. Keep an eye on it and reduce the oven temperature to 325°F (160°C) if it looks dark before the interior is baked.

Variation

For extra apple flavor and texture, add ¹/₂ cup (125 mL) chopped dried apples when stirring the liquid into the dry ingredients in step 4.

- 9- by 5-inch (2 L) metal loaf pan, greased or lined with parchment paper

¹/₂ cup	dried apple slices	125 mL
¹/₂ cup	dried plum wedges	125 mL
1 cup	boiling water or unsweetened apple juice	250 mL
1¹/₂ cups	all-purpose flour	375 mL
1 cup	whole wheat flour	250 mL
2 tsp	baking powder	10 mL
¹/₂ tsp	baking soda	2 mL
¹/₂ tsp	salt	2 mL
¹/₂ tsp	ground cinnamon	2 mL
²/₃ cup	packed brown sugar	150 mL
2	eggs	2
¹/₄ cup	vegetable oil or butter, melted	50 mL
2 tsp	vanilla extract	10 mL

1. In a large heatproof measuring cup or bowl, combine apples, plums and boiling water; let stand for 30 minutes or until fruit is very soft and water has cooled to room temperature.

2. Meanwhile, preheat oven to 350°F (180°C).

3. In a large bowl, whisk together all-purpose and whole wheat flours, baking powder, baking soda, salt and cinnamon. Set aside.

4. Using an immersion blender, or transferring to a blender, purée fruit mixture until fairly smooth. Pulse in brown sugar, eggs, oil and vanilla until blended. Pour over dry ingredients and stir just until moistened.

5. Spread batter in prepared pan, smoothing top. Bake for 50 to 60 minutes or until a tester inserted in the center comes out clean. Let cool in pan on a wire rack for 10 minutes. Transfer loaf to rack to cool completely.

Crisp Savory Cornbread

Corn kernels and sage add an extra lift to this classic cornbread recipe. Baked in a thin layer, it has a crispy crust, making it perfect for Cornbread, Apple and Sausage Stuffing (page 171) or to eat warm out of the oven.

Makes 1 loaf

Tip

If using the cornbread for stuffing, you can make it a day ahead. Wrap it in plastic wrap and store it at room temperature. If you're eating it on its own, it's best enjoyed soon after it's baked.

Variation

For a softer cornbread, use a 9-inch (23 cm) round metal cake pan and increase the baking time to about 30 minutes.

• *13- by 9-inch (3 L) metal cake pan, lined with parchment paper or greased*

¼ cup	dried corn kernels	50 mL
½ tsp	crumbled dried sage	2 mL
½ tsp	minced dried garlic	2 mL
1 cup	milk	250 mL
1 cup	cornmeal	250 mL
1 cup	all-purpose flour	250 mL
1 tbsp	granulated sugar	15 mL
2 tsp	baking powder	10 mL
½ tsp	salt	2 mL
¼ tsp	baking soda	1 mL
¼ tsp	freshly ground black pepper	1 mL
2	eggs	2
½ cup	butter, melted	125 mL
¼ cup	plain yogurt or sour cream (not fat-free)	50 mL

1. In a small saucepan, combine corn, sage, garlic and milk; bring just to a simmer over medium-low heat (do not let boil). Remove from heat and let cool. Cover and refrigerate for at least 3 hours, until corn is soft, or for up to 1 day.

2. Meanwhile, preheat oven to 400°F (200°C).

3. In a large bowl, combine cornmeal, flour, sugar, baking powder, salt, baking soda and pepper. Set aside.

4. Whisk eggs, butter and yogurt into milk mixture. Pour over dry ingredients and stir just until moistened.

5. Spread batter in prepared pan, smoothing top. Bake for about 20 minutes or until a tester inserted in the center comes out clean and edges are crispy and golden. Let cool in pan on a wire rack for 10 minutes. Transfer cornbread to rack to cool completely.

Pear and Ginger Pound Cake

Fragrant, fruity pears are accented with ginger in this buttery cake. Though not a true pound cake, it is as rich and delicious as you'd expect.

Makes 1 loaf, about 12 slices

Variations

Replace the pears with dried peach or apple slices.

Add $1/2$ cup (125 mL) finely chopped bittersweet (dark) chocolate, stirring it in as you combine the wet and dry ingredients.

• 8- by 4-inch (1.5 L) metal loaf pan, greased or lined with parchment paper

$1/2$ cup	dried pear slices, chopped	125 mL
6	slices dried gingerroot	6
1 cup	milk	250 mL
$3/4$ cup	butter, cut into small pieces	175 mL
$2^1/3$ cups	all-purpose flour	575 mL
$1^1/2$ tsp	baking powder	7 mL
$1/2$ tsp	salt	2 mL
1 cup	granulated sugar	250 mL
3	eggs, at room temperature	3
1 tsp	vanilla extract	5 mL

1. In a saucepan, combine pears, ginger and milk; heat over medium heat just until bubbles form around the edge of the pan. Remove from heat and stir in butter. Let stand for about 30 minutes or until butter is melted, pears are soft and mixture is cooled to room temperature.

2. Meanwhile, preheat oven to 350°F (180°C).

3. In a large bowl, combine flour, baking powder and salt. Set aside.

4. Transfer ginger to a cutting board and finely mince. Return to saucepan. Whisk in sugar, eggs and vanilla just until blended. Pour over dry ingredients and stir just until moistened.

5. Spread batter in prepared pan, smoothing top. Bake for about 1 hour or until a tester inserted in the center comes out clean. Let cool in pan on a wire rack for 15 minutes. Transfer cake to rack to cool completely.

Honey Berry Pound Cake

Plump berries add even more delight to this dense, honey-sweetened cake. Serve it plain or topped with softly whipped cream or ice cream for a fabulous dessert.

Makes 1 loaf, about 12 slices

Tip

You can use dried strawberry slices, raspberries or blueberries, or a mixture. If using strawberry slices, chop or snip them into small pieces before steaming. If using raspberries, break them into smaller pieces after steaming.

- Steamer basket or heatproof sieve
- 8- by 4-inch (1.5 L) metal loaf pan, greased or lined with parchment paper

½ cup	dried berries (see tip, at left)	125 mL
⅔ cup	butter, softened	150 mL
⅓ cup	granulated sugar	75 mL
3	eggs, at room temperature	3
⅓ cup	liquid honey	75 mL
1 tbsp	vanilla extract	15 mL
1⅓ cups	all-purpose flour	325 mL
½ tsp	baking powder	2 mL

1. In steamer basket set over a saucepan of simmering water, steam berries, covered, for 5 to 10 minutes or until soft and plump. Transfer to a plate lined with paper towels and let cool.

2. Meanwhile, preheat oven to 350°F (180°C).

3. In a large bowl, using an electric mixer, beat butter and sugar until light and fluffy. Beat in eggs until blended. Beat in honey and vanilla. Using a wooden spoon, stir in about half the flour and the baking powder. Stir in the remaining flour just until blended. Gently fold in berries just until evenly distributed.

4. Spread batter in prepared pan, smoothing top. Bake for about 45 minutes or until a tester inserted in the center comes out clean. Let cool in pan on a wire rack for 20 minutes. Transfer cake to rack to cool completely.

Black Forest Cookies

Cherries and as much chocolate as you can squeeze into a cookie make these an extremely decadent treat.

Makes about 3 dozen cookies

Tips

If your dried cherries are very soft and pliable, you can skip step 1 and stir them into the dough without steaming.

Store in a cookie tin at room temperature for up to 1 week or freeze in a rigid airtight container for up to 3 months.

- *Steamer basket or heatproof sieve*
- *Large baking sheets, lined with parchment paper*

$1/2$ cup	dried sour or sweet cherries, chopped	125 mL
$1 1/4$ cups	all-purpose flour	300 mL
$1/3$ cup	unsweetened cocoa powder, sifted	75 mL
$1/2$ tsp	baking soda	2 mL
$1/4$ tsp	salt	1 mL
$3/4$ cup	butter, softened	175 mL
$1/2$ cup	granulated sugar	125 mL
$1/3$ cup	packed brown sugar	75 mL
1	egg	1
$1 1/2$ tsp	vanilla extract	7 mL
$1/2$ cup	semisweet chocolate chips	125 mL

1. In steamer basket set over a saucepan of simmering water, steam cherries, covered, for about 5 minutes or until soft and plump. Transfer to a plate lined with paper towels and let cool.

2. Meanwhile, preheat oven to 350°F (180°C).

3. In a bowl, combine flour, cocoa, baking soda and salt. Set aside.

4. In a large bowl, using an electric mixer, beat butter, granulated sugar and brown sugar until light and fluffy. Beat in egg and vanilla until well blended. Using a wooden spoon, gradually stir in flour mixture just until blended. Stir in chocolate chips and cherries.

5. Drop dough by heaping tablespoonfuls (15 mL) onto prepared baking sheets, at least 3 inches (7.5 cm) apart. Bake for 8 to 10 minutes or until firm around the edges but still slightly soft in the center. Let cool on pans on wire racks for 10 minutes. Using a metal spatula, carefully transfer cookies to racks to cool completely.

Oatmeal Cranberry Cookies

Classic oatmeal cookies get even better with the addition of home-dried cranberries. They are hard to resist warm out of the oven . . . we bet you can't eat just one.

Makes about 5 dozen cookies

Tips

Store in a cookie tin at room temperature for up to 1 week or freeze in a rigid airtight container for up to 3 months.

To freeze unbaked dough, drop onto baking sheet as directed and freeze until firm. Transfer to an airtight container and freeze for up to 3 months. To bake, place on prepared baking sheets and let stand at room temperature for 15 minutes. Bake as directed, increasing the time by about 5 minutes, if necessary.

Variations

Replace half the cranberries with raisins. There's no need to steam the raisins.

Add ½ cup (125 mL) white baking chips or chopped white chocolate with the cranberries in step 4.

- Steamer basket or heatproof sieve
- Large baking sheets, lined with parchment paper

1 cup	dried cranberries	250 mL
2 cups	quick-cooking rolled oats	500 mL
1 cup	all-purpose flour or whole wheat flour	250 mL
1 tsp	baking soda	5 mL
½ tsp	ground cinnamon	2 mL
¼ tsp	salt	1 mL
1 cup	butter, softened	250 mL
1 cup	packed brown sugar	250 mL
1	egg	1
1 tbsp	vanilla extract	15 mL

1. In steamer basket set over a saucepan of simmering water, steam cranberries, covered, for about 15 minutes or until soft and plump. Transfer to a plate lined with paper towels and let cool.

2. Meanwhile, preheat oven to 350°F (180°C).

3. In a bowl, combine oats, flour, baking soda, cinnamon and salt. Set aside.

4. In a large bowl, using an electric mixer, beat butter and brown sugar until light and fluffy. Beat in egg and vanilla until well blended. Using a wooden spoon, gradually stir in oat mixture just until blended. Stir in cranberries.

5. Drop dough by heaping tablespoons (15 mL) onto prepared baking sheets, about 2 inches (5 cm) apart. Bake for about 10 minutes or until golden around the edges but still slightly soft in the center. Let cool on pans on wire racks for 2 minutes. Using a metal spatula, carefully transfer cookies to racks to cool completely.

Lavender Shortbread Cookies

Dried lavender from your garden gives an exotic floral touch to classic shortbread cookies. They make an elegant addition to afternoon tea or a bridal shower sweet table. Wrapped decoratively, they are a wonderful gift.

**Makes about
3 dozen cookies**

Tip

Store in a cookie tin at room temperature for up to 1 week or freeze in a rigid airtight container for up to 3 months.

Variation

Lemon Lavender Shortbread Cookies:
Add 1 tsp (5 mL) grated lemon zest with the lavender in step 1.

- Preheat oven to 300°F (150°C)
- Baking sheets, lined with parchment paper
- Decorative cookie stamp (optional)

1/2 cup	granulated sugar	125 mL
1/4 tsp	dried lavender flowers	1 mL
1 cup	unsalted butter, softened	250 mL
1 3/4 cups	all-purpose flour	425 mL
1/4 tsp	salt	1 mL
	Granulated sugar	

1. In a mini chopper or food processor, purée sugar and lavender until sugar is almost powdered and lavender is very finely chopped.

2. In a large bowl, using an electric mixer, beat lavender sugar and butter until light and fluffy. Using a wooden spoon, stir in flour and salt until a soft dough forms.

3. Roll heaping teaspoonfuls (5 mL) of dough into 1-inch (2.5 cm) balls. Place 2 inches (5 cm) apart on prepared baking sheets. Using a cookie stamp or the bottom of a drinking glass dipped in granulated sugar, press each ball lightly to flatten to about 1/2-inch (1 cm) thickness.

4. Bake in preheated oven for about 20 minutes or until set and bottoms just start to turn light golden. Let cool on pans on wire racks for 5 minutes. Transfer cookies to racks to cool completely.

Cranberry Newtons

Use your own dried cranberries to make the jewel-colored filling in these treats. You can feel good about serving these to your family.

Makes about 2 dozen cookies

Tips

Store layered with parchment or waxed paper in an airtight plastic container at room temperature for up to 3 days or in the freezer for up to 3 months.

If you have dark gray or black baking sheets, watch that the cookies don't get too dark. You may need to decrease the oven temperature to 350°F (180°C).

- Parchment paper
- Large baking sheet(s)

Filling

1 cup	dried cranberries	250 mL
½ cup	granulated sugar	125 mL
1½ cups	water	375 mL
½ tsp	grated orange zest	2 mL

Dough

½ cup	butter, softened	125 mL
1 cup	packed brown sugar	250 mL
1	egg	1
2 tsp	vanilla extract	10 mL
1½ cups	all-purpose flour	375 mL
½ cup	whole wheat flour	125 mL
½ tsp	salt	2 mL
½ tsp	ground cinnamon (optional)	2 mL

1. *Prepare the filling:* In a small saucepan, combine cranberries, sugar and water; let stand for 15 minutes. Bring to a boil over medium heat, stirring often. Reduce heat and boil gently, stirring often, for about 15 minutes or until filling is a thick, jammy consistency. Stir in orange zest and let cool completely.

2. *Prepare the dough:* In a large bowl, using an electric mixer, beat butter and brown sugar until light and fluffy. Beat in egg and vanilla until well blended. Using a wooden spoon, stir in all-purpose and whole wheat flours, salt and cinnamon (if using) until a soft dough forms. Gather into a ball.

3. Place dough between two sheets of parchment paper and roll out to a 15- by 12-inch (38 by 30 cm) rectangle. Remove top piece of paper and cut dough lengthwise into three 5-inch (12.5 cm) strips. Spoon one-third of the filling along the bottom half of each strip, leaving a 1-inch (2.5 cm) border at the bottom. Moisten border with water and fold top half of dough over filling, pressing to seal edge. Slide paper onto a baking sheet and refrigerate for about 30 minutes or until dough is firm.

Variation

Classic Fig Newtons:
Replace the cranberries
with chopped dried fig
wedges and decrease
the sugar in the filling
to ¼ cup (50 mL).
Omit the orange zest,
if desired.

4. Meanwhile, preheat oven to 375°F (190°C).

5. Place filled strips at least 2 inches (5 cm) apart on baking
sheet, using another parchment-lined sheet if necessary.
Bake, in batches if necessary, for about 20 minutes or until
edges are golden and top is firm. Using a sharp knife and
a firm, straight downward motion, cut hot cookies into
1½-inch (4 cm) pieces. Let cool on pan on a wire rack for
10 minutes. Transfer cookies to rack to cool completely.

Secret-Ingredient Fudgy Brownies

The secret ingredient (dried plums) provides moisture and tenderness to these brownies, making them delightfully decadent while being much lower in fat than regular brownies. The flavor of the plums works surprisingly well with chocolate.

Makes 16 brownies

Tip

Cooled brownies can be individually wrapped in plastic wrap, then overwrapped in foil or placed in a freezer bag or airtight container and frozen for up to 2 months.

• 8-inch (2 L) square metal baking pan, lined with foil or parchment paper, leaving a 2-inch (5 cm) overhang

1/4 cup	dried purple or blue plum wedges	50 mL
1/2 cup	boiling water	125 mL
2/3 cup	all-purpose flour	150 mL
1/2 cup	unsweetened cocoa powder, sifted	125 mL
1/2 tsp	baking powder	2 mL
1/4 tsp	salt	1 mL
3/4 cup	granulated sugar	175 mL
1	egg	1
1/4 cup	butter, melted	50 mL
1 tsp	vanilla extract	5 mL

1. In a heatproof measuring cup or bowl, combine plums and boiling water; let stand for about 30 minutes or until plums are very soft and water is cooled to room temperature.

2. Meanwhile, preheat oven to 350°F (180°C).

3. In a large bowl, whisk together flour, cocoa, baking powder and salt. Set aside.

4. Using an immersion blender, or transferring to a blender, purée plums until fairly smooth. Pulse in sugar, egg, butter and vanilla until blended. Pour over dry ingredients and stir just until moistened.

5. Spread batter in prepared pan, smoothing top. Bake for about 20 minutes or until top is puffed and a tester inserted in the center comes out with a few moist crumbs clinging to it. Let cool completely in pan on a wire rack. Using foil overhang as handles, transfer brownies to a cutting board and cut into squares.

Intense Chocolate Banana Brownies

Mashed fresh bananas tend to give a brownie batter a cake-like texture instead of a fudgy texture. By using dried bananas, you keep the fantastic brownie texture while getting the terrific flavor combination of chocolate and bananas.

Makes 12 large or 24 small brownies

Tip

Cooled brownies can be individually wrapped in plastic wrap, then overwrapped in foil or placed in a freezer bag or airtight container and frozen for up to 2 months.

- Preheat oven to 350°F (180°C)
- 13- by 9-inch (3 L) metal baking pan, lined with foil or parchment paper, leaving a 2-inch (5 cm) overhang

1 cup	butter, cut into cubes	250 mL
6 oz	bittersweet (dark) chocolate, chopped	175 g
¾ cup	dried banana slices, finely chopped	175 mL
1 cup	all-purpose flour	250 mL
¼ cup	unsweetened cocoa powder, sifted	50 mL
¼ tsp	salt	1 mL
1½ cups	granulated sugar	375 mL
4	eggs	4
1 tbsp	vanilla extract	15 mL
½ cup	chopped toasted pecans (optional)	125 mL

1. In a saucepan, melt butter and chocolate over low heat, stirring until smooth. Remove from heat and stir in bananas. Let cool slightly.

2. In a bowl, combine flour, cocoa and salt. Set aside.

3. In a large bowl, whisk together sugar and eggs until light and creamy; whisk in chocolate mixture and vanilla. Stir in dry ingredients just until blended. Stir in pecans (if using).

4. Spread batter in prepared pan, smoothing top. Bake in preheated oven for about 25 minutes or until a tester inserted in the center comes out with a few moist crumbs clinging to it. Let cool completely in pan on a wire rack. Using foil overhang as handles, transfer brownies to a cutting board and cut into squares.

Banana Chocolate Chip Granola Bars

Making your own granola bars is cost-effective, and they're much more nutritious than most store-bought ones. You can vary the flavor by adding other dried fruits in place of or along with the bananas and blueberries— try chopped mango or strawberry slices.

Makes 12 bars

Tip

Store in an airtight container at room temperature for up to 2 days or in the refrigerator for up to 1 week. For longer storage, wrap bars individually in plastic wrap, then overwrap in foil or place in a freezer bag or an airtight container and freeze for up to 2 months.

- *Preheat oven to 350°F (180°C)*
- *8-inch (2 L) square metal baking pan, lined with foil or parchment paper, leaving a 2-inch (5 cm) overhang*

1 1/2 cups	quick-cooking rolled oats	375 mL
1/2 cup	finely chopped dried banana slices	125 mL
1/2 cup	semisweet chocolate chips	125 mL
1/4 cup	dried blueberries or chopped dried cherries	50 mL
1/4 cup	ground flax seeds	50 mL
1/4 cup	chopped toasted nuts (optional)	50 mL
1/4 cup	packed brown sugar	50 mL
1	egg	1
1/3 cup	liquid honey	75 mL
1/4 cup	butter, melted	50 mL
1 tsp	vanilla extract	5 mL

1. In a large bowl, combine oats, bananas, chocolate chips, blueberries, flax seeds and nuts (if using). Set aside.

2. In another bowl, whisk together brown sugar, egg, honey, butter and vanilla. Pour over dry ingredients and stir until evenly coated.

3. Press batter into prepared pan. Bake in preheated oven for about 30 minutes or until golden brown. Let cool in pan on a wire rack for 15 minutes. Using foil overhang as handles, transfer cake to a cutting board. Cut into bars and let cool on board until firm.

Desserts

Bumbleberry Crisp

Berries, apples and rhubarb combine for a unique flavor that can't be replicated with just one fruit. The combination has become a favorite for pies and crisps. This crisp uses graham cracker crumbs for the topping, for a different twist.

Serves 4

Tip

Top with lightly sweetened whipped cream or a scoop of ice cream for a nice finishing touch.

- *Preheat oven to 375°F (190°C)*
- *4-cup (1 L) shallow glass baking dish*

1 cup	dried apple slices	250 mL
1/4 cup	dried strawberry slices	50 mL
1/4 cup	dried blueberries	50 mL
1/4 cup	dried raspberries	50 mL
1/4 cup	granulated sugar	50 mL
2 tbsp	dried rhubarb slices	25 mL
1 cup	unsweetened apple juice, orange juice or water	250 mL
1 cup	graham cracker crumbs	250 mL
1/4 cup	cold butter, cut into pieces	50 mL
1 tsp	vanilla extract	5 mL
2 tbsp	cornstarch	25 mL
2 tbsp	cold water	25 mL

1. In baking dish, combine apples, strawberries, blueberries, raspberries, sugar, rhubarb and juice. Cover and bake in preheated oven for about 20 minutes or until fruit starts to soften and juice is bubbling.

2. Meanwhile, place graham cracker crumbs in a bowl. Using a pastry blender or two knives, cut in butter until clumps form. Stir in vanilla.

3. In a small bowl, dissolve cornstarch in water. Uncover baking dish and stir cornstarch mixture into fruit; sprinkle with crumb mixture. Bake, uncovered, for 20 minutes or until fruit is bubbling, liquid is thickened and topping is crisp. Let stand for at least 5 minutes before serving or let cool to room temperature.

Apple Cherry Crumble

Cherries add a touch of color and a nice flavor to this all-time favorite dessert.

Serves 4

Variations

Add ¼ cup (50 mL) chopped pecans, walnuts or almonds to the topping after cutting in the butter.

Replace half the apples with dried pear slices. Soak pears in 1 cup (250 mL) hot water for 15 minutes before combining in baking dish. Drain, reserving liquid. Measure liquid and add enough apple juice or water to make 1 cup (250 mL) total.

- *Preheat oven to 375°F (190°C)*
- *4-cup (1 L) shallow glass baking dish*

2 cups	dried apple slices	500 mL
¼ cup	dried cherries (sweet or sour)	50 mL
¼ cup	packed brown sugar	50 mL
1 tbsp	all-purpose flour	15 mL
½ tsp	ground cinnamon	2 mL
1 cup	unsweetened apple juice or water	250 mL

Crumble Topping

½ cup	quick-cooking rolled oats	125 mL
½ cup	packed brown sugar	125 mL
¼ cup	all-purpose flour	50 mL
¼ tsp	ground cinnamon	1 mL
¼ cup	cold butter, cut into pieces	50 mL

1. In baking dish, combine apples, cherries, brown sugar, flour, cinnamon and juice. Cover and bake in preheated oven for about 20 minutes or until fruit starts to soften and juice is bubbling.

2. *Meanwhile, prepare the topping:* In a bowl, combine oats, brown sugar, flour and cinnamon. Using a pastry blender or two knives, cut in butter until crumbly.

3. Uncover baking dish and sprinkle crumb mixture over fruit. Bake, uncovered, for 20 minutes or until fruit is bubbling, liquid is thickened and topping is golden and crisp. Let stand for at least 5 minutes before serving or let cool to room temperature.

Apple Peach Cobbler

A cobbler combines tender fruit with a fluffy biscuit topping and is a warming, comforting dessert for those cold winter evenings. By using dried fruits, you can pair apples and peaches, which aren't usually in season together but taste terrific in combination.

Serves 4

Tip

For the best texture, cobblers are best served within a couple of hours of baking. Add the topping and pop it in the oven before you sit down to dinner, so it's hot out of the oven when you're ready for dessert.

Variation

Add ¼ cup (50 mL) raisins or dried cherries or blueberries with the fruit and increase the juice by 2 tbsp (25 mL).

- Preheat oven to 375°F (190°C)
- 8-inch (2 L) square glass baking dish, greased

1 cup	dried apple slices	250 mL
1 cup	dried peach slices	250 mL
¼ cup	granulated sugar	50 mL
1 tbsp	all-purpose flour	15 mL
1 cup	unsweetened apple juice, peach nectar or water	250 mL

Topping

¼ cup	granulated sugar	50 mL
½ cup	milk	125 mL
¼ cup	plain yogurt (not fat-free)	50 mL
¼ cup	butter, melted	50 mL
1 cup	all-purpose flour	250 mL
1 tsp	ground cinnamon or ginger	5 mL
½ tsp	baking powder	2 mL
¼ tsp	baking soda	1 mL
¼ tsp	salt	1 mL
	Granulated sugar	

1. In prepared baking dish, combine apples, peaches, sugar, flour and juice. Cover and bake in preheated oven for about 20 minutes or until fruit starts to soften and juice is bubbling.

2. *Meanwhile, prepare the topping:* In a large bowl, whisk together sugar, milk, yogurt and butter. Without stirring, add flour, cinnamon, baking powder, baking soda and salt. Using a fork, stir just until moistened.

3. Uncover baking dish and pour batter over fruit, spreading gently to cover evenly. Sprinkle with sugar. Bake, uncovered, for about 30 minutes or until a tester inserted in the center of the topping comes out clean. Let stand for at least 5 minutes before serving or let cool to room temperature.

Burnished Cranberry Custard Pie

Combine a creamy custard, tangy cranberries and a caramelized sugar coating, and you get a stunning pie fit for any occasion.

Serves 6 to 8

Tips

Prepare your favorite recipe for the pie shell or use a store-bought frozen one. This amount of filling fits a pie crust that is 1 inch (2.5 cm) deep. If buying a frozen shell, you may need a "deep-dish" one.

If you have a blowtorch or a kitchen torch, use it to brown the topping. You won't need the ice cubes around the pie, because it's much faster than broiling and the custard doesn't get heated too much.

Extra egg whites can be stored in an airtight container in the refrigerator for up to 2 days or frozen for up to 6 months.

Variation

Add a lemony twist by whisking 2 tsp (10 mL) grated lemon zest into the filling in step 2.

- Preheat oven to 425°F (220°C)
- Rimmed baking sheet
- Pie weights or beans
- Steamer basket or heatproof sieve

1	9-inch (23 cm) pie shell, unbaked, chilled	1
½ cup	granulated sugar	125 mL
3	eggs	3
3	egg yolks	3
1 cup	milk	250 mL
1 cup	whipping (35%) cream	250 mL
1 tsp	vanilla extract	5 mL
½ cup	dried cranberries	125 mL
	Granulated sugar	
	Ice cubes	

1. Place prepared pie shell on baking sheet and prick all over with a fork. Line with parchment paper or foil and fill with pie weights. Bake in bottom third of preheated oven for about 15 minutes or until edges are firm.

2. Meanwhile, in a bowl, whisk together sugar, eggs, egg yolks, milk, cream and vanilla until blended.

3. Remove paper and weights from pie crust. Reduce oven temperature to 325°F (160°C). Pour custard filling into hot crust. Bake for about 30 minutes or until filling is set at the edges and slightly jiggly in the center. Let cool completely on pan on a wire rack. Refrigerate for at least 3 hours, until chilled, or for up to 1 day.

4. Meanwhile, in steamer basket set over a saucepan of simmering water, steam cranberries, covered, for about 15 minutes or until plump and soft. Place on a plate lined with paper towels and let cool.

5. Up to 4 hours before serving, preheat broiler. Return pie to baking sheet and sprinkle evenly with cranberries. Sprinkle a thin layer of sugar over pie, including the crust. Place ice cubes around pie on baking sheet. Broil, rotating sheet as necessary, for about 5 minutes or until sugar is bubbling and browned. Let cool for at least 5 minutes or refrigerate for up to 4 hours.

Year-Round Berry Cream Pie

With dried berries on hand, you can whip up this simple, luscious pie any day of the year and it'll taste just like summer.

Serves 6 to 8

Tip

If you want to make the pie 1 day ahead, brush the inside of the cooled pie crust with 1 oz (30 g) melted white or dark chocolate and let it cool before adding the filling. This will prevent the crust from getting soggy.

- Steamer basket or heatproof sieve

$1/2$ cup	dried strawberry slices	125 mL
	Water	
$1/4$ cup	dried blueberries	50 mL
$1/4$ cup	dried raspberries	50 mL
1	envelope ($1/4$ oz/7 g) unflavored gelatin powder	1
1 tsp	vanilla extract	5 mL
$1 1/2$ cups	whipping (35%) cream	375 mL
$1/2$ cup	confectioner's (icing) sugar, sifted	125 mL
1	9-inch (23 cm) pie crust, baked and cooled	1

1. In a saucepan, combine strawberries and $3/4$ cup (175 mL) water; let stand for 15 minutes or until slightly softened.

2. Meanwhile, in steamer basket set over another saucepan of simmering water, steam blueberries and raspberries, covered, for about 5 minutes or until plump and soft. Let cool.

3. In a small bowl, sprinkle gelatin over $1/4$ cup (50 mL) water and let stand for 5 minutes or until softened.

4. Heat strawberry mixture over medium heat just until simmering and strawberries are soft. Reduce heat to low, stir in gelatin mixture and heat, stirring, for about 1 minute or just until gelatin has dissolved. Transfer to a bowl and let cool to room temperature. Stir in blueberries, raspberries and vanilla.

5. In a chilled bowl, using an electric mixer, whip cream until soft peaks form. Gradually beat in confectioner's sugar and whip until firm peaks form. Fold one-quarter of the whipped cream into the berry mixture. Fold berry mixture into the remaining cream just until blended. Spread into pie crust, decoratively swirling top.

6. Refrigerate for at least 1 hour, until filling is set, or for up to 8 hours.

Pecan Cranberry Butter Tarts

Mini pecan pies with a burst of fruit flavor from the cranberries are sure to be a hit at bake sales and buffets or as a dessert served with ice cream.

Makes 12 tarts

Tips

These delicate and sometimes sticky tarts are much easier to remove from individual foil or metal tart tins than from a muffin pan.

To toast this small amount of pecans, in a small dry skillet over medium heat, toast chopped pecans, stirring constantly, for about 3 minutes or until toasted and fragrant. Transfer to a bowl and let cool.

- Preheat oven to 400°F (200°C)
- Steamer basket or heatproof sieve
- Baking sheet

¼ cup	dried cranberries	50 mL
⅓ cup	packed brown sugar	75 mL
1	egg	1
¼ cup	corn syrup	50 mL
1 tbsp	butter, softened	15 mL
1 tsp	cider vinegar or white vinegar	5 mL
½ tsp	vanilla extract	2 mL
12	tart shells (each 2½ inches/6 cm), unbaked, chilled	12
2 tbsp	toasted chopped pecans	25 mL

1. In steamer basket set over a saucepan of simmering water, steam cranberries, covered, for about 15 minutes or until plump and soft. Place on a plate lined with paper towels and let cool.

2. In a liquid measuring cup with a spout, whisk together brown sugar, egg, corn syrup, butter, vinegar and vanilla until well blended (some small pieces of butter will remain).

3. Place tart shells on baking sheet and sprinkle cranberries and pecans evenly in bottoms. Carefully pour syrup mixture over berries and nuts, dividing evenly and leaving about ¼ inch (0.5 cm) of the shell above the filling.

4. Bake in bottom third of preheated oven for 10 to 15 minutes or until pastry is golden and filling is puffed. Let cool on pan on a wire rack for 5 minutes. Carefully loosen pastry from tart tin if any syrup has spilled over edge. Let cool completely.

Blueberry Maple Butter Tarts

Butter tarts are a Canadian treasure. They're often made with raisins or just with the gooey, sweet filling. This version highlights two other Canadian favorites: blueberries and maple syrup.

Makes 12 tarts

Tips

Pure maple syrup is essential for these tarts. Don't try to use maple-flavored pancake syrup.

Use store-bought frozen tart shells or prepare your favorite recipe. These were tested with tart shells that were about ¾ inch (2 cm) deep.

- *Preheat oven to 400°F (200°C)*
- *Steamer basket or heatproof sieve*
- *Baking sheet*

¼ cup	dried blueberries	50 mL
⅓ cup	packed brown sugar	75 mL
1	egg	1
⅓ cup	pure maple syrup	75 mL
1 tbsp	butter, softened	15 mL
1 tsp	freshly squeezed lemon juice	5 mL
12	tart shells (each 2½ inches/6 cm), unbaked, chilled	12

1. In steamer basket set over a saucepan of simmering water, steam blueberries, covered, for about 5 minutes or until plump and soft. Place on a plate lined with paper towels and let cool.

2. In a liquid measuring cup with a spout, whisk together brown sugar, egg, maple syrup, butter and lemon juice until well blended (some small pieces of butter will remain).

3. Place tart shells on baking sheet and sprinkle blueberries evenly in bottoms. Carefully pour syrup mixture over berries, dividing evenly and leaving about ¼ inch (0.5 cm) of the shell above the filling.

4. Bake in bottom third of preheated oven for 10 to 15 minutes or until pastry is golden and filling is puffed. Let cool on pan on a wire rack for 5 minutes. Carefully loosen pastry from tart tin if any syrup has spilled over edge. Let cool completely.

Strawberry Rhubarb Tarts

With dried fruit, these tarts — usually reserved for early summer — can be enjoyed any time of year. For extra decadence, spoon a little custard into the bottom of the tarts before adding the fruit filling.

Makes 12 tarts

Tip

If you want to fill the tarts ahead of serving, brush the inside of the cooled shells with 1 to 2 oz (30 to 60 g) melted white or dark chocolate and let it cool before adding the filling. This will prevent the crust from getting soggy. The filled tarts can then be refrigerated for up to 8 hours.

¼ cup	dried rhubarb slices	50 mL
¾ cup	water, divided	175 mL
½ cup	granulated sugar	125 mL
¼ cup	dried strawberry slices	50 mL
4 tsp	cornstarch	20 mL
2 tbsp	freshly squeezed lemon or orange juice	25 mL
¼ tsp	vanilla extract	1 mL
12	baked tart shells (each 2½ inches/6 cm)	12

1. In a saucepan, combine rhubarb and ½ cup (125 mL) of the water; let stand for 30 minutes or until slightly softened. Stir in sugar and strawberries; bring to a boil over medium heat. Reduce heat and boil gently, stirring occasionally, for about 8 minutes or until fruit is plump and tender and liquid is reduced by about half.

2. In a bowl, whisk cornstarch into the remaining water. Drizzle into saucepan and cook, stirring, for about 1 minute or until sauce is thickened and clear. Transfer to a bowl and let cool. Cover and refrigerate for about 2 hours, until chilled, or for up to 1 day.

3. To serve, spoon fruit filling into tart shells.

Apple, Raisin and Pecan Strudels

Frozen phyllo pastry is one of those ingredients that's handy to have on hand for last-minute dessert creations. With a pantry full of dried fruits as well, you can create these delightful strudels in a jiffy.

Serves 4

Tips

When working with phyllo, keep it covered with a slightly damp tea towel to prevent it from drying out.

The strudels can be assembled, covered and refrigerated for up to 1 hour before baking. Alternatively, bake them up to 4 hours ahead of time and reheat in 350°F (180°C) oven for about 10 minutes just before serving.

Variations

Reduce the apple juice in step 2 to 2 tbsp (25 mL) and add 2 tbsp (25 mL) brandy or rum.

Replace the raisins with dried cherries or cranberries or use a mixture.

• *Baking sheet, lined with parchment paper*

1 cup	chopped dried apples	250 mL
¼ cup	raisins	50 mL
1 cup	unsweetened apple juice, divided	250 mL
2 tbsp	all-purpose flour	25 mL
2 tbsp	granulated sugar	25 mL
¼ tsp	ground cinnamon	1 mL
8	sheets phyllo pastry	8
3 tbsp	butter, melted	45 mL
	Ground cinnamon	
	Granulated sugar	
¼ cup	toasted chopped pecans	50 mL
	Caramel sauce, warmed	

1. In a saucepan, combine apples, raisins and ¾ cup (175 mL) of the apple juice; bring to a boil over medium heat. Reduce heat and simmer, stirring often, for about 10 minutes or until apples are plump and liquid is slightly reduced.

2. In a small bowl, whisk the remaining apple juice into flour. Stir into saucepan, then stir in sugar and cinnamon. Simmer, stirring constantly, for about 5 minutes or until mixture is thick. Remove from heat and let cool to room temperature.

3. Preheat oven to 425°F (220°C).

4. Lay one sheet of phyllo on a large work surface and brush lightly with butter; sprinkle with a light dusting of cinnamon and sugar. Place a second sheet on top and brush with butter. Starting about 1 inch (2.5 cm) from one long side of sheet, in the center, spoon one-quarter of the apple mixture in a 4- by 2-inch (10 by 5 cm) rectangle; sprinkle with one-quarter of the pecans. Starting at the edge closest to you, fold pastry and filling over once. Fold both short ends toward the center. Roll up and place seam side down on prepared baking sheet. Brush outside of strudel with butter and sprinkle with cinnamon and sugar. Repeat to make 3 more strudels.

5. Bake strudels for about 15 minutes or until golden brown. Drizzle caramel sauce on plates and top with hot or warm strudels.

Blueberry Lemon Cheesecake

Cheesecake never goes out of style for a special treat. Make it even more special with dried blueberries and a burst of fresh lemon.

Serves 10 to 12

Tip

For restaurant-style presentation, run a sharp knife under warm water and wipe lightly, leaving the knife slightly moist, and cut cake, rinsing and wiping the knife between each cut.

- *Preheat oven to 300°F (150°C)*
- *Steamer basket or heatproof sieve*
- *9-inch (23 cm) springform pan, bottom lined with parchment paper*

¹/₂ cup	dried blueberries	125 mL
2 cups	lemon or vanilla cookie crumbs	500 mL
¹/₄ cup	butter, melted	50 mL
3	packages (each 8 oz/250 g) cream cheese, softened	3
³/₄ cup	granulated sugar	175 mL
2 tbsp	cornstarch or all-purpose flour	25 mL
4	eggs, at room temperature	4
2 tsp	grated lemon zest	10 mL
¹/₂ cup	whipping (35%) cream	125 mL
2 tsp	vanilla extract	10 mL

1. In steamer basket set over a saucepan of simmering water, steam blueberries, covered, for about 10 minutes or until very soft and plump. Transfer to a plate lined with paper towels and let cool.

2. Meanwhile, in a bowl, combine cookie crumbs and butter. Press into bottom and 1 inch (2.5 cm) up the sides of prepared pan. Freeze until firm.

3. In a bowl, using an electric mixer, beat cream cheese until fluffy. Beat in sugar and cornstarch until smooth. Beat in eggs, one at a time, until well blended. Beat in lemon zest, cream and vanilla until blended.

4. Pour half the cheesecake batter into frozen crust. Sprinkle blueberries evenly over top. Carefully pour the remaining batter over blueberries.

5. Bake in preheated oven for about 70 minutes or until edges are set and center is just slightly jiggly. Run a sharp knife carefully around the edge of the cake. Let cool completely in pan on a wire rack. Cover loosely and refrigerate for at least 6 hours, until chilled, or for up to 2 days.

Chocolate Potato Cake

Believe it or not, potatoes add wonderful moisture to this chocolate cake. Jay and Jennifer discovered this trick while living on Prince Edward Island, where world-famous potatoes are grown.

Serves 8 to 10

Tips

Let egg whites come to room temperature before beating to get maximum volume.

Be sure the bowl and beaters are very clean and dry before adding egg whites. Any trace of oil or fat will prevent the whites from beating to a stiff meringue, and you won't get a light, airy cake.

High-quality chocolate with 55% to 70% cacao is best for the ganache.

- Preheat oven to 350°F (180°C)
- 9-inch (23 cm) springform pan, bottom lined with parchment paper

½ cup	dried potato cubes	125 mL
¾ cup	water	175 mL
1¼ cups	all-purpose flour	300 mL
½ cup	unsweetened cocoa powder, sifted	125 mL
1 tsp	baking powder	5 mL
¼ tsp	salt	1 mL
3	eggs, separated	3
¾ cup	granulated sugar, divided	175 mL
½ cup	butter, softened	125 mL
2 tsp	vanilla extract	10 mL
Ganache		
⅔ cup	whipping (35%) cream	150 mL
6 oz	bittersweet (dark) chocolate, chopped	175 g

1. In a small saucepan, combine potatoes and water; bring to a boil over medium heat. Reduce heat to medium-low, cover, leaving lid slightly ajar, and boil gently, stirring occasionally, for 15 minutes or until potatoes are soft. Using a potato masher, mash potatoes with liquid until fairly smooth. Let cool completely.

2. In a bowl, combine flour, cocoa, baking powder and salt. Set aside.

3. In a small bowl, using an electric mixer, beat egg whites until foamy. Gradually beat in 2 tbsp (25 mL) of the sugar in a thin, steady stream. Continue to beat just until stiff, glossy peaks form. Set aside.

4. In a separate bowl, using an electric mixer, beat butter and the remaining sugar until fluffy. Beat in egg yolks until well blended. Beat in potato mixture and vanilla until smooth. Stir in flour mixture just until moistened. Fold in one-third of the egg whites until blended. Gently fold in the remaining egg whites just until no longer visible.

Variation

Decorate this cake with your favorite chocolate icing or chocolate-flavored whipped cream instead of the ganache.

5. Spread batter in prepared pan, smoothing top. Bake in preheated oven for about 40 minutes or until a tester inserted in the center comes out clean. Let cool in pan on a wire rack for 20 minutes. Run a knife around the edge of the cake and remove ring. Let cool completely.

6. *Prepare the ganache:* In a saucepan, heat cream over medium heat until steaming and bubbles form around the edge. Remove from heat and gently whisk in chocolate just until melted. Let cool slightly, until no longer steaming but still pourable.

7. Remove cake from pan bottom and place on a serving plate. Pour ganache in the center of the cake and let it flow across the cake and slightly down the sides, gently nudging with a spatula if necessary. Let cool for about 15 minutes or refrigerate for up to 1 day. Let warm slightly at room temperature before serving.

Double Apple Streusel Cake

Though the flavor of this cake is reminiscent of a crisp fall day, it's absolutely delicious at any time of year.

Serves 12

Tip

For extra decadence, serve this cake warm on a pool of caramel sauce and top with a scoop of vanilla bean or butterscotch ripple ice cream.

- *Preheat oven to 350°F (180°C)*
- *9-inch (23 cm) springform pan, bottom lined with parchment paper*

Streusel

1/3 cup	all-purpose flour	75 mL
1/3 cup	packed brown sugar	75 mL
1/2 tsp	ground cinnamon or ginger	2 mL
2 tbsp	butter, melted	25 mL

Cake

3/4 cup	chopped dried apples	175 mL
3/4 cup	unsweetened applesauce	175 mL
1 1/2 cups	all-purpose flour	375 mL
1 tsp	baking powder	5 mL
1 tsp	ground cinnamon or ginger	5 mL
1/2 tsp	baking soda	2 mL
1/4 tsp	salt	1 mL
2/3 cup	packed brown sugar	150 mL
1/2 cup	butter, softened	125 mL
1	egg	1
2 tsp	vanilla extract	10 mL

1. *Prepare the streusel:* In a bowl, mash together flour, brown sugar, cinnamon and butter until crumbly. Set aside.

2. *Prepare the cake:* In a bowl, combine apples and applesauce; set aside.

3. In another bowl, combine flour, baking powder, cinnamon, baking soda and salt. Set aside.

4. In a separate bowl, using an electric mixer, beat brown sugar and butter until fluffy. Beat in egg and vanilla until blended. Stir in flour mixture alternately with apple mixture, making 3 additions of flour and 2 of apple.

5. Spread batter in prepared pan, smoothing top. Sprinkle with streusel. Bake in preheated oven for 50 to 60 minutes or until a tester inserted in the center comes out clean. Let cool in pan on a wire rack for 20 minutes. Run a knife around the edge of the cake and remove ring. Serve warm or let cool completely.

Pear and Dried Blueberry Mascarpone Shortcake

With little effort at all, a store-bought pound cake, or one you've got stashed in the freezer, gets dressed up with a rich, scrumptious topping.

Serves 4

Tip

Use clean kitchen scissors to cut the dried pears into small pieces.

Variation

If mascarpone isn't available, soften $1/3$ cup (75 mL) cream cheese and, using an electric mixer, whip with the sugar until light. Fold in $1/4$ cup (50 mL) whipped cream before adding the fruit.

$1/4$ cup	finely chopped dried pears	50 mL
$1/4$ cup	dried blueberries	50 mL
$1/4$ cup	water	50 mL
$1/4$ cup	Marsala, sherry or other sweet wine	50 mL
$1/2$ cup	mascarpone cheese	125 mL
2 tbsp	granulated sugar	25 mL
8	slices pound cake, each about $1/2$ inch (1 cm) thick	8

1. In a small saucepan, combine pears, blueberries, water and Marsala; let stand for 15 minutes or until fruit starts to soften. Bring to a boil over medium heat, stirring often. Reduce heat and simmer, stirring, for about 5 minutes or until fruit is soft and liquid is syrupy. Remove from heat and let cool completely.

2. In a bowl, combine mascarpone and sugar; gently fold in fruit mixture, leaving some streaks of white.

3. Place 1 slice of cake on each plate and top with a dollop of the mascarpone mixture. Perch another slice of cake on top and spoon the remaining mascarpone mixture on cake.

Tropical Fruit Upside-Down Cake

Classic upside-down cake is updated with a mixture of tropical fruits and the zesty flavors of lime and ginger. Serve slightly warm with ice cream or a dollop of lightly sweetened whipped cream for that extra-special touch.

Serves 6 to 8

Tips

The parchment paper provides insurance that the fruit will come out on top of the cake and won't stick to the pan.

This cake is best served the day it is made. For best results, time it so the cake comes out of the oven just before you sit down for your main course. The fruit can be simmered up to 4 hours ahead of assembling the cake. Cover it once it has cooled.

- *Preheat oven to 350°F (180°C)*
- *9-inch (23 cm) round metal cake pan, bottom lined with parchment paper*

3	dried pineapple quarter rings	3
¼ cup	chopped dried mango slices	50 mL
¼ cup	chopped dried papaya slices	50 mL
¼ cup	packed brown sugar	50 mL
¾ cup	unsweetened pineapple or apple juice	175 mL
½ tsp	grated lime zest	2 mL
1 tbsp	freshly squeezed lime juice	15 mL
Cake		
1½ cups	all-purpose flour	375 mL
1½ tsp	ground ginger	7 mL
1 tsp	baking powder	5 mL
½ tsp	baking soda	2 mL
¼ tsp	salt	1 mL
¼ tsp	ground allspice	1 mL
⅔ cup	packed brown sugar	150 mL
½ cup	butter, softened	125 mL
1	egg	1
1 tsp	vanilla extract	5 mL
⅔ cup	plain yogurt (not fat-free)	150 mL

1. In a saucepan, combine pineapple, mangos, papaya, brown sugar, pineapple juice and lime juice; bring to a boil over medium heat, stirring gently until sugar is dissolved. Reduce heat and simmer, stirring occasionally, for about 10 minutes or until fruit is tender and liquid is syrupy. Remove from heat and stir in lime zest. Let cool to room temperature.

2. *Prepare the cake:* In a bowl, combine flour, ginger, baking powder, baking soda, salt and allspice. Set aside.

Variation

Add 2 tbsp (25 mL) dark rum or brandy to the fruit mixture just before assembling the cake.

3. In a separate bowl, using an electric mixer, beat brown sugar and butter until fluffy. Beat in egg and vanilla until blended. Stir in flour mixture alternately with yogurt, making 3 additions of flour and 2 of yogurt.

4. Arrange fruit decoratively in bottom of prepared pan and pour in syrup. Gently drop batter by spoonfuls over fruit and carefully smooth top.

5. Bake in preheated oven for 50 to 60 minutes or until a tester inserted in the center comes out clean. Let cool in pan on a wire rack for 10 minutes. Invert a large plate on top of cake pan and flip over to unmold cake onto plate. If necessary, rearrange fruit on top of cake. Serve warm or let cool completely.

Berry-Studded Angel Food Cake

Light, fluffy angel food cake gets a flavor lift with the addition of dried berries. Top each slice with a spoonful of sweetened whipped cream for a heavenly dessert.

Serves 10 to 12

Tips

Cake-and-pastry flour is a soft, lower-protein flour that makes delicate cakes. You may find flour labeled just "cake flour," and you can use this interchangeably. It tends to clump, so to get an accurate amount, it is essential to sift before spooning it into the measuring cup.

Be sure the bowl and beaters are very clean and dry before adding egg whites. Any trace of oil or fat will prevent the whites from beating to a stiff meringue, and you won't get a light, airy cake.

- *Preheat oven to 350°F (180°C)*
- *Steamer basket or heatproof sieve*
- *10-inch (4 L) tube pan, ungreased*

¼ cup	dried blueberries	50 mL
¼ cup	dried raspberries	50 mL
¼ cup	dried strawberry slices	50 mL
1 cup	sifted cake-and-pastry flour (see tip, at left)	250 mL
1½ cups	granulated sugar, divided	375 mL
½ tsp	salt	2 mL
1½ cups	egg whites (about 11), at room temperature	375 mL
1½ tsp	cream of tartar	7 mL
1 tsp	vanilla extract	5 mL

1. In steamer basket set over a saucepan of simmering water, steam blueberries and raspberries, covered, for about 10 minutes or until very soft and plump. Transfer to a plate lined with paper towels and let cool.

2. In the same steamer basket, steam strawberries, covered, for about 10 minutes or until very soft and plump. Transfer to a cutting board and chop into small pieces; add to plate with other berries. Set aside.

3. In a bowl, using a dry fine-mesh sieve, sift together flour, ¾ cup (175 mL) of the sugar and the salt. Sift into another bowl and then back into the original bowl (sifting a total of 3 times).

4. In a large metal or glass bowl, using an electric mixer, beat egg whites until foamy. Beat in cream of tartar until egg whites thicken. Gradually beat in the remaining sugar in a thin, steady stream. Continue to beat just until stiff, glossy peaks form.

5. Sift one-third of the flour mixture over egg whites. Using a rubber spatula, gently fold in just until blended. Repeat with the remaining flour mixture in 2 more additions. Fold in vanilla.

Tip

Angel food cake freezes well. Wrap in plastic wrap, then overwrap in foil or place in an airtight container and freeze for up to 3 months. Thaw for a few hours at room temperature before serving.

6. Pour about one-quarter of the batter into tube pan. Sprinkle with half the berries. Pour half the remaining batter over berries, smoothing top. Sprinkle with the remaining berries, then pour the remaining batter over top. Gently run a narrow spatula or a knife through the batter to remove any large air pockets. Smooth top.

7. Bake in preheated oven for about 40 minutes or until top is golden and springs back when lightly touched. Immediately invert pan onto a wire rack, perching on the rim of the pan or placing the tube over an inverted funnel to lift cake in the air, if necessary. Let cool completely. Gently run a knife around the edge of the cake and press bottom through to remove ring. Invert cake onto a serving platter and carefully remove the bottom and tube section, letting cake drop onto platter.

Tropical Fruit Compote

Fruit compote is essentially just fruit simmered with liquid and sugar, but "compote" makes it sound so much fancier! Serve it on its own, in a bowl with crisp cookies or spooned over shortcakes or ice cream.

Serves 4

Variations

For extra island flair, add 1 to 2 tbsp (15 to 25 mL) dark rum with the vanilla.

Add 1 slice dried gingerroot with the fruit for extra zing; discard before adding the vanilla.

1½ cups	chopped mixed dried tropical fruit (pineapple, papaya, mangos, kiwifruit, melons)	375 mL
2 tbsp	packed brown sugar or liquid honey	25 mL
1½ cups	unsweetened pineapple juice, apple juice or mango nectar	375 mL
½ tsp	vanilla extract	2 mL

1. In a saucepan, combine fruit, brown sugar and juice; bring to a boil over medium heat. Reduce heat and simmer, stirring often, for about 10 minutes or until fruit is tender and liquid is slightly syrupy.

2. Remove from heat and stir in vanilla. Let cool slightly and serve warm, or let cool completely.

Rhubarb Peach Compote

Fresh rhubarb is usually reserved for spring and early summer, but dried rhubarb shines at any time of year, especially when combined with fragrant peaches. Serve this simple, saucy dessert with shortbread cookies or spooned over ice cream.

Serves 4

1 cup	dried peach slices	250 mL
¼ cup	dried rhubarb slices	50 mL
1 cup	unsweetened orange juice or peach nectar	250 mL
½ cup	water	125 mL
¼ cup	granulated sugar	50 mL

1. In a saucepan, combine peaches, rhubarb, juice and water; let stand for 30 minutes or until slightly softened.

2. Stir in sugar and bring to a boil over medium heat. Reduce heat and boil gently, stirring occasionally, for about 8 minutes or until fruit is plump and tender and liquid is slightly syrupy. Let cool slightly and serve warm, or let cool completely.

Lavender Custard

A versatile custard is even better when it's infused with home-dried lavender. The delicate floral flavor works wonderfully with the sweet cream.

Makes about 1¹⁄₂ cups (375 mL)

Tips

Use this custard as the base for a fruit tart. It works particularly well with strawberries, apples or citrus.

Fold a little whipped cream into the cooled custard and use to garnish pies or shortcake.

Thin with a little more cream and drizzle on plates for a dessert garnish.

1¹⁄₂ cups	table (18%) cream	375 mL
3	egg yolks	3
¹⁄₃ cup	granulated sugar	75 mL
2 tbsp	all-purpose flour	25 mL
1 tsp	dried lavender flowers	5 mL
1 tbsp	butter	15 mL
1 tsp	vanilla extract	5 mL

1. Place cream in a glass measuring cup and microwave on Medium (50%) power for about 3 minutes or just until steaming (or heat in a saucepan over medium heat, stirring often).

2. In a heavy-bottomed saucepan, whisk together egg yolks and sugar until pale. Whisk in flour and lavender. Set pan over medium heat and gradually whisk in heated cream. Bring almost to a boil, whisking constantly. Reduce heat to medium-low and cook, whisking constantly, for about 5 minutes or until thickened.

3. Strain through a fine-mesh sieve into a cool bowl, discarding lavender. Stir in butter and vanilla until butter is melted. Place plastic wrap directly on surface of custard and refrigerate for at least 4 hours, until chilled, or for up to 1 day.

Dried Cherry Rice Pudding

Short-grain rice creates a luscious, creamy pudding that is a far cry from the stodgy boarding school versions of old. With the addition of dried cherries, it becomes a dessert fit for company.

Serves 4 to 6

Tip

You'll need to use a deep saucepan because the milk mixture bubbles up while the rice is simmering. If your stove doesn't go low enough to keep the rice at a gentle simmer and the food seems to be sticking to the bottom, use a simmer plate to diffuse the heat or occasionally remove the pan from the burner to cool it off.

Variation

Add 2 tbsp (25 mL) finely chopped dried pears or apples with the cherries and add a pinch of freshly grated nutmeg.

½ cup	short-grain white rice (such as Arborio)	125 mL
¼ cup	dried cherries (sour or sweet), chopped if large	50 mL
¼ cup	granulated sugar	50 mL
¼ tsp	salt	1 mL
¼ tsp	ground cinnamon	1 mL
1½ cups	milk (approx.)	375 mL
1 cup	table (18%) or whipping (35%) cream	250 mL
1 tsp	vanilla extract	5 mL

1. In a deep saucepan, combine rice, cherries, sugar, salt, cinnamon, milk and cream; bring to a simmer over medium heat, stirring often. Reduce heat to low, cover and simmer gently, stirring occasionally, for about 25 minutes or until rice is very tender. Be careful the milk doesn't burn on the bottom.

2. Stir in vanilla. Let cool slightly and serve warm. The pudding will thicken considerably upon standing. To thin, if desired, stir in a little more milk before serving.

PART 3

Cooking on the Trail with Dehydrated Foods

Everything You Need to Know About Camp Food

About the Recipes

With a little advance planning, making your own camp food is really easy. There are many packaged products on the market, and you can buy a wide array of ready-mixed dried foods at outdoor stores. Of course, the quality varies greatly between brands — and so does the price. As with anything you make from scratch, by preparing camp food with your own dried products you can control exactly what ingredients you add and be sure you'll like the flavor. With these recipes, you don't have to sacrifice quality and taste for convenience. You can have it all!

The recipes in this section take advantage of convenient dried ingredients to make tasty, nutritious and quick foods with a minimum of work. Many of them require only the addition of water to be ready to serve, so they're perfect for the campsite, cottage, cabin or roadside meal.

We've taken fuel efficiency into consideration, and in many of the recipes you'll start by soaking the ingredients in cold water to get the rehydration started, then heat and cook for a minimum amount of time. If time is of the essence, you can usually heat the food right away and cook it a little longer, rather than cold-soaking. We've noted recipes where this won't work well.

For many recipes, we have provided amounts for one serving, and you can multiply as necessary to make the number of servings you need. Multiple amounts of dry ingredients can be mixed together in the same bags or containers; just keep in mind that you'll need a pan large enough to cook the larger amount of food.

We do use a few commercially prepared dried ingredients. Instant skim milk powder and powdered eggs are readily available, convenient and of far better quality than anything you can make at home. In combination with your own dried foods, these convenience foods make packing supplies and preparing recipes a breeze.

The most important thing is to plan ahead. Make sure you have enough food for the entire trip and all of the equipment you'll need to prepare it. Read the recipes before you leave home and bring the serving and cooking instructions with you. Then savor your made-from-scratch camp meals!

Equipment

In general, these recipes were designed to use small camping-style saucepans and skillets, to keep your equipment needs at a minimum.

Essential

- Small saucepan with lid: A 2-cup (500 mL) pan will work for the single portions of these recipes. If you don't have a lid, pack some foil to cover the pan when necessary. It can usually be wiped off and reused multiple times.
- Small skillet with lid: You'll need one that's about 6 inches (15 cm) in diameter to prepare single servings or a larger one if you're cooking for more. A cast-iron skillet is particularly helpful if you plan to cook over a wood fire, because it holds the heat well, but you certainly won't want one if you're toting your supplies in a backpack. A skillet can always sub in for a saucepan, but some things (like pancakes) won't work in a saucepan; if you can only bring one vessel, choose the skillet.
- Wooden or other heatproof spoon or spatula
- Paring knife and/or small serrated knife
- Measuring cup for water: Bring a plastic liquid measuring cup or mark measures on a water bottle with permanent marker before you leave home.
- Camp stove: Though a wood fire will work for most cooking, it helps to pack a small portable burner to make sure you can still heat your food if you can't make a fire. There's always the risk of bad weather, wet wood or restrictions on burning.

Optional (But Very Helpful)

- Metal or foil baking pan: Make sure it is fire-safe and uncoated (not a nonstick surface) and bring foil to wrap it in after it's been over a fire to protect your other gear from the soot (it's tricky to wash it all off).
- Cast-iron griddle that goes over a campfire or camp stove: This works well for cooking larger portions of pancakes, biscuits and pan breads.
- Bowls or containers with tight-fitting lids: These are handy when ingredients need to be soaked in water before cooking. By using a bowl, you won't tie up your saucepan, which you may need for other things.
- Pancake flipper

Things to Consider When Meal Planning

Will there be potable running water available?
No: Choose recipes that require the least amount of water to prepare. Pack enough water for each recipe you plan to cook, plus what you'll need to drink and extra in case of spillage.
Yes: You can bring foods that require larger quantities of water. Pack a jug or bottle to tote the water from the source to your site.

Do you plan to cook solely over a wood campfire?
Yes: Choose recipes that require as little cooking time as possible, and some that don't require any cooking at all, just in case a fire isn't possible or takes too long to get hot.

Is there a cooler or refrigeration available?
Yes: You can bring some fresh ingredients to combine with the dried foods.
No: Make sure all of the ingredients you pack are non-perishable at room temperature for the length of time you'll be toting them.

Do you have to tote everything in your backpack?
Yes: Choose recipes that indicate "just add water"; that provide the most amount of energy with the least bulk (e.g., grains versus potatoes and pasta); and that can be made in the same saucepan or skillet for the entire trip.

Will you be hiking, climbing or paddling all day?
Yes: Choose high-energy foods, particularly for breakfast and lunch, and pack snacks that don't require cooking to eat between mealtimes.

Packaging, Storing and Transporting

- For ease and space efficiency, sealable bags are good for short-term ingredient storage; however, bags can allow minute amounts of air and moisture transfer, so they're not recommended for longer storage. If you make a larger batch of mixed dried ingredients and want to store it for longer than 1 month, store it in a glass jar or airtight plastic container and transfer to the sealable bag or smaller container as you pack for your trip.
- You can place small sealable bags together in one larger sealable bag or an airtight container, but be sure not to pack foods with strong flavors and aromas in the same container with milder-flavored foods (e.g., keep onions in a separate container from your pancake mix).
- On a small piece of paper, jot the ingredients, the amount of water you'll need to prepare the recipe and the basic gist of the cooking instructions. Staple it to the bag (above the seal) so it's right where you need it when it's time to cook.
- Pack a separate sealable bag with seasonings and condiments such as salt and pepper, a small plastic bottle of vegetable oil (if necessary) and packets of

ketchup, soy sauce, mustard, jam, honey and sugar, just in case. A few condiments can go a long way in perking up flavors.

- Plan the meals for your trip and pack food in reverse order of when you'll need it. Keep the equipment and condiments on top, since you'll need them each time.

Tips for Group Meals

If you're camping with a large group, there are different ways to approach the task of preparing and packing meals for the trip. A group effort is likely easier than everyone packing their own food individually.

One approach is to delegate each meal to a different person or family. They can gather and pack all the dried items necessary for each dish they're responsible for preparing. Do the math in advance: if a recipe feeds four, and you have 12 people, you'll need to triple every ingredient in the recipe. It's much easier for one person to prepare a large recipe than it is for three people to prepare the recipe individually.

Another approach is to assign different people to dry larger amounts of specific items, rather than having everyone dry a little bit of each. Decide on the menu and plan well ahead, at the beginning of the harvest season. Then divide up the items for each person or family to dry. For instance, one person or family can do all of the carrots, onions and potatoes, another can do the meats and other vegetables, and someone else can do the fruits and grains. Keep seasonality in mind and make sure that one person (or part of the group) won't be overwhelmed by the need to dry everything on their list all at once. Once you've dried enough ingredients, gather everyone together and package the recipes for the trip. Working together turns a rather mundane activity into an event. (This can work even if you're not taking a trip: it can be fun to gather a group together to pack up meals to make at home.)

Menu Plans

By taking the time to prepare and plan for your camping trip, you can make sure that all of your meals are easy to find, easy to prepare, satisfying and delicious. Some trips require a very tight timeline to reach your destinations before dark or to rendezvous at a specific time and place. A well-planned menu can remove some of the time-management challenges that a day in the wilderness or on the road can present.

Don't forget, just because you're cooking in the bush or on the road, food doesn't need to be inferior to what you'd eat at home. Bring small containers of sea salt, a pepper grinder and some hot pepper flakes for seasoning. Find compromises as far as weight goes. If you're backpacking, pick one or two things you can live without, such as an alarm clock or an extra book, and trade them in for some good Parmesan cheese (it's hard, dry and travels fairly well in cool weather) or a small plastic bottle of olive oil. Bring maple sugar granules to sprinkle on your porridge, or dried bananas, raisins and coconut flakes for garnishes on curry night. If you're traveling by canoe or kayak rather than on foot, it will be easier to carry a greater variety of food, but do keep in mind any possible portages!

When packing for your trip, put the ingredients for each recipe into labeled sealable plastic bags, then put the recipe bags for each meal into larger sealable bags labeled Breakfast 1, Lunch 1, etc. Organize the bags by days, packing the last day's food at the bottom of your pack and working your way up to the first day. Keep one bag with all of your condiments handy at the top.

For the following menus, we've assumed that you will eat your first prepared meal on the first evening, but it's very easy to adjust the order to accommodate your schedule. And, of course, these recipes are just suggestions. Substitute recipes you prefer, but do keep in mind flavor and texture balance and the equipment you'll have at the campsite.

Light Camping

Here are two menu plans for a variety of easily prepared meals that provide high amounts of energy for hitting the trails, tackling the river or scaling the cliffs. For light camping, we've kept equipment, preparation and stove use to a minimum, taking into consideration that you're likely cooking on a single-burner stove or over a campfire.

If you're wilderness camping, take along a strong waterproof bag that can be used to hang your food from a tree or a pole to prevent animals from raiding your pantry.

2-Day Menu

Supper 1:	Smoked Sausage Risotto (page 300)
	Citrus Marinated Chickpea Salad (page 305)
	Raspberry Chocolate Pudding (page 329)
Breakfast 1:	Brown Rice, Maple and Berry Porridge (page 257)
	Cottage Cheese Breakfast Biscuits (page 253)
Lunch 1:	Hearty Minestrone Soup (page 260)
	Sesame Teriyaki Veggie Trail Mix (page 319)
	Tropical Fruit Compote (page 331)
Supper 2:	Cajun Shrimp and Rice (page 296)
	Warm Broccoli, Leek and Raisin Salad (page 304)
	Cheese and Herb Skillet Biscuits (page 316)
	Campfire Apple Crumble (page 325)
Breakfast 2:	Granola Pancakes (page 249)
	Warm Peaches with Ginger (page 330)
Lunch 2:	Almost-Instant Mac and Cheese (page 288)
	No-Bake Blueberry Cheesecakes (page 326)

5-Day Menu

Supper 1:	Chicken and Potato Stew (page 270)
	Broccoli and Cottage Cheese Gratin (page 307)
	Banana Peanut Butter S'mores (page 324)
Breakfast 1:	Scrambled Huevos Rancheros (page 244)
Lunch 1:	Peppered Beef and Noodles (page 276)
	Sesame Teriyaki Veggie Trail Mix (page 319)
Supper 2:	Vegetable Bean Chili (page 266)
	Chili Cornmeal Cakes (page 315)
	Fruit-Studded Bannock on a Stick (page 323)
Breakfast 2:	Blueberry Pancakes (page 250)
Lunch 2:	Moroccan Couscous with Chickpeas (page 301)
	Wasabi Tofu and Vegetable Trail Mix (page 321)
Supper 3:	Tex-Mex Beef Fajitas (page 279)
	Spanish Brown Rice (page 314)
	Pumpkin Pie Pudding (page 327)
Breakfast 3:	Wake Up! Omelets (page 245)
	Campfire Hash Browns (page 248)
Lunch 3:	Wheat Berries Parmesan (page 302)
	Brown Rice, Apple and Cranberry Salad (page 306)
	GORP with a Twist (page 318)
Supper 4:	Teriyaki Tofu Stir-Fry (page 277)
	Egg Noodles with Teriyaki Veggies (page 313)
	Apple Spice Rice Pudding (page 328)
Breakfast 4:	Brown Rice, Maple and Berry Porridge (page 257)
Lunch 4:	One-Pot Simple Spaghetti (page 290)
	Jerky 'n' Veg Trail Mix (page 320)
	Tropical Fruit Compote (page 331)
Supper 5:	Lemon Honey Garlic Chicken (page 287)
	Stovetop Scalloped Potatoes (page 309)
	Moroccan Braised Beans and Lentils (page 311)
	Campfire Apple Crumble (page 325)
Breakfast 5:	Jerked Beef Hash with Potatoes and Peppers (page 247)
Lunch 5:	Tofu, Vegetable and Fruit Curry (page 273)
	Warm Peaches with Ginger (page 330)

Heavy Camping

When you're traveling by car, canoe, horse, motorcycle, RV or boat, or setting up camp once and staying put, you have a little more flexibility in your menu planning than if you're carrying all of your food and equipment on your back. It's easier to bring along an extra pot for cooking more than one dish at a time or a cooler to include fresh ingredients like meat, chicken, milk and eggs to mix in with your dried items. A good option is to do some baking ahead and freeze items like the Apple and Dried Plum Loaf (page 199), which you can use as an ice block until it has thawed and then enjoy on the second or third day of your trip.

It's also likely that you can bring along a more sophisticated camp stove with multiple burners. If you're using an RV or a boat, you may have a barbecue that you can use as an oven, if desired.

These menus include dried and fresh items in combination. Menu suggestions designated with an asterisk (*) are recipes from Part 2 that can be made ahead and packaged to bring along. Plan on consuming fresh or premade items early in your trip and save the recipes that use only dried foods for later on.

2-Day Menu

Supper 1:	Curried Chicken with Apples (page 274) *or* barbecued chicken
	Moroccan Braised Beans and Lentils (page 311)
	Pumpkin Pie Pudding (page 327)
Breakfast 1:	Strawberry Pan Bread (page 255)
	Peanut Banana Chews* (page 183)
Lunch 1:	Beef and Barley Soup (page 262)
	Cheese and Herb Skillet Biscuits (page 316)
	Tropical Fruit Compote (page 331)
Supper 2:	Catch of the Day Foil-Packet Fish (page 283)
	Easy Mushroom Risotto (page 298)
	Warm Broccoli, Leek and Raisin Salad (page 304)
	Campfire Apple Crumble (page 325)
Breakfast 2:	Sweet Cornmeal Pancakes (page 251) with Berry Sauce (page 332)
Lunch 2:	Beef Stroganoff (page 275)
	Warm Peaches with Ginger (page 330)

7-Day Menu

Supper 1:	Chicken à la King (page 285)
	Broccoli and Cottage Cheese Gratin (page 307)
	Intense Chocolate Banana Brownies* (page 209)
Breakfast 1:	Cinnamon Apple Multigrain Porridge (page 258)
	Cranberry Pecan Muffins* (page 189)
Lunch 1:	Veggie Pasta (page 291)
	Black Forest Cookies* (page 203)
Supper 2:	Tex-Mex Beef Fajitas (optional: use fresh steaks) (page 279)
	Cajun Rice and Black Beans (page 295)
	Banana Peanut Butter S'mores (page 324)
Breakfast 2:	Cornbread Johnny Cakes (page 252)
	Tropical Fruit Compote (page 331)
Lunch 2:	Teriyaki Tofu Stir-Fry (page 277)
	Mixed dried fruit or fresh fruit
Supper 3:	Venison Chili (page 269)
	Potatoes "Anna" and Onion Gratin (page 310)
	Apple and Dried Plum Loaf* (page 199)
Breakfast 3:	Wake Up! Omelets (page 245)
	Campfire Hash Browns (page 248)
Lunch 3:	Chicken Noodle Soup (page 261)
	GORP with a Twist (page 318)
Supper 4:	Shrimp and Herb Pasta (page 292)
	Warm Broccoli, Leek and Raisin Salad (page 304)
	Apple Spice Rice Pudding (page 328)
Breakfast 4:	Jerked Beef Hash with Potatoes and Peppers (page 247)
Lunch 4:	No-Luck Corn Chowder (page 265)
	Jerky 'n' Veg Trail Mix (page 320)
	No-Bake Blueberry Cheesecakes (page 326)

continued on next page

Supper 5:	Smoked Sausage Risotto (page 300)
	Citrus-Marinated Chickpea Salad (page 305)
	Raspberry Chocolate Pudding (page 329)
Breakfast 5:	Scrambled Huevos Rancheros (page 244)
	Mexican Tortilla Triangles* (page 178)
Lunch 5:	Almost-Instant Mac and Cheese (page 288)
	Warm Peaches with Ginger (page 330)
Supper 6:	Tofu, Lentil and Peanut Stovetop "Meatloaf" (page 280)
	Jerky and Vegetable Pasta Salad (page 293)
	Campfire Apple Crumble (page 325)
Breakfast 6:	Blueberry Pancakes (page 250)
	Tropical Fruit Compote (page 331)
Lunch 6:	Hearty Minestrone Soup (page 260)
	Cottage Cheese Breakfast Biscuits (page 253)
Supper 7:	Orange and Sweet Pepper Chicken (page 286)
	Moroccan Braised Beans and Lentils (page 311)
	Fruit-Studded Bannock on a Stick (page 323)
Breakfast 7:	Banana Nut Oatmeal (page 256)
Lunch 7:	Chipotle Beef Chili (page 268)
	Cornbread Johnny Cakes (page 252)

Breakfast

Scrambled Huevos Rancheros

You won't believe that a few simple ingredients mixed with a little water can taste so good until you try it. Add more vegetables if you've got them on hand.

Serves 1

Tip

If desired, toast tortilla wedges in a dry skillet over medium heat or over a campfire before cooking the eggs.

Variation

In place of fresh eggs, use 2 tbsp (25 mL) powdered eggs and add them to the bag with the leather when you prep at home. Add 3 tbsp (45 mL) extra water when softening the leather mixture.

Prep at Home

1	2-inch (5 cm) square Salsa Leather	1
1 tbsp	dried cooked black beans	15 mL
1	small flour tortilla, cut into wedges	1

To Serve

2 tbsp	water	25 mL
2	eggs (see variation, at left)	2
	Vegetable oil	

Prep at Home

1. Tear leather into very small pieces. In a sealable plastic bag, combine leather and beans. Seal and store at room temperature for up to 1 month. Place tortilla wedges in another bag; seal and store at room temperature for up to 5 days.

To Serve

1. In a bowl, pour water over the leather mixture. Let soak for about 15 minutes or until leather starts to soften. Using a fork, whisk in eggs until blended.

2. In a skillet, heat a thin layer of oil over medium-low heat. Add egg mixture and cook, stirring, for about 2 minutes or until eggs are just set. Serve eggs with tortilla wedges.

Wake Up! Omelets

This breakfast will give your day a terrific kick-start. Add some toast and a piece of fruit on the side, and you'll be raring to go.

Serves 1

Tip

Use scissors to snip tomatoes, chile peppers and onions into very small pieces.

Prep at Home

2 tbsp	powdered eggs	25 mL
1 tsp	finely chopped dried tomatoes	5 mL
1 tsp	finely chopped dried hot chile peppers	5 mL
1 tsp	finely chopped dried onions	5 mL
1 tsp	crumbled dried parsley	5 mL
Pinch	chili powder	Pinch
Pinch	ground cumin	Pinch
Pinch	salt	Pinch

To Serve

⅓ cup	water	75 mL
	Vegetable oil	

Prep at Home

1. In a sealable plastic bag, combine eggs, tomatoes, chile peppers, onions, parsley, chili powder, cumin and salt. Seal and store at room temperature for up to 1 month.

To Serve

1. In a bowl, combine egg mixture and water. Let stand for 15 minutes or until vegetables are softened. Using a fork, whisk until frothy.

2. In a skillet, heat a thin layer of oil over medium-low heat. Add egg mixture and swirl to coat pan evenly. Cook, without stirring, for about 3 minutes or until eggs are just set.

> ### Fresh Addition
>
> Omit the powdered eggs when prepping at home and decrease the water to 3 tbsp (45 mL). Whisk in 2 to 3 fresh eggs after rehydrating the vegetable mixture.

Beef Jerky, Scrambled Egg and Mushroom Wrap

Need a power-packed breakfast? This is sure to satisfy even the hungriest camper.

Serves 1

Tips

If desired, warm the tortillas in the skillet before adding the oil and eggs, or wrap in foil and warm over the campfire.

Add a spoonful of Anytime Salsa (page 161) with the egg mixture when wrapping it in the tortillas.

Prep at Home

½ oz	beef jerky (any flavor), torn into small pieces	15 g
3 tbsp	powdered eggs	45 mL
1 tbsp	dried mushroom slices, crumbled	15 mL
1 tsp	snipped dried chives	5 mL
⅛ tsp	dried thyme	0.5 mL
Pinch	salt	Pinch

To Serve

6 tbsp	water	90 mL
	Vegetable oil	
2	small flour tortillas	2

Prep at Home

1. In a sealable plastic bag, combine jerky, eggs, mushrooms, chives, thyme and salt. Seal and store at room temperature for up to 1 month.

To Serve

1. In a bowl, combine jerky mixture and water. Cover and let stand for 20 minutes or until jerky and mushrooms start to soften. Using a fork, whisk until frothy.

2. In a skillet, heat a thin layer of oil over medium-low heat. Add egg mixture and cook, stirring, for about 2 minutes or until eggs are just set.

3. Spoon half the egg mixture in the center of each tortilla. Fold up bottom and fold in both sides to enclose filling.

Fresh Addition

Omit the powdered eggs when prepping at home and decrease the water to 3 tbsp (45 mL). Whisk in 3 fresh eggs after rehydrating the jerky mixture.

Jerked Beef Hash with Potatoes and Peppers

Hearty jerky and potatoes give a terrific start to a busy day of trekking or paddling.

Serves 1

Tip

This can also be cooked over a campfire. Use a foil pan or a flameproof skillet covered with foil or a lid. Place covered pan on a rack over the hot fire and cook for about 20 minutes or until potatoes are tender. Uncover and cook, stirring occasionally, for 5 to 10 minutes or until liquid is evaporated and potatoes start to brown.

Prep at Home

½ oz	Jerk Beef Jerky, torn into small pieces	15 g
½ cup	dried potato cubes	125 mL
1 tbsp	dried onion pieces	15 mL
1 tbsp	dried green bell pepper pieces	15 mL
1 tbsp	dried red bell pepper pieces	15 mL
½ tsp	crumbled dried cilantro or oregano	2 mL
⅛ tsp	salt	0.5 mL

To Serve

1¼ cups	water	300 mL

Prep at Home

1. In a sealable plastic bag, combine jerky, potatoes, onions, green and red peppers, cilantro and salt. Seal and store at room temperature for up to 1 month.

To Serve

1. In a skillet, combine jerky mixture and water. Cover and let stand for 30 minutes or until potatoes start to soften.

2. Bring to a boil over medium heat. Reduce heat to low, cover and simmer for about 15 minutes or until potatoes are soft. Uncover and simmer, increasing heat as necessary, for about 5 minutes or until liquid is evaporated and potatoes start to brown.

Campfire Hash Browns

Serve these with a side of bacon or grilled sausages for a classic campfire breakfast.

Serves 1

Tip

Turn this into a side dish for supper by adding $\frac{1}{2}$ tsp (2 mL) Cajun seasoning or $\frac{1}{4}$ tsp (1 mL) minced dried lemon zest and replace the paprika with crumbled dried dill.

• *Foil pan or flameproof skillet, with foil or lid to cover*

Prep at Home

$\frac{1}{2}$ cup	dried potato cubes	125 mL
1 tbsp	dried onion pieces	15 mL
1 tsp	crumbled dried parsley	5 mL
$\frac{1}{2}$ tsp	snipped dried chives	2 mL
$\frac{1}{4}$ tsp	salt	1 mL
$\frac{1}{4}$ tsp	pepper	1 mL
Pinch	paprika	Pinch

To Serve

1 cup	water	250 mL

Prep at Home

1. In a sealable plastic bag, combine potatoes, onions, parsley, chives, salt, pepper and paprika. Seal and store at room temperature for up to 1 month.

To Serve

1. In foil pan, combine potato mixture and water. Cover and let stand for 30 minutes or until potatoes start to soften. Meanwhile, prepare campfire.

2. Place covered pan on a rack over the hot fire and cook for about 20 minutes or until potatoes are tender. Uncover and cook, stirring occasionally, for 5 to 10 minutes or until liquid is evaporated and potatoes start to brown.

Granola Pancakes

Hearty pancakes are a terrific start to the day. You can customize the flavor by adding different fruit and spices.

Makes about 4 pancakes

Tip
To toast a small amount of nuts, in a small dry skillet over medium heat, toast chopped nuts, stirring constantly, for about 2 minutes or until fragrant. Transfer to a bowl and let cool.

Variation
If powdered eggs aren't available, substitute powdered egg replacer, using the package instructions to substitute for 1 egg. Alternatively, omit the powdered eggs when prepping at home and decrease the water to 6 tbsp (90 mL). Whisk in 1 fresh egg with the oil.

Prep at Home

2 tbsp	dried cooked grains (barley, wheat berries, whole oats, wild rice)	25 mL
2 tbsp	dried cranberries or raisins	25 mL
1/2 cup	all-purpose flour	125 mL
1 tbsp	powdered eggs	15 mL
1 tbsp	packed brown sugar	15 mL
1 tbsp	toasted finely chopped almonds or pecans	15 mL
1/2 tsp	baking powder	2 mL
1/4 tsp	ground cinnamon or nutmeg	1 mL
Pinch	salt	Pinch

To Serve

1/2 cup	water	125 mL
	Vegetable oil	

Prep at Home

1. In a mini chopper or small food processor, process grains until finely chopped and about one-quarter is powdery. Transfer to a sealable plastic bag and add cranberries. In another bag, combine flour, eggs, brown sugar, almonds, baking powder, cinnamon and salt. Seal both bags and store at room temperature for up to 1 month.

To Serve

1. In a bowl, combine grain mixture and water. Cover and let stand for 30 minutes or until grains start to soften. Stir in 1 tsp (5 mL) oil. Shake flour mixture in bag to mix and pour into grain mixture. Stir just until evenly moistened.

2. Heat a skillet over medium heat until warmed. Add a thin layer of oil. Pour in about 1/4 cup (50 mL) batter per pancake. Cook for 2 to 3 minutes or until bubbles break on the surface but don't fill in and bottom is golden. Turn and cook for about 2 minutes or until golden brown. Repeat with remaining batter, adding oil to the pan and adjusting heat as necessary.

Blueberry Pancakes

There's nothing like classic pancakes studded with your own dried blueberries to make a good camping trip even better.

Makes about 4 pancakes

Variation

If powdered eggs aren't available, substitute powdered egg replacer, using the package instructions to substitute for 1 egg. Alternatively, omit the powdered eggs when prepping at home and decrease the water to 6 tbsp (90 mL). Whisk in 1 fresh egg with the oil.

Prep at Home

½ cup	all-purpose flour	125 mL
1 tbsp	powdered eggs	15 mL
1 tbsp	instant skim milk powder	15 mL
2 tsp	granulated sugar	10 mL
½ tsp	baking powder	2 mL
Pinch	salt	Pinch
2 tbsp	dried blueberries, chopped	25 mL

To Serve

½ cup	water	125 mL
	Vegetable oil	

Prep at Home

1. In a sealable plastic bag, combine flour, eggs, milk powder, sugar, baking powder and salt. Place blueberries in another bag. Seal both bags and store at room temperature for up to 1 month.

To Serve

1. In a bowl, combine blueberries and water. Let stand for 15 minutes or until blueberries are softened. Stir in 1 tsp (5 mL) oil. Shake flour mixture in bag to mix and pour into blueberry mixture. Stir just until evenly moistened.

2. Heat a skillet over medium heat until warmed. Add a thin layer of oil. Pour in about ¼ cup (50 mL) batter per pancake. Cook for 2 to 3 minutes or until bubbles break on the surface but don't fill in and bottom is golden. Turn and cook for about 2 minutes or until golden brown. Repeat with remaining batter, adding oil to the pan and adjusting heat as necessary.

Sweet Cornmeal Pancakes

With a slather of jam, a drizzle of syrup or simply on their own, these delightful pancakes are sure to start your day off right.

**Makes about
4 pancakes**

Variations

If powdered eggs aren't available, substitute powdered egg replacer, using the package instructions to substitute for 1 egg. Alternatively, omit the powdered eggs when prepping at home and decrease the water to 6 tbsp (90 mL). Whisk in 1 fresh egg with the oil.

Add 2 tbsp (25 mL) chopped dried fruit or berries with the corn.

Prep at Home

2 tbsp	dried corn kernels	25 mL
1/2 cup	all-purpose flour	125 mL
2 tbsp	cornmeal	25 mL
1 tbsp	granulated sugar	15 mL
1 tbsp	powdered eggs	15 mL
1 tbsp	instant skim milk powder	15 mL
1/2 tsp	baking powder	2 mL
Pinch	salt	Pinch

To Serve

1/2 cup	water	125 mL
	Vegetable oil	

Prep at Home

1. In a mini chopper or small food processor, process corn until finely chopped. Transfer to a sealable plastic bag. In another bag, combine flour, cornmeal, sugar, eggs, milk powder, baking powder and salt. Seal both bags and store at room temperature for up to 1 month.

To Serve

1. In a bowl, combine corn and water. Cover and let stand for 20 minutes or until corn is tender. Stir in 1 tsp (5 mL) oil. Shake flour mixture in bag to mix and pour into corn mixture. Stir just until evenly moistened.

2. Heat a skillet over medium heat until warmed. Add a thin layer of oil. Pour in about 1/4 cup (50 mL) batter per pancake. Cook for 2 to 3 minutes or until bubbles break on the surface but don't fill in and bottom is golden. Turn and cook for about 2 minutes or until golden brown. Repeat with remaining batter, adding oil to the pan and adjusting heat as necessary.

Fresh Addition

Fry an egg and sandwich it between two pancakes for a heartier breakfast. Drizzle the egg with a little ketchup, if desired.

Cornbread Johnny Cakes

This traditional simple cake was introduced to early settlers by Native North Americans. There are many theories about the origin of the name, but it is most commonly said to be a derivation of "journey cakes" or "Shawnee cakes." We've added fruit and spice to liven up the flavor.

Serves 1 or 2

Tip

Serve topped with Berry Sauce (page 332) or Tropical Fruit Compote (page 331), or simply with a drizzle of honey or maple syrup.

Variation

Substitute chopped dried apples or blueberries for the cherries.

• *6- to 8-inch (15 to 20 cm) nonstick or cast-iron skillet*

Prep at Home

1 cup	cornmeal	250 mL
1 tbsp	packed brown sugar	15 mL
1 tsp	baking powder	5 mL
¼ tsp	salt	1 mL
¼ tsp	ground ginger	1 mL
¼ cup	dried corn kernels	50 mL
1 tbsp	dried sweet cherries, chopped	15 mL

To Serve

1 cup	water	250 mL
	Vegetable oil	

Prep at Home

1. In a sealable plastic bag, combine cornmeal, brown sugar, baking powder, salt and ginger. Place corn and cherries in another bag. Seal both bags and store at room temperature for up to 1 month.

To Serve

1. In a saucepan, bring water to a boil over high heat. Remove from heat and add corn mixture. Cover and let stand for about 10 minutes or until corn is softened. Shake cornmeal mixture in bag to mix and pour into corn mixture. Using a fork, stir just until evenly moistened. Let stand for 10 minutes.

2. Meanwhile, heat skillet over medium-low heat until warm. Add a thin layer of oil. Spread the batter in skillet. Reduce heat to low, cover and cook for about 5 minutes or until bottom is golden brown. Flip cake and cook, uncovered, for about 2 minutes or until browned. Cut into quarters and serve hot.

Cottage Cheese Breakfast Biscuits

Sweet biscuits studded with fruit are a nice change from cereal in the morning. Any extras can be packed along and eaten with a slice of cheese or a smear of nut butter for a snack.

Makes 4 biscuits

Tip

These can be cooked over a campfire. Just heat the pan on a rack over the hottest part of the fire, then move it to the cooler edge to cook the biscuits. The timing will depend on the fire, so keep an eye on them.

- 6- to 8-inch (15 to 20 cm) skillet, preferably cast-iron, with lid or foil to cover

Prep at Home

¾ cup	all-purpose flour	175 mL
2 tbsp	powdered dried cottage cheese	25 mL
2 tbsp	granulated sugar	25 mL
1 tsp	baking powder	5 mL
½ tsp	ground cinnamon or ginger	2 mL
¼ tsp	salt	1 mL
¼ cup	chopped dried fruit (apples, pears, peaches, cherries, berries)	50 mL

To Serve

⅔ cup	water	150 mL
	Vegetable oil or butter	

Prep at Home

1. In a sealable plastic bag, combine flour, cottage cheese, sugar, baking powder, cinnamon and salt. Seal and store at room temperature for up to 1 week or in the refrigerator for up to 6 months. Place fruit in another bag; seal and store at room temperature for up to 6 months.

To Serve

1. In a bowl, combine fruit and water. Cover and let stand for 15 minutes or until fruit is softened.

2. Meanwhile, heat skillet over medium heat until warmed.

3. Shake flour mixture in bag to mix and pour into fruit mixture. Using a fork, stir just until evenly moistened.

4. Add a thin layer of oil to skillet. Spoon dough into 4 mounds in skillet. Reduce heat to low, cover and cook for 3 minutes. Uncover and cook for about 1 minute or until bottoms are golden brown and edges are no longer shiny. Flip over and cook for about 2 minutes or until biscuits are puffed and firm. Serve hot.

Jerky, Cheese and Dried Tomato Biscuits

Savory biscuits add new life to breakfast. They're satisfying on their own and also make a nice change from toast, served with scrambled eggs or an omelet.

Makes 4 biscuits

Tip

Let extra biscuits cool and seal in a plastic bag for a snack later in the day. Wrap in foil and heat over a campfire to refresh them.

- 6- to 8-inch (15 to 20 cm) skillet, preferably cast-iron, with lid or foil to cover

Prep at Home

½ oz	beef or other meat jerky (any flavor), broken into very small pieces	15 g
1 tbsp	finely chopped dried tomatoes	15 mL
1 tsp	crumbled dried parsley	5 mL
1 tsp	crumbled dried basil or oregano	5 mL
¾ cup	whole wheat flour	175 mL
2 tbsp	powdered dried cottage cheese	25 mL
2 tsp	granulated sugar	10 mL
1 tsp	baking powder	5 mL
¼ tsp	salt	1 mL

To Serve

½ cup	water	125 mL
	Vegetable oil or butter	

Prep at Home

1. In a sealable plastic bag, combine jerky, tomatoes, parsley and basil. In a separate bag, combine flour, cottage cheese, sugar, baking powder and salt. Seal both bags and store at room temperature for up to 1 week or in the refrigerator for up to 6 months.

To Serve

1. In a saucepan, bring water to a boil over high heat. Remove from heat and add jerky mixture. Cover and let stand for about 30 minutes or until jerky is soft and water is cooled to room temperature.

2. Meanwhile, heat skillet over medium heat until warmed.

3. Shake flour mixture in bag to mix and pour into jerky mixture. Using a fork, stir just until evenly moistened.

4. Add a thin layer of oil to skillet. Spoon dough into 4 mounds in skillet. Reduce heat to low, cover and cook for 3 minutes. Uncover and cook for about 1 minute or until bottoms are golden brown and edges are no longer shiny. Flip over and cook for about 2 minutes or until biscuits are puffed and firm. Serve hot.

Strawberry Pan Bread

Heartier than a pancake but just as easy, this strawberry studded bread makes a nice breakfast served with yogurt and fresh fruit.

Serves 2

Tip

This can be cooked over a campfire. Just heat the pan on a rack over the hottest part of the fire, then move it to the cooler edge to cook the bread. The timing will depend on the fire, so peek under the lid frequently (but don't lift it off).

- 6- to 8-inch (15 to 20 cm) skillet, preferably cast-iron, with lid or foil to cover

Prep at Home

¼ cup	all-purpose flour	50 mL
¼ cup	whole wheat flour	50 mL
1 tbsp	instant skim milk powder or buttermilk powder	15 mL
1 tbsp	packed brown sugar	15 mL
½ tsp	baking powder	2 mL
⅛ tsp	salt	0.5 mL
2 tbsp	chopped dried strawberries	25 mL
¼ tsp	finely chopped dried orange or lemon zest	1 mL

To Serve

⅓ cup	water or orange juice	75 mL
	Vegetable oil or butter	

Prep at Home

1. In a sealable plastic bag, combine all purpose and whole wheat flours, milk powder, brown sugar, baking powder and salt. Seal and store at room temperature for up to 2 weeks or in the refrigerator for up to 6 months. Place strawberries and orange zest in another bag; seal and store at room temperature for up to 6 months.

To Serve

1. In a bowl, combine strawberry mixture and water. Cover and let stand for 10 minutes or until fruit is softened.

2. Meanwhile, heat skillet over medium heat until warmed.

3. Shake flour mixture in bag to mix and pour into berry mixture. Using a fork, stir just until evenly moistened.

4. Add a thin layer of oil to skillet. Spread dough in skillet. Reduce heat to low, cover and cook for about 8 minutes or until bottom is brown and top is no longer shiny. Uncover, flip over and cook for about 1 minute or until bottom is dry. Cut into quarters and serve hot.

Banana Nut Oatmeal

Whole oats are hearty and tasty and have a more toothsome texture than rolled oats. Try them with dried bananas and pecans and you'll never go back to the instant kind.

Serves 1

Tip

Place the oat mixture in a covered bowl and measure the water before you go to sleep. When you wake up, mix them together, then get the stove ready and wash up. The soaking time will be finished before you know it, and a hot breakfast will be just minutes away.

Variation

Substitute quick-cooking rolled oats for the dried cooked whole oats. Reduce the soaking time to 15 minutes and reduce the cooking time to 2 to 3 minutes.

Prep at Home

1/3 cup	dried cooked whole oats	75 mL
1 tbsp	dried banana slices	15 mL
1 tbsp	toasted chopped pecans (see tip, page 249)	15 mL
1 tbsp	instant skim milk powder	15 mL
1 tsp	packed brown sugar (or to taste)	5 mL
Pinch	ground nutmeg (optional)	Pinch
Pinch	salt	Pinch

To Serve

1 cup	water (approx.)	250 mL

Prep at Home

1. In a mini chopper or small food processor, process oats until finely chopped and about one-quarter is powdery. Transfer to a sealable plastic bag and add bananas, pecans, milk powder, brown sugar, nutmeg (if using) and salt. Seal and store at room temperature for up to 1 month.

To Serve

1. In a saucepan, combine oat mixture and water. Cover and let stand for 30 minutes or until oats start to soften.

2. Uncover and bring to a boil over medium heat, stirring often. Reduce heat and simmer, stirring often, for about 5 minutes or until oats are tender and porridge is thickened. Thin with more water, if desired.

Apple, Cranberry and Sage Relish (page 159),
Sweet Red Pepper and Basil Vinaigrette (page 156)
and Pear, Raisin and Walnut Chutney (page 160)

Dried Cantaloupe Slices (page 27) and Honeydew Melon (page 29)

Muesli Muffins (page 193) and Blueberry Scones (page 194)

Dried Bananas (page 26),
Mangos (page 30), Figs (page 29)
and Pineapple Rings (page 31)

Strawberry Rhubarb Tarts (page 219)

Dried Strawberries (page 32) and Kiwifruit (page 29)

GORP with a Twist (page 318)

Chipotle Beef Chili (page 268)
and Chili Cornmeal Cakes (page 315)

Brown Rice, Maple and Berry Porridge

This hearty, nutritious hot cereal makes a nice change from regular oatmeal. Grinding the dried cooked rice slightly gives the cereal a creamy texture — perfect for a chilly morning.

Serves 1

Tip

You can find maple sugar granules at farmers' markets and specialty food stores. If you can't find them, use 1 tsp (5 mL) packed brown sugar or granulated sugar, or omit them for an unsweetened version.

Variation

Replace the berries with your favorite dried fruit. Try chopped figs, apples, pears, peaches or raisins.

Prep at Home

½ cup	dried cooked long-grain brown rice	125 mL
2 tbsp	dried berries, chopped if large	25 mL
2 tbsp	instant skim milk powder (optional)	25 mL
2 tsp	maple sugar granules	10 mL
Pinch	salt	Pinch

To Serve

1 cup	water	250 mL

Prep at Home

1. In a mini chopper or small food processor, process rice until finely chopped and about one-quarter is powdery. Transfer to a sealable plastic bag and add berries, milk powder (if using), maple sugar and salt. Seal and store at room temperature for up to 1 month.

To Serve

1. In a saucepan, combine rice mixture and water. Cover and let stand for 20 minutes or until rice starts to soften.

2. Uncover and bring to a boil over medium heat, stirring often. Reduce heat and simmer, stirring often, for about 5 minutes or until rice is tender and porridge is thickened.

Cinnamon Apple Multigrain Porridge

Hot cooked multigrain porridge usually takes 30 minutes or more to cook — not practical for a camp stove! Now you can get all the benefits of whole grains in a fraction of the cooking time with dried cooked whole grains.

Serves 1

Variations

Use 6 tbsp (90 mL) of any combination of dried cooked whole grains.

In place of the whole oats, substitute dried cooked steel-cut or large-flake rolled oats. Break the sheet into small pieces and grind until very finely chopped with some powder. Measure, then add the other grains and grind again.

Add 1 tbsp (15 mL) dried cranberries or blueberries and 1 tbsp (15 mL) toasted chopped almonds with the apples.

Prep at Home

2 tbsp	dried cooked whole oats	25 mL
2 tbsp	dried cooked long-grain brown rice	25 mL
1 tbsp	dried cooked wheat berries	15 mL
1 tbsp	dried cooked whole or pot barley	15 mL
1 tsp	flax seeds (whole or ground)	5 mL
2 tbsp	chopped dried apples	25 mL
1 tbsp	instant skim milk powder	15 mL
1 tsp	packed brown sugar (or to taste)	5 mL
$1/8$ tsp	ground cinnamon	0.5 mL
Pinch	salt	Pinch

To Serve

1 cup	water (approx.)	250 mL

Prep at Home

1. In a mini chopper or small food processor, process oats, rice, wheat berries, barley and flax seeds until finely chopped and about one-quarter is powdery. Transfer to a sealable plastic bag and add apples, milk powder, brown sugar, cinnamon and salt. Seal and store at room temperature for up to 1 month.

To Serve

1. In a saucepan, combine oat mixture and water. Cover and let stand for 30 minutes or until grains start to soften.

2. Uncover and bring to a boil over medium heat, stirring often. Reduce heat and simmer, stirring often, for about 5 minutes or until grains are tender and porridge is thickened. Thin with more water, if desired.

Main Courses

Hearty Minestrone Soup

This classic soup can be made with ease with your own dried ingredients. The tomato sauce leather adds a boost of flavor with little work.

Serves 1

Tip

Use a spice grinder or mini chopper to grind dried garlic slices into powder.

Prep at Home

1	1-inch (2.5 cm) square Tomato Pasta Sauce Leather	1
½ cup	dried cooked fusilli	125 mL
¼ cup	dried cooked red kidney beans or Romano beans	50 mL
2 tbsp	crumbled beef jerky (optional, any flavor)	25 mL
1 tbsp	dried carrot pieces	15 mL
1 tbsp	dried celery slices	15 mL
¼ tsp	crumbled dried basil	1 mL
Pinch	powdered dried garlic	Pinch

To Serve

1½ cups	water	375 mL

Prep at Home

1. Tear leather into small pieces. In a sealable plastic bag, combine leather, fusilli, beans, jerky (if using), carrots, celery, basil and garlic. Seal and store at room temperature for up to 1 month (or up to 6 months if jerky is not used).

To Serve

1. In a saucepan, combine vegetable mixture and water. Let stand for 15 minutes or until vegetables start to soften.

2. Bring to a boil over medium heat, stirring often. Reduce heat and boil gently, stirring often, for about 10 minutes or until vegetables are softened.

> **Fresh Addition**
>
> Top hot soup with 1 tbsp (15 mL) shredded cheese.

Chicken Noodle Soup

Even on the best camping trip, a little comfort food might be in order. Here's the chicken noodle soup that you won't believe came out of your pack.

Serves 1

Tip

Dried chicken tends to keep a toothsome texture even when rehydrated. Chopping it into very small pieces does help to soften it.

Prep at Home

1 oz	Sea Salt and Peppercorn Chicken Jerky or Cajun Chicken Jerky, finely chopped	30 g
1 tbsp	dried carrot pieces, finely chopped	15 mL
1 tbsp	dried celery slices, finely chopped	15 mL
1 tbsp	dried onion pieces, finely chopped	15 mL
1 tbsp	dried chopped parsley	15 mL
1/4 tsp	salt	1 mL
1/8 tsp	freshly ground black pepper	0.5 mL
1/4 cup	broken spaghettini	50 mL

To Serve

2 cups	water	500 mL

Prep at Home

1. In a sealable plastic bag, combine chicken, carrots, celery, onions, parsley, salt and pepper. Place spaghettini in another bag. Seal both bags and store at room temperature for up to 1 month.

To Serve

1. In a saucepan, bring water to a boil. Add chicken mixture, remove from heat, cover and let stand for 20 minutes or until chicken starts to soften.

2. Uncover and bring to a boil over medium heat, stirring often. Add spaghettini. Reduce heat and boil gently, stirring often, for about 10 minutes or until pasta is tender.

Beef and Barley Soup

Start with a flavored jerky, add a few dried vegetables and you've got a scrumptious soup to enjoy.

Serves 1

Tip

Heating the water before adding the beef mixture speeds up the soaking time and gives a better texture to the barley. If you don't want to fire up the stove twice, you can soak the mixture in cold water for about 1 hour or until the barley is softened.

Prep at Home

½ oz	Maple and Whisky Ground Beef Jerky or Southwestern Ground Beef Jerky, broken into small pieces	15 g
2 tbsp	dried cooked barley	25 mL
1 tbsp	dried carrot pieces, finely chopped	15 mL
1 tbsp	dried celery slices, finely chopped	15 mL
2 tsp	dried onion pieces or leek slices, finely chopped	10 mL
¼ tsp	crumbled dried thyme	1 mL
¼ tsp	salt	1 mL
⅛ tsp	freshly ground black pepper	0.5 mL

To Serve

2 cups	water	500 mL

Prep at Home

1. In a sealable plastic bag, combine beef, barley, carrots, celery, onions, thyme, salt and pepper. Seal and store at room temperature for up to 1 month.

To Serve

1. In a saucepan, bring water to a boil. Add beef mixture, remove from heat, cover and let stand for 20 minutes or until beef starts to soften.

2. Uncover and bring to a boil over medium heat, stirring often. Reduce heat and boil gently, stirring often, for about 10 minutes or until beef and barley are tender.

Fresh Addition

Add a dash of hot pepper sauce, Worcestershire sauce or steak sauce for an extra kick of flavor.

Hamburger Soup

The secret ingredient (instant coffee) in this one comes from Jennifer's mom, Patricia, who always added a touch to enrich the broth when she made hamburger soup. You'll be surprised at the fabulous flavor for a just-add-water soup.

Serves 1

Variation

Flavored ground meat jerky can be used in place of the ground beef. Try Herb and Garlic Ground Meat Jerky, Maple and Whisky Ground Meat Jerky, or Southwestern Ground Meat Jerky, broken into very small pieces.

Prep at Home

2 tbsp	dried cooked ground beef	25 mL
1 tbsp	finely chopped dried tomatoes	15 mL
1 tbsp	dried carrot pieces, finely chopped	15 mL
1 tbsp	dried celery slices, finely chopped	15 mL
1 tbsp	dried mushroom slices, crumbled	15 mL
1 tsp	dried onion pieces, finely chopped	5 mL
1/2 tsp	instant coffee granules	2 mL
1/4 tsp	paprika	1 mL
1/4 tsp	crumbled dried rosemary	1 mL
1/4 tsp	salt	1 mL
	Freshly ground black pepper	

To Serve

2 cups	water	500 mL

Prep at Home

1. In a sealable plastic bag, combine beef, tomatoes, carrots, celery, mushrooms, onions, coffee granules, paprika, rosemary, salt and pepper to taste. Seal and store at room temperature for up to 1 month.

To Serve

1. In a saucepan, combine beef mixture and water. Cover and let stand for 15 minutes or until vegetables start to soften.

2. Uncover and bring to a boil over medium heat, stirring often. Reduce heat and boil gently, stirring often, for about 10 minutes or until beef and vegetables are tender.

Fisherman's Chowder

This tasty fish chowder will make you proud of your catch and your cooking skills. Serve with biscuits for a hearty meal after a hard day's work.

Serves 1

Tip

Crumbled dried potato slices cook quickly and add body to the chowder. You can break them into small pieces by hand or pulse them in a mini chopper.

Variation

Pack ½ oz (15 g) dried cooked shrimp, finely chopped, to add with the potato mixture just in case you don't catch a keeper.

Prep at Home

¼ cup	crumbled dried potato slices	50 mL
1 tbsp	dried celery slices, finely chopped	15 mL
1 tbsp	dried carrot pieces, finely chopped	15 mL
1 tbsp	instant skim milk powder	15 mL
1 tbsp	all-purpose flour	15 mL
1 tsp	dried leek slices or onion pieces, finely chopped	5 mL
¼ tsp	crumbled dried thyme or rosemary	1 mL
¼ tsp	salt	1 mL
Pinch	cayenne pepper	Pinch

To Serve

2 cups	water	500 mL
1	fresh fish, filleted, skinned and cut into bite-size pieces	1

Prep at Home

1. In a sealable plastic bag, combine potatoes, celery, carrots, milk powder, flour, leeks, thyme, salt and cayenne. Seal and store at room temperature for up to 1 month.

To Serve

1. In a saucepan, combine potato mixture and water. Let stand for 15 minutes or until vegetables start to soften.

2. Bring to a boil over medium heat, stirring often. Reduce heat and boil gently, stirring often, for about 10 minutes or until vegetables are almost tender. Stir in fish, reduce heat and simmer for about 5 minutes or until fish flakes easily with a fork and vegetables are tender.

No-Luck Corn Chowder

*If the big one got away
and you had your heart
set on chowder, a
steaming bowl of this
corn version, complete
with dumplings, makes
a fine consolation prize.*

Serves 1

Tip
Don't be tempted to lift
the lid when cooking
dumplings. You need to
keep the heat and steam
in the pan for proper
cooking.

Variation
Substitute ¼ cup
(50 mL) dried sweet
potato cubes and 1 tbsp
(15 mL) dried red bell
pepper pieces for the
Sweet Potato and Red
Pepper Leather.

Prep at Home

¼ cup	crumbled Sweet Potato and Red Pepper Leather	50 mL
¼ cup	dried corn kernels	50 mL
2 tbsp	crumbled dried potato slices	25 mL
2 tbsp	instant skim milk powder	25 mL
1 tbsp	dried celery slices	15 mL
¼ tsp	crumbled dried thyme	1 mL
¼ tsp	paprika	1 mL
¼ tsp	salt	1 mL
	Freshly ground black pepper	

Dumplings

⅓ cup	all-purpose flour	75 mL
1 tbsp	instant skim milk powder	15 mL
1 tsp	crumbled dried parsley	5 mL
½ tsp	baking powder	2 mL
Pinch	salt	Pinch
Pinch	freshly ground black pepper	Pinch

To Serve

2⅓ cups	water, divided	575 mL

Prep at Home

1. In a sealable plastic bag, combine leather, corn, potatoes, milk powder, celery, thyme, paprika, salt and pepper to taste. Seal and store at room temperature for up to 1 month.

2. *For the dumplings:* In another bag, combine flour, milk powder, parsley, baking powder, salt and pepper. Seal and store at room temperature for up to 1 month.

To Serve

1. In a saucepan, combine corn mixture and 2 cups (500 mL) of the water. Let stand for 20 minutes or until corn starts to soften.

2. Bring to a boil over medium heat, stirring often. Reduce heat to low, cover and simmer, stirring occasionally, for about 15 minutes or until vegetables are almost tender.

3. Meanwhile, in a bowl, stir dumpling mixture to blend. Add the remaining water and, using a fork, stir just until moistened. Drop by spoonfuls on top of simmering chowder. Cover and simmer for about 10 minutes or until dumplings are puffed and a tester inserted in a dumpling comes out clean.

Vegetable Bean Chili

A spicy mixture of beans and vegetables, this satisfying chili is even better served over rice or with toast.

Serves 1

Tip

Chipotle pepper powder is available at well-stocked spice or bulk food stores and some supermarkets. If you can't find it, you can grind a dry chipotle pepper in a spice grinder.

Prep at Home

¼ cup	dried cooked black beans or chickpeas	50 mL
¼ cup	dried cooked kidney beans	50 mL
2 tbsp	finely chopped dried tomatoes	25 mL
1 tbsp	dried red or green bell pepper pieces	15 mL
1 tbsp	dried mushroom slices, crumbled	15 mL
1 tbsp	dried onion pieces	15 mL
¾ tsp	chili powder	3 mL
½ tsp	crumbled dried oregano	2 mL
Pinch	chipotle pepper powder	Pinch
Pinch	salt	Pinch

To Serve

1⅓ cups	water	325 mL

Prep at Home

1. In a sealable plastic bag, combine black beans, kidney beans, tomatoes, red peppers, mushrooms, onions, chili powder, oregano, chipotle powder and salt. Seal and store at room temperature for up to 1 month.

To Serve

1. In a saucepan, combine bean mixture and water. Let stand for 20 minutes or until vegetables start to soften.

2. Bring to a boil over medium heat, stirring often. Reduce heat and boil gently, stirring often, for about 10 minutes or until vegetables are soft and chili is thickened.

Fresh Addition

Serve on top of torn fresh lettuce, sprinkle with diced avocado and serve with tortilla chips for a taco salad.

Tofu Chili

You can't beat a rich-flavored chili that's warm, hearty and filling after a day of extreme trekking.

Serves 1

Tip

Barbecue sauce leather adds a deep, rich flavor to the chili. If you don't have it, increase the chili powder to 1 tsp (5 mL) and stir in some liquid barbecue sauce before serving.

Prep at Home

1	1-inch (2.5 cm) square Barbecue Sauce Leather	1
¼ cup	dried crumbled tofu	50 mL
¼ cup	dried cooked kidney or black beans	50 mL
2 tbsp	finely chopped dried tomatoes	25 mL
1 tbsp	dried grated carrots	15 mL
1 tbsp	dried onion pieces	15 mL
1 tbsp	dried celery slices	15 mL
1 tsp	crumbled dried parsley	5 mL
½ tsp	chili powder	2 mL
¼ tsp	finely chopped dried garlic	1 mL
¼ tsp	ground cumin	1 mL
¼ tsp	salt	1 mL

To Serve

1¼ cups	water	300 mL

Prep at Home

1. Tear leather into small pieces. In a sealable plastic bag, combine leather, tofu, beans, tomatoes, carrots, onions, celery, parsley, chili powder, garlic, cumin and salt. Seal and store at room temperature for up to 1 month.

To Serve

1. In a saucepan, bring water to a boil. Add leather mixture, remove from heat, cover and let stand for 15 minutes or until tofu is softened.

2. Uncover and bring to a boil over medium heat, stirring often. Boil, stirring often, for about 10 minutes or until vegetables are soft and chili is thickened.

Chipotle Beef Chili

A super-satisfying hot bowl of chili is made even better with a touch of smoky heat from the chipotles and your own dried vegetables and jerky.

Serves 1

Tip

Chipotle pepper powder is available at well-stocked spice or bulk food stores and some supermarkets. If you can't find it, you can grind a dry chipotle pepper in a spice grinder.

Prep at Home

½ oz	Cajun Beef Jerky or Southwestern Ground Beef Jerky, broken into small pieces	15 g
¼ cup	dried cooked kidney or black beans	50 mL
2 tbsp	finely chopped dried tomatoes	25 mL
1 tbsp	dried red or green bell pepper pieces	15 mL
2 tsp	dried onion pieces	10 mL
½ tsp	crumbled dried oregano	2 mL
½ tsp	chili powder	2 mL
Pinch	chipotle pepper powder	Pinch
Pinch	salt	Pinch

To Serve

1¼ cups	water	300 mL

Prep at Home

1. In a sealable plastic bag, combine beef, beans, tomatoes, red peppers, onions, oregano, chili powder, chipotle powder and salt. Seal and store at room temperature for up to 1 month.

To Serve

1. In a saucepan, combine beef mixture and water. Cover and let stand for 30 minutes or until vegetables start to soften.

2. Uncover and bring to a boil over medium heat, stirring often. Reduce heat and boil gently, stirring often, for about 15 minutes or until vegetables are soft.

> **Fresh Additions**
>
> Replace ¼ cup (50 mL) of the water with beer.
> Sprinkle with shredded Cheddar cheese or dollop with sour cream to serve.

Venison Chili

This chili has a little kick from the spices and rich venison flavor. Serve with corn cakes or tortilla chips, and this meal will make the top five list of camping memories.

Serves 1

Variation

If you don't have tomato paste leather, use 2 tbsp (25 mL) finely chopped dried tomatoes.

Prep at Home

1	2-inch (5 cm) piece Tomato Paste Leather	1
1/2 oz	Southwestern Ground Venison Jerky or Cajun Venison Jerky, broken into small pieces	15 g
1/4 cup	dried cooked chickpeas, kidney beans or black beans	50 mL
1 tbsp	dried grated carrots	15 mL
1 tbsp	dried mushroom slices, crumbled	15 mL
2 tsp	dried onion pieces	10 mL
1/2 tsp	crumbled dried oregano	2 mL
3/4 tsp	chili powder	3 mL
1/4 tsp	salt	1 mL
Pinch	hot pepper flakes	Pinch

To Serve

1 1/4 cups	water	300 mL

Prep at Home

1. Tear leather into very small pieces. In a sealable plastic bag, combine leather, venison, chickpeas, carrots, mushrooms, onions, oregano, chili powder, salt and hot pepper flakes. Seal and store at room temperature for up to 1 month.

To Serve

1. In a saucepan, combine venison mixture and water. Cover and let stand for 30 minutes, mashing leather occasionally, until vegetables start to soften.

2. Uncover and bring to a boil over medium heat, stirring often. Reduce heat and boil gently, stirring often, for about 15 minutes or until vegetables and venison are tender and chili is slightly thickened.

Fresh Addition

Top with a dollop of sour cream and some diced avocado.

Chicken and Potato Stew

A stick to your ribs stew is just what you need when there's a chill in the air and you've had an active day. This is an all-in-one meal, but a biscuit or bread on the side might be in order to sop up the sauce.

Serves 1

Variation

Substitute your favorite dried vegetables in place of the squash, carrots and celery. Just be sure to use a total of about ¼ cup (50 mL).

Prep at Home

1 oz	Maple and Grainy Dijon Chicken Jerky or Sea Salt and Peppercorn Chicken Jerky, finely chopped	30 g
¼ cup	dried potato cubes	50 mL
2 tbsp	dried winter squash cubes	25 mL
1 tbsp	dried carrot pieces	15 mL
1 tbsp	dried celery slices	15 mL
1 tbsp	all-purpose flour	15 mL
1 tsp	crumbled dried parsley	5 mL
¼ tsp	crumbled dried tarragon or thyme	1 mL
¼ tsp	salt	1 mL
	Freshly ground black pepper	

To Serve

1½ cups	water	375 mL

Prep at Home

1. In a sealable plastic bag, combine chicken, potatoes, squash, carrots, celery, flour, parsley, tarragon, salt and pepper to taste. Seal and store at room temperature for up to 1 month.

To Serve

1. In a saucepan, combine chicken mixture and water. Cover and let stand for 30 minutes or until jerky starts to soften.

2. Uncover and bring to a boil over medium heat, stirring often. Reduce heat and boil gently, stirring often, for about 15 minutes or until potatoes and chicken are tender and liquid is slightly thickened.

Viking Stew

The name of this stew comes from Jay's childhood. It's what his mom called a stew when she used all of the leftover bits of vegetables from the fridge to make it. The kids thought it was fantastic and even dressed in costume to eat it. It wasn't until years later that they realized it had nothing to do with Norsemen or ships, but rather that their fridge was a Viking brand! You can clean out your dried goods pantry for this version.

Serves 1

Variation

Replace ¼ cup (50 mL) of the water with beer.

Prep at Home

1	1-inch (2.5 cm) square Tomato Pasta Sauce Leather or Barbecue Sauce Leather	1
1 oz	meat jerky (any type), broken into small pieces	30 g
¼ cup	dried potato cubes or crumbled dried potato slices	50 mL
¼ cup	dried vegetables (any type)	50 mL
1 tbsp	all-purpose flour	15 mL
1 tsp	crumbled dried herbs	5 mL
½ tsp	finely chopped dried garlic	2 mL
¼ tsp	salt	1 mL
¼ tsp	freshly ground black pepper	1 mL

To Serve

1½ cups	water	375 mL

Prep at Home

1. Tear leather into very small pieces. In a sealable plastic bag, combine leather, jerky, potatoes, vegetables, flour, herbs, garlic, salt and pepper. Seal and store at room temperature for up to 1 month.

To Serve

1. In a saucepan, combine leather mixture and water. Cover and let stand for 30 minutes, mashing leather occasionally, until vegetables start to soften.

2. Uncover and bring to a boil over medium heat, stirring often. Reduce heat and boil gently, stirring often, for about 15 minutes or until potatoes and meat are tender and liquid is slightly thickened.

Fresh Addition

Spice the stew up with a little hot pepper sauce before serving.

Venison, Potato and Apple Stew

When you need something warm and hearty on a crisp night, this is the stew that will satisfy you.

Serves 1

Variations

You can use any type of meat or poultry jerky in this stew in place of the venison.

Barbecue sauce leather adds a good depth of flavor to this stew. If you don't have it, add a splash of liquid barbecue sauce or steak sauce before serving.

Prep at Home

1	1-inch (2.5 cm) square Barbecue Sauce Leather	1
½ oz	Sea Salt and Peppercorn Venison Jerky or Maple and Grainy Dijon Venison Jerky, broken into small pieces	15 g
¼ cup	dried potato slices, broken into pieces	50 mL
2 tbsp	dried apple slices	25 mL
1 tbsp	dried carrot pieces	15 mL
1 tbsp	dried celery slices	15 mL
¼ tsp	crumbled dried rosemary or thyme	1 mL
¼ tsp	salt	1 mL
Pinch	dry mustard	Pinch
	Freshly ground black pepper	

To Serve

1½ cups	water	375 mL

Prep at Home

1. Tear leather into very small pieces. In a sealable plastic bag, combine leather, venison, potatoes, apples, carrots, celery, rosemary, salt, mustard and pepper to taste. Seal and store at room temperature for up to 1 month.

To Serve

1. In a saucepan, combine leather mixture and water. Cover and let stand for 30 minutes, mashing leather occasionally, until vegetables start to soften.

2. Uncover and bring to a boil over medium heat, stirring often. Reduce heat and boil gently, stirring often, for about 15 minutes or until potatoes and venison are tender and liquid is slightly thickened.

Tofu, Vegetable and Fruit Curry

There's dazzling color and flavor and a variety of textures in this satisfying vegetarian curry.

Serves 1

Tips

For the lime flesh, dry whole lime slices, then cut off the rind. Chop the flesh into small pieces.

Heating the water to soak the tofu gives it a much better texture than cold-soaking.

Prep at Home

1/4 cup	dried crumbled tofu	50 mL
2 tbsp	dried cooked lentils	25 mL
2 tbsp	dried mushroom slices, crumbled	25 mL
2 tbsp	dried red bell pepper pieces	25 mL
1 tbsp	finely chopped dried peaches or apricots	15 mL
1 tbsp	raisins	15 mL
1 tbsp	sweetened shredded coconut or finely chopped dried coconut	15 mL
1 tbsp	chopped dried lime flesh (optional)	15 mL
2 tsp	dried onion pieces	10 mL
1/2 tsp	curry powder	2 mL
1/4 tsp	finely chopped dried gingerroot	1 mL
1/4 tsp	salt	1 mL

To Serve

1 1/4 cups	water	300 mL

Prep at Home

1. In a sealable plastic bag, combine tofu, lentils, mushrooms, red peppers, peaches, raisins, coconut, lime (if using), onions, curry powder, ginger and salt. Seal and store at room temperature for up to 1 month.

To Serve

1. In a saucepan or skillet, bring water to a boil. Add tofu mixture, remove from heat, cover and let stand for 15 minutes or until tofu is softened.

2. Uncover and bring to a boil over medium heat, stirring often. Boil, stirring often, for about 5 minutes or until mixture is hot and liquid is absorbed.

Fresh Addition

Serve with lime wedges to squeeze over top and add a dollop of plain yogurt.

Curried Chicken with Apples

Fragrant spices and sweet apples warm up a simple chicken dish. Serve it over rice or with lentils.

Serves 1

Variation

If you like a fiery hot curry, use a hot curry powder or add ⅛ tsp (0.5 mL) cayenne pepper.

Prep at Home

1 oz	Sea Salt and Peppercorn Chicken Jerky, finely chopped	30 g
¼ cup	dried sweet potato cubes	50 mL
2 tbsp	dried apple slices	25 mL
2 tbsp	dried red bell pepper pieces	25 mL
1 tbsp	dried onion pieces	15 mL
1 tsp	crumbled dried cilantro or parsley	5 mL
½ tsp	curry powder	2 mL
¼ tsp	ground cumin	1 mL
¼ tsp	finely chopped dried gingerroot	1 mL
¼ tsp	salt	1 mL

To Serve

1½ cups	water	375 mL

Prep at Home

1. In a sealable plastic bag, combine chicken, sweet potatoes, apples, red peppers, onions, cilantro, curry powder, cumin, ginger and salt. Seal and store at room temperature for up to 1 month.

To Serve

1. In a saucepan, combine chicken mixture and water. Cover and let stand for 30 minutes or until chicken starts to soften.

2. Uncover and bring to a boil over medium heat, stirring often. Reduce heat and boil gently, stirring often, for about 15 minutes or until potatoes are tender and liquid is slightly thickened.

Beef Stroganoff

This simplified version of the classic noodle, beef and mushroom dish will surprise you because it's so easy and tasty.

Serves 1

Variation

Other flavors of beef jerky can be used. Try Cajun Beef Jerky, Herb and Garlic Ground Beef Jerky or Maple and Whisky Ground Beef Jerky.

Prep at Home

½ oz	Sea Salt and Peppercorn Beef Jerky, broken into small pieces	15 g
2 tbsp	dried mushroom slices	25 mL
2 tsp	crumbled dried parsley	10 mL
¼ tsp	paprika	1 mL
1 cup	broad egg noodles (about 2 oz/60 g)	250 mL
2 tbsp	instant skim milk powder	25 mL
1 tbsp	crumbled dried cottage cheese	15 mL

To Serve

1¼ cups	water	300 mL
	Salt and pepper	

Prep at Home

1. In a sealable plastic bag, combine beef, mushrooms, parsley and paprika. In another bag, combine noodles, milk powder and cottage cheese. Seal both bags and store at room temperature for up to 1 month.

To Serve

1. In a saucepan, combine beef mixture and water. Cover and let stand for 15 minutes or until beef starts to soften.

2. Uncover and bring to a boil over high heat. Stir in noodle mixture, reduce heat and boil gently, stirring often, for about 5 minutes or until noodles are tender. Season to taste with salt and pepper.

Fresh Addition

Omit the cottage cheese when prepping at home and stir in 2 tbsp (25 mL) sour cream after removing from heat.

Peppered Beef and Noodles

Plenty of flavor and all four food groups in one pot make this a winner. The other campers will surely be curious about the fantastic aromas emanating from your site.

Serves 1

Prep at Home

$1/2$ oz	Peppercorn Ground Beef Jerky Strips, broken into small pieces	15 g
1 cup	broad egg noodles (about 2 oz/60 g)	250 mL
$1/4$ cup	instant skim milk powder	50 mL
2 tbsp	halved dried red bell pepper slices	25 mL
$1/2$ tsp	crumbled dried basil	2 mL
$1/4$ tsp	salt	1 mL
	Freshly ground black pepper	

To Serve

$1 1/4$ cups	water	300 mL

Prep at Home

1. In a sealable plastic bag, combine beef, noodles, milk powder, red peppers, basil, salt and pepper to taste. Seal and store at room temperature for up to 1 month.

To Serve

1. In a saucepan, combine beef mixture and water. Cover and let stand for 15 minutes or until beef starts to soften.

2. Uncover and bring to a boil over high heat. Reduce heat and boil gently, stirring often, for about 5 minutes or until noodles and peppers are tender.

> **Fresh Addition**
>
> At the end, stir in 1 cup (250 mL) baby spinach until wilted.

Teriyaki Tofu Stir-Fry

The idea for this super-easy, satisfying recipe was given to Jennifer and Jay by their friend Christopher Campbell, a professional photographer, avid camper and fervent foodie.

Serves 1

Tip

To make dried crumbled teriyaki tofu, marinate crumbled tofu in Teriyaki Jerky marinade (page 67) and dry according to the instructions on page 54.

Variation

Substitute $\frac{1}{2}$ oz (15 g) chopped Asian Ground Meat Jerky for the tofu.

Prep at Home

$\frac{1}{3}$ cup	dried cooked long-grain brown rice	75 mL
$\frac{1}{4}$ cup	dried crumbled teriyaki tofu (see tip, at left)	50 mL
1 tbsp	dried grated carrots	15 mL
1 tbsp	dried zucchini or red bell pepper slices	15 mL
1 tbsp	dried cauliflower florets, broken into small pieces	15 mL
$\frac{1}{4}$ tsp	finely chopped dried gingerroot	1 mL

To Serve

$1\frac{1}{4}$ cups	water	300 mL

Prep at Home

1. In a sealable plastic bag, combine rice, tofu, carrots, zucchini, cauliflower and ginger. Seal and store at room temperature for up to 2 weeks or refrigerate for up to 1 month.

To Serve

1. In a saucepan or skillet, bring water to a boil. Add rice mixture, remove from heat, cover and let stand for 15 minutes or until tofu is softened.

2. Uncover and bring to a boil over medium heat, stirring often. Boil, stirring often, for about 5 minutes or until mixture is hot and liquid is absorbed.

Bean Fajitas

Make your own fried beans right over the camp stove. You'll love the terrific "fresh" flavor.

Serves 1

Tip

If desired, warm the tortillas in a skillet or wrap in foil and warm over the campfire.

Prep at Home

1	2-inch (5 cm) square Salsa Leather	1
½ cup	dried cooked black beans	125 mL
1 tbsp	dried onion slices	15 mL
1 tbsp	dried red or green bell pepper pieces	15 mL
Pinch	salt	Pinch

To Serve

1 cup	water	250 mL
2	flour tortillas	2

Prep at Home

1. Tear leather into very small pieces. In a sealable plastic bag, combine leather, beans, onions, red peppers and salt. Seal and store at room temperature for up to 1 month.

To Serve

1. In a saucepan or skillet, combine bean mixture and water. Let stand for 20 minutes, mashing leather occasionally, until vegetables start to soften.

2. Bring to a boil over medium heat, stirring often. Reduce heat and boil gently, stirring often and mashing beans, for about 5 minutes or until mixture is thick and hot.

3. Spoon half the bean mixture into the center of each tortilla. Fold up bottom and fold in both sides to enclose filling.

> **Fresh Addition**
>
> Spoon 1 tbsp (15 mL) shredded Monterey Jack, pepper Jack or Cheddar cheese and 1 tbsp (15 mL) sour cream over the bean mixture before folding the tortilla.

Tex-Mex Beef Fajitas

Hearty fajitas, a campfire — just add a cold beer, and you've got a fiesta under the stars.

Serves 1

Tip

If desired, warm the tortillas in a skillet or wrap in foil and warm over the campfire.

Prep at Home

1	2-inch (5 cm) square Salsa Leather	1
1 oz	Cajun Beef Jerky or Southwestern Ground Beef Jerky, broken into small pieces	30 g
¼ cup	dried red and/or green bell pepper slices	50 mL
1 tbsp	dried cooked black or kidney beans	15 mL
1 tbsp	dried onion slices	15 mL
¼ tsp	finely chopped dried hot chile peppers (optional)	1 mL
Pinch	salt	Pinch

To Serve

1 cup	water	250 mL
2	flour tortillas	2

Prep at Home

1. Tear leather into very small pieces. In a sealable plastic bag, combine leather, beef, red peppers, beans, onions, chile peppers (if using) and salt. Seal and store at room temperature for up to 1 month.

To Serve

1. In a saucepan or skillet, combine beef mixture and water. Let stand for 20 minutes, mashing leather occasionally, until vegetables start to soften.

2. Bring to a boil over medium heat, stirring often. Reduce heat and boil gently, stirring often and mashing beans, for about 10 minutes or until mixture is thick and hot.

3. Spoon half the beef mixture into the center of each tortilla. Fold up bottom and fold in both sides to enclose filling.

Fresh Additions

Omit the jerky when prepping at home and add 4 oz (125 g) fresh boneless beef grilling steak, cut into thin strips. Sauté it separately in a skillet, then stir into the cooked bean mixture. Alternatively, grill a whole piece of steak, slice it thinly, then stir into bean mixture for the last minute.

Sprinkle with a little shredded Monterey Jack or pepper Jack cheese before folding the tortillas.

Tofu, Lentil and Peanut Stovetop "Meatloaf"

Moisture, lots of texture and great flavor — you won't miss the meat in this loaf, which can be made on a stove or over a campfire.

Serves 1

Tip
This can be cooked over a campfire. Place the wrapped loaf in a flameproof metal or foil pan and cook over the moderately hot part of the fire. It may take a little longer to heat through, but you should hear it sizzling once it's hot.

- *9-inch (23 cm) square piece of foil*
- *Skillet with a lid*

Prep at Home

¼ cup	dried Basic Veggie Burger Blend	50 mL
¼ cup	dried crumbled tofu	50 mL
¼ cup	chopped peanuts	50 mL
¼ cup	chopped dried tomatoes	50 mL
1 tsp	dried roasted onions	5 mL
1 tsp	crumbled dried parsley	5 mL
¼ tsp	salt	1 mL
¼ tsp	freshly ground black pepper	1 mL

To Serve

⅔ cup	water	150 mL
	Vegetable oil	

Prep at Home
1. In a sealable plastic bag, combine veggie burger blend, tofu, peanuts, tomatoes, onions, parsley, salt and pepper. Seal and store at room temperature for up to 1 month.

To Serve
1. In a saucepan, bring water to a boil. Add tofu mixture, remove from heat, cover and let stand for 15 minutes or until tofu is softened and liquid is absorbed.

2. Oil the center of the foil square. Form tofu mixture into a loaf about 4 by 2 by 1 inch (10 by 5 by 2.5 cm) in size and place on the oiled foil. Wrap tightly.

3. Place the foil package in a skillet over low heat. Cover and cook for 10 minutes, then flip foil package and heat for about 8 minutes or until loaf is heated through.

Veggie Burger on a Stick

Start with your own dried grain and lentil blend, add in dried veggies and peanut butter, and voila! You've got a fantastic veggie burger to cook over the campfire.

Serves 1

Variation

To make burger patties instead, shape mixture into two ½-inch (1 cm) thick patties. Heat a thin layer of oil in a skillet over medium heat and cook patties, turning once, for about 5 minutes or until both sides are golden brown and inside is hot.

- Two ½-inch (1 cm) thick sticks, at least 2 feet (60 cm) long
- Two 8-inch (20 cm) pieces of foil

Prep at Home

¼ cup	dried Basic Veggie Burger Blend	50 mL
3 tbsp	quick-cooking rolled oats	45 mL
2 tsp	dried grated carrots	10 mL
½ tsp	finely chopped dried onions	2 mL
½ tsp	crumbled dried parsley	2 mL
¼ tsp	salt	1 mL
Pinch	ground cumin	Pinch
Pinch	ground coriander	Pinch
	Freshly ground black pepper	

To Serve

¼ cup	water	50 mL
2 tsp	natural peanut butter or almond butter	10 mL
½ tsp	freshly squeezed lime juice (optional)	2 mL

Prep at Home

1. In a sealable plastic bag, combine veggie burger blend, oats, carrots, onions, parsley, salt, cumin, coriander and pepper to taste. Seal and store at room temperature for up to 1 month.

To Serve

1. Prepare campfire.

2. In a bowl, combine burger mixture and water. Let stand for 15 minutes or until grains are softened and liquid is absorbed. Stir in peanut butter and lime juice (if using).

3. Wrap a square of foil around one end of each stick, covering at least 4 inches (10 cm). Divide mixture in half and squeeze one piece around the foil-wrapped section of each stick, making sure it is about ½ inch (1 cm) thick on all sides of the stick.

4. Cook burgers on sticks over the fire, holding them over a medium-hot area if possible and turning often, until golden brown and firm.

Tomato and Herb Tofu

Pack more protein into your meal by replacing pasta with tofu seasoned with zesty Italian flair.

Serves 1

Variation

Substitute 1 tsp (5 mL) plain dried onions for the roasted onions.

Prep at Home

½ cup	dried shredded tofu	125 mL
2 tbsp	finely chopped dried tomatoes	25 mL
1 tbsp	dried roasted onions	15 mL
1 tsp	crumbled dried basil	5 mL
1 tsp	dried parsley	5 mL
½ tsp	crumbled dried oregano	2 mL
¼ tsp	crumbled dried roasted garlic or finely chopped dried garlic	1 mL
¼ tsp	salt	1 mL
Pinch	hot pepper flakes	Pinch

To Serve

1 cup	water	250 mL

Prep at Home

1. In a sealable plastic bag, combine tofu, tomatoes, onions, basil, parsley, oregano, garlic, salt and hot pepper flakes. Seal and store at room temperature for up to 1 month.

To Serve

1. In a saucepan, bring water to a boil. Add tofu mixture, remove from heat, cover and let stand for 15 minutes or until tofu is softened.

2. Uncover and bring to a boil over medium heat, stirring often. Boil, stirring often, for about 8 minutes or until tomatoes are soft and liquid is absorbed.

Fresh Addition

Top with shredded mozzarella or Parmesan cheese.

Catch of the Day Foil-Packet Fish

If you happen to be lucky enough to make a good catch, here's a simple recipe to dress up that prize fish. (If you go into town and find a good fish market, you never have to divulge the truth.)

Serves 1

Variation

If you want to use dried lemon slices, pack them separately from the leek mixture and soak them in boiling water for about 15 minutes or until softened, then drain before stuffing the fish. Omit the extras for serving on top.

- *12-inch (30 cm) square piece of foil*
- *Grill rack (for campfire cooking)*

Prep at Home

1 tbsp	dried leek slices or onion pieces	15 mL
1 tsp	dried garlic slices	5 mL
¼ tsp	crumbled dried thyme	1 mL
¼ tsp	salt	1 mL
¼ tsp	freshly ground black pepper	1 mL

To Serve

1 tbsp	butter, softened, divided	15 mL
½	lemon, sliced	½
1	whole fresh fish, dressed and scaled (1 to 2 lbs/500 g to 1 kg)	1

Prep at Home

1. In a sealable plastic bag, combine leeks, garlic, thyme, salt and pepper. Seal and store at room temperature for up to 1 month.

To Serve

1. Prepare campfire (if using) and position grill rack over fire.

2. Spread half the butter across the center of the foil. Stuff the leek mixture, 2 of the lemon slices and the remaining butter in the cavity of the fish. Place on the buttered foil and wrap tightly.

3. Place on grill rack over hot coals or in a skillet over medium heat on a stove and cook for about 10 minutes per inch (2.5 cm) of thickness, turning once, until fish flakes easily with a fork. Serve with the remaining lemon slices to squeeze over top.

Fire-Grilled Fish Stuffed with Red Peppers, Lime and Oregano

A hint of wood smoke makes fresh-caught fish all the better. The lime and savory seasonings add moisture and zest.

Serves 1

Variations

If you want to use dried lime slices, pack them separately from the vegetable mixture and soak them in boiling water for about 15 minutes or until softened, then drain before stuffing the fish.

To cook in a skillet on a stove, heat oil over medium-high heat. Add fish, reduce heat to medium-low and cook as directed in step 4.

- Grill rack

Prep at Home

1 tbsp	dried red bell pepper pieces	15 mL
1 tbsp	dried onion pieces	15 mL
1 tsp	finely chopped dried garlic	5 mL
1/2 tsp	crumbled dried oregano	2 mL
1/4 tsp	salt	1 mL
1/4 tsp	freshly ground black pepper	1 mL

To Serve

2 tbsp	water	25 mL
1	lime, sliced	1
1	whole fresh fish, dressed and scaled (1 to 2 lbs/500 g to 1 kg)	1
1 tbsp	olive or vegetable oil	15 mL

Prep at Home

1. In a sealable plastic bag, combine peppers, onions, garlic, oregano, salt and pepper. Seal and store at room temperature for up to 1 month.

To Serve

1. Prepare campfire and position grill rack over fire.

2. In a bowl, combine vegetable mixture and water. Let stand for about 15 minutes or until softened. Carefully drain off any excess water, trying not to lose the herbs.

3. Stuff the cavity of the fish with lime slices and vegetable mixture. Secure with toothpicks or skewers, or tie with soaked string. Brush the outside of the fish with olive oil.

4. Place on grill rack and cook over medium coals for about 10 minutes per inch (2.5 cm) of thickness, turning once, until the skin is crisp and golden brown and fish flakes easily with a fork.

Chicken à la King

This classic dish never goes out of style. You might have to forgo the puff pastry shell at the campfire, but biscuits would be just as nice alongside.

Serves 1

Tip

Dried chicken tends to keep a toothsome texture even when rehydrated. Chopping it into very small pieces does help to soften it.

Prep at Home

1 oz	Maple and Grainy Dijon Chicken Jerky or Sea Salt and Peppercorn Chicken Jerky, finely chopped	30 g
1 tbsp	dried onion pieces	15 mL
1 tbsp	dried mushroom slices, crumbled	15 mL
1 tbsp	dried carrot pieces	15 mL
1 tbsp	dried green peas	15 mL
1 tbsp	instant skim milk powder	15 mL
1 tbsp	all-purpose flour	15 mL
$1/4$ tsp	crumbled dried thyme	1 mL
$1/4$ tsp	dry mustard	1 mL
$1/4$ tsp	salt	1 mL
	Freshly ground black pepper	

To Serve

$1^1/_2$ cups	water	375 mL

Prep at Home

1. In a sealable plastic bag, combine chicken, onions, mushrooms, carrots, peas, milk powder, flour, thyme, mustard, salt and pepper to taste. Seal and store at room temperature for up to 1 month.

To Serve

1. In a saucepan, combine chicken mixture and water. Cover and let stand for 30 minutes or until chicken starts to soften.

2. Uncover and bring to a boil over medium heat, stirring constantly. Reduce heat and simmer, stirring often, for about 15 minutes or until chicken and vegetables are tender and liquid is slightly thickened.

Orange and Sweet Pepper Chicken

Oranges and red bell peppers are such a fresh-tasting combination, you won't believe you made this dish from dried ingredients. Serve it over rice or pasta.

Serves 1

Tip

This is a thin sauce that soaks nicely into rice or pasta. If you prefer a thickened sauce, whisk $\frac{1}{2}$ tsp (2 mL) cornstarch into 1 tbsp (15 mL) cold water and stir into the sauce for the last 2 minutes of cooking.

Prep at Home

1 oz	Sea Salt and Peppercorn Chicken Jerky or Teriyaki Chicken Jerky, finely chopped	30 g
2 tbsp	dried red bell pepper slices	25 mL
1 tbsp	dried onion slices	15 mL
1 tbsp	dried carrot slices	15 mL
$\frac{1}{2}$ tsp	finely chopped dried orange zest	2 mL
$\frac{1}{4}$ tsp	salt	1 mL
$\frac{1}{4}$ tsp	paprika	1 mL
	Freshly ground black pepper	

To Serve

$1\frac{1}{4}$ cups	water	300 mL

Prep at Home

1. In a sealable plastic bag, combine chicken, red peppers, onions, carrots, orange zest, salt, paprika and pepper to taste. Seal and store at room temperature for up to 1 month.

To Serve

1. In a saucepan, combine chicken mixture and water. Cover and let stand for 30 minutes or until chicken starts to soften.

2. Uncover and bring to a boil over medium heat, stirring constantly. Reduce heat and simmer, stirring often, for about 15 minutes or until chicken and vegetables are tender and liquid is slightly thickened.

Fresh Addition

Omit the dried chicken when prepping at home and add 4 oz (125 g) fresh chicken, thinly sliced, to the saucepan after it comes to a simmer; simmer until chicken is no longer pink inside.

Lemon Honey Garlic Chicken

Even if you're hundreds of miles away from the nearest Chinese takeout, you can have a fast dinner with that classic flavor you love. It's worth toting a few fresh ingredients for the best lemon and honey taste. Serve over rice or noodles.

Serves 1

Tip

This is a thin sauce that nicely soaks into rice or coats noodles. If you prefer a thickened sauce, whisk $1/2$ tsp (2 mL) cornstarch into 1 tbsp (15 mL) cold water and stir into the sauce for the last 2 minutes of cooking.

Prep at Home

1 oz	Teriyaki Chicken Jerky, finely chopped	30 g
1 tbsp	dried green bean pieces	15 mL
1 tbsp	dried onion pieces	15 mL
1 tsp	crumbled dried parsley	5 mL
$1/2$ tsp	finely chopped dried garlic	2 mL
$1/2$ tsp	finely chopped dried lemon zest	2 mL
Pinch	salt	Pinch
Pinch	hot pepper flakes	Pinch

To Serve

1 cup	water	250 mL
2 tbsp	freshly squeezed lemon juice	25 mL
1 tsp	liquid honey	5 mL

Prep at Home

1. In a sealable plastic bag, combine chicken, green beans, onions, parsley, garlic, lemon zest, salt and hot pepper flakes. Seal and store at room temperature for up to 1 month.

To Serve

1. In a saucepan, combine chicken mixture and water. Cover and let stand for 30 minutes or until chicken starts to soften.

2. Uncover and bring to a boil over medium heat, stirring constantly. Reduce heat and simmer, stirring often, for about 15 minutes or until chicken and vegetables are tender and liquid is slightly thickened. Stir in lemon juice and honey.

Almost-Instant Mac and Cheese

Made from scratch, this macaroni and cheese, which needs just a couple of minutes on the stove to heat up, might just become your new favorite.

Serves 1

Prep at Home

1 cup	dried cooked macaroni	250 mL
2 tbsp	crumbled dried cottage cheese	25 mL
2 tbsp	skim milk powder	25 mL
¼ tsp	dry mustard	1 mL
¼ tsp	crumbled dried basil (optional)	1 mL
	Salt and pepper	

To Serve

1 cup	water	250 mL

Prep at Home

1. In a sealable plastic bag, combine macaroni, cottage cheese, milk powder, mustard, basil (if using) and salt and pepper to taste. Seal and store at room temperature for up to 2 weeks or refrigerate for up to 3 months.

To Serve

1. In a saucepan, combine macaroni mixture and water. Let stand for 15 minutes or until pasta is softened.

2. Bring to a boil over medium heat, stirring constantly. Reduce heat and boil gently, stirring often, for about 1 minute or until sauce is reduced and thickened.

Fresh Additions

Add drained canned tuna or fresh grilled fish.
Add chopped fresh tomatoes or the traditional squeeze of ketchup.

No-Cook Pasta and Sauce

Pack this as a "just in case" meal for the time when you run out of camp stove fuel or the fire just won't start. Dried cooked pasta rehydrates wonderfully in room-temperature water. You'll never eat that stuff out of a can again.

Serves 1

Tip

This can be served hot. Just combine in a saucepan instead of a bowl, let stand as directed, then uncover and heat over medium heat until bubbling.

Prep at Home

1	4-inch (10 cm) square Tomato Pasta Sauce Leather	1
1 cup	dried cooked fusilli	250 mL
1 tbsp	grated Parmesan cheese	15 mL
1/2 tsp	crumbled dried basil or oregano	2 mL
Pinch	freshly ground black pepper	Pinch

To Serve

1 cup	water	250 mL

Prep at Home

1. Tear leather into small pieces. In a sealable plastic bag, combine leather, fusilli, Parmesan, basil and pepper. Seal and store at room temperature for up to 2 weeks or refrigerate for up to 3 months.

To Serve

1. In a bowl, combine leather mixture and water. Cover and let stand for 30 minutes, mashing leather occasionally, until pasta is tender.

One-Pot Simple Spaghetti

The tomato sauce leather and jerky pack such a punch of flavor, you won't believe how fast and easy this one-pot meal is.

Serves 1

Tip

The smaller the leather pieces are, the better the texture of the sauce once it's rehydrated.

Prep at Home

1	2-inch (5 cm) square Tomato Pasta Sauce Leather	1
2 tbsp	crumbled Herb and Garlic Ground Beef Jerky	25 mL
1 tbsp	dried mushroom slices	15 mL
1 tbsp	finely chopped dried tomatoes	15 mL
¼ tsp	salt	1 mL
Pinch	hot pepper flakes	Pinch
½ cup	broken spaghettini	125 mL

To Serve

1½ cups	water	375 mL

Prep at Home

1. Tear leather into small pieces. In a sealable plastic bag, combine leather, beef, mushrooms, tomatoes, salt and hot pepper flakes. Place spaghettini in another bag. Seal both bags and store at room temperature for up to 1 month.

To Serve

1. In a saucepan, combine leather mixture and water. Let stand for 30 minutes or until mushrooms are softened.

2. Bring to a boil over medium heat, stirring often. Stir in spaghettini. Reduce heat and boil gently, stirring occasionally, for about 8 minutes or until pasta is tender and sauce is reduced and thickened.

Fresh Addition

Top with freshly grated Parmesan cheese or another shredded cheese.

Veggie Pasta

Color and flavor abound in this just-add-water pasta dish. Serve it on its own or as a side to grilled steak, sausage or fish.

Serves 1

Variation

Substitute other dried vegetables in your pantry for the mushrooms, zucchini or peppers. Try roasted onions, asparagus, hot chile peppers or green peas.

Prep at Home

1 cup	dried cooked fusilli	250 mL
2 tbsp	finely chopped dried tomatoes	25 mL
1 tbsp	dried mushroom slices, crumbled	15 mL
1 tbsp	dried zucchini slices	15 mL
1 tbsp	dried bell pepper pieces	15 mL
1 tbsp	grated Parmesan cheese	15 mL
1/2 tsp	crumbled dried basil	2 mL
1/4 tsp	crumbled dried oregano	1 mL
1/4 tsp	finely chopped dried garlic	1 mL
1/4 tsp	salt	1 mL
	Freshly ground black pepper	

To Serve

1 1/4 cups	water	300 mL

Prep at Home

1. In a sealable plastic bag, combine fusilli, tomatoes, mushrooms, zucchini, bell peppers, Parmesan, basil, oregano, garlic, salt and pepper to taste. Seal and store at room temperature for up to 2 weeks or refrigerate for up to 3 months.

To Serve

1. In a saucepan, combine fusilli mixture and water. Let stand for 20 minutes or until vegetables start to soften.

2. Bring to a boil over medium heat, stirring constantly. Reduce heat and boil gently, stirring often, for about 3 minutes or until pasta and vegetables are tender and liquid is reduced.

Shrimp and Herb Pasta

A primavera-style pasta makes a nice meal on a steamy summer night. If you've packed some white wine, chill it in the lake and uncork it (or unscrew it!) to enjoy with this dinner.

Serves 1

Variations

Substitute chopped dried asparagus or green beans for the peas.

Use whatever herbs you like. Tarragon, sage or rosemary would also be nice.

Prep at Home

1/2 oz	dried shrimp, chopped into very small pieces	15 g
2 tbsp	finely chopped dried tomatoes	25 mL
1 tbsp	dried onion pieces or leek slices, finely chopped	15 mL
1 tbsp	dried green peas	15 mL
1 tbsp	instant skim milk powder	15 mL
1/2 tsp	crumbled dried roasted garlic	2 mL
1/2 tsp	crumbled dried basil	2 mL
1/4 tsp	crumbled dried oregano	1 mL
Pinch	crumbled dried thyme	Pinch
1/4 tsp	salt	1 mL
	Freshly ground black pepper	
1 cup	dried cooked fusilli	250 mL

To Serve

1 1/4 cups	water	300 mL

Prep at Home

1. In a sealable plastic bag, combine shrimp, tomatoes, onions, peas, milk powder, garlic, basil, oregano, salt and pepper to taste. Place fusilli in another bag. Seal both bags and store at room temperature for up to 2 weeks or refrigerate for up to 3 months.

To Serve

1. In a saucepan or skillet, bring water to a boil. Add shrimp mixture, remove from heat, cover and let stand for 20 minutes or until shrimp is softened.

2. Stir in fusilli and bring to a boil over medium heat, stirring often. Boil, stirring often, for about 5 minutes or until pasta and vegetables are tender.

Jerky and Vegetable Pasta Salad

All you need to do is boil water to make this delicious pasta salad. Get it started, then set up camp. By the time the tent is up, your dinner will be soaked and ready to eat.

Serves 1

Variation

Omit the dried herbs when prepping at home and replace the vinegar and oil with 1 tbsp (15 mL) prepared basil pesto or other pesto.

Prep at Home

$1/2$ oz	Maple and Grainy Dijon Jerky or Cajun Jerky	15 g
2 tbsp	finely chopped dried tomatoes	25 mL
1 tbsp	dried zucchini slices	15 mL
1 tbsp	dried asparagus or green bean pieces	15 mL
$1/2$ tsp	crumbled dried basil	2 mL
$1/4$ tsp	crumbled dried rosemary	1 mL
$1/4$ tsp	finely chopped dried garlic	1 mL
1 cup	dried cooked fusilli	250 mL
1 tbsp	grated Parmesan cheese	15 mL
$1/4$ tsp	salt	1 mL
	Freshly ground black pepper	

To Serve

1 cup	water	250 mL
1 tbsp	vinegar (any flavor)	15 mL
1 tsp	olive or vegetable oil	5 mL

Prep at Home

1. In a sealable plastic bag, combine jerky, tomatoes, zucchini, asparagus, basil, rosemary and garlic. In another bag, combine fusilli, Parmesan, salt and pepper to taste. Seal both bags and store at room temperature for up to 2 weeks or refrigerate for up to 3 months.

To Serve

1. In a saucepan, bring water to a boil. Add jerky mixture, remove from heat, cover and let stand for 10 minutes or until jerky and vegetables start to soften.

2. Stir in fusilli mixture, cover and let stand for about 20 minutes or until pasta is tender and cooled to room temperature. Stir in vinegar and oil.

Caribbean Spiced Rice and Beans

Spiced-up rice is very nice. This classic dish gives a tropical twist to your meal.

Serves 1

Tip

Heating the water before adding the rice mixture speeds up the soaking time and gives a better texture to the rice. If you don't want to fire up the stove twice, you can soak the mixture in cold water for about 1 hour or until the rice is softened.

Prep at Home

1/3 cup	dried cooked long-grain brown or white rice	75 mL
1/4 cup	dried cooked kidney or black beans	50 mL
1 tbsp	dried grated carrots	15 mL
1 tbsp	finely chopped dried pineapple	15 mL
1 tsp	finely chopped dried onions	5 mL
1/2 tsp	curry powder	2 mL
1/4 tsp	salt	1 mL
Pinch	ground allspice or ginger	Pinch
Pinch	hot pepper flakes (optional)	Pinch

To Serve

1 1/4 cups	water	300 mL

Prep at Home

1. In a sealable plastic bag, combine rice, beans, carrots, pineapple, onions, curry powder, salt, allspice and hot pepper flakes (if using). Seal and store at room temperature for up to 2 weeks or refrigerate for up to 1 month.

To Serve

1. In a saucepan or skillet, bring water to a boil. Add rice mixture, remove from heat, cover and let stand for 15 minutes or until rice is softened.

2. Uncover and bring to a boil over medium heat, stirring often. Boil, stirring often, for about 5 minutes or until mixture is hot and liquid is absorbed.

Fresh Addition

Serve with fresh lime or lemon wedges to squeeze over top.

Cajun Rice and Black Beans

Jumping with flavor and color, this rice and bean dish is sure to spice up your meal.

Serves 1

Tips

Heating the water before adding the rice mixture speeds up the soaking time and gives a better texture to the rice. If you don't want to fire up the stove twice, you can soak the mixture in cold water for about 1 hour or until the rice is softened.

If you like it fiery, use a generous pinch or $\frac{1}{8}$ tsp (0.5 mL) cayenne pepper.

Prep at Home

$\frac{1}{3}$ cup	dried cooked long-grain brown rice	75 mL
$\frac{1}{4}$ cup	dried cooked black beans	50 mL
2 tbsp	finely chopped dried tomatoes	25 mL
1 tbsp	dried onion pieces	15 mL
1 tbsp	dried celery slices	15 mL
1 tbsp	dried green bell pepper pieces	15 mL
$\frac{1}{4}$ tsp	salt	1 mL
$\frac{1}{4}$ tsp	crumbled dried thyme	1 mL
$\frac{1}{4}$ tsp	paprika	1 mL
Pinch	cayenne pepper	Pinch

To Serve

$1\frac{1}{3}$ cups	water	325 mL

Prep at Home

1. In a sealable plastic bag, combine rice, beans, tomatoes, onions, celery, green peppers, salt, thyme, paprika and cayenne. Seal and store at room temperature for up to 1 month.

To Serve

1. In a saucepan or skillet, bring water to a boil. Add rice mixture, remove from heat, cover and let stand for 15 minutes or until rice is softened.

2. Uncover and bring to a boil over medium heat, stirring often. Boil, stirring often, for about 5 minutes or until mixture is hot and liquid is absorbed.

Cajun Shrimp and Rice

A quick version of jambalaya will elevate your camp cuisine to new heights.

Serves 1

Tips

Heating the water before adding the rice mixture speeds up the soaking time and gives a better texture to the rice. If you don't want to fire up the stove twice, you can soak the mixture in cold water for about 1 hour or until the rice is softened.

Dried shrimp tends to keep a firm texture even when rehydrated. Chopping it into very small pieces does help to soften it.

Variations

Add 1 tbsp (15 mL) finely chopped smoked pepperette sausage or Cajun Chicken Jerky to the shrimp mixture.

Use a 2-inch (5 cm) square of Tomato Pasta Sauce Leather, torn into very small pieces, in place of the dried tomatoes.

Prep at Home

½ oz	dried cooked shrimp, chopped into very small pieces	15 g
⅓ cup	dried cooked long-grain brown or white rice	75 mL
2 tbsp	finely chopped dried tomatoes	25 mL
1 tbsp	dried onion pieces	15 mL
1 tbsp	dried red bell pepper pieces	15 mL
½ tsp	crumbled dried parsley	2 mL
¼ tsp	crumbled dried thyme	1 mL
¼ tsp	salt	1 mL
⅛ tsp	cayenne pepper	0.5 mL

To Serve

1¼ cups	water	300 mL

Prep at Home

1. In a sealable plastic bag, combine shrimp, rice, tomatoes, onions, red peppers, parsley, thyme, salt and cayenne. Seal and store at room temperature for up to 1 month.

To Serve

1. In a saucepan or skillet, bring water to a boil. Add shrimp mixture, remove from heat, cover and let stand for 15 minutes or until rice is softened.

2. Uncover and bring to a boil over medium heat, stirring often. Boil, stirring often, for about 5 minutes or until mixture is hot and liquid is absorbed.

Beef and Veggie Fried Rice

This one-dish meal has lots of color and texture to delight the eye and the palate. Save up those packets of soy sauce when you get takeout and pack them to add that extra burst of flavor.

Serves 1

Tip

Heating the water before adding the rice mixture speeds up the soaking time and gives a better texture to the rice. If you don't want to fire up the stove twice, you can soak the mixture in cold water for about 1 hour or until the rice is softened.

Prep at Home

½ oz	Teriyaki Beef Jerky or Asian Ground Meat Jerky, broken into small pieces	15 g
⅓ cup	dried cooked long-grain brown or white rice	75 mL
1 tbsp	dried onion pieces	15 mL
1 tbsp	dried carrot slices	15 mL
1 tbsp	dried green or red bell pepper pieces	15 mL
1 tbsp	dried broccoli florets, broken into small pieces	15 mL
¼ tsp	finely chopped dried garlic	1 mL
¼ tsp	finely chopped dried gingerroot	1 mL
Pinch	hot pepper flakes	Pinch

To Serve

1⅓ cups	water	325 mL
1 tbsp	soy sauce (or to taste)	15 mL

Prep at Home

1. In a sealable plastic bag, combine beef, rice, onions, carrots, green peppers, broccoli, garlic, ginger and hot pepper flakes. Seal and store at room temperature for up to 1 month.

To Serve

1. In a saucepan or skillet, bring water to a boil. Add beef mixture, remove from heat, cover and let stand for 15 minutes or until rice is softened.

2. Uncover and bring to a boil over medium heat, stirring often. Boil, stirring often, for about 5 minutes or until mixture is hot and liquid is absorbed. Stir in soy sauce.

Easy Mushroom Risotto

Although risotto is usually made with short-grain rice, this version uses slightly chopped long-grain rice, with added creaminess from the cottage cheese. It's sure to earn you a reputation as a campsite gourmet.

Serves 1

Variation

Substitute 1 tsp (5 mL) crumbled roasted garlic for the plain dried garlic.

Prep at Home

½ cup	dried cooked long-grain white or brown rice	125 mL
2 tbsp	dried mushroom slices, crumbled	25 mL
1 tbsp	finely chopped dried leeks or onions	15 mL
1 tbsp	powdered dried cottage cheese	15 mL
½ tsp	finely chopped dried garlic	2 mL
½ tsp	crumbled dried tarragon	2 mL
¼ tsp	salt	1 mL
	Freshly ground black pepper	

To Serve

1 cup	water	250 mL

Prep at Home

1. In a mini chopper, pulse rice until chopped and about one-quarter is powdery. Transfer to a sealable plastic bag and add mushrooms, leeks, cottage cheese, garlic, tarragon, salt and pepper to taste. Seal and store at room temperature for up to 1 month.

To Serve

1. In a saucepan, combine rice mixture and water. Cover and let stand for 30 minutes or until mushrooms are softened.

2. Uncover and bring to a boil over medium heat, stirring often. Reduce heat to low, cover and simmer, stirring twice, for about 10 minutes or until rice is tender. Uncover and simmer, stirring, until liquid is absorbed and rice is creamy.

Chicken and Tomato Risotto

Dried tomatoes and a blend of herbs add lots of flavor to this hearty risotto.

Serves 1

Tip

Dried chicken tends to keep a toothsome texture even when rehydrated. Chopping it into very small pieces does help to soften it.

Prep at Home

½ cup	dried cooked long-grain white rice	125 mL
1 oz	Sea Salt and Peppercorn Chicken Jerky, finely chopped	30 g
2 tbsp	chopped dried tomatoes	25 mL
1 tbsp	powdered dried cottage cheese	15 mL
½ tsp	crumbled dried basil	2 mL
¼ tsp	crumbled dried oregano	1 mL
¼ tsp	finely chopped dried garlic	1 mL
Pinch	crumbled dried rosemary	Pinch
¼ tsp	salt	1 mL
	Freshly ground black pepper	

To Serve

1¼ cups	water	300 mL

Prep at Home

1. In a mini chopper, pulse rice until chopped and about one-quarter is powdery. Transfer to a sealable plastic bag and add chicken, tomatoes, cottage cheese, basil, oregano, garlic, rosemary, salt and pepper to taste. Seal and store at room temperature for up to 2 weeks or refrigerate for up to 3 months.

To Serve

1. In a saucepan, combine rice mixture and water. Cover and let stand for 30 minutes or until chicken starts to soften.

2. Uncover and bring to a boil over medium heat, stirring often. Reduce heat to low, cover and simmer, stirring twice, for about 10 minutes or until rice is tender. Uncover and simmer, stirring, until liquid is absorbed and rice is creamy.

Smoked Sausage Risotto

With its fabulous flavor and satisfying texture, this quick risotto will have you singing "O Sole Mio" around the campfire.

Serves 1

Tips

It is best to buy prepared dried sausage, as it is difficult to get a safe product when drying sausage at home.

Short-grain rice is traditionally used for risotto, but it doesn't dry and rehydrate as well as long-grain. Pulsing the rice in the mini chopper first adds some creaminess to the texture.

Variation

In place of sausage, substitute crumbled Herb and Garlic Ground Meat Jerky or Southwestern Ground Meat Jerky.

Prep at Home

1/2 cup	dried cooked long-grain white rice	125 mL
1	2-inch (5 cm) square Tomato Pasta Sauce Leather	1
1/4 cup	thinly sliced dried smoked pepperette sausage (see tip, at left)	50 mL
1 tbsp	dried onion pieces	15 mL
1 tbsp	grated Parmesan cheese	15 mL
1/2 tsp	crumbled dried basil	2 mL
Pinch	salt	Pinch
	Freshly ground black pepper	

To Serve

1 1/4 cups	water	300 mL

Prep at Home

1. In a mini chopper, pulse rice until chopped and about one-quarter is powdery. Tear leather into small pieces. In a sealable plastic bag, combine rice, leather, sausage, onions, Parmesan, basil, salt and pepper to taste. Seal and store at room temperature for up to 2 weeks or refrigerate for up to 3 months.

To Serve

1. In a saucepan, combine rice mixture and water. Cover and let stand for 30 minutes, mashing leather occasionally, until leather is soft.

2. Uncover and bring to a boil over medium heat, stirring often. Reduce heat to low, cover and simmer, stirring twice, for about 10 minutes or until rice is tender. Uncover and simmer, stirring, until liquid is absorbed and rice is creamy.

Moroccan Couscous with Chickpeas

When spiked with spices, dried fruit and the added protein of chickpeas, couscous makes a quick meal that gives a touch of the exotic to your campsite.

Serves 1

Tip

To toast a small amount of nuts, in a small dry skillet over medium heat, toast chopped nuts, stirring constantly, for about 2 minutes or until fragrant. Transfer to a bowl and let cool.

Prep at Home

2 tbsp	dried cooked chickpeas	25 mL
1 tbsp	dried grated carrots	15 mL
1 tbsp	chopped dried apricots	15 mL
1 tbsp	raisins	15 mL
1/4 tsp	ground cumin	1 mL
1/4 tsp	ground coriander	1 mL
1/8 tsp	salt	0.5 mL
Pinch	finely chopped dried orange or lemon zest	Pinch
Pinch	ground cinnamon	Pinch
Pinch	cayenne pepper or black pepper	Pinch
1/4 cup	couscous (preferably whole wheat)	50 mL
1 tbsp	toasted sliced almonds	15 mL

To Serve

2/3 cup	water	150 mL

Prep at Home

1. In a sealable plastic bag, combine chickpeas, carrots, apricots, raisins, cumin, coriander, salt, orange zest, cinnamon and cayenne. In another bag, combine couscous and almonds. Seal both bags and store at room temperature for up to 1 month.

To Serve

1. In a saucepan, combine chickpea mixture and water. Let stand for 30 minutes or until chickpeas are softened.

2. Bring to a boil over high heat, stirring often. Remove from heat and stir in couscous mixture. Cover and let stand for 5 minutes or until liquid is absorbed. Fluff with a fork.

Fresh Addition

Sprinkle 1 tbsp (15 mL) freshly squeezed orange or lemon juice over top, or serve with orange wedges.

Wheat Berries Parmesan

Wheat berries have a toothsome texture and make a nice change from rice or pasta. This recipe is hearty enough for a main course and is also nice as a side dish.

Serves 1

Variation

Replace the leather with 1 tbsp (15 mL) finely chopped dried tomatoes and add ¼ tsp (1 mL) crumbled dried roasted garlic or minced dried garlic and an extra ¼ tsp (1 mL) dried basil.

Prep at Home

1	2-inch (5 cm) square Tomato Pasta Sauce Leather	1
½ cup	dried cooked wheat berries	125 mL
1 tbsp	grated Parmesan cheese	15 mL
¼ tsp	crumbled dried basil	1 mL
	Freshly ground black pepper	

To Serve

1 cup	water	250 mL

Prep at Home

1. Tear leather into small pieces. In a sealable plastic bag, combine leather, wheat berries, Parmesan, basil and pepper to taste. Seal and store at room temperature for up to 2 weeks or refrigerate for up to 1 month.

To Serve

1. In a saucepan, combine leather mixture and water. Let stand for 30 minutes, mashing leather occasionally, until wheat berries start to soften.

2. Bring to a boil over medium heat, stirring often. Reduce heat and boil gently, stirring often, for about 10 minutes or until wheat berries are tender and liquid is absorbed.

Side Dishes and Accompaniments

Warm Broccoli, Leek and Raisin Salad

Start this salad before your other dishes to give it time to soak and cool down. It makes a refreshing, tender-crisp side to fish or stew.

Serves 1

Prep at Home

¼ cup	dried broccoli florets	50 mL
1 tbsp	dried leek slices, finely chopped	15 mL
1 tbsp	raisins	15 mL
½ tsp	crumbled dried oregano	2 mL
¼ tsp	finely chopped lemon or orange zest	1 mL
¼ tsp	finely chopped dried garlic	1 mL
Pinch	salt	Pinch

To Serve

⅓ cup	water	75 mL
1 tbsp	olive oil	15 mL
2 tsp	lemon juice, orange juice or vinegar	10 mL

Prep at Home

1. In a sealable plastic bag, combine broccoli, leeks, raisins, oregano, lemon zest, garlic and salt. Seal and store at room temperature for up to 1 month.

To Serve

1. In a saucepan, bring water to a boil. Add broccoli mixture, remove from heat, cover and let stand for 30 minutes, stirring occasionally, until broccoli is tender and cooled to room temperature and most of the liquid is absorbed. Stir in oil and lemon juice.

Fresh Addition

Add sliced fresh oranges with the oil and juice.

Citrus-Marinated Chickpea Salad

A simple salad is sometimes just what you need. Whether it's alongside grilled fresh-caught fish, a burger or a rice dish, it's sure to perk up the meal.

Serves 1

Prep at Home

⅓ cup	dried cooked chickpeas	75 mL
2 tbsp	dried red bell pepper pieces	25 mL
1 tsp	dried red onion pieces	5 mL
½ tsp	crumbled dried tarragon	2 mL
¼ tsp	finely chopped dried lemon or orange zest	1 mL
⅛ tsp	salt	0.5 mL
	Freshly ground black pepper	

To Serve

½ cup	water	125 mL
1 tbsp	lemon juice or orange juice	15 mL
1 tsp	olive oil	5 mL

Prep at Home

1. In a sealable plastic bag, combine chickpeas, red peppers, red onions, tarragon, lemon zest, salt and pepper to taste. Seal and store at room temperature for up to 1 month.

To Serve

1. In a bowl, combine chickpea mixture and water. Let stand for 30 minutes, stirring occasionally, until chickpeas and vegetables are softened. Stir in lemon juice and oil.

Fresh Addition

Add a fresh orange, peeled and cut into segments, with the juice.

Brown Rice, Apple and Cranberry Salad

This salad is terrific served with a biscuit as a light lunch. It also makes a satisfying side dish for grilled fish or chicken.

Serves 1

Tip

You can leave out the vinegar — it just adds a little fresh zing.

Prep at Home

¼ cup	dried cooked long-grain brown rice	50 mL
2 tbsp	finely chopped dried apples	25 mL
1 tbsp	dried cranberries	15 mL
1 tsp	dried leek slices or onion pieces, finely chopped (optional)	5 mL
1 tsp	crumbled dried parsley	5 mL
⅛ tsp	salt	0.5 mL
	Freshly ground black pepper	

To Serve

½ cup	water	125 mL
1 tbsp	cider vinegar or unsweetened apple juice	15 mL

Prep at Home

1. In a sealable plastic bag, combine rice, apples, cranberries, leeks (if using), parsley, salt and pepper to taste. Seal and store at room temperature for up to 1 month.

To Serve

1. In a saucepan, bring water to a boil. Add rice mixture, remove from heat, cover and let stand for 20 minutes or until rice is tender and cooled to room temperature and most of the liquid is absorbed. Stir in vinegar.

Broccoli and Cottage Cheese Gratin

Turn a classic side dish into a camp cuisine wonder. Serve alongside a meat or rice dish.

Serves 1

Variation

Replace half or all of the broccoli with dried cauliflower florets.

Prep at Home

¼ cup	dried broccoli florets	50 mL
1 tbsp	crumbled dried cottage cheese	15 mL
1 tsp	dried onion pieces, finely chopped	5 mL
½ tsp	powdered dried roasted garlic (optional)	2 mL
	Freshly ground black pepper	
2 tbsp	coarse dried bread crumbs	25 mL
1 tbsp	grated Parmesan cheese	15 mL

To Serve

½ cup	water	125 mL

Prep at Home

1. In a sealable plastic bag, combine broccoli, cottage cheese, onions, garlic (if using) and pepper to taste. In another bag, combine bread crumbs and Parmesan. Seal both bags and store at room temperature for up to 2 weeks or refrigerate for up to 3 months.

To Serve

1. In a saucepan, combine broccoli mixture and water. Cover and let stand for 20 minutes or until broccoli starts to soften.

2. Uncover and bring to a boil over medium heat. Reduce heat and simmer, stirring occasionally, for about 5 minutes or until broccoli is tender and most of the liquid is absorbed. Remove from heat, sprinkle with bread crumb mixture and let stand for 5 minutes.

Curried Squash and Chickpeas

Pair this spiced side dish with a rice dish or grilled meat or fish.

Serves 1

Prep at Home

1/4 cup	dried butternut squash cubes	50 mL
2 tbsp	dried cooked chickpeas	25 mL
1 tbsp	chopped dried mangos, apricots or raisins	15 mL
1 tsp	dried onion pieces	5 mL
1 tsp	crumbled dried cilantro	5 mL
1/4 tsp	finely chopped dried garlic	1 mL
1/4 tsp	curry powder	1 mL
1/4 tsp	salt	1 mL
1/8 tsp	ground cumin	0.5 mL
1/8 tsp	ground coriander	0.5 mL
Pinch	cayenne pepper	Pinch

To Serve

1/2 cup	water	125 mL

Prep at Home

1. In a sealable plastic bag, combine squash, chickpeas, mangos, onions, cilantro, garlic, curry powder, salt, cumin, coriander and cayenne. Seal and store at room temperature for up to 1 month.

To Serve

1. In a saucepan, combine squash mixture and water. Cover and let stand for 20 minutes or until starting to soften.

2. Uncover and bring to a boil over medium heat, stirring often. Reduce heat and simmer, stirring occasionally, for about 10 minutes or until squash is tender and most of the liquid is absorbed.

Fresh Addition

Add a squeeze of fresh lime or lemon juice before serving.

Stovetop Scalloped Potatoes

You don't need an oven and an hour to bake these creamy, herb-scented potatoes. They make a nice change from rice or pasta as a side to grilled pork, steak or sausages, or even just with some flavorful jerky.

Serves 1

Variation

Replace ¼ cup (50 mL) of the potatoes with dried sweet potato slices.

Prep at Home

½ cup	dried potato slices	125 mL
2 tbsp	instant skim milk powder	25 mL
1 tbsp	dried onion pieces or slices	15 mL
¼ tsp	salt	1 mL
Pinch	freshly ground black pepper	Pinch
Pinch	crumbled dried rosemary (or any other herb)	Pinch

To Serve

½ cup	water	125 mL

Prep at Home

1. In a sealable plastic bag, combine potatoes, milk powder, onions, salt, pepper and rosemary. Seal and store at room temperature for up to 1 month.

To Serve

1. In a saucepan, combine potato mixture and water. Cover and let stand for 30 minutes.

2. Uncover and bring to a boil over medium heat, stirring often. Reduce heat and simmer, gently stirring occasionally, for about 10 minutes or until potatoes are tender and sauce is thickened. Remove from heat and let stand for 5 minutes.

Potatoes "Anna" and Onion Gratin

The traditional dish "Pommes Anna" was named for a French courtesan. We're not sure Anna did much camping, but if she did, she surely would have been very impressed with this just-add-water version.

Serves 1

Tip

We generally try to avoid using stock or bouillon powder because of the high salt content and added fillers, but this dish really does benefit from the extra flavor stock powder provides. Look for one that is lower in sodium and has the most natural ingredients possible.

Prep at Home

½ cup	dried potato slices	125 mL
2 tbsp	dried onion slices	25 mL
½ tsp	vegetable or chicken stock powder (see tip, at left)	2 mL
¼ tsp	salt	1 mL
Pinch	freshly ground black pepper	Pinch
2 tbsp	coarse dried bread crumbs	25 mL
1 tbsp	grated Parmesan cheese	15 mL

To Serve

½ cup	water	125 mL

Prep at Home

1. In a sealable plastic bag, combine potatoes, onions, stock powder, salt and pepper. In another bag, combine bread crumbs and Parmesan. Seal both bags and store at room temperature for up to 2 weeks.

To Serve

1. In a saucepan, combine potato mixture and water. Cover and let stand for 30 minutes.

2. Uncover and bring to a boil over medium heat, stirring often. Reduce heat and simmer, gently stirring occasionally, for about 10 minutes or until potatoes are tender and liquid is almost absorbed. Remove from heat, sprinkle with bread crumb mixture and let stand for 5 minutes.

Moroccan Braised Beans and Lentils

Fragrant spices and a variety of textures might make this side dish take over as the main feature of your meal.

Serves 1

Variation

In place of the squash, you can use a 2-inch (5 cm) square of Roasted Winter Squash Leather or Sweet Potato and Red Pepper Leather, torn into very small pieces.

Prep at Home

¼ cup	dried cooked lentils	50 mL
¼ cup	dried cooked red kidney or black beans	50 mL
1 tbsp	finely chopped dried tomatoes	15 mL
1 tbsp	finely chopped dried winter squash	15 mL
½ tsp	crumbled dried mint	2 mL
¼ tsp	finely chopped dried lemon zest	1 mL
¼ tsp	salt	1 mL
⅛ tsp	ground cinnamon	0.5 mL
⅛ tsp	ground cumin	0.5 mL
⅛ tsp	paprika	0.5 mL

To Serve

1 cup	water	250 mL

Prep at Home

1. In a sealable plastic bag, combine lentils, beans, tomatoes, squash, mint, lemon zest, salt, cinnamon, cumin and paprika. Seal and store at room temperature for up to 1 month.

To Serve

1. In a saucepan or skillet, combine lentil mixture and water. Let stand for 15 minutes or until vegetables start to soften.

2. Bring to a boil over medium heat, stirring often. Reduce heat and boil gently, stirring often, for about 5 minutes or until vegetables are tender and liquid is absorbed.

Ramen-Style Noodles with Beans, Carrots and Onions

Toss out the seasoning packet in a ramen noodle soup (it's full of stuff you wouldn't want to eat) and add your own nutritious dried vegetables instead. The noodles themselves are fast and convenient.

Serves 1

Variation
Add 1 tbsp (15 mL) powdered Spinach Leather with the vegetables for an extra nutrition boost.

Prep at Home

1 tbsp	dried green bean pieces	15 mL
1 tbsp	dried carrot slices	15 mL
1 tbsp	dried onion pieces	15 mL
1 tbsp	dried celery slices	15 mL
1 tsp	crumbled dried parsley	5 mL
$\frac{1}{2}$ tsp	finely chopped dried garlic	2 mL
$\frac{1}{4}$ tsp	finely chopped dried gingerroot	1 mL
1	package (about $2\frac{1}{2}$ oz/80 g) instant ramen noodles, broken	1

To Serve

1 cup	water	250 mL
1 tbsp	lime juice	15 mL
2 tsp	soy sauce	10 mL

Prep at Home
1. In a sealable plastic bag, combine green beans, carrots, onions, celery, parsley, garlic and ginger. Place noodles in another bag. Seal both bags and store at room temperature for up to 1 month.

To Serve
1. In a saucepan, combine vegetable mixture and water. Let stand for 30 minutes or until vegetables are softened.

2. Bring to a boil over medium heat, stirring often. Reduce heat and simmer for about 5 minutes or until vegetables are tender. Stir in noodles, lime juice and soy sauce; heat until noodles are tender.

Egg Noodles with Teriyaki Veggies

Colorful vegetables and tender noodles in a lightly seasoned teriyaki sauce make a terrific side dish for plain grilled chicken or fish.

Serves 1

Variation

Add 1 tbsp (15 mL) finely chopped dried pineapple or mango to the vegetable mixture.

Prep at Home

2 tbsp	dried green or red bell pepper slices	25 mL
1 tbsp	dried onion slices	15 mL
1 tbsp	dried carrot slices	15 mL
1 tbsp	dried green peas	15 mL
1 tsp	packed brown sugar	5 mL
1/4 tsp	finely chopped dried gingerroot	1 mL
1/2 cup	fine egg noodles	125 mL

To Serve

2/3 cup	water	150 mL
1 tbsp	thin teriyaki sauce	15 mL

Prep at Home

1. In a sealable plastic bag, combine green peppers, onions, carrots, peas, brown sugar and ginger. Place noodles in another bag. Seal both bags and store at room temperature for up to 1 month.

To Serve

1. In a saucepan, combine vegetable mixture and water. Let stand for 15 minutes or until vegetables are softened.

2. Bring to a boil over medium heat, stirring often. Stir in noodles and teriyaki sauce. Reduce heat and boil gently, stirring often, for about 5 minutes or until vegetables and noodles are tender.

Spanish Brown Rice

Seriously, a recipe with three ingredients that tastes great? You have to try it to believe it.

Serves 1

Variation

If you don't have salsa leather, use 2 tsp (10 mL) finely chopped dried tomatoes, 1 tsp (5 mL) finely chopped dried red bell peppers and a pinch of cayenne pepper.

Prep at Home

1	2-inch (5 cm) square Salsa Leather	1
1/3 cup	dried cooked long-grain brown rice	75 mL
1/4 tsp	crumbled dried thyme	1 mL

To Serve

1/2 cup	water	125 mL

Prep at Home

1. Tear leather into small pieces. In a sealable plastic bag, combine leather, rice and thyme. Seal and store at room temperature for up to 1 month.

To Serve

1. In a saucepan or skillet, bring water to a boil. Add leather mixture, remove from heat, cover and let stand for 15 minutes, mashing leather occasionally, until rice is softened.

2. Uncover and bring to a boil over medium heat, stirring often. Boil, stirring often, for about 5 minutes or until mixture is hot and liquid is absorbed.

Chili Cornmeal Cakes

Serve these flavorful biscuits with soup or stew to round out a hearty meal perfectly.

Makes 4 biscuits

Tip

If you don't have dried chile peppers, substitute $\frac{1}{8}$ tsp (0.5 mL) cayenne pepper.

• 6- to 8-inch (15 to 20 cm) skillet, preferably cast-iron, with lid or foil to cover

Prep at Home

1 tbsp	dried corn kernels	15 mL
1 tsp	crumbled dried parsley	5 mL
$\frac{1}{2}$ tsp	finely chopped dried hot chile peppers	2 mL
$\frac{1}{2}$ tsp	chili powder	2 mL
$\frac{1}{2}$ cup	all-purpose flour	125 mL
$\frac{1}{4}$ cup	cornmeal	50 mL
2 tbsp	instant skim milk powder	25 mL
1 tsp	granulated sugar	5 mL
1 tsp	baking powder	5 mL
$\frac{1}{4}$ tsp	salt	1 mL

To Serve

$\frac{1}{2}$ cup	water or beer	125 mL
	Vegetable oil or butter	

Prep at Home

1. In a sealable plastic bag, combine corn, parsley, chile peppers and chili powder. In another bag, combine flour, cornmeal, milk powder, sugar, baking powder and salt. Seal both bags and store at room temperature for up to 1 month.

To Serve

1. In a bowl, combine corn mixture, water and 2 tsp (10 mL) oil. Let stand for 15 minutes or until corn starts to soften.

2. Shake flour mixture in bag to mix and pour into corn mixture. Using a fork, stir just until evenly moistened. Let stand for 5 minutes.

3. Meanwhile, heat skillet over medium heat until warmed. Add a thin layer of oil. Spoon dough into 4 mounds in skillet. Reduce heat to low, cover and cook for 3 minutes. Uncover and cook for about 1 minute or until bottoms are golden brown and edges are no longer shiny. Flip over and cook for about 2 minutes or until biscuits are puffed and firm. Serve hot.

Fresh Addition

Add 1 tbsp (15 mL) shredded Cheddar or Monterey Jack cheese with the flour mixture.

Cheese and Herb Skillet Biscuits

The dried cottage cheese adds a fabulous gooeyness to these herb biscuits. Serve them with eggs for breakfast or with soup or stew for lunch or dinner.

Makes 4 biscuits

Tip

These can be cooked over a campfire. Just heat the pan on a rack over the hottest part of the fire, then move it to the cooler edge to cook the biscuits. The timing will depend on the fire, so keep an eye on them.

● *6- to 8-inch (15 to 20 cm) skillet, preferably cast-iron, with lid or foil to cover*

Prep at Home

¾ cup	all-purpose flour	175 mL
2 tbsp	powdered dried cottage cheese	25 mL
2 tsp	granulated sugar	10 mL
2 tsp	crumbled dried parsley	10 mL
1½ tsp	crumbled dried herbs (basil, oregano, thyme, chives)	7 mL
1 tsp	baking powder	5 mL
¼ tsp	salt	1 mL
Pinch	freshly ground black pepper	Pinch

To Serve

½ cup	water or beer	125 mL
	Vegetable oil or butter	

Prep at Home

1. In a sealable plastic bag, combine flour, cottage cheese, sugar, parsley, herbs, baking powder, salt and pepper. Seal and store at room temperature for up to 1 week or refrigerate for up to 6 months.

To Serve

1. Heat skillet over medium heat until warmed.

2. In a bowl, combine flour mixture and water. Using a fork, stir just until evenly moistened.

3. Add a thin layer of oil to skillet. Spoon dough into 4 mounds in skillet. Reduce heat to low, cover and cook for 3 minutes. Uncover and cook for about 1 minute or until bottoms are golden brown and edges are no longer shiny. Flip over and cook for about 2 minutes or until biscuits are puffed and firm. Serve hot.

> **Fresh Addition**
>
> Add ¼ cup (50 mL) diced ham or other deli meat or 2 tbsp (25 mL) minced smoked salmon when mixing the dough.

Snacks, Baked Goods and Desserts

GORP with a Twist

"Good Old Raisins and Peanuts" has come a long way since we were kids. Combine as many dried fruits and nuts as you like to get your favorite combination, and pack several bags to satisfy munchies on the go.

**Makes about
3¹/₂ cups (875 mL)**

Tip

Be sure to drink plenty of water when snacking on dried fruits. You need to replace the liquid you'd normally get from fresh fruit.

¹/₂ cup	dried cranberries	125 mL
¹/₂ cup	raisins	125 mL
¹/₂ cup	chopped dried apricots	125 mL
¹/₂ cup	chopped dried pineapple	125 mL
¹/₂ cup	salted peanuts	125 mL
¹/₂ cup	salted cashews or almonds	125 mL
¹/₄ cup	dried sweet or sour cherries	50 mL
¹/₄ cup	dried strawberry slices	50 mL
¹/₄ cup	toasted pumpkin seeds	50 mL

1. In a sealable plastic bag or bags, combine cranberries, raisins, apricots, pineapple, peanuts, cashews, cherries, strawberries and pumpkin seeds. Seal and store at room temperature for up to 1 month.

Sesame Teriyaki Veggie Trail Mix

This colorful homemade mix is sure to satisfy the munchies when you're on the trail.

Makes about 2 cups (500 mL)

Tips

Small pieces of vegetables work well for this recipe, so use chopped or sliced vegetables that are similar in size.

Use a thin teriyaki sauce (the consistency of soy sauce) for this recipe. Those with thickeners, such as cornstarch, won't dry properly.

- *Leather sheet or parchment paper*

1 1/2 cups	mixed dried vegetables (bell peppers, peas, carrots, green beans)	375 mL
1/2 cup	chopped almonds	125 ml
2 tbsp	sesame seeds	25 mL
2 tbsp	thin teriyaki sauce	25 mL

1. In a bowl, combine vegetables, almonds, sesame seeds and teriyaki sauce; toss to coat evenly.

2. Spread mixture onto leather sheet, spacing vegetables out as much as possible. Dry at 135°F (58°C), stirring and spreading out vegetables once or twice, for 2 to 3 hours or until no longer sticky. Let cool completely on trays. Store in an airtight container at room temperature for up to 1 month.

Jerky 'n' Veg Trail Mix

Protein on the go never tasted so good. Keep a bag of this handy in your pocket for those days of hard trekking or paddling. It's sure to get you through to the next meal break.

Makes about 2¹/₂ cups (625 mL)

**Makes about
2¹⁄₂ cups (625 mL)**

Tip
Be sure to drink plenty of water when snacking on dried foods. You need to replace the liquid you'd normally get from fresh foods.

Variation
Use your favorite dried vegetables in place of the peas and red peppers. Mix in dried fruits, if you like. Try pineapple or melon for something different.

¹⁄₂ cup	dried green peas	125 mL
¹⁄₂ cup	dried cooked chickpeas	125 mL
¹⁄₂ cup	dried red bell pepper pieces	125 mL
¹⁄₂ cup	dried tomatoes, chopped	125 mL
¹⁄₂ cup	Cajun Jerky or Maple and Grainy Dijon Jerky, broken into small pieces	125 mL

1. In a sealable plastic bag, combine peas, chickpeas, red peppers, tomatoes and jerky. Seal and store at room temperature for up to 1 month.

Wasabi Tofu and Vegetable Trail Mix

This will perk you up with its hot wasabi flavor and high protein and energy content. If you like it really hot, feel free to add more wasabi.

Makes about 2¹/₂ cups (625 mL)

Tip
Be sure to drink plenty of water when snacking on dried foods to replace the water you'd normally get from fresh foods.

● *Leather sheet or parchment paper*

¹/₂ cup	dried crumbled tofu	125 mL
¹/₂ cup	dried cooked chickpeas	125 mL
¹/₂ cup	dried cauliflower florets, broken into small pieces	125 mL
¹/₂ cup	dried broccoli florets, broken into small pieces	125 mL
¹/₄ cup	dried carrot slices	50 mL
¹/₄ cup	dried green peas	50 mL
1 tsp	sesame seeds	5 mL
1 tsp	wasabi powder	5 mL
¹/₂ tsp	finely chopped dried gingerroot	2 mL
2 tbsp	freshly squeezed lime juice	25 mL

1. In a bowl, combine tofu, chickpeas, cauliflower, broccoli, carrots, peas, sesame seeds, wasabi powder, ginger and lime juice; toss to coat evenly.

2. Spread mixture onto leather sheet, spacing vegetables out as much as possible. Dry at 135°F (58°C), stirring and spreading out vegetables once or twice, for 2 to 3 hours or until no longer sticky. Let cool completely on trays. Store in an airtight container at room temperature for up to 1 month.

Tomato Herb Popcorn Seasoning

Whether you have a campfire corn popper, use the microwave at the camp recreation center or buy the nifty type in the foil pan, popcorn is a camp snack tradition. This seasoning will make it even better.

Makes about 4 cups (1 L)

Tip

Be sure the mini chopper bowl, blade and lid are completely dry before chopping the leather mixture. Any bit of moisture will prevent it from processing properly.

Prep at Home

1	2-inch (5 cm) square Tomato Paste Leather	1
¼ tsp	crumbled dried basil	1 mL
¼ tsp	crumbled dried oregano	1 mL
¼ tsp	crumbled dried parsley	1 mL
¼ tsp	salt	1 mL

To Serve

4 cups	hot popped popcorn	1 L
1 tbsp	melted butter	15 mL

Prep at Home

1. Tear leather into small pieces. In a mini chopper, pulse leather, basil, oregano, parsley and salt until very finely chopped, then process until as fine a powder as possible. Transfer to a sealable plastic bag, seal and store at room temperature for up to 1 month.

To Serve

1. In a bowl, combine hot popcorn, butter and seasoning; toss to coat evenly.

Fruit-Studded Bannock on a Stick

Bannock is a traditional bread baked over a wood fire. This slightly sweet fruit version makes a nice simple dessert or snack.

Serves 2 to 4

Tip

If you don't have refrigeration, shortening is best for room-temperature storage. Use trans fat–free shortening, if available. If you do have refrigeration available to store the flour mixture until serving, use the butter — it tastes great!

- *Four ¹/₂-inch (1 cm) thick sticks, at least 2 feet (60 cm) long*
- *Four 8-inch (20 cm) pieces of foil*

Prep at Home

¹/₂ cup	all-purpose flour	125 mL
1 tbsp	instant skim milk powder	15 mL
1 tbsp	granulated sugar	15 mL
¹/₂ tsp	baking powder	2 mL
¹/₄ tsp	ground cinnamon (optional)	1 mL
¹/₈ tsp	salt	0.5 mL
1 tbsp	cold shortening or butter	15 mL
¹/₄ cup	chopped dried fruit (apples, pears, peaches, cherries, berries)	50 mL

To Serve

¹/₄ cup	water	50 mL
	Vegetable oil or melted butter	

Prep at Home

1. In a bowl, combine flour, milk powder, sugar, baking powder, cinnamon (if using) and salt. Using a pastry blender or two knives, cut in shortening until fine crumbs form. Transfer to a sealable plastic bag. Place fruit in another bag. Seal both bags and store at room temperature for up to 1 month (or in the refrigerator if butter was used).

To Serve

1. Prepare campfire.

2. In a bowl, combine fruit and water. Let stand for 10 minutes or until fruit starts to soften.

3. Shake flour mixture in bag to mix and pour into fruit mixture. Using a fork, stir just until a soft dough forms. Gather with your hands and lightly knead in the bowl just until dough holds together.

4. Wrap a square of foil around one end of each stick, covering at least 4 inches (10 cm). Divide dough in quarters and squeeze one piece around the foil-wrapped section of each stick, making sure dough is about ¹/₂ inch (1 cm) thick on all sides of the stick.

5. Cook bannock on sticks over the fire, holding it over a medium-hot area if possible and turning often, until golden brown and firm.

Banana Peanut Butter S'mores

A camping trip wouldn't be the same without at least one feast on s'mores. This version takes it up a notch with the addition of dried bananas and peanut butter. Look out: other campers will be sneaking over to see what all the oohing and aahing is about.

Makes 4 s'mores

Variation

Replace the peanut butter with almond butter or another nut butter, or omit it.

- *Four 12-inch (30 cm) squares of foil*
- *Grill rack or flat rocks to place close to fire*

8	graham crackers	8
¼ cup	peanut butter	50 mL
¼ cup	dried banana slices	50 mL
4	1-inch (2.5 cm) pieces thin chocolate bar (or ¼ cup/50 mL chocolate chips)	4
4	large marshmallows, cut in half lengthwise	4

1. Prepare campfire and place grill rack over fire, if using.

2. Place one cracker in the center of each square of foil. Spread crackers with half the peanut butter and top each with one-quarter of the banana slices and 1 piece of chocolate. Place 2 marshmallow halves, cut side down, on top of the chocolate. Spread the remaining peanut butter on one side of the remaining graham crackers and place on top to sandwich. Wrap sandwiches tightly with foil.

3. Place on grill rack or on flat rocks close to the fire. Heat for about 10 minutes or until heated through and chocolate is melted. Let stand for 2 minutes before unwrapping.

Campfire Apple Crumble

Apple crumble is always a terrific dessert. Made over a campfire and topped with sweet cookies, it is even better than terrific!

Serves 2

Tip

You can find maple sugar granules at farmers' markets and specialty food stores.

Variation

Substitute dried pears for the apples and ground ginger for the cinnamon.

- *Shallow flameproof metal or foil baking pan (for campfire cooking)*

Prep at Home

½ cup	dried apple slices	125 mL
1 tbsp	packed brown sugar or maple sugar granules	15 mL
½ tsp	finely chopped dried lemon zest (optional)	2 mL
¼ tsp	ground cinnamon	1 mL
½ cup	crumbled oatmeal or ginger cookies	125 mL

To Serve

¾ cup	water	175 mL

Prep at Home

1. In a sealable plastic bag, combine apples, brown sugar, lemon zest (if using) and cinnamon. Place cookie crumbs in another bag. Seal both bags and store at room temperature for up to 1 month.

To Serve

1. In baking pan or a saucepan, combine apple mixture and water. Let stand for 15 minutes or until apples start to soften.

2. Simmer over a campfire or over low heat on a stove, stirring occasionally, for about 10 minutes or until apples are plump and hot. Sprinkle with cookie crumbs. Serve hot or warm.

No-Bake Blueberry Cheesecakes

These might be a little different from any other cheesecakes you've made, but they give the same sweet and fruity dessert satisfaction.

Serves 1

Tip

If you have a cooler or refrigerator, the prepared cheesecake can be covered and chilled for up to 1 day.

Prep at Home

¼ cup	dried blueberries	50 mL
¼ cup	powdered dried cottage cheese	50 mL
1 tbsp	granulated sugar	15 mL
Pinch	finely chopped dried lemon zest	Pinch
2 tbsp	graham wafer crumbs	25 mL

To Serve

½ cup	water	125 mL

Prep at Home

1. In a sealable plastic bag, combine blueberries, cottage cheese, sugar and lemon zest. Place graham crumbs in another bag. Seal both bags and store at room temperature for up to 2 weeks or refrigerate for up to 3 months.

To Serve

1. In a saucepan, bring water to a boil. Stir in blueberry mixture, remove from heat, cover and let stand for about 30 minutes, stirring occasionally, until mixture is thick and cooled to room temperature. Scrape into a bowl, if desired, and serve sprinkled with graham crumbs.

Pumpkin Pie Pudding

Jennifer was on a camping trip in Oregon during Canadian Thanksgiving (in mid-October), and there wasn't a pumpkin pie to be found. She improvised by making a pudding with canned pumpkin and creating a water bath to cook over the campfire. It did cook — eventually. This version is much, much easier and much less smoky tasting (definitely a plus!).

Serves 1

Tips

If the leather is pliable, you can tear or crumble it by hand; if it's crisp, you can tear it into pieces and pulse it in a mini chopper or spice grinder.

If you don't have pumpkin pie spice, use $1/8$ tsp (0.5 mL) each ground cinnamon and ginger and a pinch of ground nutmeg.

Prep at Home

$1/4$ cup	crumbled Roasted Pumpkin Leather or Roasted Winter Squash Leather	50 mL
1 tbsp	packed brown sugar	15 mL
1 tbsp	instant skim milk powder	15 mL
1 tsp	cornstarch	5 mL
$1/4$ tsp	pumpkin pie spice	1 mL

To Serve

$2/3$ cup	water	150 mL

Prep at Home

1. Tear leather into very small pieces. In a sealable plastic bag, combine leather, brown sugar, milk powder, cornstarch and pumpkin pie spice. Seal and store at room temperature for up to 1 month.

To Serve

1. In a saucepan, stir pumpkin mixture to make sure it's evenly blended. Gradually stir in water. Let stand for 15 minutes or until pumpkin starts to soften.

2. Bring to a boil over medium heat, stirring often. Reduce heat and boil gently, stirring constantly, for about 2 minutes or until thickened. Serve hot or let cool.

Apple Spice Rice Pudding

Rice pudding is one of Jennifer's all-time favorite desserts. The addition of dried apples and warm spices makes it even better.

Serves 1

Variation

Replace the apples with 1 tbsp (15 mL) each finely chopped dried peaches and dried cherries.

Prep at Home

⅓ cup	dried cooked long-grain white or brown rice	75 mL
2 tbsp	finely chopped dried apples	25 mL
2 tbsp	instant skim milk powder	25 mL
1 tbsp	packed brown sugar	15 mL
1 tsp	powdered eggs (optional)	5 mL
¼ tsp	ground cinnamon	1 mL
Pinch	ground nutmeg or ginger	Pinch
Pinch	salt	Pinch

To Serve

1 cup	water	250 mL

Prep at Home

1. In a mini chopper or small food processor, process rice until finely chopped and about one-quarter is powdery. Transfer to a sealable plastic bag and add apples, milk powder, brown sugar, powdered eggs (if using), cinnamon, nutmeg and salt. Seal and store at room temperature for up to 1 month.

To Serve

1. In a saucepan, combine rice mixture and water. Cover and let stand for 20 minutes or until rice starts to soften.

2. Uncover and bring to a boil over medium heat, stirring often. Reduce heat and simmer, stirring often, for about 5 minutes or until rice is tender and pudding is creamy and thickened.

Raspberry Chocolate Pudding

Chocolate is always a good choice for dessert, and when it's cooked into an easy pudding, spiked with raspberries and served warm, you might be tempted to eat dessert first!

Serves 1

Prep at Home

2 tbsp	skim milk powder	25 mL
1 tbsp	granulated sugar	15 mL
1 tbsp	unsweetened cocoa powder	15 mL
1 tsp	cornstarch	5 mL
2 tbsp	dried raspberries	25 mL

To Serve

$1/2$ cup	water	125 mL

Prep at Home

1. In a sealable plastic bag, combine milk powder, sugar, cocoa and cornstarch, mashing to break up any lumps of cocoa. Add raspberries. Seal and store at room temperature for up to 1 month.

To Serve

1. In a small saucepan, stir raspberry mixture to make sure it's evenly blended. Gradually stir in water. Bring to a boil over medium heat, stirring often. Reduce heat and boil gently, stirring constantly, for about 2 minutes or until thickened. Serve hot or let cool.

Fresh Addition

Add $1/4$ tsp (1 mL) vanilla extract after removing the pudding from the heat.

Warm Peaches with Ginger

Peaches and ginger are a delightful combination, whether served in a bowl on their own or with cookies, over cake or on biscuits.

Serves 1

Tips

You can find maple sugar granules at farmers' markets and specialty food stores.

If you have a spice grinder, use it to finely chop or powder the dried gingerroot slices, chopping 1 to 2 tbsp (15 to 25 mL) at a time and storing it in an airtight container. Alternatively, use a sharp knife, though it's a little more work.

Prep at Home

⅓ cup	dried peach slices	75 mL
1 tsp	packed brown sugar or maple sugar granules	5 mL
¼ tsp	minced dried gingerroot	1 mL

To Serve

⅓ cup	water	75 mL

Prep at Home

1. In a sealable plastic bag, combine peaches, brown sugar and ginger. Seal and store at room temperature for up to 1 month.

To Serve

1. In a small saucepan, combine peach mixture and water. Let stand for 15 minutes or until peaches start to soften.

2. Bring just to a simmer over medium heat, stirring often. Serve hot or let cool.

Tropical Fruit Compote

A little taste of the tropics is just the thing to warm you up at the campsite on a chilly evening.

Serves 1

Tip

To make vanilla sugar: In a food processor, mini chopper or blender, combine 1 cup (250 mL) granulated sugar and half a vanilla bean, cut into thirds; process until vanilla is very finely chopped. Transfer to an airtight container and let stand for at least 1 week or for up to 3 months. Sift through a fine-mesh sieve to remove any large pieces of vanilla. Return to airtight container for up to 1 year from the date you made it.

Prep at Home

⅓ cup	chopped mixed dried tropical fruit (pineapple, papaya, mango, kiwifruit, melon)	75 mL
2 tsp	vanilla sugar (see tip, at left)	10 mL

To Serve

½ cup	water	125 mL

Prep at Home

1. In a sealable plastic bag, combine fruit and vanilla sugar. Seal and store at room temperature for up to 1 month.

To Serve

1. In a small saucepan, combine fruit mixture and water. Let stand for 15 minutes or until fruit starts to soften.

2. Bring just to a simmer over medium heat, stirring often. Serve hot or let cool.

Fresh Addition

Replace the water with fruit juice and add a splash of rum after removing the compote from the heat.

Berry Sauce

If you happen to pick up some ice cream or a cake to eat at your campsite, add this berry sauce to turn it into a fancy dessert. It's also delicious served over pancakes for breakfast.

Serves 1 to 2

Variation

Berry Cherry Sauce: Use ¼ cup (50 mL) mixed dried berries and 1 tbsp (15 mL) dried cherries.

Prep at Home

⅓ cup	mixed dried berries	75 mL
1 tbsp	vanilla sugar (see tip, page 331)	15 mL
½ tsp	minced dried orange or lemon zest	2 mL

To Serve

½ cup	water	125 mL

Prep at Home

1. In a sealable plastic bag, combine berries, vanilla sugar and orange zest. Seal and store at room temperature for up to 1 month.

To Serve

1. In a small saucepan, combine fruit mixture and water. Let stand for about 15 minutes or until berries start to soften.

2. Bring just to a simmer over medium heat, stirring often. If desired, mash berries slightly for a thicker sauce. Serve hot or let cool.

Other Uses
for Your
Dehydrator

Pet Treats

Making your own homemade pet treats is much easier than you'd expect. We've created recipes here that rival the pricy gourmet treats available at boutique pet stores, and you can make them for a fraction of the cost in your dehydrator.

Keep in mind that dogs and cats don't care for sweetening and salt as much as humans do, so don't be tempted to season up their treats as you'd prefer. They'll be delighted with the naturally good-tasting ingredients.

As with all dehydrating, for high-quality, safe preserved foods, always use high-quality, fresh ingredients. Don't use anything to make pet treats that you wouldn't feel safe feeding to your family. The recipes here avoid the use of any foods that are toxic to animals, so don't make substitutions unless you're sure a food is safe.

You should always introduce new foods to your pets gradually to avoid stomach upset. So, when you try a new recipe, give your pets just one treat to start to make sure they tolerate the ingredients well.

And of course, check with your veterinarian if you have any questions about your pets' dietary requirements before feeding them these treats.

Apple Oat Crisps

Ever since they tasted these crispy treats, Jennifer and Jay's dogs, Daisy and Snoopy, go crazy every time they smell anything with apples in the dehydrator.

Makes about 50 crisps

Tip

Steel-cut oats are less refined, and therefore more nutritious, than rolled oats. If you prefer, use large-flake (old-fashioned) rolled oats in place of the steel-cut oats and cook according to package directions.

• *Leather sheets or parchment paper*

1 cup	steel-cut oats	250 mL
3 cups	water	750 mL
2	apples, cored and chopped	2
½ tsp	ground cinnamon	2 mL

1. In a saucepan, combine oats and water; bring to a boil over high heat. Reduce heat to low and cook, stirring often, for about 30 minutes or until oats are tender and thick. Measure out 3 cups (750 mL) and transfer to a shallow dish; let cool completely. Reserve any extra for another use.

2. In a food processor, pulse apples and cinnamon until very finely chopped. Add oats and pulse until mixture is fairly smooth and has the consistency of paste.

3. Spread out to about ¼-inch (0.5 cm) thickness, as evenly as possible, on leather sheets, leaving it slightly thicker around the edges. Dry at 130°F (55°C) for 5 to 8 hours or until top is very firm and it is easy to lift from the sheet. Flip onto a cutting board and peel off sheet. Cut into 2- by 1-inch (5 by 2.5 cm) rectangles, or desired size.

4. Transfer pieces to mesh drying racks, moist side down, and dry for about 2 hours or until firm and crisp. Let cool completely on trays or on wire racks. Store in a cookie tin at room temperature for up to 3 months.

Veggie and Brown Rice Crisps

You'll fool your dogs into thinking these are something decadent when, really, they're just pure, healthy ingredients made into colorful, crispy treats.

Makes about 60 small or 20 large crisps

Tip

Use fine-mesh tray liners such as Clean-A-Screen, if necessary, to prevent the mixture from slipping through the trays and sticking.

2 cups	coarsely chopped carrots	500 mL
	Cold water	
2½ cups	cooked long-grain brown rice, cooled	625 mL
1 cup	frozen green peas, thawed	375 mL
¼ cup	salt-free tomato paste	50 mL
½ tsp	crumbled dried basil or oregano	2 mL

1. In a saucepan, cover carrots with cold water by about ¼ inch (0.5 cm); bring to a boil over high heat. Reduce heat and boil gently for about 7 minutes or until carrots are soft. Drain, reserving cooking water. Let carrots cool.

2. In a food processor, purée carrots, rice, peas, tomato paste and basil, gradually adding 1 to 2 tbsp (15 to 25 mL) of the reserved cooking water if necessary to make a thick, smooth paste.

3. Scoop out 1 tsp (5 mL) of carrot mixture for small crisps or 1 tbsp (15 mL) for large crisps. With moistened fingers, pat out to a rounded rectangle about ¼ inch (0.5 cm) thick. Place at least ½ inch (1 cm) apart on fine-mesh drying trays. Repeat with the remaining mixture, dipping your fingers in water often to prevent sticking.

4. Dry at 130°F (55°C) for 5 to 6 hours for small or 6 to 8 hours for large or until crisp and dry throughout. Let cool completely on trays or on wire racks. Store in a cookie tin at room temperature for up to 3 months.

Peanut Butter and Jelly Drops

*You might have to hide
these to keep the people
in your house from
snacking on them —
they're that good!*

**Makes about
100 small or
60 large drops**

Variations

Use large-flake (old-
fashioned) rolled oats in
place of the steel-cut
oats and cook according
to package directions.

Replace half the berries
with $^1/_2$ cup (125 mL)
mashed ripe banana.

- *Leather sheets or parchment paper*

$^1/_2$ cup	steel-cut oats	125 mL
$1^1/_2$ cups	water	375 mL
1 cup	unsalted roasted peanuts	250 mL
1 cup	mixed berries (thawed and drained if frozen)	250 mL

1. In a saucepan, combine oats and water; bring to a boil over high heat. Reduce heat to low and cook, stirring often, for about 30 minutes or until oats are tender and thick. Measure out $1^1/_2$ cups (375 mL) and transfer to a shallow dish; let cool completely. Reserve any extra for another use.

2. In a food processor, pulse peanuts until finely ground and starting to clump together. Add berries and purée until fairly smooth. Add oats and pulse until blended.

3. Drop level teaspoonfuls (5 mL) of peanut mixture for small drops or rounded teaspoonfuls for large drops onto leather sheets, leaving at least 1 inch (2.5 cm) between drops. Using a moistened spatula or fingers, spread out to about $^1/_4$-inch (0.5 cm) thickness. Dry at 130°F (55°C) for about 6 hours or until tops are very firm and drops are easy to lift from sheet.

4. Transfer drops to mesh drying racks, moist side down, and dry for about 3 hours or until firm and crisp. Let cool completely on trays or on wire racks. Store in an airtight container at room temperature for up to 1 month.

Chicken and Sweet Potato Snacks

You won't believe how fast tails wag when your furry friends have a taste of these nutritious snacks.

Makes about 100 small or 60 large cookies

Tips

Choose the size that is appropriate for your dog. Make sure it's big enough that he has to chew and that it won't get stuck in between his rows of teeth.

Treats made with meat, even lean dehydrated meat, last longer if stored in the refrigerator, though they can be stored at room temperature for short periods.

1 lb	lean ground chicken	500 g
2 cups	cubed sweet potato (about 1)	500 mL
½ cup	water	125 mL

1. In a large skillet, over medium heat, cook chicken, breaking up with a spoon, until it starts to release liquid. Stir in sweet potato and water. Reduce heat to medium-low, cover and boil gently, stirring occasionally, for about 15 minutes or until potatoes are soft and chicken is no longer pink. Remove lid, increase heat to medium-high and boil until excess liquid is evaporated. Transfer to a shallow dish and let cool completely.

2. In a food processor, purée chicken mixture until very smooth.

3. Scoop out level teaspoonfuls (5 mL) of chicken mixture for small snacks or rounded teaspoonfuls for large snacks and roll into a ball. With moistened fingers, press into a rounded rectangle about ¼ inch (0.5 cm) thick. Place at least ½ inch (1 cm) apart on mesh drying trays. Repeat with the remaining mixture, dipping your fingers in water often to prevent sticking.

4. Dry at 155°F (68°C) for about 6 hours or until crisp and dry throughout. Let cool completely on trays or on wire racks. Store in an airtight container at room temperature for up to 2 weeks or refrigerate for up to 3 months.

Minty Lamb and Rice Cookies

Gourmet food for your dogs? Why not? They'll think you're the best chef around when they taste these cookies.

Makes about 100 small or 60 large cookies

Tip

Treats made with meat, even lean dehydrated meat, last longer if stored in the refrigerator, though they can be stored at room temperature for short periods. Even small amounts of fat in the meat can go rancid if kept at warmer temperatures for too long.

1 lb	lean ground lamb	500 g
1½ cups	cooked brown rice	375 mL
½ cup	water (approx.)	125 mL
¼ cup	fresh mint leaves (or 1 tbsp/15 mL crumbled dried mint)	50 mL

1. In a large skillet, over medium heat, cook lamb, breaking up with a spoon, until it starts to release liquid. Stir in rice and water. Reduce heat and boil gently, stirring occasionally, for 5 to 8 minutes or until lamb is no longer pink. Transfer to a shallow dish and let cool completely.

2. In a food processor, purée lamb mixture and mint until smooth, adding a little more water if necessary to make a thick, smooth paste.

3. Scoop out level teaspoonfuls (5 mL) of lamb mixture for small cookies or rounded teaspoonfuls for large cookies and roll into a ball. With moistened fingers, press into a rounded rectangle about ¼ inch (0.5 cm) thick. Place at least ½ inch (1 cm) apart on mesh drying trays. Repeat with the remaining mixture, dipping your fingers in water often to prevent sticking.

4. Dry at 155°F (68°C) for about 6 hours or until crisp and dry throughout. Let cool completely on trays or on wire racks. Store in an airtight container at room temperature for up to 2 weeks or refrigerate for up to 3 months.

Venison, Apple and Barley Cookies

Use up cuts of venison that aren't popular with your human family members and you'll delight the canine ones for sure with these healthy, crispy cookies.

Makes about 100 small or 60 large cookies

Tips

If you don't have ground venison, use a food processor to pulse raw chopped venison until fairly finely chopped, then cook as directed in step 1. Be sure to clean the food processor well.

Whole barley is more nutritious than the more refined pot or pearl barley; however, if it's not available, you can substitute pot or pearl barley.

8 oz	lean ground venison	250 g
1½ cups	cooked whole barley, cooled	375 mL
½ cup	water (approx.)	125 mL
1 cup	chopped apple	250 mL

1. In a large skillet, over medium heat, cook venison, breaking up with a spoon, until it starts to brown. Stir in barley and water. Reduce heat and boil gently, stirring occasionally, for 5 to 8 minutes or until venison is no longer pink and liquid is almost absorbed. Transfer to a shallow dish and let cool completely.

2. In a food processor, purée venison mixture and apple until smooth, adding a little more water if necessary to make a thick, smooth paste.

3. Scoop out level teaspoonfuls (5 mL) of venison mixture for small cookies or rounded teaspoonfuls for large cookies and roll into a ball. With moistened hands, press into a rounded rectangle about ¼ inch (0.5 cm) thick. Place at least ½ inch (1 cm) apart on mesh drying trays. Repeat with the remaining mixture, dipping your fingers in water often to prevent sticking.

4. Dry at 155°F (68°C) for about 6 hours or until crisp and dry throughout. Let cool completely on trays or on wire racks. Store in an airtight container at room temperature for up to 2 weeks or refrigerate for up to 3 months.

Chicken Liver and Garlic Jerky

These highly nutritious snacks cost a fraction of the price of the "gourmet" packaged versions.

Makes about 8 oz (250 g)

Tips

Lining the drying trays with parchment paper makes these treats dry more quickly and get crisper, and makes it much easier to lift the sheet from the tray. Another bonus: you don't have to worry about the liver and garlic flavors transferring to the plastic of a leather sheet.

If desired, use metal paper clips to fasten the parchment paper to the drying trays to prevent it from blowing around in the dehydrator.

Break the jerky into pieces that are an appropriate size for your dog. Make sure they're big enough that she has to chew and that they won't get stuck in between her rows of teeth.

- *Preheat oven to 350°F (180°C)*
- *Rimmed baking sheet, lined with parchment paper*
- *Mesh drying trays, lined with parchment paper*

2 lbs	chicken livers	1 kg
12	cloves garlic (about 4 oz/125 g)	12

1. Spread out livers and garlic as much as possible on prepared baking sheet. Bake in preheated oven for about 25 minutes or until livers are no longer pink inside. Let cool completely.

2. In a food processor, purée livers and garlic to make a thick, smooth paste.

3. Using a moistened offset or rubber spatula, spread paste out to $1/4$-inch (0.5 cm) thickness, as evenly as possible, on prepared drying trays. Dry at 155°F (68°C) for about 2 hours or until firm and easy to lift from the parchment paper. Break into bite-size pieces.

4. Transfer pieces to mesh drying trays and dry for about 4 hours or until very firm, crisp and dry throughout. Let cool completely on trays or on wire racks. Store in an airtight container at room temperature for up to 2 weeks or refrigerate for up to 3 months.

Tuna and Rice Snacks

Your cats will be delighted with these snacks made from two simple, nutritious ingredients.

Makes about 4 oz (125 g)

Tip

If you have a large food processor that doesn't work for this amount of ingredients, you can do it in batches in a mini chopper or use an immersion blender in a tall cup. You may need to add more juice to improve puréeing; just be sure not to make the mixture too wet to handle.

| 1 | can (6 oz/170 g) water-packed low-sodium tuna | 1 |
| 1 cup | cooked brown rice, cooled | 250 mL |

1. Drain juice from tuna, reserving juice. In a food processor, purée tuna and rice until smooth, adding enough of the reserved juice to make a thick, smooth paste.

2. Scoop out ¼ tsp (1 mL) paste and, with moistened fingers, roll into a ball. Press to ¼-inch (0.5 cm) thickness. Place at least ¼ inch (0.5 cm) apart on mesh drying trays. Repeat with the remaining paste, dipping your fingers in water often to prevent sticking.

3. Dry at 155°F (68°C) for 2 to 3 hours or until very firm, crisp and dry throughout. Let cool completely on trays. Store in an airtight container at room temperature for up to 2 weeks or refrigerate for up to 3 months.

White Fish Jerky

With just one ingredient and your dehydrator, you can make jerky that your cats will love.

Makes about 4 oz (125 g)

Variation

Replace the tilapia with salmon, cutting it into ¼-inch (0.5 cm) thick bite-size pieces. Blot off any excess fat after baking in step 1. Store salmon jerky in the refrigerator — its higher fat content can cause rancidity more quickly than leaner fish.

- *Preheat oven to 350°F (180°C)*
- *Rimmed baking sheet, lined with parchment paper*

1 lb	skinless tilapia, catfish or other low-fat whitefish fillets	500 g

1. Slice each fish fillet into quarters lengthwise. Slice crosswise into slices about ¼ inch (0.5 cm) thick. Place on prepared baking sheet, spreading out as much as possible. Bake in preheated oven for about 10 minutes or until firm and opaque. Let cool completely.

2. Place fish pieces on fine-mesh drying trays, discarding any accumulated liquid. Dry at 155°F (68°C) for 4 to 6 hours or until very firm and dry throughout. Let cool completely on a tray lined with paper towels to blot off any excess fat. Store in an airtight container at room temperature for up to 2 weeks or refrigerate for up to 3 months.

Catnip Jerky

Some cats go crazy for catnip. When you combine it with chicken liver in this jerky, it will really drive them wild.

Makes about 4 oz (125 g)

Tips

Lining the drying trays with parchment paper makes these treats dry more quickly and get crisper, and makes it much easier to lift the sheet from the tray. Another bonus: you don't have to worry about the liver flavor transferring to the plastic of a leather sheet.

If desired, use metal paper clips to fasten the parchment paper to the drying trays to prevent it from blowing around in the dehydrator.

If you grow your own catnip, use it fresh in these treats or dry it for later use, following the directions for mint on page 24. Dried catnip can be purchased at pet food stores.

- *Preheat oven to 350°F (180°C)*
- *Rimmed baking sheet, lined with parchment paper*
- *Mesh drying trays, lined with parchment paper*

1 lb	chicken livers	500 g
2 tbsp	fresh catnip leaves (or 2 tsp/10 mL crumbled dried)	25 mL

1. Spread out livers as much as possible on prepared baking sheet. Bake in preheated oven for about 25 minutes or until no longer pink inside. Let cool completely.

2. In a food processor, purée livers and catnip to make a thick, smooth paste.

3. Using a moistened offset or rubber spatula, spread paste out to ¼-inch (0.5 cm) thickness, as evenly as possible, on prepared drying trays. Dry at 155°F (68°C) for about 2 hours or until firm and easy to lift from the parchment paper. Break into bite-size pieces.

4. Transfer pieces to mesh drying trays and dry for about 4 hours or until very firm, crisp and dry throughout. Let cool completely on trays or on wire racks. Store in an airtight container at room temperature for up to 2 weeks or refrigerate for up to 3 months.

Gifts

Gifts from the kitchen are always a welcome treat. When you use ingredients you dried yourself to create the gifts, they become even more special and will be appreciated that much more. In this chapter, you'll find a selection of recipes that require minimal work and ingredients, but make wonderful gifts.

Packaging makes a world of difference when you're giving food as a gift, so get creative with jars, containers, decorative bags and ribbons or ties. Be sure to label the ingredients and include the preparation instructions. A hand-printed recipe card, a small piece of paper tied into a scroll or a pretty gift tag are just a few ways you can both dress up your gift and include the necessary information.

Fruit and Herb Tea Blends

Many fruits, flowers and herbs can be made into tea. You need only your imagination and your palate to concoct delicious blends. Some of these suggestions incorporate store-bought loose tea leaves; others just include herbs and fruits you can dry yourself.

Each blend makes about ¼ cup (50 mL)

Tip

If you're buying loose tea leaves, high-quality and yes, more expensive, tea really is superior to the cheaper versions. It's worth the splurge for the finest flavor.

Ginger Lemon Tea

¼ cup	loose black tea leaves	50 mL
1 tsp	finely chopped dried lemon zest	5 mL
½ tsp	finely chopped dried gingerroot	2 mL

Blueberry Lemon Tea

2 tbsp	loose black tea leaves	25 mL
2 tbsp	dried blueberries, crushed	25 mL
1 tsp	finely chopped dried lemon zest	5 mL

Apple Cinnamon Tea

2 tbsp	loose black tea leaves	25 mL
2 tbsp	finely chopped dried apples	25 mL
Pinch	ground cinnamon	Pinch

Lavender Lemon Tea

¼ cup	loose black tea leaves	50 mL
1 tsp	dried lavender flowers	5 mL
½ tsp	finely chopped dried lemon zest	2 mL

Vanilla Peach Tea

3 tbsp	loose black tea leaves	45 mL
1 tbsp	finely chopped dried peaches	15 mL
1	¼-inch (0.5 cm) piece vanilla bean, minced	1

Berry Green Tea

3 tbsp	loose green tea leaves	45 mL
1 tbsp	dried cranberries	15 mL
1 tsp	finely chopped dried strawberries	5 mL

Mint Green Tea

3 tbsp	loose green tea leaves	45 mL
1 tbsp	crumbled dried mint	15 mL

Strawberry Mint Tea

¼ cup	crumbled dried mint	50 mL
1 tbsp	finely chopped dried strawberries	15 mL

Orange Mint Tea

¼ cup	crumbled dried mint	50 mL
1 tsp	finely chopped dried orange zest	5 mL

Tropical Mint Tea

2 tbsp	crumbled dried mint	25 mL
1 tbsp	finely chopped dried mango	15 mL
1 tbsp	finely chopped dried pineapple	15 mL

Savory Herb and Lemon Tea

3	dried bay leaves, crumbled	3
2 tbsp	crumbled dried rosemary	25 mL
1 tbsp	crumbled dried thyme	15 mL
2 tsp	finely chopped dried lemon zest	10 mL
¼ tsp	whole black peppercorns	1 mL

1. In a bowl, combine tea leaves, herbs and/or fruit as called for. Transfer to a jar with a tight-sealing lid, a decorative bag or a tin. Seal tightly and let stand for at least 1 week to let flavors blend. Store in a cool, dark place for up to 1 year.

Write out these directions on a recipe card to attach to the package:

To brew tea, add about 1 tsp (5 mL) tea blend for each 6-oz (175 mL) cup of boiling water. Let stand for about 5 minutes or until desired strength. Strain through a sieve into cup.

Cranberry Ginger Scone Mix

Short of delivering hot, fresh-baked scones, what could be a more delightful gift than a scone mix made with your own dried cranberries and ginger? The recipients will be able to make tender, yummy scones just by adding water and giving the mixture a quick stir.

Makes 5 batches (each batch makes 8 to 10 scones)

Tips

If buttermilk powder is unavailable, substitute skim milk powder and reduce the baking soda to 2 tsp (10 mL).

Real butter does make wonderful scones; however, the mix will need to be stored in the refrigerator and you'll need to make a notation on the recipe card for the recipient to do the same. If using shortening to make a shelf-stable mix, look for shortening with zero trans fat.

Variation

Substitute other chopped dried berries for the cranberries and/or grated dried orange or lemon zest for the ginger.

- 5 decorative bags or jars with tight-fitting lids

9 cups	cake-and-pastry flour (2½ lbs/1.25 kg)	2.25 L
1 cup	buttermilk powder	250 mL
⅔ cup	granulated sugar	150 mL
¼ cup	baking powder	50 mL
1 tbsp	baking soda	15 mL
1 tbsp	salt	15 mL
1 lb	butter or shortening, cubed and chilled (see tip, at left)	500 g
2 cups	dried cranberries, finely chopped	500 mL
¼ cup	dried grated gingerroot	50 mL

1. In a large bowl, whisk together flour, buttermilk powder, sugar, baking powder, baking soda and salt. Using a pastry blender, cut in butter until crumbly. Stir in cranberries and ginger.

2. Divide into 5 equal portions (about 3¼ cups/800 mL each) and place in bags or jars. Tie tightly or seal and store in the refrigerator for up to 1 month (if using butter) or in a cool, dry place for up to 2 months (if using shortening).

Write out these directions on a recipe card to attach to the package:

Cranberry Ginger Scones
In a bowl, using a fork, stir the scone mix. Quickly stir in ¾ cup (175 mL) water just until a sticky dough forms. Drop 8 to 10 large spoonfuls on a baking sheet lined with parchment paper. Bake in a 450°F (230°C) oven for 10 to 12 minutes or until golden and firm to the touch. Serve warm with butter and/or preserves.

Vegetable Soup Mix

Gift the gift of your garden's bounty in this pretty, delicious dried soup mix. Package it up, attach the cooking instructions and wait for the rave reviews.

Makes 1 batch (serves 4)

- *Clear jar with a tight-fitting lid or a sturdy decorative bag*

½ cup	dried corn kernels	125 mL
½ cup	dried carrot pieces	125 mL
1 tbsp	dried celery slices	15 mL
1 tbsp	dried onion pieces	15 mL
¼ cup	dried red bell pepper pieces	50 mL
1 tsp	crumbled dried parsley	5 mL
1 tsp	salt	5 mL
½ tsp	crumbled dried basil	2 mL
½ tsp	minced dried garlic	2 mL
¼ tsp	freshly ground black pepper	1 mL
¼ cup	red lentils	50 mL

1. In jar or bag, carefully add in order to layer: corn, carrots, celery, onions, red peppers, parsley, salt, basil, garlic, pepper and lentils. Seal tightly and store at room temperature for up to 6 months.

Write out these directions on a recipe card to attach to the package:

Vegetable Soup
In a large pot, combine soup mix and 9 cups (2.25 L) water; bring to a boil over high heat. Reduce heat and simmer, stirring occasionally, for about 30 minutes or until vegetables are tender and flavor is well blended.

Housewarming Just-Add-Water Chili Mix

When someone has just moved into a new house, they're lucky to be able to find the kitchen amid all of the boxes, let alone any ingredients. A gift of this hearty chili mix will be a welcome treat. If they've got people helping them move, make them a double batch.

Makes 1 batch (serves 4)

Tip

Complete the gift by including a bag of tortilla chips or a batch of Mexican Tortilla Triangles (page 178), some disposable plastic bowls and cutlery and a package of paper napkins. A few chilled beers would also likely be a welcome addition!

- Clear jar with a tight-fitting lid or a sturdy decorative bag

1 cup	dried cooked kidney or black beans	250 mL
1 cup	dried cooked chickpeas	250 mL
1/2 cup	finely chopped dried tomatoes	125 mL
1/4 cup	dried red or green bell pepper pieces	50 mL
2 tbsp	dried onion pieces	25 mL
2 tsp	crumbled dried oregano	10 mL
1 tsp	chili powder	5 mL
1/2 tsp	salt	2 mL
1/4 tsp	chipotle pepper powder	1 mL

1. In jar or bag, combine beans, chickpeas, tomatoes, red peppers, onions, oregano, chili powder, salt and chipotle powder. Seal tightly and store at room temperature for up to 6 months.

Write out these directions on a recipe card to attach to the package:

Chili
In a pot, combine chili mix and 5 cups (1.25 L) water; let stand for 30 minutes or until vegetables start to soften. Bring to a boil over medium heat. Reduce heat and boil gently, stirring often, for about 15 minutes or until vegetables are soft.

Fruit and Oat Muffin Mix

A homemade mix to make muffins from scratch will be even more of a treat when it's chock full of your own home-dried fruits.

Makes 1 batch (makes 12 muffins)

Tips

For best results, use dried fruits that are soft and pliable, since they won't get soaked before going into the batter.

Give a jar of homemade jam along with the muffin mix, or make it a part of a bigger kitchen gift with a nice bowl, a whisk and a silicone spatula or a shiny new muffin pan.

● *Clear jar with a tight-fitting lid or a sturdy decorative bag*

1 cup	all-purpose flour	250 mL
1 cup	whole wheat flour	250 mL
¾ cup	quick-cooking rolled oats	175 mL
¾ cup	granulated sugar	175 mL
⅓ cup	instant skim milk powder	75 mL
2 tsp	baking powder	10 mL
1 tsp	ground cinnamon	5 mL
½ tsp	ground ginger	2 mL
¼ tsp	salt	1 mL
¾ cup	finely chopped mixed dried fruit (apples, pears, peaches, bananas, pineapple, berries, cherries)	175 mL
½ cup	chopped toasted walnuts or pecans (optional)	125 mL

1. In a bowl, combine all-purpose and whole wheat flours, oats, sugar, milk powder, baking powder, cinnamon, ginger and salt. Pour into jar or bag. Add fruit and nuts (if using). Seal tightly and store at room temperature for up to 3 months.

Write out these directions on a recipe card to attach to the package:

Fruit and Oat Muffins
In a bowl, stir the muffin mix. In another bowl, whisk together 1 egg, 1³⁄₄ cups (425 mL) water and ¹⁄₄ cup (50 mL) melted butter or vegetable oil. Pour over dry ingredients and stir just until moistened. Spoon into a 12-cup muffin pan lined with paper liners. Bake in a 375°F (190°C) oven for 25 minutes or until tops spring back when lightly touched. Let cool in pan on a wire rack for 10 minutes. Transfer to rack to cool completely.

Crafts

Drying flowers and craft dough in your dehydrator is much faster than air-drying, ensures even drying and helps to preserve the color, especially for flowers. Different temperatures are required for flower drying and crafts than for food, so these are best to do when you're not using your dehydrator to dry food.

Lavender Wreath

A fragrant and pretty wreath is simple to make and can be used on a table, on a wall or as part of a larger dried flower creation.

Tip

This wreath can be any size you like. Just keep in mind that you want to make it bushier to start, as once dried, the individual flowers will shrink by about half.

• *Metal floral wire or twist ties*

Lavender sprigs

1. Cut lavender sprigs just as the flowers are fully formed and colored but have not started to open. Leave the stems of the sprigs as long as possible. Shake outside to remove any dirt or bugs.

2. Hold 3 sprigs of lavender at the part of the stem closest to the flowers. Braid the 3 stems together, starting with the left stem toward the center, and complete one set of twists. Add another sprig to the new left-hand stem, starting the top of the flowers about halfway down the first set of flowers. Add another sprig to the other two stems and braid another set of twists.

3. Keep adding new stems and braiding to make a bushy braid. While braiding, start shaping stems into a ring. When ring is the desired size, tuck the ends of the last stems under the first flowers and fasten with wire. The flowers should meet on top of the wreath so that very little stem shows.

4. Place on a mesh drying tray and dry at 100°F (38°C) for 8 to 12 hours or until stems are very dry and crisp. Let cool completely.

Orange Ornaments

These ornaments can be hung on a Christmas tree or from an indoor tree or curtain rod any time of year.

Tips

If you don't paint these, they can be composted when they've lost their color and fragrance. If they are painted, they will last a little longer.

- Glue gun
- Sewing needle
- Raffia, decorative string, ribbon or elastic
- Clear craft paint (optional)
- Paint brushes (optional)
- Sparkles (optional)

Oranges

1. Using a small serrated knife, cut oranges crosswise into slices about $\frac{1}{4}$ inch (0.5 cm) thick, trimming off ends. You'll need two slices for each ornament. Cut a slit starting from the center of each slice straight out through the rind.

2. Place on mesh drying trays and dry at 130°F (55°C) for 16 to 20 hours or until very firm and dry.

3. Meanwhile, preheat glue gun. While the oranges are still warm, take two slices of about the same size and put the slits together, sliding the slices together at a 90° angle. Add a small dot of glue at the center where the two slices meet to hold them in place. Hold until glue hardens. Thread needle with raffia, insert through the top of one slice, at the center, and tie in a loop to hang.

4. If desired, paint with clear craft paint to seal. Dip edges of freshly painted rind in sparkles, if desired, for a festive look. Hang to dry completely.

Dried Rose Posy

Roses are a classic dried flower, and the dehydrator makes drying them easy and thorough. These lovely little posies make a lovely decoration or gift.

Tips

Sunflowers, cornflowers, ferns, grasses and other sturdy flowers can be dried as well. Follow the drying instructions for the roses, adjusting the time as necessary. Thin, delicate flowers don't tend to dry well; they just shrivel and lose their beauty. Keep in mind that any thick stems should be removed, as they hold a lot of water and are difficult to get thoroughly dry.

If you have a dehydrator with stacking trays, an accessory like Convert-A-Tray can increase the height between trays, allowing you to dry larger items such as flowers.

- Elastic band
- Decorative ribbon

Roses

1. Choose small roses that are starting to open but are not yet in full bloom. Be sure that the roses are not larger than the space between drying trays. Cut stems to 4 to 6 inches (10 to 15 cm) in length and snip off any thorns.

2. Place on mesh drying trays and dry at 100°F (38°C) for 8 to 16 hours or until the area around the base of the flower is firm and dry. Let cool.

3. To make the posy, gather dried roses together, setting flowers at slightly different heights to keep them in a tight, attractive bunch. Wrap elastic around the stems to hold them in place. Trim stem ends so they are even. Wrap ribbon around the elastic to cover it completely and tie a bow as desired. The posy can be placed in a vase or hung from the ribbon, either upside down or upright against a wall.

Crystallized Pansies

Pansies are edible and make lovely decorations for cakes, cupcakes, hors d'oeuvres and salads.

Tip

For optimal food safety, use pasteurized liquid egg whites if you plan to eat the pansies.

• *Pastry brush or paint brush*

> Fresh pansies
> Egg whites
> Granulated sugar

1. Trim pansy stems to about 2 inches (5 cm) in length.

2. In a bowl, whisk egg whites until just starting to get foamy. Using pastry brush, lightly paint face and underside of pansy with egg white (do not coat too thickly). Holding over a dish, sprinkle with sugar as evenly as possible, gently shaking off excess.

3. Place pansies face side up on mesh drying racks and dry at 100°F (38°C) for 4 to 8 hours or until flowers are firm and dry. Let cool. Trim off stems as desired. Store pansies in a cookie tin at a cool room temperature for up to 1 week.

Kids' Dough Creations

Jennifer has fond memories of hours spent at the kitchen table creating wonderful creatures and decorations with this dough. While they're usually baked in the oven, the dehydrator works wonderfully to ensure a hard, long-lasting craft that won't brown (as is the risk with oven baking).

Makes about 2 lbs (1 kg) dough

Tip

You can also use a rolling pin and roll this dough out as for the "Gingerbread" Tree Ornaments (page 358) and use cookie cutters to make shapes.

- *Parchment paper or foil*
- *Acrylic craft paints (optional)*
- *Clear craft varnish or paint*
- *Paint brushes*

4 cups	all-purpose flour	1 L
1 cup	salt	250 mL
1½ cups	water (approx.)	375 mL
	Food coloring (optional)	

1. In a large bowl, combine flour and salt. Using a wooden spoon, stir in water, adding just enough to make a firm, pliable dough.

2. Turn out onto a work surface and knead until dough is smooth and elastic (this may take up to 15 minutes), sprinkling with very small amounts of water periodically if dough feels too dry. If colored dough is desired, in a bowl and wearing disposable gloves, knead in food coloring to tint dough as desired. Break dough into pieces and keep covered with a damp towel.

3. On a sheet of parchment paper or foil, shape dough as desired, keeping shapes thin enough to fit between the racks of your dehydrator. Creations between ¼ and ½ inch (0.5 and 1 cm) thick will dry best. Use a small amount of water to "glue" pieces together as desired. Pinching or crimping pieces together helps them adhere. Roll out one scrap piece of dough to the same thickness as your creations to use as a test piece.

4. Place shapes on mesh drying trays and dry at 155°F (68°C) for 10 to 16 hours or until very firm and dry throughout. Break the test piece to check the inside and make sure there is no sign of moisture. Let cool completely on trays or wire racks.

5. Paint the creations with acrylic craft paints as desired. Let dry completely. Paint all sides of each creation with varnish or other clear paint to seal. Let dry.

"Gingerbread" Tree Ornaments

Save the real gingerbread cookies for eating and hang these sturdy and long-lasting crafty versions on the tree. After drying, seal them with varnish or paint, and they can be used and enjoyed year after year.

Makes about 1³/₄ lbs (875 g) dough, enough for about twenty-four 3-inch (7.5 cm) ornaments

Tips

Buy the ingredients, especially the spices, at bulk or discount stores to save money. You don't need high-quality spices, since they won't be eaten; rather, they are used to add color and aroma.

If giving these ornaments as gifts, be sure to include a note to the recipient that they are not edible!

Some dough will stick to the saucepan. Just fill the pan with cold water and let it soak to dissolve the dough. Then you can easily clean the pan.

- Parchment paper
- Cookie cutters
- Paint brushes
- Clear craft varnish or paint
- Craft glue (optional)
- Decorative ribbon, string or elastic

2 cups	baking soda	500 mL
1 cup	cornstarch	250 mL
3 tbsp	ground cinnamon	45 mL
2 tsp	ground cloves	10 mL
1¼ cups	cold water	300 mL
	Small candies for decorating (optional)	

1. In a saucepan, whisk together baking soda, cornstarch, cinnamon and cloves. Stir in water and cook over medium heat, stirring constantly, for about 5 minutes or until mixture is thickened to a stiff dough and just loses its shine. Scrape into a heatproof bowl and cover immediately with a damp paper towel and then with plastic wrap to prevent it from drying out. Let cool to room temperature.

2. Place a sheet of parchment paper on a work surface. Divide dough into pieces and work with one piece at a time, keeping remaining pieces covered with a damp towel.

3. Using a rolling pin, roll dough out to ¼-inch (0.5 cm) thickness. Using cookie cutters, cut out shapes, rerolling scraps and adding a touch of water as necessary to keep the dough smooth and pliable. Using a plastic straw or a skewer, cut a small hole in the top that will be used to thread string and hang ornaments (keep in mind that it will get slightly smaller upon drying). Roll out a scrap of dough for a test piece, making sure it is the same thickness as the ornaments.

4. Place shapes on mesh drying trays and dry at 155°F (68°C) for 3 to 5 hours or until very firm and dry throughout. Break the test piece to check the inside and make sure there is no sign of moisture. Let cool completely on wire racks.

5. Paint all sides of each ornament with varnish or other clear paint to seal. Let dry.

6. Using glue, attach candies to ornaments to decorate as desired. Let dry completely.

7. Thread decorative ribbon through the holes, leaving enough length to hang over branches.

Seed Saving

If you grow your own heirloom or heritage tomatoes, peppers, beans, sunflowers or other seed-producing plants, use your dehydrator to dry the seeds and save them to plant the next year

Tips

Hybrid plants don't produce seeds that will reproduce the same fruit or flowers, so only heirloom or heritage seeds are suitable for saving.

It is best to dry seeds longer if you're not sure whether they're ready, as any amount of moisture can cause spoilage.

1. For tomato seeds, place seeds and pulp in a fine-mesh sieve and rinse off as much pulp as possible. Drain well.

2. Spread seeds on a piece of parchment paper. Using metal paper clips, clip paper to a mesh drying tray (use a fine-mesh tray liner such as Clean-A-Screen, if necessary) to fasten it tight.

3. Dry at 95°F (35°C) for 3 to 12 hours or until seeds are firm and very dry throughout. Let cool completely. Peel off parchment paper or leave seeds on paper and transfer to an airtight container. Store at a cool room temperature until it's time to plant them.

Appendix: Dorm Room Cuisine

So you've headed off to school and only a few days in you've realized that the novelty of cafeteria food is going to fade quickly. Or perhaps you're a parent who wants to make sure that at least some of the food your child eats is not loaded with preservatives or fresh from the deep-fryer.

Many of this book's recipes require nothing more than boiling water and/or a single saucepan or skillet on a hot plate. So pack up several sealed, premeasured single-serving portions that can be used at a moment's notice, whether for early-morning breakfast or late-night studying. Don't forget to include instructions and a measuring cup for the water.

Library and Archives Canada Cataloguing in Publication

MacKenzie, Jennifer
    The dehydrator bible: includes over 400 recipes / Jennifer MacKenzie, Jay Nutt, Don Mercer.

Includes index.
ISBN 978-0-7788-0213-6

1. Cookery (Dried foods). 2. Food—Drying. I. Nutt, Jay, 1966–. II. Mercer, Don, 1949–. III. Title.

TX826.5.M33 2009   641.6'14   C2008-907636-2

Index

O

oats (uncooked)
    Apple, Cranberry and Oat Breakfast
        Crumble, 89
    Apple Cherry Crumble, 213
    Apple Cinnamon Oat Crisps, 180
    Apple Oat Crisps (dog treats), 335
    Banana Chocolate Chip Granola Bars, 210
    Banana Nut Oatmeal (variation), 256
    Cinnamon Apple Multigrain Porridge
        (variation), 258
    Fruit and Oat Muffin Mix, 351
    Muesli Muffins, 193
    Oatmeal Cranberry Cookies, 204
    Oatmeal with Fruit and Maple, 88
    Peanut Butter and Jelly Drops (dog treats),
        337
    Veggie Burger on a Stick, 281
oats (cooked), dried, 57
    Banana Nut Oatmeal, 256
    Cinnamon Apple Multigrain Porridge, 258
    Granola Pancakes, 249
olive oil, 78
One-Pot Simple Spaghetti, 290
onions, dried, 37
    Beef and Beer Stew with Turnips, Squash
        and Onions, 120
    Cassoulet with Beans, Sausage and Bread
        Crumbs, 124
    French-Style Three-Onion Soup, 104
    Mushroom, Beer and Onion Sauce, 164
    Onion Marmalade, 161
    Peppercorn Ground Meat Jerky Shepherd's
        Pie, 123
    Potatoes "Anna" and Onion Gratin, 310
    Roasted Onion Vinaigrette, 156
    Tomato Soup with Basil and Garlic, 98
onions, fresh
    Balsamic-Marinated Onion Rings, 176
    Cajun-Spiced Dried Onion Rings, 176
    Roasted Onion and Potato Soup, 103
orange zest, dried
    Citrus Ginger Creamy Wheat, 88
    Cranberry Ginger Scone Mix (variation),
        348
    Orange and Sweet Pepper Chicken, 286
    Orange Mint Tea, 346

oranges, fresh
    Citrus-Marinated Chickpea Salad (fresh
        addition), 305
    Orange Ornaments, 354
    Teriyaki Orange Simmered Beef, 122
    Warm Broccoli, Leek and Raisin Salad (fresh
        addition), 304
oregano, 24
Orzo Pasta with Basil, Pine Nuts and Raisins,
    154

P

papaya, dried, 30
    Carrot Pineapple Muffins (variation), 191
    Tropical Fruit Upside-Down Cake, 226
parchment paper, 20
Parmesan cheese
    Asparagus Risotto, 141
    Broccoli and Cottage Cheese Gratin, 307
    Dried Herb Pesto, 162
    Dried Tomato Pesto (variation), 163
    Jerky and Vegetable Pasta Salad, 293
    No-Cook Pasta and Sauce, 289
    Parmesan Cheese and Herb Breadstick Bites,
        177
    Peppercorn Ground Meat Jerky Shepherd's
        Pie, 123
    Potatoes "Anna" and Onion Gratin, 310
    Smoked Sausage Risotto, 300
    Veggie Pasta, 291
    Wheat Berries Parmesan, 302
    Zucchini and Red Pepper Fritters, 138
parsley, dried, 24
    Dried Herb Pesto, 162
parsnips, 33–34
pasta (uncooked), 78. *See also* noodles; pasta
    (cooked)
    Angel Hair Pasta with Tomatoes, Asparagus
        and Peas, 127
    Baked Macaroni Tuna Casserole, 132
    Chicken Noodle Soup, 261
    Linguini with Red Peppers, Garlic and
        Rosemary, 153
    One-Pot Simple Spaghetti, 290
    Orzo Pasta with Basil, Pine Nuts and Raisins,
        154
    Penne with Tomatoes, Artichokes and Basil,
        129

More Great Books
from Robert Rose

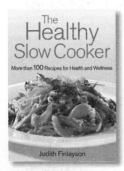

Appliance Cooking

- The Dehydrator Bible
  *by Jennifer MacKenzie,
  Jay Nutt & Don Mercer*
- The Mixer Bible
  Second Edition
  *by Meredith Deeds and
  Carla Snyder*
- The Juicing Bible
  Second Edition
  by Pat Crocker
- 200 Best Panini Recipes
  by Tiffany Collins
- 200 Best Pressure
  Cooker Recipes
  by Cinda Chavich
- 300 Slow Cooker
  Favorites
  by Donna-Marie Pye
- The 150 Best Slow
  Cooker Recipes
  by Judith Finlayson
- Delicious &
  Dependable Slow
  Cooker Recipes
  by Judith Finlayson
- 125 Best Vegetarian
  Slow Cooker Recipes
  by Judith Finlayson
- The Healthy Slow
  Cooker
  by Judith Finlayson
- The Best Convection
  Oven Cookbook
  by Linda Stephen
- 250 Best American
  Bread Machine
  Baking Recipes
  *by Donna Washburn
  and Heather Butt*
- 250 Best Canadian
  Bread Machine
  Baking Recipes
  *by Donna Washburn
  and Heather Butt*

Baking

- The Cheesecake Bible
  by George Geary
- 1500 Best Bars, Cookies,
  Muffins, Cakes & More
  by Esther Brody
- The Complete Book
  of Baking
  by George Geary
- The Complete Book
  of Bars & Squares
  by Jill Snider
- The Complete Book
  of Pies
  by Julie Hasson
- 125 Best Chocolate
  Recipes
  by Julie Hasson
- 125 Best Cupcake
  Recipes
  by Julie Hasson
- Complete Cake
  Mix Magic
  by Jill Snider

Healthy Cooking

- The Vegetarian Cook's
  Bible
  by Pat Crocker
- The Vegan Cook's
  Bible
  by Pat Crocker
- 125 Best Vegetarian
  Recipes
  *by Byron Ayanoglu
  with contributions from
  Algis Kemezys*
- The Smoothies Bible
  by Pat Crocker
- 125 Best Vegan
  Recipes
  *by Maxine Effenson Chuck
  and Beth Gurney*

- 200 Best Lactose-Free Recipes
  by Jan Main
- 500 Best Healthy Recipes
  Edited by Lynn Roblin, RD
- Complete Gluten-Free Cookbook
  by Donna Washburn and Heather Butt

- 125 Best Gluten-Free Recipes
  by Donna Washburn and Heather Butt
- The Best Gluten-Free Family Cookbook
  by Donna Washburn and Heather Butt
- Diabetes Meals for Good Health
  Karen Graham, RD
- Canada's Diabetes Meals for Good Health
  Karen Graham, RD

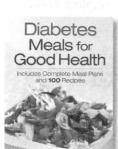

- America's Complete Diabetes Cookbook
  Edited by Katherine E. Younker, MBA, RD
- Canada's Complete Diabetes Cookbook
  Edited by Katherine E. Younker, MBA, RD

Recent Bestsellers

- 125 Best Soup Recipes
  by Marylin Crowley and Joan Mackie
- The Convenience Cook
  by Judith Finlayson
- 125 Best Ice Cream Recipes
  by Marilyn Linton and Tanya Linton

- Easy Indian Cooking
  by Suneeta Vaswani
- Baby Blender Food
  by Nicole Young
- Simply Thai Cooking
  by Wandee Young and Byron Ayanoglu

Health

- 55 Most Common Medicinal Herbs Second Edition
  by Dr. Heather Boon, B.Sc.Phm., Ph.D. and Michael Smith, B.Pharm, M.R.Pharm.S., ND
- Canada's Baby Care Book
  by Dr. Jeremy Friedman MBChB, FRCP(C), FAAP, and Dr. Norman Saunders MD, FRCP(C)

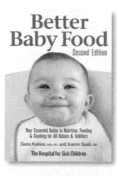

- The Baby Care Book
  by Dr. Jeremy Friedman MBChB, FRCP(C), FAAP, and Dr. Norman Saunders MD, FRCP(C)
- Better Baby Food Second Edition
  by Daina Kalnins, MSc, RD, and Joanne Saab, RD
- Better Food for Pregnancy
  by Daina Kalnins, MSc, RD, and Joanne Saab, RD

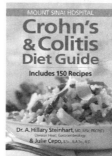

- Crohn's & Colitis
  by Dr. A. Hillary Steinhart, MD, MSc, FRCP(C)
- Crohn's & Colitis Diet Guide
  by Dr. A. Hillary Steinhart, MD, MSc, FRCP(C), and Julie Cepo, BSc, BASc, RD

Wherever books are sold

Robert ROSE

Also Available
from Robert Rose

The Complete Book of
Pickling

250 recipes from pickles &
relishes to chutneys & salsas

Jennifer MacKenzie

ISBN 978-0-7788-0216-7 $24.95 Canada / $24.95 U.S.

For more great books, see previous pages

Robert
ROSE